MW00803982

Action Research

Sara Miller McCune founded SAGE Publishing in 1965 to support the dissemination of usable knowledge and educate a global community. SAGE publishes more than 1000 journals and over 800 new books each year, spanning a wide range of subject areas. Our growing selection of library products includes archives, data, case studies and video. SAGE remains majority owned by our founder and after her lifetime will become owned by a charitable trust that secures the company's continued independence.

Los Angeles | London | New Delhi | Singapore | Washington DC | Melbourne

Action Research

*Using Strategic Inquiry to Improve
Teaching and Learning*

S. Michael Putman
The University of North Carolina at Charlotte

Tracy Rock
The University of North Carolina at Charlotte

Los Angeles | London | New Delhi
Singapore | Washington DC | Melbourne

FOR INFORMATION:

SAGE Publications, Inc.
2455 Teller Road
Thousand Oaks, California 91320
E-mail: order@sagepub.com

SAGE Publications Ltd.
1 Oliver's Yard
55 City Road
London EC1Y 1SP
United Kingdom

SAGE Publications India Pvt. Ltd.
B 1/I 1 Mohan Cooperative Industrial Area
Mathura Road, New Delhi 110 044
India

SAGE Publications Asia-Pacific Pte. Ltd.
3 Church Street
#10-04 Samsung Hub
Singapore 049483

Acquisitions Editor: Terri Accomazzo
Development Editor: Lucy Berbeo
Editorial Assistant: Erik Helton
Production Editor: Olivia Weber-Stenis
Copy Editor: Terri Lee Paulsen
Typesetter: C&M Digitals (P) Ltd.
Proofreader: Tricia Currie-Knight
Indexer: Judy Hunt
Cover Designer: Candice Harman
Marketing Manager: Kara Kindstrom

Copyright © 2018 by SAGE Publications, Inc.

All rights reserved. No part of this book may be reproduced or utilized in any form or by any means, electronic or mechanical, including photocopying, recording, or by any information storage and retrieval system, without permission in writing from the publisher.

Printed in the United States of America

Library of Congress Cataloging-in-Publication Data

Names: Putman, S. Michael, author. | Rock, Tracy, author.
Title: Action research : using strategic inquiry to improve teaching and learning / S. Michael Putman, The University of North Carolina at Charlotte; Tracy Rock, The University of North Carolina at Charlotte.
Description: Thousand Oaks, California : Sage Publications, Inc., 2017. | Includes index.
Identifiers: LCCN 2016031396 | ISBN 9781506307985 (pbk. : alk. paper)
Subjects: LCSH: Action research in education.
Classification: LCC LB1028.24 .P88 2017 | DDC 370.72—dc23
LC record available at https://lccn.loc.gov/2016031396

This book is printed on acid-free paper.

17 18 19 20 21 10 9 8 7 6 5 4 3 2 1

Brief Contents

PREFACE   xii

ABOUT THE AUTHORS   xix

PHASE I—TASK DEFINITION   1

CHAPTER 1: WHAT IS ACTION RESEARCH?   2

PHASE II—GOAL SETTING AND PLANNING   25

CHAPTER 2: IDENTIFYING A RESEARCH TOPIC   26

CHAPTER 3: CREATING A REVIEW OF LITERATURE   44

CHAPTER 4: CREATING A RESEARCH PLAN   71

CHAPTER 5: METHODS OF DATA COLLECTION   98

PHASE III—ENACTING   127

CHAPTER 6: ANALYZING THE DATA   128

PHASE IV—ADAPTATION   153

CHAPTER 7: REFLECTING ON RESULTS
AND PLANNING FOR ACTION   154

CHAPTER 8: THE ACTION RESEARCH REPORT:
SHARING RESULTS   171

CHAPTER 9: LEADING A COLLABORATIVE
ACTION RESEARCH TEAM   195

APPENDIX A: EXAMPLES OF ACTION RESEARCH REPORTS   221

APPENDIX B: POTENTIAL PUBLICATION OUTLETS
FOR ACTION RESEARCH   247

GLOSSARY   249

INDEX   255

Detailed Contents

PREFACE   xii

    Acknowledgments   xvi

ABOUT THE AUTHORS   xix

PHASE I—TASK DEFINITION   1

CHAPTER 1: WHAT IS ACTION RESEARCH?   2

    Guiding Questions   2

    Chapter Aims and Goals   2

    Setting the Context: Research in the Age of Accountability   2

        Why Conduct Research?   3

        What Is Action Research?   5

          Planning   7

          Acting   8

          Observing   8

          Reflecting   8

        Common Approaches to Research   10

        Action Research and Teaching   11

        Contexts for Teacher Action Research   15

    Taking Action: Using the CAPES Framework   16

    Summary   19

    Key Terms   20

    Case in Point: Introducing the Research Log   20

        One Elementary Teacher's Journey: Preliminary
          Research Log Entry   21

        One Secondary Teacher's Journey: Preliminary Research Log Entry   22

    Activities and Additional Resources   23

PHASE II—GOAL SETTING AND PLANNING   25

CHAPTER 2: IDENTIFYING A RESEARCH TOPIC   26

    Guiding Questions   26

    Chapter Aims and Goals   26

    Setting the Context: Choosing a Research Topic   27

        Formulate a Personal Educational Philosophy   28

        Narrow the Focus: Your Classroom, Your Experiences   29

Taking Action: Developing the Research Topic   32

    Reflect Further on the Topic   32

    Write the Problem Statement   34

    Generate Solutions to the Problem   34

    Develop the Research Question   35

Developing a Plan or a Product: Completing a Topic Proposal Form   37

Evaluating Against the Standards: Are You Ready to Move On?   37

    Checklist: Developing the Topic for Action Research   39

    Checklist: Developing a Research Question   39

Summary   40

Key Terms   40

Case in Point: Developing a Topic   40

    One Elementary Teacher's Journey: Research Log Entry   41

    One Secondary Teacher's Journey: Research Log Entry   42

Activities and Additional Resources   42

CHAPTER 3: CREATING A REVIEW OF LITERATURE   44

Guiding Questions   44

Chapter Aims and Goals   44

Setting the Context: Sources of Information   45

    Types of Resources   46

      Peer-reviewed resources   49

      Primary or secondary sources   49

Taking Action: Locating and Synthesizing Information   50

    Online Inquiries   51

    Google Scholar   53

    University Libraries   53

    Education Resources Information Center   54

    Other Sources of Information   55

    Selection of Relevant Literature   56

    Organize and Summarize Your Information   58

    Write the Synthesis of Literature   60

Developing a Plan or a Product: Writing the Synthesis of Literature   63

Evaluating Against the Standards: Are You Ready to Move On?   64

    Checklist: Synthesis of Literature   65

Summary   65

Key Terms   66

Case in Point: Annotated Bibliography Entries   66

    One Elementary Teacher's Journey: Annotated Bibliography Entries   66

    One Secondary Teacher's Journey: Annotated Bibliography Entries   67

Activities and Additional Resources   68

CHAPTER 4: CREATING A RESEARCH PLAN   71

Guiding Questions   71

Chapter Aims and Goals   71

Setting the Context: Examining Characteristics and
Components of Research Methods   72

     Research Terminology   73

     Research Methods   77

         Qualitative Methods   77

         Quantitative Methods   78

         Mixed Methods Research   79

     Data Sources and Collection Methods   81

     Ethical Considerations in Action Research   83

         Informed Consent   84

     Institutional Review Board   87

Taking Action: Developing a Preliminary Research Plan   90

Developing a Plan or a Product: Initiating the
Research Plan Proposal Form   91

Evaluating Against the Standards: Are You Ready to Move On?   92

     Checklist: Preliminary Research Plan   92

Summary   93

Key Terms   93

Case in Point: Research Plan (Pre-implementation)   94

     One Elementary Teacher's Journey: Research Log Entry   94

     One Secondary Teacher's Journey: Research Log Entry   95

Activities and Additional Resources   96

CHAPTER 5: METHODS OF DATA COLLECTION   98

Guiding Questions   98

Chapter Aims and Goals   98

Setting the Context: Choosing Data Collection Methods   98

Validity and Reliability   100

     Reliability   101

     Validity   102

Sources of Data   104

     Qualitative Data Sources   104

         Observations and anecdotal notes   104

         Interviews   107

         Journals and reflective logs   109

         Less common qualitative sources   110

     Quantitative Data Sources   110

         Surveys and questionnaires   110

         Records and artifacts   112

         Attitude and rating scales   113

         Observations   115

Taking Action: Selecting Data Collection Methods   116

Developing a Plan or a Product: Revising the Research Plan
    Proposal Form and Creating a Timeline   117

    Research Plan   120

    Timeline   120

Evaluating Against the Standards: Are You Ready to Move On?   121

    Checklist: Research Plan (Revised) and Timeline   121

Summary   121

Key Terms   122

Case in Point: Revising the Research Plan and Timeline   122

    One Elementary Teacher's Journey: Research Log Entry #2   122

    One Secondary Teacher's Journey: Research Log Entry #2   123

Activities and Additional Resources   125

PHASE III—ENACTING   **127**

CHAPTER 6: ANALYZING THE DATA   **128**

Guiding Questions   128

Chapter Aims and Goals   128

Setting the Context: Analyzing Your Data   129

    Generalizability   130

    Preparing for Data Analysis   130

    Qualitative Analysis   131

    Quantitative Analysis   134

       Descriptive statistics   135

       Inferential statistics   137

    Mixed Methods Approaches to Data Analysis   142

Taking Action: Selecting the Method of Data Analysis   143

    Using Formative Data   144

Developing a Plan or a Product: Completing the Research Plan
    Proposal Form and Timeline   144

Evaluating Against the Standards: Are You Ready to Move On?   145

    Checklist: Research Plan and Timeline   145

Summary   146

Key Terms   146

Case in Point: Final Research Plan and Timeline   146

    One Elementary Teacher's Journey: Research Log Entry #3   146

    One Secondary Teacher's Journey: Research Log Entry #3   148

Activities and Additional Resources   151

PHASE IV—ADAPTATION   **153**

CHAPTER 7: REFLECTING ON RESULTS AND PLANNING FOR ACTION   **154**

Guiding Questions   154

Chapter Aims and Goals   154

Setting the Context: Reflecting on the Results of Action Research   155

    Importance of Reflection   156

    Constructing Meaning From Results   157

    Generating New Questions for Future Study   161

     Planning for action   161

Taking Action: Creating a Plan for Action   164

Developing a Plan or a Product: Completing a Plan of Action   164

Evaluating Against the Standards: Are You Ready to Move On?   165

    Checklist: Self-Reflection   165

    Checklist: Action Plan   166

Summary   166

Key Terms   166

Case in Point: Reflecting on Results   166

    One Elementary Teacher's Journey: Research Log Entry #4   167

    One Secondary Teacher's Journey: Research Log Entry #4   168

Activities and Additional Resources   169

CHAPTER 8: THE ACTION RESEARCH REPORT: SHARING RESULTS   171

Guiding Questions   171

Chapter Aims and Goals   171

Setting the Context: Determining the Audience, Format, and Outlet   172

    Action Research Report Format   175

    Action Research Summary Format   177

    Action Research Presentation Format   177

    Writing the Action Research Report   179

    Publishing Your Work   180

Taking Action: Crafting the Abstract and Policy Implication Statements   181

    Writing an Abstract   182

    Elaborating on Implications   182

Developing a Product: Creating the Action Research Report Outline,
Presentation, and Summary   184

    Action Research Report Outline   184

    Action Research Presentation   186

    Action Research Summary   186

Evaluating Against the Standards: Are You Ready to Move On?   187

    Checklist: Action Research Report   187

    Checklist: Action Research Summary   187

Moving Forward: Potential Challenges   188

Summary   188

Key Terms   189

Case in Point: Action Research Summary   189

    One Elementary Teacher's Journey: The Action Research Summary   189

    One Secondary Teacher's Journey: The Action Research Summary   191

Activities and Additional Resources   193

CHAPTER 9: LEADING A COLLABORATIVE
ACTION RESEARCH TEAM   195

Guiding Questions   195

Chapter Aims and Goals   195

Setting the Context: Organizing for Collaborative Action Research   196

    Building Community   197

    Professional Learning Communities   200

    Community of Practice   201

    Virtual Learning Communities   202

Taking Action: Collaborative Action Research   204

    Beginning the Conversation and Planning for Success   205

        Leadership   205

        Assessing the climate and inviting critical participants   206

    Planning Collaborative Action Research   209

    Implementation of Collaborative Action Research   213

    Examining the Results and Preparing for the Next Iteration   214

Developing the Product: Forming the Collaborative
Action Research Team   215

Summary   215

Key Terms   216

Case in Point: Developing a Collaborative Action Research Study   216

    One School's Journey: Preliminary Steps in Developing the
    Collaborative Plan   216

Activities and Additional Resources   218

APPENDIX A: EXAMPLES OF ACTION RESEARCH REPORTS   221

Examining the Impact of Readers' Theater on Struggling Readers'
Fluency Levels   221

Using an Investigation Model in Ninth-Grade Science Class:
Impact on Lower-Level Readers   232

APPENDIX B: POTENTIAL PUBLICATION OUTLETS FOR ACTION
RESEARCH   247

GLOSSARY   249

INDEX   255

Preface

PURPOSE OF THE BOOK

Having guided more than 200 teachers through the action research process over the past eight years, we have seen many teachers engage in the use of data to make decisions about their instruction and the learning that is occurring within their classrooms. However, the anecdotal evidence collected over this time has revealed a hesitation on the part of teachers to proactively plan investigations that involve specifically collecting and analyzing data to arrive at conclusions regarding the success of an intervention in improving students' achievement. The common explanation for this revolves around feeling underprepared to engage in research, which is viewed as something that occurs outside of teaching. As university instructors who teach action research, our goal is to counteract these feelings through our instruction. In seeking to attain this goal, we have previewed and adopted a variety of popular texts to use within our courses in our attempts to alleviate teachers' concerns. Regardless of the text, though, we've never found a perfect match that addressed both the needs of the teachers we work with and the courses of action required to effectively plan action research in a school setting. Teachers have repeatedly mentioned the disconnect between the texts and their day-to-day experiences. In essence, the texts needed to be written in a more practitioner-oriented fashion, gradually scaffolding teachers' knowledge of and comfort within the process, making action research a manageable procedure that could be incorporated into the practices of planning, assessment, and reflection that were already taking place in the classroom.

Given this knowledge and these experiences, this book was specifically written with educators in mind. It is intended to be very practical and useful, containing specific examples that are relevant to teachers' everyday reality. While many educators are confident in their abilities to use data to facilitate decision making, fewer feel prepared to conduct systematic and methodologically sound interventions and measure the impact on student learning outcomes. Thus, we seek to prepare teachers to think about assessment to guide decision making as well as to be proactive in planning interventions that can be used to determine the educational effectiveness of various instructional strategies. Action research should be completed as an opportunity for a teacher to use what is available within her classroom to study and reflect on her own practices and the proficiencies of her students with her attention toward what worked and what didn't. In this way, the recursive cycle associated with the spiral of action research becomes more readily applicable within the classroom context.

By extension, our experiences have taught us that many teachers feel at ease when processes and procedures are systematic, logical, and comprehensible. Taking this into account, the book was organized using a model of self-regulation to ensure these attributes could be reflected in the overall design and structure we created to lead readers through the process. Within the model, referred to as CAPES, chapters of the book are organized into the following primary sections:

- Setting the **Context**—This section is directed toward activating readers' prior knowledge about the topic introduced in the chapter and subsequently developing new insights about the underlying information pertinent to the specific step in the action research process addressed by the chapter.

- Taking **Action**—This section of the chapter moves the readers beyond the content introduced in the Setting the Context section and requires them to implement strategies that are directly associated with a task related to the specific phase of the action research process they are engaged in.

- Developing a Plan or **Product**—The primary goal of this section of each chapter is to describe and finalize the development of a tangible product that matches the focus of the chapter. This product is the result of what was begun in the Taking Action section.

- **Evaluating** the Product Against the **Standards**—This section represents an extension of Developing a Product, as the reader will compare the finished product to a series of questions or statements within a checklist. The checklist is intended to represent a general set of standards to frame the particular step of the action research the teacher is engaged in. If the product addresses the items in the checklist, the reader is ready to move on. If not, another examination of the context and intended actions is recommended, with modifications to the product as necessary.

Looking at this process across a single chapter, the Setting the Context of Chapter 3 introduces the various sources of information that can be used to locate literature and provides an overview of the process for searching for literature. In Taking Action, the reader takes preliminary steps to locate, select, and summarize information in preparation for constructing a synthesis of literature. The synthesis is then written (Developing a Plan or Product) and is compared to the checklist within the Evaluating the Product Against the Standards section of the chapter. If the synthesis successfully addresses the items within the checklist, the reader proceeds to Chapter 4. If not, the reader is recommended to revisit the information obtained within the search.

In sum, use of the CAPES process guides the reader through the relevant stages of the action research process, including identifying a topic to investigate, creating a synthesis of literature, developing a plan to collect and analyze data collection, sharing results, and finally, reflecting on the next phase of the process. The teachers we have worked with have collectively praised our process for engaging them in each of the steps in the action research process as they were able to proceed in what initially seemed to be an overwhelming process to effectively build an action research report. In writing this text, our purpose is to share this process—helping practitioners and prospective teachers to see teachers are researchers and subsequently enabling and supporting them to engage in this process.

AUDIENCE FOR THE BOOK

Acknowledging our experiences working with teachers, one of the principal reasons for writing this book was to address the needs of practitioners in the field. However, the orientation of the book toward proactive planning as part of an organized, efficient process for developing and conducting an action research study will help readers at a variety of levels, including practicing teachers, preservice candidates, educational leaders, and administrators.

Acknowledging these different audiences, we see the primary use of the text as a primary or supplemental resource in a graduate-level action research class or professional development seminar. Given the focus on methods and processes that incorporate formative data that is readily available to teachers, we feel practitioners will be able to make direct associations between classroom instruction and the action research process. The text will also reinforce how action research can improve the teaching and learning process by reinforcing or changing perceptions about the use of informal data, including anecdotal notes or observations, in the research process. A unique aspect of the text is the inclusion of a chapter focused on collaborative action research, and thus instructional leaders, including administrators, instructional coaches, and department chairs, may find the information in Chapter 9 especially relevant for developing the capacity to facilitate and lead the action research process for a larger group.

By extension, given the increasing emphasis on developing the capacity of educators to understand, analyze, and use data, there is a need to incorporate these processes as part of teacher preparation. We feel that the general framework of the text, focused on systematically conducting interventions and gathering data to guide decision making, could enable its use within upper-level undergraduate courses focused on differentiation or data-based instructional design.

BOOK OUTLINE

The book has been divided into four phases, each with a distinct purpose in preparing the reader to engage in the action research process. Engaging with each chapter will not only help the reader build knowledge of the various considerations and procedures encompassed within the process, but will result in a tangible product that will represent a completed action research study, including considerations for developing collaborative projects in the future.

Phase I, Task Definition, introduces foundational aspects of the action research process. The reader is presented with the recursive cycle of the four phases of action research as well as how action research is differentiated from notions of "traditional" research. Setting the stage for the organization of the chapters in the phases that follow, the reader is also introduced to the self-regulatory model that is used as an organizational feature throughout the text.

In Phase II, Goal Setting and Planning, the reader will take initial steps toward planning the action research investigation. After reflecting upon a personal educational philosophy and classroom experiences, the reader will select a research topic and explore related literature about the topic. Using the information gained through the examination of the various sources of literature on the topic as well as knowledge of the context of practice, the reader is introduced to the processes necessary to develop a research plan. This encompasses descriptions of research methods as well as the various sources of data and methods of collection that are practical and feasible within a classroom. Phase II concludes with the construction of a preliminary research plan and a timeline for implementation of the activities associated with the research.

Phase III, Enacting, transitions the reader from thinking about data collection to focusing on the considerations and methods for analyzing data. The intent is to help the reader finalize the research plan and subsequently conduct the activities associated with the action research investigation.

In Phase IV, Adaptation, the reader engages in the reflective processes necessary to interpret the results obtained through the action research process. A significant emphasis is placed on helping the reader determine necessary action steps for future iterations of the action research cycle. Subsequently, various methods of sharing the results are presented and discussed as ways the reader can expand the audience for the work, creating opportunities for expanding the influence of the implications. The final chapter moves the reader beyond the individual action research report, as it focuses on the notion of community and presents considerations and suggestions for expanding the action research process to encompass a collaborative action research team.

BOOK FEATURES

We feel that the self-regulatory approach and the consistency among the organizational structure of each chapter are important facets of the book that will enhance readers' understanding of the action research process. Notably, the text will more effectively support readers in the development of the artifacts associated with each chapter as they gradually build the action research investigation using CAPES. There are a number of other features that are imbedded into each chapter that will add to this support as well as provide relevance of the text to the intended audience.

Each chapter incorporates multiple opportunities for the reader to actively reflect upon the content within the "Note"-able Thoughts feature. We have included "Note"-able Thoughts as a way to encourage the reader to stop and think about how the content relates to prior knowledge or experience related to the chapter topic or to take a specific action that will help develop the artifact for the chapter. Each chapter also includes sidebars referred to as Voices From the Field. The sidebars consist of vignettes constructed by the authors based on multiple journal entries where teachers describe their actual experiences conducting action research, from development of a plan and literature review, through data analysis and planning additional cycles. This feature is intended to emphasize that conducting action research within the parameters of regular classroom duties is manageable.

The Case in Point examples were built into the text to ensure the reader could see what each phase of the action research process could look like for an elementary or secondary teacher. Each chapter includes the specific artifact associated with the content presented in the chapter, constructed by the authors based on real teacher action research projects from different levels. For example, Chapter 4 concludes by illustrating what a preliminary research plan looks like. The Case in Point examples are the same throughout the book, and we have included a full action research report example for each of them within Appendix A. We felt that by providing a consistent example of two action research studies throughout the book, the reader will be able to see how all of the phases of the action research process are interconnected and how the process develops to help the researcher reach conclusions and implications.

Tech Connections are intended to highlight ways that technology can be used to facilitate the research process, including searching literature, collecting, storing, or analyzing data, or communicating with peers within the collaborative action research process. We have included at least one example in each chapter.

Other practical tools that are threaded throughout the chapters:

- Templates for creating various artifacts (e.g., research plan)

- End-of-chapter summaries

- Key terms (bolded within chapter text; listed at the end of the chapter)

- End-of-chapter activities that present opportunities to further engage with chapter content

- Additional resources pertinent to each chapter topic

- Visual examples of models, outlines, and concepts related to content

- Glossary

DIGITAL RESOURCES

edge.sagepub.com/putman

SAGE edge offers a robust online environment you can access anytime, anywhere, and features an impressive array of free tools and resources to keep you on the cutting edge of your learning experience.

<u>**SAGE edge for Instructors**</u> supports your teaching by making it easy to integrate quality content and create a rich learning environment for students.

- **Test banks** provide a diverse range of pre-written options as well as the opportunity to edit any question and/or insert your own personalized questions to effectively assess students' progress and understanding.

- Editable, chapter-specific **PowerPoint® slides** offer complete flexibility for creating a multimedia presentation for your course.

- EXCLUSIVE! Access to full-text **SAGE journal articles** that have been carefully selected to support and expand on the concepts presented in each chapter.

- **Multimedia content** appeals to students with different learning styles.

- **Lecture notes** summarize key concepts by chapter to help you prepare for lectures and class discussions.

SAGE edge for Students provides a personalized approach to help you accomplish your coursework goals in an easy-to-use learning environment.

- Mobile-friendly **eFlashcards** strengthen your understanding of key terms and concepts.

- Mobile-friendly practice **quizzes** allow you to independently assess your mastery of course material.

- A complete online **action plan** includes tips and feedback on your progress and allows you to individualize your learning experience.

- **Learning objectives** reinforce the most important material.

- **Multimedia** web links make it easy to mine internet resources, further explore topics, and answer critical thinking questions.

- EXCLUSIVE! Access to full-text **SAGE journal articles** that have been carefully chosen to support and expand on the concepts presented in each chapter.

ACKNOWLEDGMENTS

There are multiple people that must be acknowledged for their support, assistance, and encouragement during the process of writing this book. First, and foremost, this undertaking would not have been possible without the patience and understanding of our families. Many evenings and weekends were given up to ensure we met our deadlines and delivered a text that we could be proud of.

We would also like to thank multiple students who contributed feedback and artifacts that appear in our Voices From the Field and the Case in Point examples. We were able to construct relevant and meaningful representations of teachers' thinking and work products based on the hundreds of action research projects we have facilitated over the years. We would especially like to thank Laura Handler, who provided helpful comments on several chapters that were proving to be challenging to conceptualize and develop.

We would also like to thank our editorial team at SAGE Publications. Terri Accomazzo (acquisitions editor) has been our primary contact and support throughout this entire process. Her positivity, timely communication, and thorough feedback made this a very smooth and seamless process. Thanks also to Lucy Berbeo (development editor) and Erik Helton (editorial assistant) for their support and prompt responses to our questions.

Finally, we would like to extend our gratitude to the following reviewers of the various chapters for their feedback and comments. Your suggestions were greatly appreciated and resulted in numerous improvements that are reflected throughout.

Valerie Allison, Susquehanna University

Tamarah M. Ashton, California State University, Northridge

Ruth Ban, Barry University

Dawn Behan, Mount Mercy University

Ann Bender, Marian University

Drinda E. Benge, North Carolina State University

Ann Bassett Berry, Plymouth State University

Tyrone Bynoe, University of Michigan, Flint

Susan H. Cogdill, Kent State University

Jasmine Diaz, Miami Dade College

Phillip Diller, Shippensburg University

Eleni Coukos Elder, Tennessee State University

Marc Ryan Flett, West Virginia University

Johanna Flip-Hanke, Sonoma State University

Timothy J. Frederiks, Centenary College

Ochieng' K'Olewe, McDaniel College

Malissa A. Scheuring Leipold, Iona College

Joellen Maples, St. John Fisher College

J. Sabrina Mims-Cox, California State University, Los Angeles

Kristin T. Rearden, University of Tennessee

Gerene K. Starratt, Barry University

Denise H. Stuart, University of Akron

Michelle Szpara, Cabrini College

Martin J. Wasserberg, University of North Carolina, Wilmington

Stephanie Wexler-Robock, Iona College

About the Authors

S. Michael Putman is a professor and the department chair in the Department of Reading and Elementary Education at the University of North Carolina at Charlotte. During his 20 years in education, he has taught at a variety of levels, from preschool through doctoral-level classes. He has taught various courses in pedagogy, action research, and literacy at two different institutions during his career in higher education. He has served as an advisor for over 200 action research studies as well as over 100 behavioral intervention studies, all conducted by teachers. His research interests are focused on the development of teacher self-efficacy and intercultural competencies through field experiences, self-regulation, and the relationship of affective variables on literacy outcomes, including those associated with online inquiry. Dr. Putman has published five books, nine book chapters, and 22 journal articles. He has also published a variety of non-refereed articles, primarily describing methods to effectively integrate technology into literacy instruction. Dr. Putman currently serves a co-editor for *Literacy Research and Instruction*. He is an avid runner and has completed 17 marathons.

Tracy Rock is a professor in the Department of Reading and Elementary Education in the College of Education at UNC Charlotte. Her teaching and research interests include inquiry models of teacher professional development, social studies education, and service learning. She teaches courses in the undergraduate, master's, and doctoral programs in the College of Education. She is a Faculty Fellow for the Center for Teaching and Learning at UNC Charlotte, where she provides professional development workshops, webinars, private consultations, and peer observations for faculty across the campus. Dr. Rock has advised numerous action research studies conducted by both practicing teachers and teacher candidates. She has also conducted research on the Action Research process and has published her work in the *Journal of Teacher Education and Teacher Education Quarterly*. Dr. Rock is the recipient of several teaching awards including the Teaching Fellows Teaching Excellence Award in 2007, the 2014 UNC Charlotte Bank of America Award for Teaching Excellence, and the 2015 North Carolina Board of Governor's Award for Teaching Excellence.

PHASE I
Task Definition

CHAPTER 1

What Is Action Research?

GUIDING QUESTIONS

After reading this chapter, you should be able to answer the following questions:

- What is action research?
- What are the stages of action research?
- What types of research methods are available for action research?
- Why should teachers conduct action research?
- What is CAPES, and how can it be used to frame action research?

CHAPTER AIMS AND GOALS

This chapter is meant to serve as an introduction to action research and the related processes associated with completing an action research study. First, we will discuss what action research is, defining it and describing each of the relevant stages that you will engage in as you progress through the research process. Second, we'll briefly overview the various types of methods associated with action research and the potential sources of data that are generally available in classrooms. Third, the links between teaching and action research and the subsequent impact on practices will be detailed. Finally, we will introduce CAPES, a framework of self-regulation that will provide the foundation for organizing your work and will help you to consider various perspectives as you develop and complete the action research study.

SETTING THE CONTEXT: RESEARCH IN THE AGE OF ACCOUNTABILITY

Data driven, rigor, closing the gap, and *evidence based* are just a few terms that have taken added importance in an era where teachers are increasingly held accountable for ensuring students meet specific educational outcomes while in their classroom. Acknowledging that opinions differ, there are some teachers who view these words with hesitation, perhaps because of their association with a teaching context that seems to be less about teaching and more about test taking and establishing career readiness. However, what if data could be used more to inform instruction than drive it? What if, by systematically using data, we could be more effective at improving our instruction? Perhaps the aforementioned words would have less association with the accountability movement and greater connection to effective teaching practices.

With the passage of No Child Left Behind in 2001, the age of accountability was introduced. As a result of this legislation, teachers and schools experienced a heightened sense of urgency toward meeting adequate yearly progress and ensuring students were prepared to take and pass standardized tests used to assess whether the "necessary" progress had been made. Recent accountability methods, such as those legislated within the Every Child Succeeds Act and associated with President Obama's educational initiatives (i.e., Race to the Top), have continued to place pressure on teachers to ensure students are progressing toward "college and career readiness." Furthermore, there has been an increase in the use of value-added measurements and growth measures, which have a specific focus on the outcomes of students, but are also used to quantify whether a given teacher was successful in producing a year (or more) of academic growth in her students (Fusarelli & Fusarelli, 2015; Sindelar, Washburn-Moses, Thomas, & Leko, 2014).

Within a climate characterized by data-gathering activity and the resulting large number of data points that we now have access to, we must step back and look at how all of this information can be beneficial to our teaching practices. External mandates aside, practicing and prospective teachers must thoughtfully plan instruction, critically examine its impact on students, and reflect on how they can successfully use data from assessments to improve both their practices and the achievement of students. The goal of such reflection is to produce "practical improvement, innovation, change or development of social practice, and . . . better understanding of . . . practices" (Zuber-Skerritt, 1996, p. 83). It is at the intersection of planning, evaluation, and reflection that action research resides.

"NOTE"-ABLE THOUGHTS

Given that many teachers do feel some nervousness when presented with the idea of conducting research, take a minute and think about what *research* means to you. Write a definition or list a few statements that capture your views of what research is or entails.

WHY CONDUCT RESEARCH?

During our careers in higher education, we have helped many teachers navigate the action research process. It is not uncommon for these teachers to express that they are intimidated by any process that includes the word *research*. What comes to mind immediately for them are images of statistical formulas and numerical analyses that have little perceived impact on classroom practices. However, as part of our work, we have tried to remind them that there are many different kinds of research and multiple ways to collect and analyze data beyond statistics. Our task, and the goal of this book, is to help you begin to think more broadly about the notion of research. There are certainly forms that rely on numerical data, and there are many quantitative sources of data that are available in the classroom, including tests, quizzes, and scored homework assignments. We also need to be cognizant of the other sources of data that are often a regular part of our practice, though, including observations, anecdotal notes, work samples, and student conferences. Research can and should combine the various sources whenever possible to help us consider multiple possibilities and develop potentially stronger conclusions. A quote from Charles Kettering nicely summarizes the preceding thoughts and helps us think about the practical significance of research. Kettering said:

> Research is a high-hat word that scares a lot of people. It needn't. It is rather simple. Essentially, research is nothing but a state of mind—a friendly, welcoming attitude toward change . . . going out to look for change instead of waiting for it to come. Research . . . is an effort to do things better. . . . It is the problem solving mind as contrasted with the let-well-enough-alone mind. . . . It is the "tomorrow" mind instead of the "yesterday" mind. (Boyd, 1957, p. 216)

Johnson (2000) further elaborates, telling educators, "Research can: inform us, educate us, answer questions, prompt new questions, create reflection and discussion, challenge what we do as educators, and clarify education situations" (p. 3). For the purposes of this book, we define **research** as systematic processes used to examine specific questions or topics with the intent of developing new knowledge or conclusions.

Teachers and researchers are thought to have different traits, goals, interests, and concerns. Yet, teaching and research do not have to be mutually exclusive, even though society (teachers included) often views the activities as separate. We would argue the differences are not as pronounced as some may think. In fact, we would argue that there are strikingly similar characteristics: teachers are problem solvers as they think about ways to reach that one student in the classroom who has trouble grasping a concept; teachers are deep thinkers as they reflect on the lessons taught and how they can be improved; and finally they are collaborators as they form professional learning communities with peers to examine topics and discuss how they may impact students. Teachers take on many roles and responsibilities in their daily classroom activities; however, the role of teacher as researcher may be the role most needed to promote professional development and improved classroom practice. "When teachers focus on their own concerns, they solve pressing problems without depending on the bureaucracy, and students benefit at once" (Evans, 1991, p. 11).

However, as much as we hate to admit it, we (as teachers) are sometimes resistant to change, especially when it is forced upon us, as the recent policies focused solely on data and accountability have been. We tend to patiently wait out the "swings in the pendulum" as we go about the daily business of helping children learn. In thinking further on Kettering's idea, we may need to shift our mind-set to actively thinking about conducting our own research, whether formal or informal, to develop our own conclusions and to lead the narrative, instead of being reactive to the constantly shifting landscape that is teaching. It's a subtle shift in our practices, but if we are going to be required to collect data, let's use it to our advantage and think about how *teacher* and *researcher* can become more synonymous in both meaning and action.

"NOTE"-ABLE THOUGHTS

Are teaching and research mutually exclusive? Can you be both a teacher and a researcher? Explain the rationales for your responses.

WHAT IS ACTION RESEARCH?

Kurt Lewin, whom most scholars acknowledge as one of the first people to conceptualize action research, sought to describe a process that could simultaneously combine experimental approaches for research with social programs while advancing both theory and action for research and social progress. He noted, "Research that produces nothing but books will not suffice" (Lewin, 1946, p. 208). To accomplish the goals for this new process, Lewin proposed a paradigm for **action research** that began with an objective to reach, then proceeded in a spiral of stages of analysis, fact-finding, planning, and execution (Lewin, 1946). Lewin suggested that the cycle begins with a general idea for the research that is confirmed by the collection of data and ongoing "reconnaissance" or fact-finding to confirm the individual's interpretation of the situation as well as a proposed plan to address it. Once the necessary reconnaissance is complete, the researcher develops a plan and implements the steps necessary to carry out the plan, while active monitoring is utilized within the evaluation of the process as the researcher engages in rethinking, reflecting, and replanning. This replanning phase sets the stage for the next cycle of the action research, hence the spiral-like pattern associated with the process. Ultimately, this process serves as a means of formative assessment that results in modifications or revisions to the original plan as necessitated by what the data revealed, leading the researcher successively closer to the objective of the research. Stephen Kemmis (1988) captured the essence of the essential characteristics of Lewin's model in a widely accepted representation of the action research "spiral" (see Figure 1.1). Kemmis' model established the ideas of reconnaissance, planning, first action step, monitoring, reflecting, rethinking, and evaluation as the key components of action research.

■ ■ ■ VOICES FROM THE FIELD

Within our work with teachers, graduate students, and researchers, we've found that people often find it helpful to hear the voices of those who they can identify with and are engaging in action research in the "real world." Acknowledging this preference, we've incorporated our Voices From the Field anecdotes to share reflections and comments about the action research process.

As you engage with these thoughts, reading about some successes and challenges related to the process, we hope you will gain insights and guidance on the topic that is the focus of the chapter. Ultimately, we hope our Voices From the Field will help you plan and implement an action research study that flows smoothly and efficiently from start to finish.

FIGURE 1.1 A Representation of Lewin's Action Research Cycle

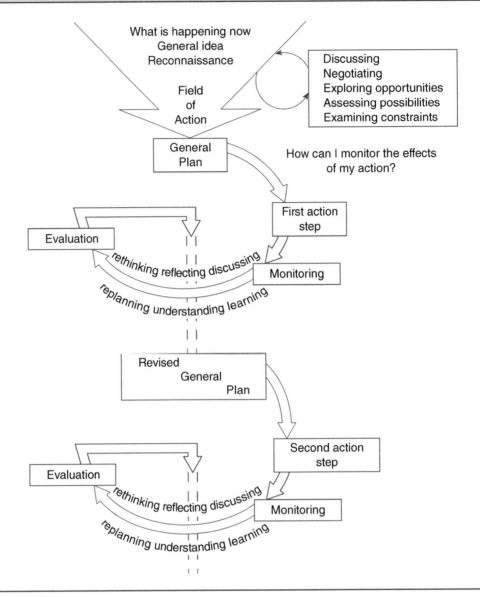

SOURCE: *Action Research in Retrospect and Prospect* (p. 29), by Stephen Kemmis, 1988, Victoria, Australia: Deakin University Press, distributor. Copyright 1988 Deakin University. Reprinted with permission. All rights reserved.

Since Lewin's initial ideas were set forth regarding what constituted action research, others (see Kemmis & McTaggart, 1992; McKernan, 1991; McNiff & Whitehead, 2011) have continued to provide additional refinements and clarification to illuminate ideas concerning action research. These ideas characterize action research as

- including researchers who are direct participants within the process as they critically and systematically examine their own practice and context, intending to improve them through the action research process;

- requiring the collection of various forms of data (evidence) and the use of diverse methods to document changes throughout the ongoing, cyclical process; and

- starting small as the researcher attempts to create relevant, usable conclusions within the current situation and gradually expand the process through active evaluation and reflection upon the results.

As previously noted, the process of action research has been theorized to be recursive and cyclical, meaning that it continues to reform and be refined through additional studies, yet it is important to note that it does not typically proceed in a linear fashion. It is possible that action researchers may find themselves having to revisit or repeat some of the steps or perhaps having to engage with them in a different order (Mertler, 2014).

"NOTE"-ABLE THOUGHTS

Define action research in your own words. Consider, how do the actions taken by an "action researcher" differ from someone who conducts what we could consider traditional research?

While there are many notable authors and books that have addressed action research, *The Action Research Planner* (Kemmis, McTaggart, & Nixon, 2014) has been influential in many of our current understandings of the processes associated with action research, having originally proposed the now familiar "spiral" of action research (see Figure 1.1). There is now a revised and more simplified version, which is pictured in Figure 1.2. In the spiral, the researcher develops a plan, implements the plan (acts), systematically observes the results of the actions, and then reflects on the results. Through active reflection, the researcher then uses the information from the first cycle to plan, act, observe, and reflect within a second one. This spiral provides the opportunity for the researcher to continue to refine his or her planning and actions, subsequently improving practices and outcomes for the chosen area of focus (Sagor, 2000). Each phase of the action research cycle is characterized by a distinct purpose and set of actions.

Planning. The purpose of the **planning** phase is to create a plan of action to improve what is currently happening. The plan should be (a) forward-looking to assist you in examining new potential for your current practice, (b) flexible to adjust to unforeseen

---

FIGURE 1.2 Spiral of Action Research

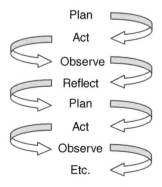

Plan
Act
Observe
Reflect
Plan
Act
Observe
Etc.

---

effects and unrecognized constraints, and (c) strategic in its ability to go beyond current constraints and empower you to act more appropriately and effectively.

Acting. The **acting** phase requires thoughtful and deliberate implementation of the plan. As you put the ideas to work, you will reflect back on the plan, but you are not controlled by the plan. Acting is fluid and dynamic, and it involves immediate decisions about what is to be done and wise judgment of how to address real circumstances. You should remain flexible, aware, and open to change as ideas are put into practice. "Three action gains should be kept in mind: the improvement of practice, the improvement of understanding (individually and collaboratively), and the improvement of the situation in which the action takes place" (Kemmis & McTaggart, 1982, p. 9).

Observing. The purpose of the **observing** phase is to gather systematic and deliberate documentation to provide a valid basis for critical self-reflection. You will want to plan sound methods for gathering the data; however, the observation plans must be flexible and open to record the unexpected. You will want to observe the action process, the intended and unintended effects of the action, any related circumstances of and constraints on the action, and the context of the situation of the action.

Reflecting. **Reflecting** is the retrospective phase of the process that analyzes the action using what has been recorded in observation. You will engage in reflection to make sense of processes, problems, issues and constraints made apparent in the strategic action. You may find that it enhances or deepens your reflection if you engage in discussion of the data and action with other participants. "Reflection leads to the reconstruction of the meaning of the social situation and provides the basis for the revised plan" (Kemmis & McTaggart, 1982, p. 9). You will be evaluating the experience—to judge whether the intended and unintended effects were desirable. As you reflect you will identify ways to proceed with your inquiry and develop new questions for the next cycle of action research. The reflection should lead you to a clearer conception of how to act more appropriately and effectively in the situation and open your mind to new possibilities in your practice.

These core elements are consistently found in the variety of action research models that have been developed to conceptualize the action research process. For example, Ernest Stringer (2007) proposed an Action Research Helix (see Figure 1.3) where participants

---

FIGURE 1.3 Stringer's Action Research Helix

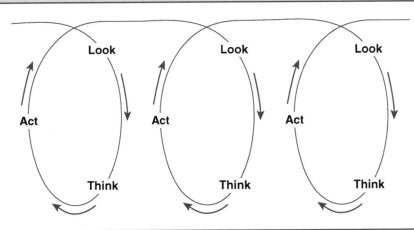

SOURCE: Adapted from *Action Research* (p. 9), by Ernest T. Stringer, 2007, Thousand Oaks, CA: Sage. Copyright 2007 by Sage. Reprinted with permission of the publisher. All rights reserved.

ACTION RESEARCH

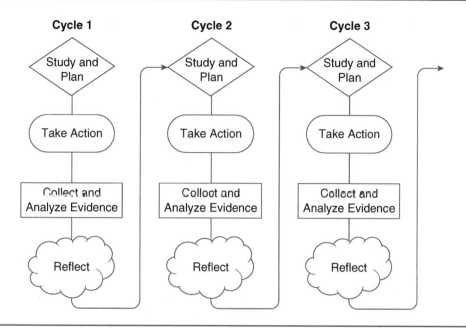

SOURCE: Adapted from *Understanding Action Research,* by Margaret Riel. Retrieved April 24, 2016, from http://cadres.pepperdine.edu/ccar/define.html. Copyright 2007 by the Center for Collaborative Action Research, Pepperdine University. Reprinted with permission of the author.

are engaged in looking, thinking, and acting phases that continually lead to a next cycle of the action research process and are repeated over time. Riel's (2007) progressive problem solving through action research model, on the other hand, engages participants in four steps: planning, taking action, collecting evidence, and reflecting (see Figure 1.4), but, similarly, these steps lead to a next cycle in a repeated process. These examples are consistent with most action research models, which begin with some type of problem of practice or topic, involve observation or monitoring of current or existing practices through the gathering and analysis of data or evidence, and result in some sort of action to be taken to improve the existing practices. This then leads to continued examination and a next stage in the action research process.

■ ■ ■ VOICES FROM THE FIELD

Jeannie Madorey, Fifth-Grade Teacher

Much of what I do as a teacher is guided by various processes. I write lesson plans, teach them, and assess student understanding of the content that was taught. Based on what the assessment reveals, I may revisit content or move to the next concepts. I think action research is very similar—you plan what you want to examine, collect data, and analyze it. For me personally, I feel that the *planning* stage of research is the most challenging. I don't

(Continued)

(Continued)

always have time or want to sit down and plan a specific intervention and examine how it worked. As a teacher, I want to jump straight into the *action* stage where I am actually teaching and conducting the intervention with my students. However, this "trial and error" approach doesn't always allow me to consider the data I have or want to collect that will indicate whether what I am doing is working. It also doesn't always guide me in how to look critically at the data. For me, the opportunity to conduct action research will hopefully allow me to slow down and focus on planning, acting, and then reflecting as part of a comprehensive process.

COMMON APPROACHES TO RESEARCH

Although we mentioned this previously, it's important to reiterate that as a teacher you have access to a wealth of data that can be used as part of the action research process. In your classroom, you may administer quizzes or tests, score projects using a rubric, or assign points for participation. These numeric scores facilitate comparisons. That is, a score of 95 usually indicates a more successful performance than a score of 87. Numeric data is associated with quantitative methods of research. The goal of **quantitative research**, in general, is to prove or disprove a hypothesis about the particular phenomenon being examined (Gall, Borg, & Gall, 2007). Quantitative approaches to research utilize computation of measures such as variability (e.g., how spread out the data is), as shown through range and standard deviation, and central tendency, including the mean, median, and mode. Quantitative data can also be used to create graphic comparisons. When using quantitative data, researchers use statistical analyses, for example, analysis of variance or correlation, to examine relationships or to engage in comparisons as they seek evidence of **statistical significance**. This term refers to results that reach a level where it is improbable that differences or relationship between variables is due to chance. The advantage of using quantitative approaches to research is that they have been deemed objective—it is difficult to argue with numbers. On the other hand, the depth of information is limited, as the results convey a number or graph that minimizes the theories and inferences that can be developed about the results.

As teachers, using a quantitative approach for our research would be appropriate if we were interested in examining the relationship between computational ability and scores on a math test or whether one class that received an instructional intervention scored higher on some measure than a class that was not exposed to it. Statistical significance is the gold standard in quantitative research, as it indicates the results of your study most likely did not happen by chance, but it has limited applicability within our classrooms. We're more prone to look for **practical significance**, or a difference that is useful within the context of our teaching or student learning. For example, after a given intervention, we may note that the students in our class answered three more math problems correctly, on average, and therefore consider the intervention to be successful. However, it is important to become familiar with the various quantitative methods as well as how to interpret the results of studies that incorporate these methods.

There is little doubt that technology has become a pervasive aspect of our everyday lives. It has also impacted the ways we conduct research. We can now easily collect data by capturing a conversation with a student on our tablet or phone, listening to it or viewing it later to note critical events or understandings that occurred during the conversation. Technology has also increased our capabilities for analyzing data, both qualitative and quantitative. Researchers are no longer required to compute by hand or calculator, but instead can store data in an electronic spreadsheet that will provide answers to a multitude of statistical questions with a series of key strokes. In each of our chapters, we'll try to highlight some way that technology can be used to facilitate the research process, including gathering literature for your synthesis, collecting, storing, or analyzing data, or even presenting the results of your study to critical stakeholders!

Qualitative research involves the use of descriptions or illustrative data to construct an understanding of a particular situation or phenomenon. You may collect notes about a student's performance during an observation, or you may record anecdotal records that can be used to help you determine general strengths and weaknesses associated with a specific task. Within qualitative approaches to research, "objects are not reduced to single variables, but [are] represented in their entirety in their everyday context ... the fields of study are not artificial situations in the laboratory but the practices and interactions of the subjects in everyday life" (Flick, 2009, p. 15). In essence, the goal of qualitative research is not to use a single value or comparison, but to use a broader set of data to construct meanings or theories through the interpretation of data. One advantage of using qualitative research methods is their adaptability to the context or conditions observed in a setting where the research is taking place. An inherent challenge in action research situations, on the other hand, is the potential subjectivity of a researcher who has a personal stake in the data and findings. As teachers, we want our students to be successful, and thus we may look for and find data that makes this a reality if we allow our own biases and perceptions to cloud the analysis. As a result, it is important that we engage in systematic collection of multiple forms of data and are deliberate and critical within the analysis of the data. Additional information about each form of methodology as well as mixed methods research will be shared in Chapter 5.

"NOTE"-ABLE THOUGHTS

Now that you have a better idea of what action research entails, think about how the process applies to teaching. Do you believe research can (or should) be a regular part of your classroom practices? What would make it beneficial? What potential challenges do you see?

ACTION RESEARCH AND TEACHING

According to Phillips and Carr (2006), "The teacher as a researcher is not an image our culture gives us" (p. 7). We tend to agree with their assessment, but also believe that *teacher* and *researcher* can be synonymous in the right context. In fact, given the opportunity, we feel teachers can change this perception by exploring ways that action research can be used in their classrooms. Various researchers have cited action research as a method to improve teaching and learning (see Darling-Hammond, 1996; Levin & Rock, 2003; Sagor, 2005; Somekh, 1995). Action research within the context of teaching represents an opportunity for teachers to bridge the gap between theory and practice in the familiar domain of their classrooms. Mills (2011) characterized action research as "research done *by* teachers *for* themselves; it is not imposed on them by someone else" (p. 5). Subsequently, it involves connected processes where research impacts practice and practice influences research. In essence, action research represents an opportunity to assess and improve teaching practices and learning by actively changing and investigating our processes and using information gained from the outcomes of the changes to reflect and inform our future practices. "Practitioners who engage in action research inevitably find it to be an empowering experience.... Relevance is guaranteed because the focus of each research project is determined by the researchers, who are also the primary consumers of the findings" (Sagor, 2000, p. 3).

Specific definitions of *action research* with direct reference to teaching vary, yet many involve descriptors such as *systematic* and *intentional*. Levin and Rock (2003) referred to action research as "systematic inquiry by teachers with the goal of improving their teaching practices" (p. 136). Kemmis and McTaggart (1992) argue, "Action research is to plan, act, observe and reflect more carefully, more systematically, and more rigorously than one usually does in everyday life" (p. 10). We would expand this definition to also encompass the idea that action research is conducted to simultaneously improve practice and student learning.

Further elaborating on the recursive cycle of planning, action, evaluation, and reflection that characterizes action research, let's think more about how action research aligns with teaching. The major goals of teacher action research are: (a) to help teachers make decisions about their classrooms, (b) to improve classroom or school practice, (c) to encourage teachers to see themselves as producers of educational knowledge, and (d) to allow teachers to clarify, elaborate, and modify theories that inform their teaching (Levin & Rock, 2003). Zuber-Skerritt (1996) suggests action research often begins with participants reflecting on a situation or practical issue that has direct relevance in their classrooms. The teacher develops a plan to address the situation or issue that involves the systematic implementation of a new teaching approach or a different way of doing something in the classroom. There is a focus on using data to explore the changes as well as to examine and to reflect upon their effectiveness. Development of teachers' skills as reflective practitioners is a significant method to help them improve within some specific aspect of their practice (Caro-Bruce, 2000; Sagor, 2005). Hendricks (2006) illustrates how action research can improve classroom and school practice (see Figure 1.5) through "systematic inquiry based on ongoing reflection" (p. 9). This model shows how a teacher may target a problem of practice and, utilizing the action research cycle, study the problem with the goal of improving their practice.

Action research can be conducted in a variety of settings. In fact, any context (or classroom) where there is a problem or situation that needs to be solved or examined in greater depth will work. Ideally, however, when teachers choose to conduct action research, it is conducted within the familiar domain of the teacher's own classroom.

FIGURE 1.5 Hendricks's Action Research Process

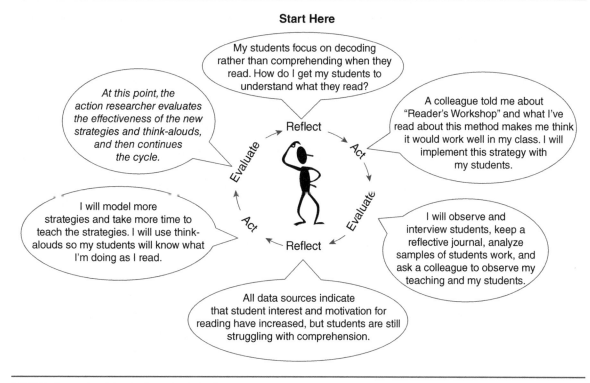

Start Here

My students focus on decoding rather than comprehending when they read. How do I get my students to understand what they read?

A colleague told me about "Reader's Workshop" and what I've read about this method makes me think it would work well in my class. I will implement this strategy with my students.

At this point, the action researcher evaluates the effectiveness of the new strategies and think-alouds, and then continues the cycle.

Reflect

Evaluate

Act

Evaluate

Act

Reflect

I will model more strategies and take more time to teach the strategies. I will use think-alouds so my students will know what I'm doing as I read.

I will observe and interview students, keep a reflective journal, analyze samples of students work, and ask a colleague to observe my teaching and my students.

All data sources indicate that student interest and motivation for reading have increased, but students are still struggling with comprehension.

SOURCE: *Improving Schools Through Action Research: A Comprehensive Guide for Educators* (p. 9), by Cher Hendricks, 2006, Boston, MA: Allyn and Bacon.

Teachers who conduct action research in their classrooms have been described as being more current in their knowledge of the field (Bennett, 1993). This could be the result of the planning that occurs within the action research process, as the teacher must be aware of current strategies and trends relative to what they have chosen to investigate. They also know the learners in their classroom, including their unique needs, and how the topic chosen for investigation fits in the broader community and school context. Collins and Duguid (1989) refer to action research as "situated learning" because it takes place in the context of practice and is *about* the context. However, it's important to note that what works in one context doesn't necessarily work in another; thus, the results of an action research study conducted in one classroom may be very different from results in a different setting.

We feel it is important to point out that action research does not represent teachers engaging in the same behaviors exhibited during a "typical" day. Kemmis and McTaggart (1992) describe action research as involving more "problem-posing" around significant instructional issues, more systematic collection evidence, and active reflection on the effects of the changes to note whether improvements were made. Given that action research is focused on teaching and learning in one's own classroom, it is only natural that there is no single process that can be generalized to all work being done by teachers. McKernan (1991) noted that action research is "methodologically eclectic" (p. 33). Teachers have a wide variety of data that is available to them on a daily basis, including scores on assessments, observations, anecdotal notes, and many others. Action research simply formalizes the collection process to ensure the teacher can actively examine and reflect upon the results, including the formative data. Table 1.1 represents a summary of the points we've made thus far to outline how what many consider to be "traditional" research compares with the form of action research engaged in by teachers.

■ ■ ■ VOICES FROM THE FIELD

Kendrick Curtis, Eighth-Grade Teacher

I've learned that action research isn't necessarily about getting the "right answer"—it's about systematically looking to improve your instruction and students' achievement by making small changes and examining the results. Each small change results in a new insight that ultimately helps guide you toward bigger changes and greater success with your students. However, I have to admit that sometimes I've found it somewhat challenging to be objective when studying my own classroom. It is hard because when you look at data on students in your class, it is easy to take it personally when you don't see improvements. I have come to the conclusion that I have been focusing on the wrong things, though. Instead of solely looking at the scores on assessments or notes from observations, I need to spend more time actively reflecting on what worked and what didn't for my students and why that was the case.

TABLE 1.1   Comparison of Traditional Educational Research and Teacher Action Research

Traditional Educational Research	Teacher as Researcher Doing Action Research
1. Problem is posed by independent researchers with little to no connection with the context.	1. Problem is posed by practitioner based on needs within the context
2. Purpose is to support hypotheses that apply across the population	2. Purpose is to construct knowledge about self, students, and learning context and to improve practice
3. Proposed actions are based on reflection upon theory	3. Proposed actions are based on reflection upon one's own understandings and perceptions
4. Focus of the research is on educational theory	4. Focus of the research is on personal practical theory
5. Colleagues are used as a source of theory and as critics of work	5. Colleagues are used as collaborators and mutual reflectors
6. Relationship with students is as observer to subjects	6. Relationship with students is learner to learner
7. Successful research brings changes in universal understanding	7. Successful research brings understanding of self, students, and learning context and action steps for improvement of practice

CONTEXTS FOR TEACHER ACTION RESEARCH

Action research can be conducted by an individual acting alone, by a group of committed colleagues in a school (or district) who are interested in a common situation, or within a teacher/researcher partnership. The latter can occur when there is a sustained relationship between various stakeholders such as might be the case in a school–university partnership (e.g., professional development school). Much of this book is focused on the individual teacher, yet the principles could be applied to any of the aforementioned situations. Collaborative inquiry, as action research conducted by a group of teachers has been referred to, is addressed in greater detail in Chapter 9, yet there are several elements that should be discussed to help you think about how action research fits within the greater school context.

Teacher action research has the power to bring action and change to an individual teacher's practice, but when it is designed with the broader school or school system context in mind, it has the potential to have greater impact. At minimum, teachers should consider aligning their inquiry into their practice with larger school/school system improvement goals or with areas of designated professional development initiatives within the school/school system. This will build broader appeal and interest to allow for administrator support and sharing of results or implications of the action research with colleagues or peers. It also increases the potential for collaborative inquiry among teams of teachers within and across schools or between practicing and prospective teachers. This will enhance the real and perceived value of the work and have a larger impact on teachers and students.

A recent trend in how schools engage teachers in professional development is to move away from the expert-led, one-day workshop models to more sustained, engaged, and collaborative team-based models. Job-embedded, collaborative professional development that is focused on using dialogue to improve student results has proven to be a more effective model, resulting in teachers feeling greater confidence and job satisfaction while diminishing the sense of isolation felt by some teachers (Walker, 2013). This emerging understanding of the importance of providing teachers with opportunities to work together to engage in data-based decision making and make explicit connections to their practice and students has led many schools to provide or increase team planning sessions for teachers, and some have engaged in extensive restructuring efforts to include the use of professional learning communities.

Broadly defined, a **professional learning community** (PLC) is "a group of people sharing and critically interrogating their practice in an ongoing, reflective, collaborative, inclusive, learning-oriented, growth-promoting way" (Stoll, Bolam, McMahon, Wallace, & Thomas, 2006, p. 223). The primary intent of the efforts to use PLCs is to engage in a collaborative, goal-driven effort aimed at improving practices and maximizing student learning. Professional learning communities have also been referred to as "inquiry teams" or "learning teams," and participants can be organized in a variety of ways, for example, by grade level or content area. This team-oriented effort provides a natural context to implement collaborative teacher action research. Reciprocally, the teacher action research process brings focus and systematic steps to guide the work of the PLC. Connecting a teacher action research project into the mission and goals of the school/school system and operating within existing team planning or PLC structures will efficiently utilize teachers' efforts to effectively improve teaching and learning through

FIGURE 1.6 Collaborative Action Research Model

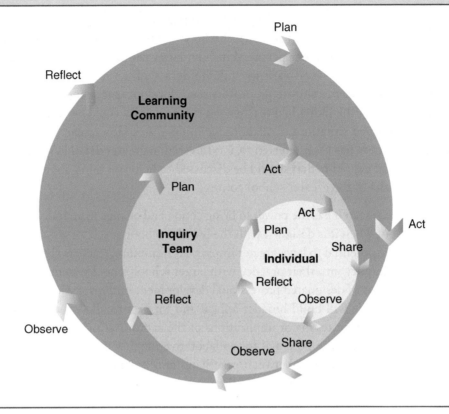

action research. In general, the process of collaborative action research remains the same; however, rather than being distinctly individual, there is a series of cycles of the action research process that proceed from the larger community to the inquiry teams to the individual (see Figure 1.6). This iterative process then reverses as the individual shares information with the inquiry teams, who subsequently reflect upon the data and share the information with the larger group. Collaborative research, including the formation and use of PLCs, will be discussed in greater detail within Chapter 9.

"NOTE"-ABLE THOUGHTS

What are your current school improvement goals? How would engaging in teacher action research fit within the context of your school or school system? What professional development initiatives is your school system currently advocating?

TAKING ACTION: USING THE CAPES FRAMEWORK

Action research has been presented throughout this chapter as a recursive cycle of planning, acting, observing, and reflecting. However, we've not addressed the specific steps, from identifying the topic to developing an action plan, which we feel are necessary to maximize the outcomes associated with your action research project. To help guide you through these steps, our chapters are organized around a self-regulatory framework, referred to as CAPES, which is built upon the principles of planning, action, and reflection. We are sure you can see the similarity of these steps with the tenets of action research. As a result, we believe by incorporating a framework for self-regulation into the action research process, it may facilitate additional attention toward the elements of action research that will ultimately help you successfully use the process in the classroom.

In general, self-regulation is characterized by the three phases mentioned above: planning, action, and reflection. Yet in their model of self-regulation, Winne and Hadwin (1998) further identify a "5-facet typology" (p. 279), referred to as COPES, which describes actions associated with a task that occur within the process of studying. The typology encompassed Conditions, Operations, Product, Evaluation, and Standards. As a result of their work with teachers, Coiro and Putman (2014) adapted the typology to conceptually fit within a revised acronym, CAPES, which was implemented within online inquiry. As part of the CAPES model (see Figure 1.7), the authors proposed a recursive cycle of behavior where learners examine the *Context* associated with a task and use this information to plan a set of *Actions* required to complete the task. The actions produce some form of *Product* that is *Evaluated* (or reflected upon) in relation to a set of *Standards*. In general, the CAPES model will provide an organizational structure for most chapters of the book. The following subheadings will be included in many of the chapters:

- Setting the *Context*. In this section of each chapter, relevant background on the topic for the chapter will be presented to develop the underlying information about the specific step in the action research process. For example, in Chapter 3, this section will describe the purpose of the review of literature. The intent is to show teachers that they are using familiar strategies such as activating prior knowledge about teaching strategies, for example, and establishing real-world connections to their practices or classrooms as they engage in reviewing literature pertinent to their study.

- Taking *Action*. This section of the chapter will synthesize information contained in the Setting the Context section and requires readers to begin to formulate and perform specific actions or enact strategies associated with the content. Referring again to Chapter 3, teachers will learn and enact strategies to find relevant literature, read primary sources, create an annotated bibliography, and begin to develop a synthesis of literature.

- Developing a Plan or *Product*. A plan or a product represents what is produced by the primary sequence of actions performed to complete a task. In general, a plan or product can be internal (i.e., a mental representation) or external (i.e., a tangible item such as a set of notes). Within the proposed text, the primary goal of this section of each chapter is to develop a tangible product that matches the focus of the chapter; for example, in Chapter 3 the product is represented by a synthesis of literature. Thus, it will function similarly to an end-of-chapter task found at the end of most texts, but it will incorporate more defined and specific directions from the Action step to reinforce what is encompassed within the product. An example of the product for the chapter will be included in the "Case in Point" section that is included at the end of each chapter (described below).

- *Evaluating* Against the *Standards*. Are you ready to move on? Whenever learners engage in self-regulatory activities, it is important that they engage in self-reflection to ensure the artifact produced within the process is aligned with the criteria used to evaluate the quality of the product. In essence, the learner is performing a monitoring (metacognitive) function relative to the task. It's important to note that the elements of Product, Evaluation, and Standards are interconnected and generally addressed simultaneously within the CAPES framework, yet they are noted separately for the purpose of the book to add clarity to what is expected for the product. The Evaluating step is characterized by a decision about the quality or qualities of the product relative to the standards. If the product is evaluated positively (e.g., the literature review is comprehensive and captures the necessary information), it is acceptable to proceed to the next step in the process. However, if the evaluation is negative, such as would be the case if a significant body of literature is missing, the learner may need to return to a previous step, such as Taking Action, to address the deficiency. A series of questions as part of a checklist will be included in each chapter and will represent a general set of standards to frame the particular step of the action research the teacher is engaged in.

Each step within the CAPES process will guide the action researcher through the relevant stages of the action research process, including:

- identifying a problem that will evolve into a research topic,

- developing research questions to guide the action research process,

- developing background knowledge and synthesizing information,

- creating a research plan to engage in systematic data collection,

- analyzing data,

- reflecting on the results of the action research, and

- developing a data-driven action plan.

A primary focus will be on building an action research report through the systematic completion of tasks (in the Taking Action section) associated with each step of the process (see Figure 1.8). Of note, prior experience has shown that it is particularly easy

FIGURE 1.7 Recursive Cycle of CAPES Framework

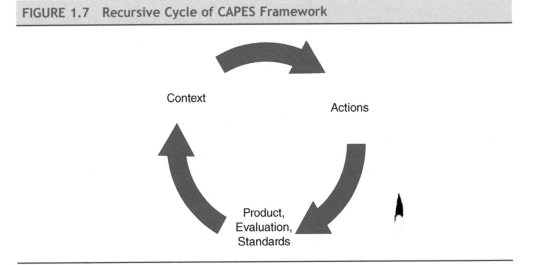

ACTION RESEARCH

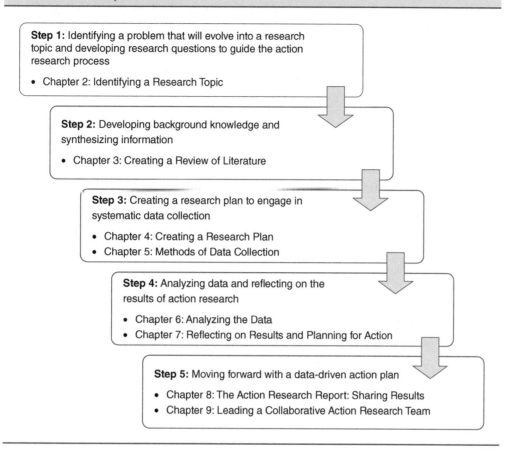

FIGURE 1.8   Steps in the Action Research Process and Their Alignment With Chapters

Step 1: Identifying a problem that will evolve into a research topic and developing research questions to guide the action research process

- Chapter 2: Identifying a Research Topic

Step 2: Developing background knowledge and synthesizing information

- Chapter 3: Creating a Review of Literature

Step 3: Creating a research plan to engage in systematic data collection

- Chapter 4: Creating a Research Plan
- Chapter 5: Methods of Data Collection

Step 4: Analyzing data and reflecting on the results of action research

- Chapter 6: Analyzing the Data
- Chapter 7: Reflecting on Results and Planning for Action

Step 5: Moving forward with a data-driven action plan

- Chapter 8: The Action Research Report: Sharing Results
- Chapter 9: Leading a Collaborative Action Research Team

to focus on the "performance" aspect of self-regulation. Performance is important since individuals who actively use various strategies improve the likelihood of successfully completing a task (Paris & Paris, 2001). Yet planning and reflection also represent vital aspects within self-regulated learning and will represent significant components in each chapter. Without behaviors such as considering the context and goal setting, teachers may not effectively engage in the tasks necessary to complete each of the relevant phases of the action research process.

SUMMARY

In this chapter, we've offered an overview of action research, providing several definitions to help develop an understanding of the process you are about to engage in. As part of the process, we noted that action research is characterized by a recursive cycle (spiral) of planning, acting, observing, and reflecting. Action research studies are eclectic in their design, meaning that there is no one right way of conducting the research, especially given the multiple forms of data that are typically available to teachers. We also established that teachers are well-suited to conduct action research for several reasons, including the availability of data and the need to continually revisit and reflect upon practices. Finally, you were introduced to the CAPES framework that will be used to guide you as you identify a topic, develop a literature review and research plan, and conduct your study. In using CAPES, you'll pay special attention to the Context that influences the manner in which your research is conducted, while constantly evaluating your progress against a set of self-identified standards that will indicate success as well as guide future iterations of the cycle.

Ultimately, the goal of any action research project is the improvement of student learning. Thus, as you engage with the chapters of the book and conduct your action research project, keep the following quote from Sagor (2000) in mind:

> Action research helps educators be more effective at what they care most about—their teaching and the development of their students. . . . When teachers have convincing evidence that their work has made a real difference in their students' lives, the countless hours and endless efforts of teaching seem worthwhile. (p. 3)

Reflecting on this and applying the principles we describe relative to action research and CAPES, you'll achieve the sought-after outcomes of your research.

Key Terms

Acting, p. 8

Action research, p. 5

Observing, p. 8

Planning, p. 7

Practical significance, p. 10

Professional learning community, p. 15

Qualitative research, p. 11

Quantitative research, p. 10

Reflecting, p. 8

Research, p. 4

Statistical significance, p. 10

Case in Point: Introducing the Research Log

Kemmis and McTaggart (1992) describe the necessity of keeping a personal journal as part of the action research process. This journal can serve as a means to record information about the progress of the ongoing study as well as the reflections about the overall process and formative results. Similarly, we feel that one of the best ways to keep track of our ongoing thoughts during the action research process is to use what we refer to as a "researcher's log." Others may refer to this personal journal by different names such as "daybook," but the function of each is similar. The intent is to capture information that will help guide you in your efforts during the study. In the Case in Point scenarios below, we will provide examples of what could be addressed in the research log as two teachers, Margaret Curtis and Matt Wells, begin to think about their students and generate some potential thoughts about a topic. Noting that readers of this book may teach a variety of grade levels, we have elected to provide examples for elementary teachers (Margaret) and secondary teachers (Matt). Both Margaret's and Matt's full action research reports are located in Appendix A for you to examine as we proceed through various steps in the action research process.

To provide some context for what you will read as part of the elementary Case in Point entries, Margaret Curtis teaches 24 second graders with a variety of learning styles and readiness levels in a Title I school near a large metropolitan area. The school where she teaches has a very diverse population, with the majority of students in the school qualifying for free or reduced-price lunch. The teachers and previous principal created a very supportive atmosphere. Recently, a change in leadership at the school resulted in a new principal who is very focused on data and its use to inform instruction. The principal has begun to consider mandating programs that prescribe instruction and facilitate the collection of data. In Margaret's graduate class, she was assigned to write a journal entry that describes her current teaching assignment, a problem or situation that is relevant to her classroom as well as interesting from her perspective, and some preliminary thoughts on what topic she will address within the action research study that is an assignment for the course. Below is her first entry into her journal, which her professor refers to as a Research Log.

In the secondary Case in Point segments, you will be introduced to Matt Wells, who teaches three sections of a ninth-grade science class in a high school located in a suburban area near a large metropolitan city. The school is classified as medium socioeconomic status, with 48% of students being eligible for free or reduced-price lunch. While the school is not Title I, it does qualify to receive state funds proportionate to the free and reduced-price lunch percentage. The student population consists mainly of Caucasian students (79%), with other race/ethnicities comprising the remainder of the population: African American (17%), Asian American (2%), American Indian/Pacific Islander (1%), and other (1%). The science department has started implementing an investigation workshop approach to teaching science at the school. There is a desire to move toward pedagogy that promotes not just the acquisition of science knowledge and skills, but also 21st-century skills that will prepare students for future college and career success. The investigation workshop approach requires development of communication and collaboration skills, information and technology skills, and critical and creative thinking skills, as students are asked to engage in problem solving, collaborate in teams, and use a variety of informational resources and technology tools to demonstrate their science content knowledge and skills. The science class sections are ability grouped based on language arts skill levels.

One Elementary Teacher's Journey: Preliminary Research Log Entry

In my classroom, I have 24 students, all either seven or eight years old. I have been teaching long enough to know what my students need to be able to do in order to be successful in third grade. My goal, as a teacher, is to ensure I help each student reach their maximum potential, while supporting them as they work toward proficiency in the second-grade standards. At the same time, I must think about building a foundation to help prepare the students to be successful at the next grade level.

In my classroom, three students are reading above grade level, five students are reading at grade level, six students are reading very close to grade level, and the remaining 10 students are reading below grade level. Many could be reading more fluently. Half of our year has passed and I am becoming very concerned about these boys and girls in the last category, since their low reading skills are impacting their entire school day. They have been making progress, but they have yet to meet quarterly goals during biweekly progress monitoring. Being able to read in an efficient manner has a huge impact on comprehending text not only in literacy, but in all content areas. Solving this problem is important to me because these students all work very hard and are motivated to become better readers, but they are not at the same levels as their peers. I do not want them to become unmotivated and lose interest, nor do I want them to lose sight of their bigger goal, which is reading to be able to understand. The majority of the students in my class who struggle with fluency are also struggling with comprehension and need more time or assistance when answering written questions about text. If my students were able to read easier and faster, I feel it wouldn't be such a daunting task to them. I feel if they can succeed at increasing their reading level, they might increase other academic skills as well.

It is my goal as a teacher to help these struggling readers make significant gains in reading in order to prepare them for the next grade level. When students leave second grade and enter third grade, the focus shifts from learning to read, to reading to learn, as they become involved in district-wide and state-wide standardized testing. During my literacy workshop, I always meet with a small group (3–5) of students who are low readers who are not proficient at a second-grade level. We meet at least two or three times a week and, whenever possible, I work with them individually, in partners, and as a small group to improve their skills. I think this is an area that I may focus on as part of my research because not only does it align with the needs of my students, but it also represents a way for me to look at the impact of my practices with a manageable group of students. I am a little fearful right now about how I am going to juggle all of my regular responsibilities, including the potential changes in curriculum that are being discussed, with completing all the work necessary for my graduate class. To say I am feeling a little stressed is probably an understatement!

One Secondary Teacher's Journey: Preliminary Research Log Entry

During professional development sessions last spring as we considered moving from direct instruction to an investigation workshop approach, we were introduced to current research that indicates that all students enjoy and are motivated by freedom of movement throughout the room and opportunities for choice. There is also research that demonstrates that with an investigative learning approach, students acquire deeper understandings of the content they study. I teach ninth-grade science to students who are divided into three sections based on their language arts proficiencies. The three sections allow for differentiation during instruction on a narrower spectrum. This way, the English instructor can select a single novel to teach the whole class, versus three novels at different reading Lexile levels for each of the three core classes. As a result, I have three science sections with different reading levels.

The third group, which has the lowest reading levels, struggles to grasp the ninth-grade science concepts. They also tend to be disengaged and many

have a poor attitude toward learning. I have already switched the first two core groups to open investigative workshops with positive success during the first six weeks of school. I am feeling more and more confident with this approach and see that it has important learning outcomes for my students. They are becoming more self-driven learners and they seem to really enjoy being in class. They like the freedom to explore ideas, test out different hypotheses, and generate new insights within their groups. I feel that they are connecting with the concepts more than what I have experienced in the past with teaching the ninth-grade curriculum. Their test scores are good, and I hope they continue to improve as they master the skills and become more familiar with their roles and responsibilities of working in their teams.

I have not yet begun to use the investigation workshop approach with my lower-ability level section of the course. I, along with my colleagues, have been hesitant to introduce this new approach because of the behavioral problems and difficulty with attention that exists in this group of students. These students struggle with complex texts, working independently, and completing tasks. Their inability to persist with a task and work effectively with others is a challenge with an open investigation approach to teaching and learning. However, I am wondering if the direct instruction approach to teaching that is very teacher controlled is actually undermining their motivation and their sense of responsibility to their own learning. I would like to try using the open investigation approach with all my students, even though many of my colleagues have warned me that the lower-level students with lower-level reading and writing abilities need more direct, explicit instruction. I am nervous and excited about this as a possible research project. I will be the first one in the science department and in the grade level to experiment with using this approach with these students. I know that there may be resistance from the students and that there is a chance of failure and disappointment with the attempt, but I feel like I need to provide the same learning opportunities for all of my students, so I am excited to really think about how to examine this aspect of my practice.

Activities and Additional Resources

1. Create a Venn diagram with *teacher* in one circle and *researcher* in the other. Fill in the diagram with adjectives or activities for each, specifically thinking about what characteristics/actions are common between the two.

2. Create a Research Log to help you consider potential topics for your action research study. Think about your classroom. Is there something that is consistently challenging for your students? Have you tried to teach something in a different way? Was it successful? Why? Alternately, if it wasn't, what may have prevented success?

3. Locate and examine your school improvement plan or discuss a strategic area of focus with an administrator or colleague(s). Consider: Is there a topic in the plan that could be influential in the development of a topic of an action research study?

In each chapter, we will provide you a set of additional resources that can be examined if you are seeking more information about a specific topic introduced within the chapter. These resources range from journal articles to books and websites. While we feel that our chapters provide you with the primary information you will need to carry out your action research study, these resources will help you expand your knowledge or provide a slightly different perspective on the action research process. In sum, they are intended to supplement what we provide in *Action Research: Using Strategic Inquiry to Improve Teaching and Learning*.

Print Resources

Armstrong, F., & Moore, M. (Eds.). (2004). *Action research for inclusive education: Changing places, changing practices, changing minds.* London, England: Routledge-Falmer.

McNiff, J., & Whitehead, J. (2011). *All you need to know about action research* (2nd ed.). Thousand Oaks, CA: Sage.

Mertler, C. A. (2014). *Action research: Improving schools and empowering educators* (4th ed.). Thousand Oaks, CA: Sage.

Meyers, E., & Rust, F. (Eds.). (2003). *Taking action with teacher action research.* Portsmouth, NH: Heinemann.

Mills, G. E. (2011). *Action research: A guide for the teacher researcher* (4th ed.). Boston, MA: Allyn & Bacon.

Zeichner, K., & Marion, R. (2001). *Practitioner resource guide for action research.* Oxford, OH: National Staff Development Council.

Student Study Site

edge.sagepub.com/putman

- Take the practice quiz.
- Review key terms with eFlashcards.
- Explore topics with video and multimedia.

References

Bennett, C. K. (1993). Teacher-researchers: All dressed up and no place to go. *Educational Leadership, 51,* 69–70.

Boyd, T. A. (1957). *Professional amateur: The biography of Charles Franklin Kettering.* New York, NY: E. P. Dutton.

Caro-Bruce, C. (2000). *Action research facilitator's handbook.* Wichita Falls, TX: National Staff Development Council.

Coiro, J., & Putman, S. M. (2014). Teaching students to self-regulate during online inquiry. In K. Wood, J. Paratore, R. McCormack, & B. Kissel (Eds.), *What's new in literacy teaching? IRA E-ssentials series.* Newark, DE: International Reading Association.

Collins, J. S., & Duguid, P. (1989). Situated cognition and the culture of learning. *Educational Researcher, 32,* 32–42.

Darling-Hammond, L. (1996). The right to learn and the advancement of teaching: Research, policy, and practice for democratic education. *Educational Researcher, 25*, 5–17.

Evans, C. (1991). Support for teachers studying their own work. *Educational Leadership, 48*, 11–13.

Flick, U. (2009). *An introduction to qualitative research* (4th ed.). Thousand Oaks, CA: Sage.

Fusarelli, L. D., & Fusarelli, B. C. (2015). Federal education policy from Reagan to Obama: Convergence, divergence, and "control." In B. S. Cooper, J. G. Cibulka, & L. D. Fusarelli (Eds.), *Handbook of education politics and policy* (2nd ed.) (pp. 189–210). New York, NY: Routledge.

Gall, M. E., Borg, W. R., & Gall, J. P. (2007). *Educational research: An introduction* (8th ed.). Boston, MA: Pearson.

Hendricks, C. (2006). *Improving schools through action research*. Boston, MA: Allyn & Bacon.

Johnson, J. (2000). *Teaching and learning mathematics: Using research to shift from the "yesterday" mind to the "tomorrow" mind*. Olympia, WA: Office of Superintendent of Public Instruction.

Kemmis, S. (1988). *Action research in retrospect and prospect*. Victoria, Australia: Deakin University Press.

Kemmis, S., & McTaggart, R. (1982). *The action research planner*. Victoria, Australia: Deakin University Press.

Kemmis, S., & McTaggart, R. (Eds.). (1992). *The action research planner* (3rd ed.). Geelong, Australia: Deakin University Press.

Kemmis, S., McTaggart, R., & Nixon, R. (2014). *The action research planner: Doing critical participatory action research*. Singapore: Springer.

Levin, B. B., & Rock, T. C. (2003). The effects of collaborative action research on preservice and experienced teacher partners in professional development schools. *Journal of Teacher Education, 54*, 135–149.

Lewin, K. (1946). Action research and minority problems. *Journal of Social Sciences, 2*, 34–46.

McKernan, J. (1991). *Curriculum action research*. London, England: Kogan Page.

McNiff, J., & Whitehead, J. (2011). *All you need to know about action research* (2nd ed.). Thousand Oaks, CA: Sage.

Mertler, C. A. (2014). *Action research: Improving schools and empowering educators* (4th ed.). Thousand Oaks, CA: Sage.

Mills, G. E. (2011). *Action research: A guide for the teacher researcher* (4th ed.). Boston, MA: Allyn & Bacon.

National Governors Association Center for Best Practices & Council of Chief State School Officers. (2010). *Common Core State Standards*. Washington, DC: Authors.

Paris, S. G., & Paris, A. H. (2001). Classroom applications of research on self-regulated learning. *Educational Psychologist, 36*, 89–101.

Phillips, D. K., & Carr, K. (2006). *Becoming a teacher through action research: Process, context, and self-study*. New York, NY: Routledge.

Riel, M. (2007). Understanding action research. Retrieved from http://cadres.pepperdine.edu/ccar/define.html

Sagor, R. (2000). *Guiding school improvement with action research*. Alexandria, VA: Association for Supervision and Curriculum Development.

Sagor, R. (2005). *The action research guidebook: A four-step process for educators and school teams*. Thousand Oaks, CA: Corwin.

Sindelar, P. T., Washburn-Moses, L., Thomas, R. A., & Leko, C. D. (2014). The policy and economic contexts of teacher education. In P. T. Sindelar, E. D. McCray, M. T. Brownell, & B. Lignugaris/Kraft (Eds.), *Handbook of research on special education teacher preparation* (pp. 3–16). New York, NY: Routledge.

Somekh, B. (1995). The contribution of action research to development in social endeavours: A position paper on action research methodology. *British Educational Research Journal, 21*, 339–355.

Stoll, L., Bolam, R., McMahon, A., Wallace, M., & Thomas, S. (2006). Professional learning communities: A review of the literature. *Journal of Educational Change, 7*, 221–258.

Stringer, E. T. (2007). *Action research* (3rd ed.). Thousand Oaks, CA: Sage.

Walker, T. (2013). No more 'Sit and Get': Rebooting teacher professional development. *NEA Today*. Retrieved from http://neatoday.org/2013/04/29/no-more-sit-and-get-rebooting-teacher-professional-development

Winne, P. H., & Hadwin, A. F. (1998). Studying as self-regulated learning. In D. J. Hacker, J. Dunlosky, & A. C. Graesser (Eds.), *Metacognition in educational theory and practice* (pp. 277–304). Mahwah, NJ: Lawrence Erlbaum Associates.

Zuber-Skerritt, O. (1996). Emancipatory action research for organisational change and management development. In O. Zuber-Skerritt (Ed.), *New directions in action research* (pp. 83–105). London, England: Falmer.

PHASE II

Goal Setting and Planning

CHAPTER 2

Identifying a Research Topic

GUIDING QUESTIONS

After reading this chapter, you should be able to answer the following questions:

- What are the initial steps for developing an action research project?

- How do you generate a topic for action research?

- How do you develop a question once you have chosen a topic?

- Once you have developed a question, how do you proceed with your action research project?

CHAPTER AIMS AND GOALS

The intent of this chapter is to initiate the strategic plan of your action research by identifying a topic of significance and to begin the process of formulating a research question to guide your study. As you proceed through this chapter, you will develop an understanding of

- how to begin the action research process,

- what makes for a meaningful and productive action research topic,

- how to narrow the focus of potential topics,

- how to clarify your topic by writing a statement of the problem,

- how action research questions are formulated, and

- how to evaluate your topic and potential research questions.

The challenge of identifying a research topic for your action research project is that there are a multitude of possibilities for you to explore. Most teachers have many questions about their students and their teaching practice. Determining what will be the focus of your action research project is the first step in developing the action research plan. The potential benefits of the action research process hinge on a carefully selected topic and well-designed research questions. This chapter will assist you in developing these first crucial initial steps of the action research process.

SETTING THE CONTEXT: CHOOSING A RESEARCH TOPIC

The purpose of teacher action research is to provide a systematic process to allow teachers to problem solve and come to better understand learning in and from their practice (Ball & Cohen, 1999). **Problems of practice**, as they are commonly referred to, are the everyday challenges that school leaders, teachers, and educators of all types face in their schools, classrooms, and educational organizations. "Most applied research begins when you select an everyday problem, interest, or concern for further study" (Machi & McEvoy, 2008, p. 16). For you, as an educator, these are challenges that likely inspire, frustrate, embolden, or push you to identify how to best support student learning. You may have already heard the term *problem of practice,* whether working with your colleagues in a professional learning community (PLC), developing a school improvement plan, discussing how your own challenges as a classroom teacher complicate your work with students, or listening to practicing teachers discuss common problems or challenges related to student achievement or learning. Whether you are attuned to them or not, problems of practice affect your work and have a significant influence on the questions you reflect upon as you think about your teaching and the context you work in. These problems are often linked to broad educational issues like the achievement gap or educational policies that directly impact your daily practice in the classroom (see additional list in Figure 2.1). It is often valuable to start with broad challenges that you face as an educator to ensure that your final, focused research topic is connected to a larger issue or problem.

FIGURE 2.1 Examples of Broadly Conceived Problems of Practice

The achievement gap

Authentic assessment

Immersion of English language learners

Common Core math implementation

Problem-based learning

Balanced literacy approach

Response to Intervention

Gender equity

Technology integration for higher-order thinking

Global competence

"NOTE"-ABLE THOUGHTS

Take a moment and think about what problems of practice are of great interest currently to the broader educational community. Is there a program that your school or school system has just implemented, such as Response to Intervention or a balanced literacy approach, that would be appropriate to research and investigate? As you consider problems of practice that interest the broader educational community, what are you most curious about? Generate an initial list of broad educational problems or issues that directly impact your classroom practice.

FORMULATE A PERSONAL EDUCATIONAL PHILOSOPHY

While studying to be teachers, we are often asked to write our personal educational philosophies. The intent of this exercise is to clearly articulate what it is that we believe and value in educational contexts. To formulate a personal educational philosophy, we consider the following:

- What do you see as the grander purpose of education in a society and community?

- What, specifically, is the role and responsibility of the teacher in the classroom?

- How do you believe students learn best?

- In general, what are your goals for your students?

- What qualities do you believe an effective teacher should have?

- Do you believe that all students can learn?

- What expectations do you have of students in your classroom?

A clear conception of your personal educational philosophy serves to guide and inspire you throughout your teaching career and should act as a centerpiece around which all of your decisions rotate. Personal educational philosophies may evolve over time, and it is important to reflect continuously on how your practice aligns with your espoused educational beliefs and values. This is significant because misalignment between your practice and personal educational philosophy often leads to internal discord that may impact your teaching effectiveness and student learning.

Early in the process of planning your action research project you will want to self-reflect on how topics of interest and potential solutions align with your personal educational beliefs and values. Will this investigation assist you in moving your practice in closer alignment with your personal educational philosophies? Will the topic of the investigation assist you in affirming, refining, or shaping your current educational beliefs and values? Will this investigation help you resolve discord that currently exists between what you believe and what you are practicing in the classroom? For this action research process to truly impact your learning, there must be the opportunity for you to test, challenge, and engage in deep reflection around your personal educational beliefs and values.

"NOTE"-ABLE THOUGHTS

Look back at the problems of practice list you generated, and think about how each one aligns with your personal educational philosophy. Are there some potential broad topics that you can discard because they do not help you move closer to operationalizing your espoused beliefs and values or your vision for what you want to happen within your classroom? Which of your potential topics have the possibility to allow you to test, challenge, and engage in deep reflection around your personal educational beliefs and values? Identify and narrow your potential topics to ones that stimulate your passion, your professional aims, and goals, and that can provide the opportunity for you to clarify and refine what you believe about teaching and learning.

NARROW YOUR FOCUS: YOUR CLASSROOM, YOUR EXPERIENCES

As you examine your narrowed list of broader educational problems or issues, begin reflecting on your day-to-day experiences in the classroom in relation to the broader problems/issues you are curious about. In order to narrow the focus of your action research you will want to begin by asking, "What is my concern in my practice?" As a reflective practitioner you probably have many aspects of your practice that you wonder about daily. We want you to dig a little deeper and consider questions you have related to student characteristics, curriculum or program implementation, classroom structures and procedures, or utilization of resources and materials. If a concern or problem of practice is not immediately apparent to you for topic identification, it may be helpful to consider the many potential categories of topics that are often utilized in teacher action research to support you in topic identification. Mertler (2009) presents a list of several categories of topics that could be considered for action research studies. The following categories and ideas are listed:

- Classroom environment—Topics in this category include the various aspects of the physical and psychosocial environments in classrooms and school buildings, and their impact on student learning.

- Instructional materials—Topics might include the appropriateness of textbooks and other printed materials with respect to gender and ethnicity, the extent to which teachers find the materials useful and to which they support the curriculum, or the perceptions that students have of those materials.

- Classroom management—Possible research topics might include the level of satisfaction that both teachers and students have with the methods of managing student behavior, the degree to which the methods of managing behavior allow students to learn without unnecessary distraction, or how limiting those methods are with respect to the ability of teachers to teach as they would like.

- Instructional methods—Topics might include the effect of a given teaching method on student learning, the impact that different teacher personality styles can have on student learning or motivation to learn, or methods of providing effective feedback to students on their academic performance.

- The relation of human growth patterns to education—Possible topics might include ways to incorporate individual students' interests and learning preferences, teaching strategies that support self-regulated learning, or those that support individual rates of learning.

- Grading and evaluation—Teachers often have questions about the effects that grades and other forms of evaluative decisions have on student motivation, stress, achievement, and attitudes, or on effective methods of incorporating authentic assessment and other nontraditional means of assessing students.

- Conferencing—Possible topics might involve the ways in which parents and teachers value individual conferences or strategies for improving the effectiveness of parent–teacher conferences (Mertler, 2009).

These topic categories may give you some insight into all the variety and possibilities of teacher action research projects. As you explore what you are most interested in, you might continue to push your thinking by asking yourself these questions: Why do I do things in a particular way? Are there things that could be done differently? If I could wave a magic wand and instantly change something that I am frustrated by, what would it be? Is there something I would like to experiment with in my practice?

■ ■ ■ VOICES FROM THE FIELD

Bailey Rogers, Sixth-Grade Teacher

Over the past few years, my district has really begun to look at how technology can be effectively incorporated into instruction. In the past two years, several schools started allowing their students to bring their own technology to school. I believe this happened for a few reasons, but mostly because students had more technology at home than at school and many students were already using it to help them in various ways as they completed assignments. The first situation is really applicable at my school. Classrooms usually have between two and four computers each, but they are often so old and slow that the students never want to use them for anything. As much as I want to incorporate technology into my instruction, it's definitely been challenging with these resources.

One teacher on my team was recently awarded a grant that allowed her to get a class set of iPads and a rolling cart. She has offered to allow me and the rest of the sixth-grade team to use them at various points during the year. I teach science and with all of the talk about having students develop 21st century skills, a burning question in my mind relates to how effective iPad use is in the classroom for different subject areas. I want to use the iPads in a way that engages the students and allows them to really explore concepts related to science, to create presentations, and as a writing resource. I really feel like the sky is the limit, but I keep wondering if there are specific advantages (or disadvantages) related to student learning when iPads are used in these ways. I have a unit coming up on thermal and chemical energy, and I have a variety of resources, both aligned with traditional instructional methods as well as a number of new resources that can be accessed through the iPad. I am leaning toward using the iPads in one class and engaging in more traditional lecture and reading-based instruction in another class. I'll compare how well each class performs on the end of unit exam and maybe interview a few students to get their perspectives. Not only will I be interested to see the results of this, but I think I will be able to share them with my team and our principal.

As you begin to identify a focus, make sure that it is a concern that you can do something about. It should not be bound by the actions of others. You need to have some level of control over the concern or problem in order to take action to resolve it or to bring meaningful change to your practice (Mills, 2011). Recognize that when you focus on a concern in your practice, it is tied to your personal values. As a result, you should select some aspect of your teaching that relates to what is important to you about your students' learning and your own personal educational philosophy, as discussed in the previous section. You will want to develop an action research plan that not only impacts your personal beliefs and understandings of teaching and learning but also has direct impact on student learning. There are many interesting areas of focus you could pursue, such as poor morale as a result of the low pay for teachers or methods the school system uses to make curriculum and instruction decisions that are implemented across schools; however, these are not topics that you have any control over or ones that will provide a solution that has the potential to document improvement in student learning. Remember, as you are beginning to bring focus to your plan, make sure you do not stray from the primary intent of teacher action research, which is the use of systematic inquiry by teachers to improve teaching practices and student learning.

As you examine teaching and learning in your classroom, it may serve you well to engage in opportunities to reflect, observe, and discuss a potential topic with colleagues. You might spend a week paying particularly close attention to the problem or area for improvement as it currently exists in your classroom. During this time, you might write down observations, reflections, and the current status of the focus area in a reflective journal (see an example in the Case in Point examples). What is working well and what is not? How are students responding to the current instruction, program, or strategies? You will want to take time to observe students in the learning environment. To facilitate this, you could videotape yourself while teaching. Then, while reviewing the tape, you could evaluate the teaching and students simultaneously. It might be valuable to invite a colleague into your classroom to observe your teaching and student learning to gain another perspective on the issue or area of concern. It can be very helpful to discuss your concern with fellow educators in your school, to let them help you focus your concern, and to let their concerns help you identify yours.

Another consideration in your topic identification should be to determine if there are any potential ethical issues within your ideas for addressing the problem of practice. As you approach the problem, you might have to wrestle with design considerations, such as whether it is ethical to deny certain students curriculum or instructional best practices, in order for you to conduct your study. You might be faced with the ethical consideration of using curriculum materials provided by politically biased groups that have more of a political agenda than an educational intention. Or you may wrestle with whether the focus of your work takes a deficit approach toward disadvantaged groups versus a strengths-based approach toward the diverse groups you teach. There are many inherent ethical issues that may present themselves as you continue to develop your topic and the plan that you will use to study it. You will need to pay attention to any ethical issues that emerge and think deeply about ways that they can be resolved in your planning that align with your personal beliefs and values and that always put the students' best interests ahead of the need to conduct the study. Being aware of and thoughtful about ethical issues should be a part of the initial steps of developing the action research plan.

As you continue to narrow your ideas for potential topics, you will want to consider if there is a way to measure or analyze the potential problems of practice. Is there data that can be collected or evidence to be evaluated? If you institute a change, the desired behaviors or intended learning outcomes must be observable or measurable. In other words, if you are looking for impact on student learning, change in behaviors, or improvement in practice you must have a way to document growth, change, or achievement.

"NOTE"-ABLE THOUGHTS

Based on your reflections of the broad educational context, your personal educational philosophy, and your specific classroom context, select a problem or concern to begin to focus on. Do this by asking yourself is there a practice, issue, or behavior you can improve? Is there a problem you can solve? Is there something you can change that might help to enhance understanding for your students? Are you able to identify strengths and weaknesses in your program or practice? What do you hope to change and why? Once you have an idea of something that can be improved, ask yourself these questions:

- Is my problem connected to a larger issue that will be of interest to the broader educational community?

- Do I have control over any aspect of the problem?

- Is the problem something that is manageable and practical?

- Will this problem allow me to test, challenge, and engage in deep reflection around my personal educational beliefs and values?

Is there some way to measure the problem, such as student exams or other assessments, audio or videotape, survey results, other statistics, or sample?

You can use the questions in "Note"-able Thoughts to test out several of your identified areas of concern within your practice. If you are unable to answer "yes" to any of the questions related to a potential topic, you will likely want to eliminate it from consideration. This will be helpful in narrowing down the focus of potential topics and allow you to identify a meaningful and productive action research topic. A research topic will be meaningful if you personally value the investigation because it will provide a solution or deeper understanding around a problem that matters to you. It will be productive if it leads to improvement in practice. It will also be meaningful if your solutions and deeper understandings of the problem have broad appeal and interest to the educational communities to which you belong. Therefore, it is important to identify the topic only after a thorough examination of your personal and professional values and the educational contexts in which you operate.

TAKING ACTION: DEVELOPING THE RESEARCH TOPIC

REFLECT FURTHER ON THE TOPIC

After identifying a topic for the action research, you may be thinking, "What do I do next?" The first action to take will be to continue to develop your thinking around the

FIGURE 2.2   Organizer for Questions to Consider While Developing Topic

Consideration	Your Response
What is your topic?	
What do you want to learn from this topic?	
What are you planning to do in order to address this topic?	
To whom will the outcome of your study be important?	
How much time do you anticipate the study requiring?	
How difficult do you anticipate it will be to conduct the study?	
Do you foresee any ethical concerns?	

Adapted from p. 68: Mertler, C. A. (2009). *Action research: Teachers as researchers in the classroom.* Los Angeles, CA: Sage.

identified research topic. The above self-reflection chart (see Figure 2.2) will assist you in recording additional ideas to support topic development.

■ ■ ■ VOICES FROM THE FIELD

Cindy Vollmer, 10th-Grade Teacher

As I began thinking about possible topics for my action research, an idea that came to mind was that one of the most prominent catch phrases currently buzzing around the educational community is "writing across the curriculum." Specifically, the National Council of Teachers of Mathematics (NCTM) has published numerous recommendations that include writing as part of math instruction. I recently read in NCTM's *Principles and Standards for School Mathematics* that "instructional programs from prekindergarten through grade 12 should enable all students to organize and consolidate their mathematical thinking through communication, communicate their mathematical thinking coherently and clearly to peers, teachers, and others, analyze and evaluate the mathematical thinking and strategies of others, and use the language of mathematics to express mathematical ideas precisely." Once I saw this information, I started thinking that the use of writing journals or logs could be beneficial to the progress of achieving some of these lofty goals.

In my classroom, I have noticed some of my students can come to the correct answer in math class, but have no idea how to explain how they arrived at that particular conclusion. These same students freeze when it comes to problem solving with word problems. Missing from my instruction has been attention to students judging the reasonableness of their solutions, and reflecting

(Continued)

(Continued)

on their thinking. Part of the reason why I feel that writing journals will be so beneficial in my math class is that I will be able to more closely monitor my students' learning. Hopefully, it will allow me to correct misconceptions earlier, guide the problem-solving process more closely, and be more in tune with my students' needs. I also feel that the students in my school lack the ability or confidence to express their logic and thought process in relation to the math work they are completing. This, combined with the push from the NCTM standards and the desire for my students to have a solid foundation in math, contribute to my consideration of the following research question: How can using writing journals in the mathematics classroom improve students' ability to understand and express mathematical concepts and problem solve?

WRITE THE PROBLEM STATEMENT

A second action step in topic development is to write the topic as a problem statement. A **problem statement** is a few sentences or a short paragraph that addresses the three elements of who, what, and how, and conveys the overall goal of the project (Pearson Education, Inc., 2008). For example:

Middle school students in a fifth-grade classroom (who) lack strategies for dividing fractions (what) as determined by scores on an end-of-chapter test administered by the teacher (how). The test scores show the average number of correct answers was 9 out of 20. The goal of the action research is to increase the number of correct answers by an average of six per student during the next four weeks (goal of the project).

OR

Kindergarten students (who) lack conceptual details in their writing and drawing related to social studies content (what) for an upcoming unit on Community Helpers as demonstrated on a pre-assessment rubric (how). The mean score of the pre-assessment rubric for drawing was 1.87 and 2.13 for writing; they need to demonstrate growth in the amount of detail in both their drawing and writing product to score at level 3, which indicates that students meet grade-level expectations, on the rubric in the post-assessment (goal of project).

The problem statement will allow you to capture the problem of practice in a concise and clear manner and allow you to communicate your action research topic in a more developed way. It will also help you to keep a tight focus on the elements and the goal of the project as you move into further developing the plan.

GENERATE SOLUTIONS TO THE PROBLEM

Once you develop the problem statement, the next question is "What am I going to do about it?" You will need to formulate a **hypothesis**, or proposed explanation, about the possible source of the problem and how to address it. Ask yourself if there is some change you could introduce to your students that would help you help them improve the quality of their learning (Henning, Stone, & Kelly, 2009). You will need to think about the problem you will be focusing on and brainstorm as many solutions to improve the problem. Maybe when you were exploring the different sources for information within your classroom context to identify a topic, you came across something you would like to try. You may have been involved in a district or school-based professional development initiative, been introduced to a potential solution to the problem in an education course, or read about how other teachers are addressing the problem in a recent professional development publication that you subscribe to. There are no limits to sources that may help you generate a potential solution. Keep an open mind and think about different ways to address the problem until you come up with at least three to five solutions. This will ensure you have enough possible solutions from which to choose.

If you need to know more before you can identify potential solutions, then talk with students to get a sense of how they see the quality of their learning, discuss ideas with colleagues, and/or seek educational resources. As you generate and consider solutions to the problem, it may be helpful to determine if there is any existing educational research or a theoretical rationale to support the use of a particular solution. You may do a brief initial search to determine if the solutions you have generated are grounded in an existing knowledge base or theory. Does there appear to be evidence within the field that the solution you are considering is a viable way to address the problem? You will want to feel confident that you will be able to build a rationale for a potential solution that is grounded in educational literature or theory. If you are unfamiliar with how to effectively search for related literature, see the Tech Connections box to get started or refer to Chapter 3 for more detailed information.

Now examine the list you have generated and select a possible solution for the problem. The choice of the solution must be one that is manageable and practical. It must be able to be carried out within the context of your practice. As part of your topic identification, the solution is critical because it is what will be investigated to see how it improves practice and student learning. Therefore, time and thought put into Step 3 is essential to success of the action research plan you develop. If you have a specific solution identified to address the problem, the action research will be more developed, focused, and productive.

DEVELOP THE RESEARCH QUESTION

The fourth and final action step in this section is to develop a specific research question. The **research question**, as the name implies, is what you will attempt to answer as a result of the actions and activities conducted within your research. It is used to guide your study. Please note that while it is possible to have more than one research question for an action research plan, we strongly recommend that you are careful not to design too many for the initial phase of the work. The research question should assist you in staying focused and should be written broadly to address the big ideas of your investigation.

TECH CONNECTIONS

As you are formulating your research topic, you will want to confirm that there is an existing literature or research base to support the use of the potential solution(s) you are considering to address your statement of the problem. Conducting an initial search of the literature at this time is valuable, as you may gain additional insights into what others have investigated or implemented. While there are a variety of tools that can assist you in this process, you might want to utilize Google Scholar (http://scholar.google.com/) initially to help with this task. Google Scholar will provide you with access to literature and research studies to assist you in determining if there is a rationale within the literature to support your thinking about the potential effectiveness of the solutions you are considering. Google Scholar functions like any other search engine, and you can enter keywords to see what exists in the literature related to your topic. If you receive a large number of results, there is a good chance that someone has researched your topic (or a similar one) in the past and you may be able to draw upon some of the information. Another resource that we've found helpful for preliminary searches is Academia.edu. Referred to as a "social networking site for academics," Academia.edu allows you to search for papers that have been posted to the site by individuals interested in sharing their work. One inherent advantage of the site, once you join, is that you can "follow" certain topics and receive notifications when additional papers associated with the particular keyword are uploaded to the site. This may be advantageous, as it diminishes the necessity of examining a long list of results, many of which may not be applicable to your given research. Given the focus of this chapter is on formulating your topic, we're limiting our information about searching to the Tech Connections. We will help you engage in a much more thorough examination of the literature/ research in Chapter 3 before finalizing your research plan in Chapters 4 and 5.

There are certain characteristics of good research questions that you should keep in mind as you set out to develop a question to guide the initial phase of your study. First, the question that you design must relate directly to the issue or problem that you have chosen to explore. If you develop more than one question, each needs to be related to the others, and together they need to be related to the overall issue or problem. Second, the question must be answerable. Although this may seem intuitive, it is necessary to make sure that an answer to the question you pose is attainable within the context of your work and resources. A good research question usually begins with *why, how,* or *what.* You will need to discard any questions that can be answered with *yes* or *no* as these are not conducive to explaining and discussing your results. You want to pose a challenging, higher-level question that demands explanations, reasons, or reveals relationship (Padak & Padak, n.d.; Pine, 2009). If you do start with a "yes or no" question, though, you are in good company. By our estimation, about 40% of the first-time researchers we work with draft one of these questions early in the question formation process.

To assist you in writing a clear, concise, and challenging question, you may want to use the research question format below (see Casas et al., 2005). This format is particularly helpful in keeping the question from becoming too lengthy. If you have worked your way through the action steps above of writing a problem statement and identifying a solution, the research question format is a structured and user-friendly approach to writing the research question. Although this format may be useful in writing the research question, it may not work for every investigation.

Example Format: What is the effect of _____ (intervention) on _____ (student description) when learning _____ (content or topic description)?

Example Questions Using Format:

1. What is the effect of SimCourt on high school students' word identification skills when developing basic foundations of reading?

2. What is the effect of the Passive Concert on the comprehension of my kindergarten students' content knowledge during our study of the Community Helpers unit?

3. What is the effect of Learning Menus on student motivation and completion of project work when learning about healthy food choices?

Other Example Questions Without Format Structure:

1. How does the Writers' Workshop approach affect my students' feelings toward writing?

2. How will the use of the cooperative learning strategies (Jigsaw II and Inside-Outside Circle) increase the achievement of seven of my students who are failing in science?

3. How will student-led discussions impact the successful completion of homework reading assignments by students?

4. What happens to student learning in my classroom when I use a project-centered approach to teaching the geography of Latin America?

DEVELOPING A PLAN OR A PRODUCT: COMPLETING A TOPIC PROPOSAL FORM

As a product for this chapter you will develop and compile your ideas to complete a Topic Proposal Form. The purpose is to clearly articulate your research topic either to gain approval by the instructor of a course that requires action research or to communicate with colleagues or administrators your initial topic proposal to generate interest and support for the developing action research plan. Following the Topic Proposal Form in this section, you will find an example to support your understanding of this product. You may also want to look ahead to the Case in Point examples to see another real-world example to support the development of your Topic Proposal Form (see Figures 2.3 and 2.4).

EVALUATING AGAINST THE STANDARDS: ARE YOU READY TO MOVE ON?

It is important before moving forward with the planning of the action research that you engage in self-reflection to ensure that the content of the Topic Proposal Form is aligned with the criteria used to evaluate the quality of the product. To support you in evaluating

FIGURE 2.3 Blank Topic Proposal Form

Topic Proposal Form

Topic:

Statement of the problem:

Research question to be studied:

Rationale—Why is this topic important to study?:

Broad educational appeal for the topic:

Personal connection/interest in the topic:

FIGURE 2.4 Completed Topic Proposal Form

Topic: The Effect of the Passive Concert on Kindergarten Learning

Statement of the problem: Kindergarten students lack conceptual details in their writing and drawing related to social studies content for an upcoming unit on Community Helpers, as demonstrated on a pre-assessment rubric. The mean score of the pre-assessment rubric for drawing was 1.87 and 2.13 for writing; they need to demonstrate growth in the amount of detail in both their drawing and writing product to score at level 3, which indicates that students meet grade-level expectations, on the rubric in the post-assessment.

Question to be studied: How will Passive Concerts affect the comprehension of my kindergarten students during our study of the unit, Community Helpers?

Personal connection/interest in the topic:

The reason I chose this question for my action research is that the whole idea of music enhancing learning is fascinating to me. I have recently had the opportunity to participate in various inservices that incorporate music and learning. The inservice highlighted that research has been conducted on the effectiveness of music and the learning of children. I have found that the effects of the music have stimulated my learning and participation. I want to incorporate these ideas into my classroom setting, and I feel that this is a wonderful opportunity.

One of the strategies introduced in the inservice workshop was the Passive Concert. The Passive Concert uses music to increase understanding and comprehension. The Passive Concert is a method of reviewing information presented to the students using Baroque-style music in conjunction with pictures and words. The music of the Baroque era has the kind of harmony and resonance that brings the mind and body into a highly effective learning state. I am intrigued by this strategy, and it aligns with my interest in finding ways to use the arts to increase student learning.

Educators' interest in the topic:

Teaching at an arts magnet elementary school reinforces my interest in this approach. I have watched my students over the last five years grow and learn while being immersed in an arts-rich curriculum. Adding this new approach should only increase the students' comprehension and add detail to their writing and drawings of the content that is taught and reviewed. Other teachers, school administrators, and parents will be very interested in what I find out through this investigation.

your work thus far, you may use the checklists in this section to carefully evaluate both your topic and the research question you have proposed in the Topic Proposal Form before sharing it with others or moving forward to the next chapter.

CHECKLIST: DEVELOPING THE TOPIC FOR ACTION RESEARCH

_____ 1. Is the topic relevant and meaningful to my everyday practice?

_____ 2. Do I have a strong interest or passion for the topic?

_____ 3. Is it a topic that other educators at my grade level, school, or beyond are interested in?

_____ 4. Is there a literature base to support my understanding of the existing knowledge of the topic or aspects of the topic?

_____ 5. Am I able to develop a concise statement of problem around my topic?

CHECKLIST: DEVELOPING A RESEARCH QUESTION

_____ 1. Is it a question that hasn't already been answered?

_____ 2. Is it a higher-level question that gets at explanations, reasons, and/or relationships? ("How does . . . ?" "What are the effects of . . . ?" "Why are . . . ?")

_____ 3. It is _not_ a "Yes/No" question.

_____ 4. Is it written in everyday language; does it avoid jargon?

_____ 5. It is not too lengthy; is it concise and clear?

_____ 6. Is it something that is manageable? I can complete it. It is _not_ too large in scope.

_____ 7. Is it something manageable within the context of my work and available resources?

_____ 8. Do I have a sense of commitment to the question or feel passionate about it?

_____ 9. Is it based in my own practice? (The further you get away from this, the more difficult it will be.)

_____ 10. Is it a challenging question? Will it provide me the opportunity to stretch myself?

_____ 11. Is it meaningful to me? Will it provide me with a deeper understanding of the topic or issue?

_____ 12. Will this question most likely lead me to other questions and additional inquiry?

SUMMARY

In this chapter, you have learned how to begin the research process by thinking about problems of practice in the broader educational community that are directly connected to an area of concern you have within your own practice. When you focus on a problem that matters to you, has the potential to improve your practice, and is of interest to the broader educational community, then you will have a meaningful, productive, and significant action research topic. This initial phase of the process is often challenging because you may find that you must wrestle between several potential ideas to explore in your practice or you may struggle coming up with a viable problem or appropriate solution to investigate. In order to narrow your focus, the chapter focused on the importance of selecting a topic that is manageable, has existing rationale within the educational literature, and stimulates your passion. It is helpful to clarify your topic by writing a statement of the problem to identify the "who," "what," "how," and the goal of the project as a useful framework to keep you focused throughout the planning and development phase of the action research process. Once you can clearly articulate the problem, the action research question can be formulated. The chapter provides you with evaluation criteria in the form of checklists to allow you to judge the effectiveness of the selected topic and formulated research question against the standards of the teacher action research literature.

As a product of this chapter, you have a developed an action research proposal form. This will be useful as you seek topic approval from a course instructor or to allow you to communicate effectively about your work with administrators and colleagues. It was also useful within the broader action research and self-regulatory processes as you engaged in observation and reflection, then strategically targeted an intended outcome for your work. The understanding you have gained about how to begin the process of action research and the proposal form you have completed provides a solid foundation within the planning phase. You will now begin the work of gathering, reading, and organizing the literature to deepen your understanding of your research question. Chapter 3 will lead you through the process of how to complete a literature review that will inform and provide additional insight to your project plan.

Key Terms

Hypothesis, p. 34
Problem(s) of practice, p. 27

Problem statement, p. 34
Research question, p. 35

Case in Point: Developing a Topic

In Chapter 1, you were introduced to Margaret Curtis, a second-grade teacher, and read her research log. In the log, she described a diverse classroom of children with a variety of learning styles and readiness levels. She expressed concern about some of her struggling readers and was unsure whether these readers would be adequately prepared to enter third grade. Margaret touched upon comprehension, motivation, fluency, and her students' need for support when creating written answers. In part 2 of her research log, she'll begin to narrow her focus by generating a list of potential topics and reflecting further upon the needs of her students.

You were also introduced in Chapter 1 to Matt Wells, a ninth-grade science teacher. In his preliminary research log entry, he described how he taught three sections of science classes that were divided by ability based on their proficiency in language arts skills. He and his colleagues had become interested in transitioning from a direct instruction approach to an open investigation approach to the teaching and learning of science in their classrooms. At the beginning of the year he transitioned to this approach with students who were working at or above grade level, but he had not yet moved away from a direct instruction approach with his below-grade-level students. He expressed the desire to begin implementing an investigative approach to the teaching and learning of science with his lower-ability grouped section of students.

One Elementary Teacher's Journey: Research Log Entry

For the last few months, I have spent a great deal of time determining what reading strategy will best support the students who are struggling in reading. As part of our classwork, Dr. Bonfil asked us to generate a list of topics that we could consider for our action research study. So far I've thought about comprehension, fluency, and motivation. These are all problems of practice with several of the students in my class. Improving comprehension and fluency is part of our school improvement goals and is monitored closely by the school system and my principal through a variety of assessments. I know that a focus on one of these areas is not only of interest to me, but also to our broader educational community and has potential to lead to a significant topic for investigation. However, those are really broad and, after conferencing with Dr. B., she noted that I needed to try and become more specific and to think about the intervention that would be most valuable for my students' reading skills and my teaching. There is so much to consider. If students can't understand what they are reading, then they will be unable to access the content necessary to build the foundation for third grade. However, as I dig a little deeper, I really think that a lack of fluency is limiting their ability to understand. The more

time they spend trying to read accurately and without pausing at individual words, the more likely they are to forget what they are reading.

I've used guided repeated readings, but the students seem to quickly become unmotivated when reading the same passage with no purpose. I have thought a lot about using Readers' Theater. My hope is that by implementing Readers' Theater on a regular basis, I will see a significant improvement in the reading rate, accuracy, and prosody of my students. Besides helping with fluency and reading skills, I also see it stimulating imagination, cooperation, motivation, and helping students develop a contagious engagement for learning. My hope is that authentic literature will come alive for my students. It might also be a different way to get students engaged with the text they are reading repeatedly. It provides them with a purpose to read fluently. Also, I believe that using this strategy will allow me to draw upon the students' multiple intelligences, especially those that are visual/spatial, bodily/kinesthetic, and interpersonal learners.

The goals I am considering for my action research study are focused on helping my students who are currently reading below grade level to become more fluent readers so that they can read words accurately, at an appropriate rate, and with expression. All second-grade students are assessed on fluency (rate and accuracy) three times a year using DIBELS. I want to see these struggling students reading on grade level, according to DIBELS, by the end of the year. I want all of my students to love reading and be great readers. I want to increase the reading fluency in my student reading below grade level.

Based on my reflections above, I have formally developed the following information to share with my course instructor for topic approval:

Topic: The Effect of Readers' Theater on Fluency

Statement of the problem: Several second-grade students in my class struggle with fluency (rate and accuracy) and are below grade level standards as assessed three times a year using DIBELS. I want to see these struggling students reading on grade level, according to DIBELS, by the end of the year.

Action research question: What is the effect of Readers' Theater on second-grade students' reading fluency?

One Secondary Teacher's Journey: Research Log Entry

As I wrote in my first entry, I am interested in studying the effect of the open investigation approach on my students with lower level language arts proficiency skills. I have not yet implemented this change to my instructional practice with this group of students due to my concerns with their behavior problems and their ability to work independently. Their scores averaged a low *C* for the first half of the first quarter. The students are all intelligent but have difficulties related to limited vocabulary, effective use of informational text comprehension strategies, and attention span. I would like to switch to open investigation with this group of students to see if, despite challenges with adapting to a new instructional approach, their scores come up. As I experiment with this in my practice, I really want to document what is happening so that I can make instructional decisions for my students based on data I collect and a systematic study of my practice rather than just on assumptions that have not been tested or evaluated. I would like to focus my research on studying the effects of how using the investigation workshop model with my lower level readers and writers impacts their science achievement scores and their attitudes about learning within the classroom. I hope to be able to find a way to effectively utilize this approach with my lower-level learners and share my findings with my colleagues. I want all of our students to develop a love for science, and I would really like to provide all of our students with the same learning opportunities.

Based on my interest in implementing the open investigation approach to teaching science with all my students and my desire to document what I learn and the effect it has on my struggling learners, I have developed the following information to share with my course instructor for topic approval:

Topic: The Effect of an Open Investigation Workshop Approach on Ninth-Grade Science Learning

Statement of the problem: In a lower level ability section of ninth-grade science, students struggle with science content and a motivation to learn. I want to see how an open investigation workshop approach impacts these students' learning and engagement during the second quarter of instruction.

Action research question: What is the effect of an open investigation workshop approach on a ninth-grade science class with students who are lower-level readers?

Activities and Additional Resources

1. Imagine a scenario where a colleague comes to you to discuss an action research project that she would like to engage in. She says that she wants to investigate experiential learning and is wondering what her next steps are. What would you suggest to her?

2. Create a fishbone diagram to brainstorm potential causes and solutions of a problem of practice identified in the first "Note"-able Thoughts reflection. Directions and a copy of the diagram can be located at: http://www.nefstem.org/teacher_guide/materials/download/planning/fishbone.doc.

3. Examine the following research questions. Determine whether each question is effectively written and, if it is not, rewrite the question to improve it.

   a) Do students' achievement scores improve when provided with direct instruction in writing strategies?

   b) What is the relationship between students' reading fluency and comprehension scores?

   c) How does the use of incentives for positive behavior impact students' engagement during instructional segments lasting more than 15 minutes?

d) How does the use of models and diagrams within instruction impact students' knowledge of the solar system?

e) Can the use of fraction strips during instruction improve students' understanding of converting mixed numbers to improper fractions?

4. Look back at the questions presented in the previous activity. Choose one and think about the problem that may be present in that particular situation. Write a problem statement that is aligned with the action research question and explicitly addresses the three elements as well as the primary objective.

Print Resources

City, E. A., Elmore, R. F., Fiarman, S. E., & Teitel, L. (2009). *Instructional rounds in education: A network approach to improving teaching and learning*. Cambridge, MA: Harvard Education Press.

Holly, M. L., Arhar, J., & Kasten, W. (2004). *Action research for teachers: Traveling the yellow brick road*. New York, NY: Prentice Hall.

Samaras, A. P. (2010). *Self-study teacher research*. Thousand Oaks, CA: Sage.

Web Resources

The Northeast Florida Science, Technology, and Mathematics Center for Education, Action research for teachers: http://www.nefstem.org/teacher_guide/prep/index.htm

Madison Metropolitan School District, Starting Points: http://oldweb.madison.k12.wi.us/sod/car/carstartingpoints.html

Madison Metropolitan School District, Guidelines for Developing a Question: http://oldweb.madison.k12.wi.us/sod/car/cardevelopquestion.html

Student Study Site

edge.sagepub.com/putman

- Take the practice quiz.
- Review key terms with eFlashcards.
- Explore topics with video and multimedia.

References

Ball, D. L., & Cohen, D. K. (1999). Developing practice, developing practitioners: Toward a practice-based theory of professional education. In L. Darling-Hammond & G. Sykes (Eds.), *Teaching as the learning profession: Handbook of policy and practice* (pp. 3–32). San Francisco, CA: Jossey-Bass.

Casas, G., Cook, C., Hogan, C., Howard, K., Thompson, D., et al. (2005). *Action research for teachers*. Jacksonville, FL: The Northeast Florida Science, Technology, and Mathematics Center for Education. Retrieved from http://www.nefstem.org/teacher_guide/prep/focus.htm

Henning, J. E., Stone, J. M., & Kelly, J. L. (2009). *Using action research to improve instruction: An interactive guide for teachers*. New York, NY: Routledge.

Machi, D., & McEvoy, B. (2008). *The literature review: Six steps to success*. Thousand Oaks, CA: Corwin.

Mertler, C. A. (2009). *Action research: Teachers as researchers in the classroom*. Los Angeles, CA: Sage.

Mills, G. E. (2011). *Action research: A guide for the teacher researcher* (4th ed.). Boston, MA: Allyn & Bacon.

Padak, N., & Padak, G. (n.d.). *Research to practice: Guidelines for planning action research projects*. Retrieved from http://literacy.kent.edu/Oasis/Pubs/0200-08.htm

Pearson Education, Inc. (2008). *Action research project guide*. Glenview, IL: Author.

Pine, G. (2009). *Teacher action research: Building knowledge democracies*. Thousand Oaks, CA: Sage.

CHAPTER 3

Creating a Review of Literature

GUIDING QUESTIONS

After reading this chapter, you should be able to answer the following questions:

- What is a synthesis of literature, and how does it relate to action research?

- What resources are available for searching for information?

- What processes can be used to effectively search for information for a synthesis of literature?

- What are different types of literature that can be read? Is there a recommended process for reading a research article?

- How can I organize and summarize information as I collect it?

- How do I organize a synthesis of literature?

CHAPTER AIMS AND GOALS

The intent of this chapter is to finalize a strategic area of focus for your action research study and to develop a synthesis of literature around the topic. As you progress through the chapter, you will develop an understanding of what a synthesis of literature consists of and how it can help you within the action research process. Along the way, we'll describe effective search techniques and methods to evaluate information about your topic. We'll also incorporate strategies to help you keep organized as you find and capture relevant information. Finally, we will describe how to summarize the literature into a comprehensive synthesis that allows you to present both broad and specific insights about the topic and the previous research that you examined during the search process.

We acknowledge not everyone will write a formal synthesis of literature as might be completed in university coursework or in a more formalized action research study. However, we believe it is important to develop knowledge of how to conduct a review for information and how to synthesize this information because it can have a significant impact on the actions you take within your study. We also feel you should see several examples of the components that can be useful in creating a synthesis of literature, and thus you'll be presented with several artifacts that will be useful in this process as you work through the content of the chapter. Even if you are not writing a formal synthesis, many of the strategies and techniques we discuss for selecting, evaluating, and summarizing information will be important for you to conduct an informed study.

SETTING THE CONTEXT: SOURCES OF INFORMATION

Before proceeding with action research, or any research for that matter, it is important to become familiar with both the topic and what other research has been conducted about the area under study. To this end, a review of literature represents an important component within the process of performing action research. Think of it as a way of immersing yourself in learning about what others have discovered about a particular topic. Sagor (1992) writes, "I would encourage anyone interested in doing good research to review the literature immediately after engaging in the problem-formulation activities" (p. 76). Many of the teachers we have worked with over the years have noted that they have gained important information through collecting literature and examining what others have done, which has helped them see effective processes for their study. It has also provided different approaches for answering the same or similar research questions. An examination of relevant literature can also help you to begin to think about your motivation and interest for the topic. While conducting a search, you'll quickly discover whether the topic you have selected will truly be one that can sustain your interest for the duration of the study.

Going back to our point about gaining information about previous work central to your topic, a review of the literature serves a vital function of showing whether the topic is well researched or whether it is a new area of study (or novel approach). In the former case, you may locate information on how others examining the same or a similar topic have approached it. Researching an area that already has a large supporting body of work will enable you to incorporate various elements into your study, including instruments and specific research methods. Using the information from other literature, you could also find additional experts or teachers who have knowledge of the subject under study and can answer questions or provide guidance as you engage in the research process. On the other hand, the review may reveal that there are a limited number of resources that you can locate about a particular topic. Does this indicate no one is interested? Quite the contrary, it may simply mean that no one has asked the same questions you are or that no one has framed their research in exactly the same way you have. You may be exploring a new topic that is only in the beginning stages of being examined. As a result, instead of locating more knowledgeable others in your search for literature, you may serve that role for others after the completion of your study!

Gloria Waters, 10th-Grade Teacher

The idea of spending a great deal of time looking at articles written by people who had likely not been in a classroom in many years was initially not appealing to me at all. In fact, I would say that I really dreaded the process and delayed starting my search much longer than I should have. However, once I began to look at descriptions of the various studies conducted to examine my topic, I started to find a wealth of resources that really helped me to refine my thinking. As it turned out, I located a dissertation where the research was very closely aligned to mine. This was a huge help, not only because I could see what data was collected, but also because the dissertation contained an instrument that the researcher validated within her study. As it turned out, I used the instrument to collect data from the students in my class and it became an important source of data.

Reviewing the literature pertinent to your topic will contribute toward the construction of a **synthesis of literature**. In essence, a synthesis of literature is a part of what many of us consider the traditional research paper, representing a culmination of all the information gathered about a particular topic. The primary purposes of the synthesis of literature are to concisely and effectively describe why your topic is significant, to provide background information on the topic to readers, and to serve as a scaffold between what is known about the topic to a description of your specific study, including your research questions. In effect, the synthesis of literature becomes a tool to help the reader understand the importance of your topic by activating and establishing their understanding of the research that preceded your work. It also allows you to demonstrate a personal understanding of the topic. In general, regardless of whether the synthesis is formally required as part of university coursework or for the development of a manuscript, we highly recommend creating the synthesis to help you organize information that will ultimately help you complete your action research. To help you in this process, we will share some information on the resources you may encounter as well as some guidance in how to categorize the information you may locate.

"NOTE"-ABLE THOUGHTS

Take a moment and think about articles you have read in the past for professional development, for a university course, or based on something you were interested in. Have you found any that were particularly influential on your practice? What made them so?

TYPES OF RESOURCES

In creating a synthesis of literature, there are several relevant topics that pertain to the resources you choose to examine. First, you'll need to consider whether you will focus your review on research-based (empirical or conceptual) or practitioner-focused literature or a combination of the two. For most action research projects, the goal should be to examine information from as many different sources of information as possible, which means that a combination is probably the best option. Furthermore, examining various types of literature allows you to see how research or theory has influenced practice and vice versa, which could be very influential in the development of your methods.

We'll begin our discussion about types and sources of literature relevant to the development of your synthesis by discussing the broad categories of work that you may find as you conduct your search. If we can help you distinguish between the forms of literature you are examining or want to examine, you'll be able to more readily evaluate whether a given piece of literature meets your needs. You'll also be able to generalize this to other sources of information. We'll start by examining the differences between practitioner-focused literature and research-based literature.

The aim of **practitioner-focused literature** is to provide strategies or techniques that help with teaching, and it is generally not written to prove something or develop deep theoretical knowledge. We think it is safe to say that the majority of the teachers we interact with prefer to read practitioner-focused literature because it fulfills the need for finding information or a strategy that has direct applicability within the classroom. In essence, something read about yesterday, with some planning, can be tried tomorrow in the classroom. That is not to say all practitioner-focused articles do not address research or do not contain elements of an investigation. We are simply saying that is not the typical purpose of literature of this form.

Research-based literature, on the other hand, may require more active reflection and thought on the part of the reader, as the purpose is to link theory and action and to describe the implementation of deliberate steps to examine a topic and arrive at conclusions related to it. The goal of research-based literature is not to describe the steps necessary for immediate implementation of a strategy. However, even given the distinctions between the practitioner-focused and research-based literature, it is not always easy to identify what type of article you are reading, and thus we hope to provide you some things to consider that may facilitate this process.

Focusing specifically on research-based literature, there are some specific elements that all research reports contain. These include

- an introduction,

- a theoretical framework and/or literature review,

- a methods section,

- a description of the results, and

- a discussion and/or implications section.

While there are additional elements you may encounter (e.g., a limitations section), this list encompasses the broader organization as well as the order in which the elements will appear in the article. Generally, published research-based literature will use subheadings to indicate the elements, which assists the reader in the identification of each. Figure 3.1 has been included to describe the purpose and information included in each of the sections listed above.

FIGURE 3.1   Elements of a Research Article

- Introduction

    o Develops the underlying purpose for the study and provides limited background information about the topic (e.g., importance, relevance)
    o Often leads to the research questions or hypothesis, which conclude the section

- Theoretical Framework/Literature Review

    o Theoretical framework—Presents the theories, concepts, or scholarly literature that informed the development of the study and relate to the broader areas under study or to describe other research on the topic
    o Literature review—Summarizes past and current research on the topic; describes how theory, research, and practice have informed understandings; further develops the necessity of the research

- Methods

    o Describes characteristics of participants
    o Provides information about instruments or forms of data
    o Explicitly details the process used to collect the data
    o Outlines the data analysis procedures that were used

- Results

    o Describes the findings that resulted from the data analysis (aligned with research question)
    o Form varies by methodology

        - Quantitative: numerically oriented, often with tables or figures to show results
        - Qualitative: more likely to use narrative descriptions to demonstrate analysis of various sources including interviews, questionnaires, observations, and so on

- Discussion or Implications

    o Summarizes the results and describes how they compare with previous research or information (literature) about the topic
    o Discusses how the information from the study may be used directly (practical implications) or how it may influence the field (theoretical implications) and provides recommendations for further research related to the topic, incorporating the findings of the study

Each section within research-based literature is useful in its own unique way and can help you with your research. For example, the theoretical framework or literature review will describe the underlying theory behind the research and provide information about what others have learned. Noting specific authors whose names appear often may lead you to search for publications by these individuals or groups, as it is likely that they have been influential in developing conclusions on the topic. The methods section describes the procedures and instruments used for the study and can help you develop a research plan, including ideas for collecting data. The discussion section serves the important function of allowing the author to expand on the results of the research, describing how the outcomes relate to previous research and the perceived underlying causes of the results. Finally, the implications describe how the results will impact or change what we currently know and provide suggestions for additional research. The latter two sections allow you to consider how your research relates to what was described and how this information could influence your study, especially if the recommendations for research present an idea that is relevant to your proposed work. As you read the sections contained in the research-based literature, we've provided a series of questions (see Figure 3.2) that may be used to organize your close examination of the description of the research. We've found that by focusing on the aspects highlighted in Figure 3.2, we can more effectively use the research to inform and guide our own studies.

Peer-reviewed resources. As you examine literature, especially research-based articles, you may come across the term *peer reviewed* and should be familiar with what this means in the greater context of your work. When a book chapter or article is peer reviewed, it has been subject to examination by experts in the field who note whether it meets certain levels of quality and scholarship. For example, the reviewers ensure the completeness of the review of literature, verify sound methodological practices (e.g., appropriate statistical analysis), and note the inclusion of a substantive contribution to the topic's knowledge base. Extending this to practitioner-focused journals, this process may also encompass examinations of applicability to the day-to-day work in the field. Peer review is presumed to result in the selection of higher-quality work for dissemination and examination. That is not to say that literature that is not peer reviewed cannot be high quality; it has simply not been vetted by experts, and thus you should exercise some caution when interpreting the work and choosing whether to use it to inform your own study.

Primary or secondary sources. As part of our work with teachers taking graduate courses, we lead them through the creation of a formal synthesis of literature within the action research process. In reading their work and discussing it with them, we've noticed

---

FIGURE 3.2   Questions to Consider While Examining Sections of a Research Article

Theoretical Framework or Literature Review Section

- What theories have formed the underlying foundation for the study? Do these match your personal philosophies?
- What previous research has been conducted on the topic?
- Who were the authors of the publications of the previous research? Are there names that appear often in the list?
- What were the results of previous research in this area?

Methods Section

- Who were the participants in the study?
- Where was the data collected?
- How did the data collection occur?
- When did the data collection occur?
- How long did it take to collect the data?
- What instruments or scales were used in the study?
- Were the instruments reliable and valid?
- Can you get access to the instruments?

Discussion/Implications Sections

- How do the findings of the current research relate to information described in the literature review?
- What reasons does the author provide as a basis for the results and their similarity/ differences to other research?
- What are the limitations of the study?
- What future directions for research are proposed by the author?

a tendency for them to read one article, and then cite information and sources that were described in the article without actually reading the work being cited. This is an easy temptation to fall into; however, you must resist! Our recommendation comes with the knowledge that the article may contain the author's personal interpretation of a work cited. Without reading the original work, you cannot be 100% sure that the information you describe about the work cited is accurate.

The issue we draw your attention to involves whether you are using what are referred to as primary or secondary sources for information. When you use a primary source, you are reading a direct description of a study written by the researcher or research team. To be precise, a **primary source** is "a document (e.g., journal article or dissertation) that was written by the individual who actually conducted the research study or who formulated the theory or opinions that are described in the document" (Gall, Borg, & Gall, 2007, p. 98). This is contrasted with a **secondary source**, which is a "publication written by authors who were not direct observers of, or participants in, the events being described" (Gall, Borg, & Gall, 2007, p. 107).

We have been asked, "Does it really matter if you use a primary or secondary source for your information?" The answer is always an emphatic "Yes!" In addition to giving what is potentially an interpretation of a study, the secondary source does not provide the specifics of the original research. For example, suppose you saw the following information in an article and were tempted to cite the authors listed: Motivation plays a critical role in the amount of reading that a student completes (Fawson & Moore, 1999; Pavonetti, Brimmer, & Cipielewski, 2002). If we simply "pulled" the citations from this sentence without examining them further, we might miss that the Fawson and Moore study really looked at the use of reading incentive programs (in general) and the perceived effects on students' motivation from the perspectives of principals, teachers, and parents. On the other hand, the Pavonetti, Brimmer, and Cipielewski study was focused on Accelerated Reader and how the program affected the reading habits of middle school students. While the sentence above is generally correct, you can see that the conclusion came from much different samples and that the latter may be more impactful on your study if you are looking for ways to measure similar programs.

"NOTE"-ABLE THOUGHTS

Reflect on the piece of literature you thought of as part of the previous "Note"-able Thoughts. Would you describe it as research based or practitioner focused? Do you think the relevant category was influential in the reason you selected it?

TAKING ACTION: LOCATING AND SYNTHESIZING INFORMATION

Now that we've built some background on the different types of literature at your disposal, let's begin to focus on finding it. For most of us, the go-to resource to find information is the Internet. Acknowledging that the Internet has simplified the process of searching for information about a particular topic, it represents one source that is not always as easy to navigate when we are really focused on finding articles around a specific topic. When we google something, typing in keywords is a strategy that is very straightforward and useful. However, keyword searches often yield millions of results (a search for "reading fluency" revealed 1.87 million matches) or lists that are too exhaustive to try and effectively find relevant information. As a result, we'll provide brief descriptions of several resources and processes that can be used within searches to ensure you have a variety of options.

TECH CONNECTIONS

Given that we've moved beyond the days of the Dewey Decimal System and the traditional card catalog, searches for information are often conducted entirely online. We may still use print resources to examine the actual information we find, but in reality our search processes and procedures are now largely electronic. As a result, much of this chapter is focused on using various technological affordances or websites to locate relevant literature. Rather than reiterate what is shared in the chapter, we'll draw your attention to using social networking tools to assist you in your search for literature. We touched briefly upon Academia.edu in Chapter 2 and believe this tool has the potential to not only provide you access to literature that is aligned with your research topic but also help put you in direct contact with other researchers who may be conducting similar work. This is an inherent advantage of using social networks—access to other people and the opportunity to discuss various elements of your research. We've heard stories of people using specific hashtags within Twitter to obtain suggestions to assist them in their ongoing research development, which we think is a great idea. As you examine opportunities to use social networking to assist you in your search for literature and to guide the development of your research, other tools to consider include ResearchGate (https://www.researchgate.net), Mendeley (https://www.mendeley.com/), and even Facebook.

ONLINE INQUIRIES

It would not be surprising if we polled readers and found most believe they are effective at searching the Internet. However, we also know the results of a search can be overwhelming when care is not taken to plan the search prior to simply typing in a few keywords. The results can also be nonrepresentative of the best resources due to the methods used by web designers to manipulate their place in the search results list. Interviews I (Mike) conducted with teachers and students revealed experiences where Wikipedia consistently held one of the first few positions in the list. This is by design! Furthermore, there is the added necessity of evaluating information that is found online. We've generally been able to trust information published in traditional sources. However, the Internet provides anyone with an Internet-enabled device and a connection to compose and publish information for billions of people to see, regardless of its accuracy.

Given this context, we will highlight a few quick methods that may help during the process of searching online for information. We advocate being very thoughtful and deliberate about the keywords that you choose to generate the most accurate list of potential sources. For example, if you searched for "homework" in Google, you'd receive 170 million results. However, if you used "homework for middle school students," you'd only have to search through 24.2 million results. While this number is obviously still too large to work with, by implementing the use of quotations, we reduced the previous results by roughly one-seventh. The point is that we must be strategic in how we search: using specific keywords, quotations, Boolean operators (*and, or*), symbols (+, –, @), and sites that enable us to find literature (e.g., research articles) as opposed to sites that contain reading fluency passages or games. Refining our search using some of the quantifiers, including: "homework assignments," "middle school," "high school," and "effectiveness," we're now down to 26,800 results. Progress! Depending on your actual topic and what you note as common results in the search, you can further refine and focus your search.

Using experience as our guide, we also recommend that you are very diligent about recording the search terms you use as you look for information. It's very frustrating when you don't do this, as you'll likely find yourself asking the question, "Where did I find that reference?" or "Didn't I already use this set of search terms?" Instead of gradually narrowing down your list of resources, you may actually find yourself expanding the number of possibilities. The use of a spreadsheet or document where you can list the key words and (potentially) record resources that were obtained as a result of the search is a good strategy. The intent is to make effective use of your time, which is not the case if you are doing the same searches over again. We've included an example organizer that may help you keep track of keywords as well as to construct annotated bibliography entries, which we have also found to be helpful when accumulating background literature (see Figure 3.3).

FIGURE 3.3 Organizer for Keeping Track of Resources During a Search for Literature

Source (citation/URL):

_____

_____

Summary:

_____

_____

_____

Reflection:

_____

_____

_____

Keywords: _____

GOOGLE SCHOLAR

While there are certainly many search engines to use, Google has created Google Scholar to facilitate the task of finding information that may be contained in research articles or more academic outlets. Personally, we often conduct searches using Scholar for several reasons. Figure 3.4 shows a screenshot of a search that we conducted using the keywords and Boolean operators we previously mentioned. As you'll note, there are still 1,510 results, but many more may be applicable to your search because the resources located through Google Scholar primarily consist of academic papers or outlets. However, you may still have to eliminate nonacademic items like the homework policy for Sweet Springs Middle School or images of homework policies that have been uploaded. We can further use several features that Google has incorporated to enable us to find literature to create our synthesis and inform our action research study. Examining the left side of the figure, you'll see that you can refine the time period that is searched, encompassing a custom range or articles found within the last one to five years. This ensures you can focus on the most up-to-date information that is relevant to your study. You may not find an article written in 1997 about using technology in your reading instruction as pertinent as one written in the past few years on the uses of podcasts or VoiceThread to develop reading and listening skills. You can also designate whether to include citations and the order that the results are presented in (i.e., relevance or date).

What is likely our favorite feature about Google Scholar, however, is the "cited by" text indicated under each article. This indicates the number of times that a particular piece of literature has been cited in other works. Obviously the higher the number, the greater the number of people who found the work relevant and important enough to include it as part of their search for literature. You can use this feature several ways. For example, if you find a particular article that meets your needs, you can click the "cited by" link and be provided with an immediate list of the additional articles that included this one in their reference list. We have found additional resources to examine using this feature, as, in many cases, the topics under study were similar to the article we were examining (and subsequently similar to our research). Furthermore, when we think about it in terms of influential works, large numbers of citations mean that the article was very noteworthy in the field of study, in some cases being a seminal article. These serve as important reference points in the development of information on your topic of study, as it is likely a citation that you'll encounter multiple times in your search for literature. Our recommendation is to make sure you locate a copy of these articles when you see them within your search. Finally, Google Scholar shows whether there is a downloadable file available for the relevant article. In looking at Figure 3.4, you can see that the first item does not appear to have a file available, but several other items in the search have pdf files that likely can be downloaded and examined, providing direct access to the content.

UNIVERSITY LIBRARIES

A second option for an electronic search for information is a university library. Most, if not all, libraries now maintain an electronic database that contains lists of the materials available about a given topic. Gone are the days of searching through the card catalog organized by the Dewey Decimal Index (many of our readers may not even know what a card catalog is!) only to find the card or book missing when a relevant resource was found. University libraries now allow you to search through specific materials and narrowly focus

FIGURE 3.4   Screenshot of Google Keyword Search

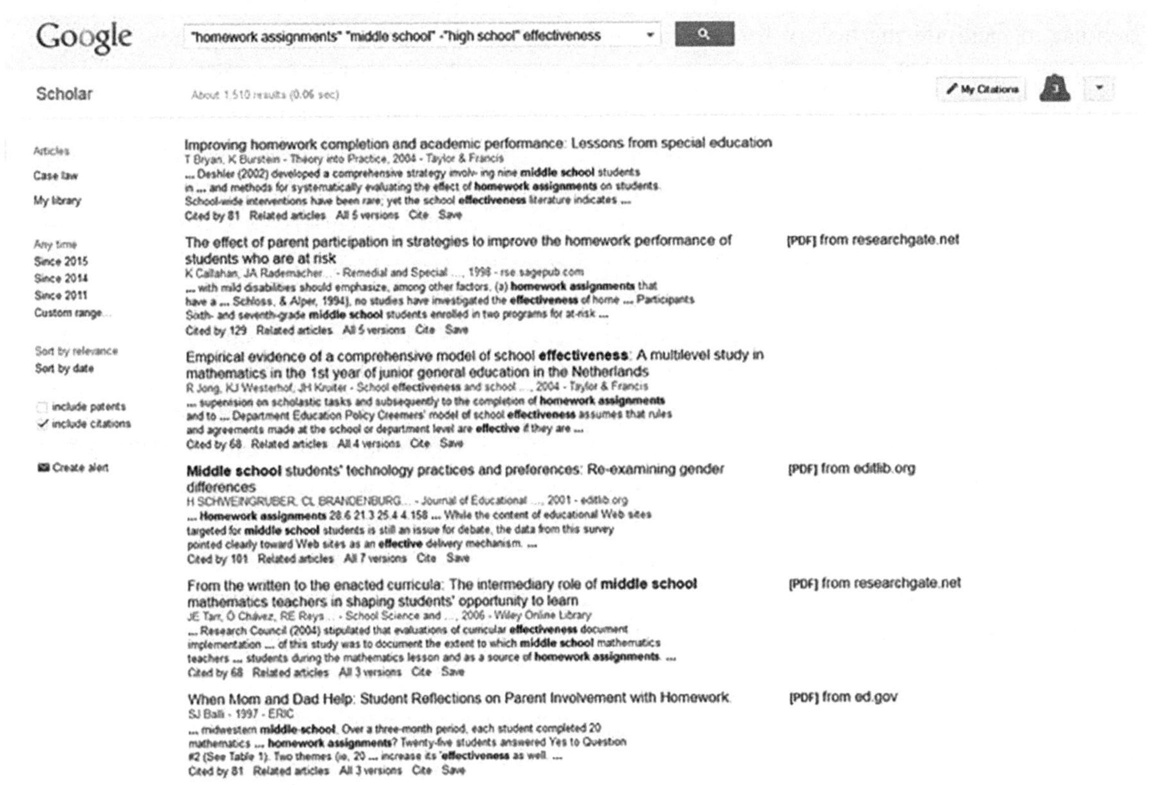

searches to find information quickly and efficiently. For example, we can search for key terms or authors within books, journals, databases, or media simply by typing in the relevant information. Advanced searches allow for more nuanced searches by date ranges, keyword, titles, or authors. The challenge for many of us, however, is that to access the actual resources, you have to be a student or faculty at the particular university. If you are, you can download those materials available electronically or check them out if they are available. If you are not, you're likely to venture back to the Internet to see if you can locate a copy of the article using the methods we've outlined previously.

EDUCATION RESOURCES INFORMATION CENTER

Probably one of the most well-known databases (for educators) is the Education Resources Information Center (ERIC), maintained by the Institute of Education Sciences. The database is an online repository of research and information and contains a variety of publication types, including journal articles, books, conference papers, and dissertations. Searching through the ERIC database is very similar to searching online. As noted on the left side of Figure 3.5, there are opportunities to refine the searches using publication date, descriptor, and source. While not visible in the screenshot in the figure, ERIC also allows users to search by author, publication type, audience, and education level. Each subsequent refinement diminishes the number of matches. Similar to online inquiries, the full text of the journal articles included in the search results are not always accessible. When the term *Direct link* is included next to the reference, the reader is sent to the website of the relevant journal, which may or may not allow access to the

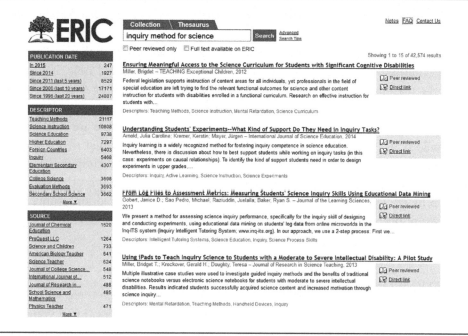

article. It is only when the words *Download full text* appear that you have direct access to the article. This can be alleviated by toggling the "Full text available on ERIC" button at the top of the page. Finally, by toggling the checkbox immediately under the search bar, you will be presented only peer-reviewed work.

OTHER SOURCES OF INFORMATION

We've briefly touched upon a few resources that can be used in your search for information. We know there are many others where you can find high-quality, relevant information. Below are some others that we think warrant examination:

- What Works Clearinghouse (http://ies.ed.gov/ncee/wwc)—A site maintained by the Institute of Education Sciences that contains more than 700 published works and over 10,000 studies focused on providing evidence of the effectiveness of various interventions.

- Professional organizations—Professional organizations often provide research and resources that can be examined by members and nonmembers. Examples of such organizations include National Council of Teachers of English (http://www.ncte.org), National Council of Teachers of Mathematics (http://www.nctm.org), National Council for the Social Studies (http://www.socialstudies.org), International Literacy Association (http://reading.org), and National Education Association (http://www.nea.org). There are others that you can likely find via a brief search.

- PsycINFO (http://www.apa.org/pubs/databases/psycinfo)—Maintained by the American Psychological Association, PsycINFO is a database that contains peer-reviewed literature, including journals, books, and dissertations, from the behavioral science and mental health fields.

- ProQuest dissertations and theses database (http://www.dc4.proquest.com/en-US/catalogs/databases/detail/pqdt.shtml)—This is a repository that includes nearly 3 million dissertations and theses completed at institutions around the world.

We have included additional resources at the end of the chapter that we believe are worth examining in addition to the ones listed so far. We should note, however, that one of the reasons we chose to outline effective Internet searching first is because we believe many of you will start your search there, finding the resources we listed as well as many others that may suit your needs. We also realize that there are still some of us who would prefer to feel an actual text in our hand, so do not forget that you can visit brick-and-mortar libraries, especially those found on university campuses. While you may not be able to check the resources out if you are not a student, it is often still possible to find print copies of archived issues of journals that may be copied for future reference. Whatever resource you choose to use, the process you use for your search can have a significant impact on the literature that you locate.

SELECTION OF RELEVANT LITERATURE

We've discussed how to locate information that might be relevant to your chosen topic; however, now it's important that you're given some methods and strategies that can be used to sift through the literature you've found and select that which is best aligned with the research you would like to conduct. When the list of potential resources is long, these decisions can be time-consuming. You certainly don't want to spend a great deal of time reading an article only to realize that it doesn't suit your purposes. Effective researchers learn to look for clues by examining information that is readily available to determine whether to conduct a thorough analysis of the piece of literature being considered. There are several ways to do this, but we are going to begin by focusing on examining abstracts, a source of information that is included in most academic literature and that will allow you to quickly determine an article's relevance to your chosen topic.

The **abstract** is a paragraph, usually containing between 100 and 250 words, that provides a brief overview of the article or chapter. According to the Purdue Online Writing Lab (n.d.), the abstract generally contains an overview of the topic, a summary of methodology (including the population being studied and the main variables involved), and the most salient findings. The abstract sometimes includes the actual research questions and can end with a conclusion or two that addresses the implications. Not all abstracts contain the latter two elements, however, and to find them you'll likely have to skim the text. The advantage of the abstract is that it may allow you to remove what was thought to be a potential source of information prior to reading it. For example, if you're planning to study methods of teaching American history to high school students, you may not want to read a paper where the subjects were fifth-grade students. That's not to say that you couldn't put the literature aside for examination later, but it's best to start with literature that is as closely aligned to your topic and sample as possible in the beginning stages. We've included an abstract from an article focused on teaching science using drawings to model science concepts (see Figure 3.6) to reinforce how the abstract can be used to quickly determine an article's focus and, subsequently, its relevance for your work.

FIGURE 3.6   Example of an Abstract

Modeling is an important approach in the teaching and learning of science. In this study, we attempt to bring modeling within the reach of young children by creating the SimSketch modeling system, which is based on freehand drawings that can be turned into simulations. This system was used by 247 children (ages ranging from 7 to 15) to create a drawing-based model of the solar system. The results show that children in the target age group are capable of creating a drawing-based model of the solar system and can use it to show the situations in which eclipses occur. Structural equation modeling predicting post-test knowledge scores based on learners' pre-test knowledge scores, the quality of their drawings and motivational aspects yielded some evidence that such drawing contributes to learning. Consequences for using modeling with young children are considered.

SOURCE: van Joolingen, W. R., Aukes, A. V., Giljers, H., & Bollen, L. (2015). Understanding elementary astronomy by making drawing-based models. *Journal of Science Education and Technology, 24*, 256–264.

Examining the abstract in Figure 3.6, you can see the researchers were investigating the use of freehand drawings in conjunction with the SimSketch modeling system to determine the impact on student learning. In this investigation, there were 247 participants between the ages of 7 and 15. Can you determine what data was collected and how long the task measuring self-regulated strategy use lasted? While this may not be distinctly evident as it is in some abstracts, we can surmise that pre-/post-test data and drawings were collected. It appears a measure was used to examine motivation, but we cannot be certain what this was based on the information included in the abstract. Figure 3.7 was included to provide you with questions that should be considered as you examine the abstracts and, subsequently, when you begin to review articles. Not all questions will apply in every case, as several more are geared toward reading the article itself, but they represent items that should help you quickly determine if further effort should be expended in examining the resource in greater depth.

Upon completion of your examination of the abstract, you will likely be able to make an initial determination about the literature's relevance to your research. In the event you are still unsure about whether to read the full article, it may be worthwhile to skim the paper and find the research question(s) in the main text if it is a research article. One thing that we've found helpful, and have often suggested to beginning researchers looking for literature, is to create three lists to help organize your search. Each list includes the following three headings: Applicable, Not Applicable, and Re-examine Later. Doing so allows you to prioritize your reading—those articles that seemed most aligned with your own research are flagged and prioritized. It may be that you get enough information for your synthesis from them or can find a sufficient number of additional citations in them to examine. The articles that may or may not be useful, based on your preliminary examination, can be put aside until you determine whether you really need them. The thinking behind the latter category is that there was something about the text that appeared to make it relevant within the initial search, and thus holding it as a resource that could be reviewed later may save some time in the long run. Given the cyclical nature of action research, there is a possibility that refinements to your original research could make the article relevant later.

FIGURE 3.7 A List of Guiding Questions to Determine the Applicability of Resources

	Abstract	**Article**
Research topic	What is the topic? How does the described topic align with the focus of your research?	
	Not Included	Does the author's rationale for choosing the topic match or extend your own?
Research question	Not Included	What are the research questions that guide the investigation? Do the questions match your chosen area of research?
Method	What are the characteristics of the participants in the study? How many participants were included? What form of data was collected as part of the investigation? What were the procedures used to complete the activities for the research? What forms of analyses were completed to develop the results and conclusions?	
Results or findings	What were the results of the study?	
	Not included	How did the findings compare to previous research and/or information in the review of literature? What were the limitations of the study?
Implications	Not included	What were the implications of the research on future research or practices?

ORGANIZE AND SUMMARIZE YOUR INFORMATION

Now that you've narrowed your search for information to literature that matches your intended topic, it's time to consider how you plan to keep track of what you've read. When I (Mike) began my doctoral program, I was incredibly inefficient at the all-important task of organizing myself prior to and during my review of literature. I took copious notes, but when I went back and read them, often several weeks or months later, they held little meaning for me. I had few options at that point beyond going back and rereading the article, and I wasted more time than I'd care to admit engaging in this behavior. As a result, I've come to recognize and understand the need and benefit of developing a plan for keeping track of what I read as well as a plan for organizing information before and while I read it.

Organizing how you keep track of the information you compile is one of the most important steps in the research process. We advocate taking notes electronically whenever possible, as computers and related devices make accumulating information and searching through it much easier than traditional, handwritten notes. Some people we know still prefer to use the traditional highlighter approach or like to write notes by hand (sometimes we're also forced to when our technology fails us). The fact is, ultimately, you will have to determine what works best for you personally for each individual article you read. However, acknowledging this, our intent is to provide at least one strategy or idea that we've used with our practicing and prospective researchers that may resonate with you.

One method, the **annotated bibliography**, is not a substitute for taking notes or highlighting, but instead is a method to develop a list of citations to books, articles, and documents that can be useful while organizing for writing. In our vision, the annotated bibliography consists of three parts: citation, summary, and reflection. Each part is intended to serve a specific role in the process of writing. First, the citation is necessary to document the source of the information. Writing the citation first ensures that you'll be able to locate the text later if you need to examine it for additional information. We know authors who use spreadsheets as a form of electronic bibliography, with a column for each respective part. This electronic bibliography allows them to search for sources by author quickly and efficiently. The added benefit of tracking entries this way (or using any electronic format) is that you can easily cut and paste each citation into a reference list later. Citation management software, such as EndNote, Zotero, and Mendeley, also helps with both the citation and summarization process (part 2 of the bibliography). One last useful organization strategy to use when you have electronic copies of the texts used in your literature review is to name the files as they would be cited within text. For example, if the authors of the text were Polly and Mims, we might name the file Polly_Mims. Again, this speeds up the ease with which you can match entries with texts, especially if you've written an accurate citation within your annotated bibliography.

To effectively explain part 2 of the annotated bibliography, we'll refer you to our previous discussion of the abstract. The abstract of an article introduces the topic, provides information about the participants and procedure, and includes a summary of the main findings. We suggest following this general pattern in your entry for the annotated bibliography, but also recommend making sure you address the forms of data and add one or two sentences describing the conclusions. The intent is to create something, in your own words, that functions much like an abstract, but that contains additional content to help you remember specific details of the text you read. The trick within part 2 is balancing the competing goals of providing yourself with a sufficient amount of detail and information while not making the summary too long. Aim for no more than eight sentences; then see if you can refine and shorten it. As you engage in this process, we're sure you'll find the level of detail that works best for you.

Finally, part 3 consists of a brief annotation evaluating the cited resource, including your personal reflection about the text. We've found a key detail to think about within this portion of the bibliography is how the article fits within your research and project. You may consider these questions:

- Was the resource helpful to you?

- How has the text contributed to your knowledge of the topic?

- Has it changed what you think or how you think about your work?

- How do the conclusions compare with other resources?

- How practical would it be to replicate the study in your current context?

Referring back to Figure 3.5, you'll see a template that could be used to develop your annotated bibliography entries. We've also included an example of an annotated bibliography entry (see Figure 3.8). Note that in our examples, we've included a space to list keywords. These are often listed in journal articles, but they are not so prevalent in other literature (e.g., book chapters). For the former, we recommend simply copying the words that are most relevant for your study, adding any that are necessary. For the latter, you will obviously need to develop your own descriptors. Using keywords in this manner will be beneficial as you sift through information, again, hopefully saving time in the long run. For more information about annotated bibliographies (and for some helpful tips about writing), we recommend visiting one of the following resources: http://www.wisc.edu/writing/Handbook/AnnotatedBibliography.html or http://owl.english.purdue.edu/owl/resource/614/01.

WRITE THE SYNTHESIS OF LITERATURE

In the preceding sections, we've set the context for finding literature that will inform your study and helped you think about how to organize your sources of information. Even though not all readers will be required to create a "formal" synthesis of literature, which might be necessary as part of university coursework, we felt it was important to provide

---

FIGURE 3.8 Example of an Annotated Bibliography Entry

Source (citation/URL):

Carbonneau, K. J., Marley, S. C., & Selig, J. P. (2013). A meta-analysis of the efficacy of teaching mathematics with concrete manipulatives. *Journal of Educational Psychology, 105*, 380–400.

Summary:

The authors examined 55 studies that compared the use of manipulatives in math instruction with control groups that provided instruction using only abstract math symbols. The results showed generally positive outcomes when manipulatives were used in instruction; however, these results were more likely when the there was a high degree of instructional support/ guidance and when use occurred with students who had reached concrete operations stage. The authors concluded that additional variables impacted the outcomes of the research and that additional considerations were needed beyond simply adding manipulatives to math instruction.

Reflection:

Based on my experiences, students may not be successful using math manipulatives if the teacher is not knowledgeable on how to demonstrate methods to apply the manipulatives to problem-solving. In thinking about my study, various manipulatives, including number lines, Base 10 blocks, Cuisenaire rods, and unifix cubes, can be incorporated within the instruction of fractions and applied to creating and solving an algorithm. It is important to understand, manipulatives do not create the learning; it is my knowledge of the concept and how I portray the purpose of the manipulative to ensure students move from concrete learning to more abstract thinking. This will be an article that I will need to refer to as I write my lit. review.

Keywords: manipulatives, mathematics, hands-on learning

---

some information as well as a few helpful hints to think about when developing the synthesis. When constructing the synthesis of literature, a visual to keep in mind regarding the organization is the shape of an inverted triangle (see Figure 3.9). You should introduce the context for your study at the beginning of the review by presenting the topic and explaining its educational and personal significance. Once this is established, begin with the primary content related to your study. In maintaining the inverted triangle analogy, begin with a broad description of the topic and the research findings about it. For example, if your research was focused on using manipulatives to solve area and perimeter problems, you might begin your review by discussing previous research on the use of manipulatives in mathematics instruction, in general. You would then gradually begin to describe research that is more pertinent to your particular study, perhaps describing investigations using manipulatives to teach computation or place value. Finally, you would get to the primary information: research on manipulatives to teach area and perimeter. It is in this section that you should not only provide information that closely relates to the work you are going to do but also conclude with how your study may extend what is currently known on the topic and your research question. On a final note, it is important within your synthesis that you describe both positive and contrary findings to ensure you are providing a balanced picture. If there are no contrary findings (or no positive), explicitly state something like, "Research has generally shown . . . to be positive" or "No studies were found that described negative effects associated with. . . ." You want your synthesis to be objective and factual, and not solely detailing the positives associated with your chosen topic.

In reading over 200 action research reports over the course of our careers, we have established a number of do's and don'ts pertinent to the development of the literature review (for additional suggestions, see Belcher, 2009). We share them here to allow you to consider them as you construct your synthesis:

DO: Write an outline before you begin to write—often you can use the keywords from your annotated bibliography to create subtopics on the outline.

DON'T: Fail to organize your sources and information before beginning to write.

FIGURE 3.9   Inverted Triangle Organizational Format for Synthesis of Literature

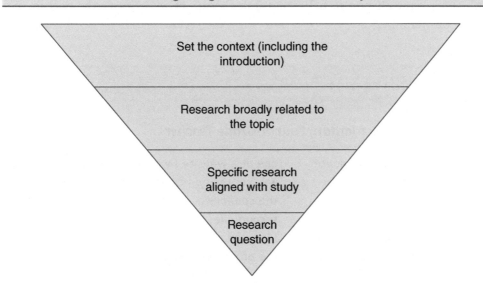

DO: Use subheadings to divide your paper, as it effectively breaks up what could be large sections of text for the reader. Keywords can be used to guide your thinking.

DON'T: Include long sections of text that don't effectively reveal changes in topic/focus.

DO: Synthesize information, especially when the literature you read reaches similar conclusions. Provide interpretations of findings within the broader context of your study.

DON'T: Write full-paragraph summaries that only address one research study at a time.

DO: Focus on paraphrasing information, putting it into your own words.

DON'T: Include too many direct quotations, especially from the same source.

DO: Include citations, especially if you use phrases like *researchers found* or *investigations have shown.*

DON'T: Omit citations if you are addressing conclusions from someone else's work.

As a bit of follow-up to our list, it is especially important to clarify why we reference synthesizing information as opposed to simply writing summaries of studies. When you synthesize information, the intent is to notice and convey patterns or relationships amongst the information presented in the literature. These patterns can help you form conclusions regarding how the literature is aligned with your own research as well as the similarities and differences among the research or findings, including the *how* and *why* behind them. As patterns are identified, they can be used for the subtopics that will constitute the headings that organize your synthesis of literature. On the other hand, while summarizing is an important skill, describing each study separately fails to convey how they are related and does not effectively (or concisely) explain to the reader the common traits or conclusions pertinent to the various literature being described. To assist you in this process, we have included some resources at the end of the chapter to help you think about how to organize the ongoing collection of literature.

■ ■ ■ VOICES FROM THE FIELD

Walker Jordan, Fourth-Grade Teacher

The professor who was teaching my graduate class recommended to our class that we use some type of organizational process to help us as we collect literature for our synthesis. After thinking about how I wanted to do this, I decided to use a synthesis matrix after seeing one at a website I was examining. The process was very easy. I created a table and labeled the columns across the top (starting with the second one) with the authors' last names. Then I labeled each row in the first column with the proposed subtopics that I thought were relevant to my question. As I read each of my articles, I took notes directly in the table in the column that aligned with the intersection of the authors' names and the subtopic. When I was done I had several pieces of paper, so I took the time to tape them together, aligning the rows pertinent to the subtopics. I was then able to scan each row and come to specific conclusions regarding the similarities and differences between each of the studies I read.

Our final recommendation is to be sure to schedule your time to write and stick to the plan. You do not have to wait until you have examined all the literature you have collected to begin writing, and we would suggest that you schedule regular sessions where you synthesize the information you have found up to that point. This is especially easy to do if you have considered an outline and how your synthesis should be organized based on the topics associated with your study. Our experiences, both as writers and as instructors of action research courses, is that it is easy to put off writing under the guise that a sufficient amount of literature hasn't been located or because there is grading or other tasks that require attention. Keeping a regular writing schedule allows you to avoid these excuses, and it keeps the information from your literature search fresh in your mind, potentially allowing a more seamless development of the literature synthesis.

DEVELOPING A PLAN OR A PRODUCT: WRITING THE SYNTHESIS OF LITERATURE

You've now reached a point where you are ready to conduct your search for literature and, for some of you, to write a synthesis of literature. The plan/products you will develop include a list of sources with a collection of notes relative to the sources and a synthesis of literature. To help begin the process of identifying sources and locating/accumulating information, we recommend thinking about the following questions:

- What resources do I have access to that I can use to seek information?

- How much time do I have to find the information?

- How will I organize my information, and what resources do I have access to that will help in this process?

- (Thinking back to Chapter 2) Do I have a strong interest or passion about this topic? Can I produce the sustained effort necessary to find a sufficient amount of literature to effectively inform my research?

Determining the answers to these questions will help you begin to develop a plan for finding information. For example, based on the amount of time you have, it will be helpful at this point to determine a timeframe for finding information and to develop a schedule for times that you will devote specifically to writing and synthesizing information as you encounter it. As you search, remember our suggestions for determining the suitability of a source before spending time reading literature that may not inform your work. We also recommend that you consider some form of electronic record keeping, specifically using either an annotated bibliography or an adaptation that allows you to quickly find information in the resources you have gathered. If you are not creating a formal, written synthesis of literature, you can skip the following section and read Evaluating Against the Standards: Are You Ready to Move On? to determine if you are ready to begin to formulate a plan for your research.

Once you've created a list of resources and found what you think is a sufficient amount of information on your chosen topic, you will need to determine how you will synthesize the information and produce the written synthesis of literature. Before you begin to write the comprehensive version of the synthesis, consider the following:

- How well do my notes represent the topic?

- What form do my notes take (electronic vs. written)? How will I search within the information I have gathered to develop the synthesis?

- If I used annotated bibliographies (or similar organizers), do I have entries for each piece of literature I read that will be used to inform my study?

- How much time is available to synthesize the information?

- What is my motivation to summarize the information (or put it all together)?

- What tools/resources (e.g., word processing software, technology) are available to create my synthesis? What knowledge do I have of each? Which of those available am I most motivated to use?

- What writing have I already completed that will contribute toward the final product?

- Have I created an outline? If so, does it reflect an organization that begins with general information and proceeds toward topics that demonstrate greater alignment with my chosen research?

- Am I being assessed, or are there specific criteria that I must meet? What are the criteria?

As we've mentioned previously, it is important to consider the use of an outline to guide your work; thus if you answered "no" to that particular question, we think it would be worthwhile to create an outline before proceeding with your writing. As you begin to write your synthesis, maintain your writing schedule and try not to engage in a renewed search for literature, at least until you have completed a draft of the synthesis. Once complete, the structure of your synthesis may match the graphic in Figure 3.8.

EVALUATING AGAINST THE STANDARDS: ARE YOU READY TO MOVE ON?

Acknowledging that not everyone will write a synthesis of literature, we will keep the questions somewhat general so they are applicable regardless of the intended outcome of this process.

CHECKLIST: SYNTHESIS OF LITERATURE

Have you:

_____1.   Located relevant information, including research studies?

_____2.   Read enough literature to give you a reasonable foundation and background on the topic?

_____3.   Read enough so that you know what other people say about your topic/area?

_____4.   Read enough research to help you build a reasonable foundation for the potential methodologies for your research?

_____5.   Organized yourself and resources via a notebook, index cards, or other method?

_____6.   Identified literature that you still might need to read?

_____7.   Developed a method of organization that represents the information collected from multiple sources in your own words?

_____8.   Recorded your personal reflections regarding the literature and its relationship to your personal experiences?

_____9.   Reviewed your research question in light of the information found as part of the search for literature to ensure that changes are not necessary?

If upon examining your responses to these questions, most, if not all of your responses, were affirmative, then you are prepared to begin to examine Chapter 4, which is focused on developing a plan for your research. If there are multiple negative responses, we suggest going back and examining the context or your plan for addressing the search for literature or development of the synthesis.

SUMMARY

We've covered a significant amount of content in this chapter. You have learned that the review of literature is an important component within the planning of an action research study, as it provides background information for your study and may facilitate decisions related to your methodology. It is important to examine research articles to help with the latter, and we can determine whether an article is research based by looking for an organizational structure that includes elements such as the literature review, methodology, and discussions. We noted that primary sources are those written directly by the author and that the peer-review process is utilized by many academic journals to ensure sound research practices and accurate citation of pertinent findings related to the topic of the research.

While many of us focus on the Internet for conducting our research, you also learned of additional resources that are important sources of information as you search for literature on your topic. This includes the Education Resources Information Center (ERIC) and professional organizations, among others. It is important to organize your information as you locate it to ensure that the process of developing conclusions about your research topic is more effectively managed. While we recommended the annotated bibliography, potentially in an electronic form, how you organize yourself must reflect your personal style and preference. Finally, if you are required to write a formal synthesis of literature, the graphic of an inverted triangle was presented to help you realize that the synthesis should progress from general information to research that is closely aligned with what you are interested in investigating.

Key Terms

Abstract, p. 56
Annotated bibliography, p. 59
Peer reviewed, p. 49

Practitioner-focused literature, p. 47
Primary source, p. 50

Research-based literature, p. 47
Secondary source, p. 50
Synthesis of literature, p. 46

Case in Point: Annotated Bibliography Entries

You've already seen how Margaret Curtis and Matt Wells have engaged in the self-reflection necessary to develop a topic and to refine what they seek to do within their action research projects in Chapter 2. Now it's time to take a look at a few of their annotated bibliography entries and the synthesis of literature that they developed around their topics. Of note, we've included one bibliography pertinent to the broader topic (fluency) and

one more refined and specific to Readers' Theater (see Figures 3.10 and 3.11) for Margaret Curtis. We have included annotated bibliographies for Matt Wells in Figures 3.12 and 3.13. To avoid making the chapter prohibitively long, we've included Margaret's and Matt's synthesis of literature as an appendix. We know that not everyone will have to craft a synthesis of literature, and thus interested readers can read these in Appendix A.

One Elementary Teacher's Journey: Annotated Bibliography Entries

FIGURE 3.10   Annotated Bibliography Entry #1 From Case in Point

Source: Rasinski, T. V., Rikli, A., & Johnston S. (2009). Reading fluency: More than automaticity? More than a concern for primary grades? *Literacy Research and Instruction, 48*, 350–361.

Summary:

According to the researchers, there is a significant correlation between fluency and comprehension. Notably, prosody, a component of fluency, has been causally linked to comprehension. This study addressed the fluency of third-, fifth-, and seventh-grade students ($n = 1,104$) in a district in Omaha, Nebraska. Instruments included the SAT9 and scores on an orally read passage scored using the Multi-Dimensional Fluency Scoring Guide. The researchers determined there was a correlation between fluency and comprehension, noting prosody was an important influence on the overall fluency scores. The researchers assert that fluency is important for ensuring students are successful in reading. The study suggests that reading fluency should continue to be a focus, particularly for struggling readers, in helping to build comprehension, even at the upper elementary grades.

Reflection:

The study helped me recognize the importance of emphasizing reading with prosody and looking beyond reading rate. The third-grade team at my school has identified words per minute as the measure they will use to assess student progress in fluency. This is important because I often see students shut down while participating in a literacy activity because it simply takes them too long to read through a text. Ultimately, if I am going to prepare students for the next grade level, shifting a focus toward prosody may help students engage with text more, build their comprehension, and limit the time and energy they spend on decoding the text. This will help to prepare them for higher grades where they will be required to read and engage with high-level, content-related text.

FIGURE 3.11   Annotated Bibliography Entry #2 From Case in Point

---

Source: Young, C., & Rasinski, T. (2009). Implementing Readers Theatre as an approach to classroom fluency instruction. *The Reading Teacher, 63*, 4–13.

Summary:

The research conducted by Young and Rasinski (2009) used Readers' Theater with primary grade students, attempting to improve their fluency and achievement. Participants were 29 (8 girls and 21 boys) second graders from a Title I school. Nine students were English-language learners and the reading levels ranged from early kindergarten to mid-third grade. The Developmental Reading Assessment and Texas Primary Reading Inventory were employed to assess the students. The results demonstrated a significant improvement (62.7 words correct per minute to 127.6 words correct per minute) over the course of the school year. The authors concluded paired reading, reading in small groups, and reading aloud seemed to have the greatest impact on improving fluency.

Reflection:

This study is very applicable since it was conducted with second graders who showed a wide range of ability, just like in my class. I like that the study used a specific schedule to organize the Readers' Theater as I think I will use something similar when I implement this for my study. I also like that the researchers extended the work with Readers' Theater into the content areas as I think that will be a tremendous benefit to my students as they begin to read to learn. Overall, this study demonstrated that Readers' Theater could be put in place with minimal time loss for teaching the district's mandated literacy program.

One Secondary Teacher's Journey: Annotated Bibliography Entries

FIGURE 3.12   Annotated Bibliography Entry #1 From Case in Point

---

Source: O'Neill, T. B. (2010). Fostering spaces of student ownership in middle school science. *Equity and Excellence in Education, 43*, 620.

Summary:

Concerned with providing empowering science learning experiences for his urban students, thus increasing their engagement and achievement, the author conducted this action research study over three years with his seventh-grade students. He sought to learn how he, as their teacher, could cultivate students' ownership for learning, and in particular, evaluate classroom structures that would support this endeavor. Through multiple sources of data, including observations, surveys, and student work, O'Neill interprets the way his relationship with students and specific practices (class zoo, student center, and teacher's phone number) positively impacted the development of student ownership. In this article he provided two vignettes to demonstrate the multiple dimensions of ownership and challenging task of balancing control in the classroom.

(Continued)

FIGURE 3.12 (Continued)

Reflection:

This article uses a similar approach in conducting action research as the author attempts to alter and interpret the role of student ownership in academic achievement in his science classes. I recognized how this construct could influence the inquiry practices I am seeking to establish as well. I appreciated how the author chose six structures (homework wall, student center, parking lot, science challenges, class zoo, teacher's phone number) to evaluate through his own observations and reflections as well as the students' opinions and responses. I felt the two vignettes allowed me a glimpse into his classroom to better understand the learning environment he sought to create and the themes of identity and control he discovered while cultivating student ownership. I wonder how these themes—and potentially others related to ownership—might emerge in my shift of instruction toward open investigations.

FIGURE 3.13 Annotated Bibliography Entry #2 From Case in Point

Source: Marx, R. W., Blumenfeld, P. C., Krajcik, J. S., Fishman, B., Soloway, E., Geier, R., & Tal, R. T. (2004). Inquiry-based science in the middle grades: Assessment of learning in urban systemic reform. *Journal of Research in Science Teaching, 41,* 1063–1080.

Summary:

This study reports middle school students' science achievement gains in the Detroit Public School system over three years of teachers using standards-based inquiry and technology-infused projects for four different curriculum units. With collaboration and support from the University of Michigan, district leaders focused on systemic reform in science education toward inquiry-based practices by engaging teachers in developing a curriculum, assessments, and offering professional development. Statistically significant increases in scores were evidenced using pre- and post-test data. Additionally, assessments were analyzed longitudinally, with effect sizes growing each year as researchers adapted practices based on students' performances on items classified as high, medium, and low cognitive levels as well as content or process-type questions. Results show that despite the challenges of an urban environment, inquiry-based learning can be an effective pedagogy for middle school science students.

Reflection:

Although this study does not specifically address students with reading deficiencies, its context describes implementing an inquiry-based curriculum in an urban environment in which students are often performing below grade level, and findings indicate strong improvements as I hope to make with my students. So many aspects of this study seem very strategic and intentional, from the development of curriculum aligned to standards to the planning of assessments to include a specific range of question types and levels. While I may not have the collaboration with a local university nor district-wide reform efforts on my side, it prompts me to reach out to other local educators to consider how I design and execute my study.

Activities and Additional Resources

1. Create a "research group" of three to five people. Each member of the group should find one article, render a decision as to whether the article is research based or practitioner focused, and then share the article with the rest of the group. Members should skim each article with the intent of classifying it as research based or practitioner focused using the characteristics described in the chapter. Once everyone has completed this task, convene the group and talk about the labels members associated with each article. Discuss any differences of opinion.

2. Access the article at the following link: http://files.eric.ed.gov/fulltext/ED505079.pdf

Direct citation: Amerine, M., Pender, L., & Schuler, K. (2009). Motivating intervention strategies to increase homework completion. Retrieved from ERIC database. (ED505079)

Read the article and summarize the main points of the study in a template like the one in Figure 3.5. Try to write this summary *without* looking back at the article. Try to capture:

- What is the research study about (i.e., what was its topic or focus)?

- How was the research conducted (i.e., what methods were used)?

   o Who were the participants?
   o What data was collected?
   o What instruments or scales were used in the study?

- What were the findings of the research (i.e., what were the results and what did the authors conclude)?

Write a complete bibliographic reference for the article using APA style. Reflect on the article and note any thoughts that come to your mind. For example, consider points on which you disagree or components that you do not understand, ideas that capture your interest, and new facts you didn't know.

3. Use the resource examination questions (see Figure 3.7) to examine the following abstract:

This study compared difference in treatment effect when Readers' Theater was implemented in two ways as an instructional intervention to promote oral reading fluency in second-grade classrooms. The study also examined the effect of Readers' Theater intervention on students at different levels of reading ability. Multiple measures were used to determine pre- and post-intervention performance of students in reading level, rate, accuracy, comprehension, and prosody. Although students in both treatment groups at all levels of ability made statistically significant gains, there was no significance between students who received Readers' Theater plus explicit instruction in aspects of fluency and students who received only the Readers' Theater intervention. Low-achievement students made significant gains in rate, retelling, and expressiveness when compared with students at average and high achievement levels. High-achievement readers made significant gains in measures of reading ability when compared with low-ability readers.

SOURCE: Keehn, S. (2003). The effect of instruction and practice through Readers Theatre on young readers' oral reading fluency. *Reading Research and Instruction, 42,* 40–61.

Databases

Academic Search Premier: https://www.ebscohost.com/academic/academic-search-premier

Child Care and Early Education Research: http://www.researchconnections.org/childcare/welcome

Education Research Complete: https://www.ebscohost.com/academic/education-research-complete

LexisNexis Academic: http://www.lexisnexis.com/hottopics/lnacademic/

Web of Science: http://webofscience.com/

WestlawNext: http://next.westlaw.com/

Citation Guides

Harvard Graduate School of Education: http://isites.harvard.edu/icb/icb.do?keyword=apa_exposed

Northern Michigan University: http://library.nmu.edu/guides/userguides/style_apa.htm

Purdue Online Writing Lab: https://owl.english.purdue.edu/owl/section/2/10/

The Writing Center (University of Wisconsin–Madison): http://www.wisc.edu/writing/Handbook/AnnotatedBibliography.html

Web Resources

Florida International University, Writing a Literature Review and Using a Synthesis Matrix: https://writingcenter.fiu.edu/resources/synthesis-matrix-2.pdf

Harvard Graduate School, Gutman Library, The Literature Review: A Research Journey: http://guides.library.harvard.edu/c.php?g=310271&p=2071511

Saint Mary's University of Minnesota, The Literature Review Matrix: http://www2.smumn.edu/deptpages/tcwritingcenter/forms_of_writing/lit_review.php#Matrix

University of Toronto, Taking Notes from Research Reading: http://www.writing.utoronto.ca/advice/reading-and-researching/notes-from-research

Student Study Site

edge.sagepub.com/putman

- Take the practice quiz.
- Review key terms with eFlashcards.
- Explore topics with video and multimedia.

References

Belcher, W. L. (2009). *Writing your journal article in 12 weeks: A guide to academic publishing.* Thousand Oaks, CA: Sage.

Carbonneau, K. J., Marley, S. C., & Selig, J. P. (2013). A meta-analysis of the efficacy of teaching mathematics with concrete manipulatives. *Journal of Educational Psychology, 105,* 380–400.

Fawson, P. C., & Moore, S. A. (1999). Reading incentive programs: Beliefs and practices. *Reading Psychology, 20,* 325–340.

Gall, M. E., Borg, W. R., & Gall, J. P. (2007). *Educational research: An introduction* (8th ed.). Boston, MA: Pearson.

Keehn, S. (2003). The effect of instruction and practice through Readers Theatre on young readers' oral reading fluency. *Reading Research and Instruction, 42,* 40–61.

Pavonetti, L. M., Brimmer, K. M., & Cipielewski, J. F. (2002). Accelerated Reader: What are the lasting effects on the reading habits of middle school students exposed to Accelerated Reader in elementary grades? *Journal of Adolescent & Adult Literacy, 46,* 300–311.

Purdue Online Writing Lab. (n.d.). *The report abstract and executive summary.* Retrieved from https://owl.english.purdue.edu/owl/resource/726/07/

Rasinski, T. V., Rikli, A., & Johnston, S. (2009). Reading fluency: More than automaticity? More than a concern for primary grades? *Literacy Research and Instruction, 48,* 350–361.

Sagor, R. (1992). *How to conduct collaborative action research.* Alexandria, VA: Association for Supervision and Curriculum Development.

van Joolingen, W. R., Aukes, A. V., Giljers, H., & Bollen, L. (2015). Understanding elementary astronomy by making drawing-based models. *Journal of Science Education and Technology, 24,* 256–264.

Young, C., & Rasinski, T. (2009). Implementing Readers Theatre as an approach to classroom fluency instruction. *The Reading Teacher, 63,* 4–13.

CHAPTER 4

Creating a Research Plan

GUIDING QUESTIONS

After reading this chapter, you should be able to answer the following questions:

- What should be considered while developing a research plan?

- What is a research design?

- What are the characteristics of qualitative research? What are common forms of qualitative data?

- What are the characteristics of quantitative research? What are common forms of quantitative data?

- What is mixed methods research?

- What are the ethical responsibilities of a teacher who conducts action research?

- What are the rights of the participant in action research?

CHAPTER AIMS AND GOALS

The next three chapters in the book are focused on helping you think about and develop the research plan that will guide your actions during your investigation. Chapter 4 is devoted to building a solid foundation for understanding the various research approaches and to help you begin to think about a research plan for your data collection. As you read it, we will help you think about what forms of data may be both available and necessary to help you answer your research question, considering the context where the research will be completed. The chapter will also address the ethical considerations necessary within the planning and implementation of the procedures associated with your study, including the rights of the participants. As you read through the chapter, we recommend that you continually reflect upon your research question to guide your thought processes and to assist you in completing a plan that enables you to be successful within your action research study.

SETTING THE CONTEXT: EXAMINING CHARACTERISTICS AND COMPONENTS OF RESEARCH METHODS

As a teacher, developing a plan for your instruction is something that you are intimately familiar with. This includes planning for each instructional segment (e.g., planning a math lesson), daily planning across all subjects, and it progresses all the way through thinking about the skills and knowledge the students in your class should develop after completing a whole year under your instruction. Without these plans in place, there is the potential for a lack of continuity or progress toward the outcomes associated with your instruction. Furthermore, you may be unable to document the successful achievement of these outcomes due to a lack of data. Within these processes, you must consider the learners in your class, the school calendar, the daily schedule, the time allocated for each instructional segment, and in some cases, whether there is actually time devoted to the subject under consideration.

We propose, and think most action researchers would agree, that planning is also vitally important within the action research process. Many elements may be very familiar to you, as you must consider who will be included in the study (participants), the location where the study will occur, how long your investigation will last, and how success will be measured. The last item, measuring success, is one you are well acquainted with, yet expectations are different as part of the action research process. As teachers, we're very familiar with documentation and the necessity of using evidence to "prove" learning. We use things like tests, quizzes, homework, and other measures, and grade these items to determine whether students were able to demonstrate the objectives that guided our instruction. These sources of data are important components within your teaching. Within the action research process, they take on added significance, as they may yield information that will facilitate conclusions relative to the question you have developed. Yet, you may also realize some of the more traditional forms of data used within your classroom are not enough and additional forms of data must be collected within your study to fully address your question.

■ ■ ■ VOICES FROM THE FIELD

Brandon Graham, Fifth-Grade Teacher

There is no doubt that my school is focused on data. We hear about it all the time. During our faculty meetings, my principal shares information about school-level data, like how we are performing on the state's assessments—where we've improved, where we still need to grow. Recently, several teachers gave a presentation about how they were using data to form groups for mini-lessons.

Sometimes all of this is a bit overwhelming. I am certainly not anti-data, but to be honest, as a language arts teacher, I am a little more focused on helping my students learn to enjoy writing and become better at it within the process. I don't really give quizzes or tests, and it is a bit harder to measure enjoyment or motivation. However, I do have the students write in their journals each day and I conference with them once a week. After I thought about this and how it related to my action research project, I decided that I could provide a specific prompt for the students to write about or ask them questions about their writing and interest near the end of a writing conference.

This data, while not representing the numeric value (score) often needed to document improvement, represents a way for me to show the impact my instruction is having on students' nonacademic traits without significantly changing what I do in my day-to-day practices.

Broadly speaking, what we are describing is your research methodology. If that is a new term for you, we understand completely, as it is not one that is typically discussed over lunch or in the workroom. To provide some clarification and build a foundation for the chapters that follow, we will describe some of the more common terminology associated with research. Learning these terms and the differences among various forms of research will help you as you begin to think about a research plan that will be developed and refined to guide and inform your thinking as you prepare to conduct your investigation. Once a clear plan is in place, the process of implementation should follow.

"NOTE"-ABLE THOUGHTS

Reflect upon the process that you use within your instructional planning. What do you consider as you plan lessons or units?

How can this process be used to help you develop the plan you will use for your action research?

RESEARCH TERMINOLOGY

Before getting too far into our discussion of the process you will use to conduct your action research study, let's start with a discussion of some of the terminology that is helpful for understanding research. We feel it is important to establish common definitions and understandings about what we are referring to when use terms like *methodology*, *method*, and *design*. It's been our experience that various authors use these words differently and sometimes interchangeably, which has a tendency to cause some confusion. While the terms are interrelated, they are distinct from one another. After reading this chapter, we want you to know and be able to identify the differences between the terms as well as to become familiar with how you may see *qualitative* and *quantitative* used with each term. Subsequently, we'll also refer to another term, *variable*, in our discussion, which we define as the factor or factors within the study that are modified or examined within the process of conducting the study.

Referring back to Chapter 1, remember that quantitative approaches to research are focused on testing a hypothesis and typically use numeric data to examine relationships or engage in comparisons. Qualitative research, on the other hand, uses descriptions or illustrative data to construct an understanding of a particular situation or phenomenon. We also mentioned (but didn't explain) that there is a third approach to research, mixed methods, which involves the combination of qualitative and quantitative approaches to potentially arrive at a greater understanding of the phenomenon under study than could be achieved by using either approach individually. Mixed methods research will be further explained and discussed in greater detail beginning on p. 79 of this chapter. Going a little deeper, the three approaches to research differ based on the assumptions about the purpose for the research, the roles and responsibilities of the researcher, the particular processes used to complete the study, and the types of studies that are undertaken. These differences are pertinent within the given definitions and descriptions of *methodology*, *methods*, and *design*.

According to Kothari (2004), "**Research methodology** is a way to systematically solve the research problem" (p. 8). It encompasses the research methods and design, explained below, but also incorporates the logic behind the selection of the methods used to conduct the research. The research papers that you examine will likely reference the methodology (e.g., ethnographic, historical, action research, survey) at or near the beginning of the methods section, although this is not always the case. Relating this back to the research approaches, there are various methodologies associated with each (see Figure 4.1) in the literature. The methodologies inform the specific methods and design of your study. For example, let's say that you have decided to conduct ethnographic research, which is a qualitative approach. The goal of such research is to examine and document the "shared patterns of behaviors, language, and actions of an intact cultural group in a natural setting over a prolonged period of time" (Creswell, 2014, p. 14). Based on this definition, we can immediately see that the researcher is going to have to spend a significant amount of time observing a group of people, documenting what occurs, then examining the data for patterns or themes that emerge. The specifics of how this occurs may differ by researcher, but the general parameters of the process are aligned with the methodology. Thinking about this further, do you see why this is considered a qualitative approach?

You may note that you do not see action research in Figure 4.1. This is by design, as an interesting thing about action research is that it doesn't fit neatly into any particular methodology. McNiff and Whitehead (2002) describe action research as

> a valid form of enquiry, with its own methodologies and epistemologies, its own criteria and standards of judgment. . . . There is general agreement that action research has an identity of its own and should not be spoken about in terms of traditional forms of research. (p. 1)

Given what we have described about action research so far, especially in Chapter 1, you can make some assumptions about the characteristics of the process; however, there is still some inherent flexibility in the methods and design of your study. We think as you read through the rest of the chapter, you'll be able to choose a method and design that is unique to your context and the research question you hope to answer.

The **research design** is your overall plan to collect the evidence necessary to reach the conclusions for your study. Creswell (2014) describes research designs as the "types of inquiry within qualitative, quantitative, and mixed methods approaches that provide specific direction for procedures" (p. 12). Given a primary function of the design is to articulate the process that will be used to ensure efficiency as well as maximize reliability and validity of the data collection and analysis, careful planning of your research design is critical to the success of the study. Quantitative designs tend to use preestablished processes. That is to say that researchers start with a hypothesis and seek to investigate the impact of an intervention or set of processes on the variable. The goal

FIGURE 4.1 Examples of Classifications of Research Methodologies

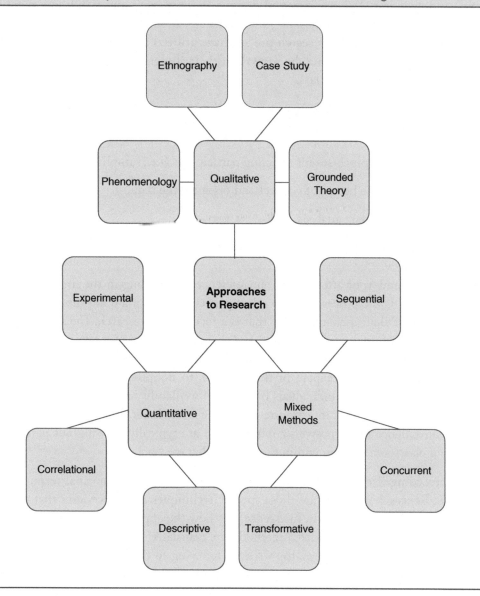

is to determine whether the hypothesis is accurate, often based upon a set of statistical procedures. Qualitative designs provide more flexibility as the focus is on providing a rich description of a case or cases and the study actually evolves through an iterative process as it progresses.

Knowledge of the primary design categories (experimental, quasi-experimental, and nonexperimental) will help you understand what you read in the literature as well as what you will need to reference for your study. The primary differences among the three types lie in how participants are assigned to groups and the presence of a comparison group. If participants are randomly assigned to groups that will be compared based on specified variables, which is often very challenging in educational contexts, it is considered **experimental design**. **Quasi-experimental design**, on the other hand, means there are groups that will be compared, but group membership was not randomly assigned. Finally, **nonexperimental designs** do not include a comparison group.

This would be the case if you simply used your class and compared their scores on a pre- and post-test. Nonexperimental designs are very common within investigations utilizing qualitative approaches. In our experiences, about 85% of the teachers we have guided through the action research process have utilized a nonexperimental design, as their intent was to determine the growth of their students as opposed to conducting comparisons with another class.

Regardless of the selected design, the researcher must consider each of the following prior to the start of the study:

- criteria and processes for selecting participants (i.e., sampling),

- procedures to be used to collect and organize the data,

- methods of data analysis, and

- a timeline to conduct the activities associated with the research

We'd like to draw your attention to our reference to sampling in the first bullet of the list. **Sampling** is the process used to select participants from among the population, or all entities that share a characteristic that is a focus of the research. The select group of participants is referred to as the sample, and there are a variety of methods used to create the sample, from random selection, where all members of a group have an equal chance of being selected to participate in the research, to nonprobabilistic sampling, which involves the selection of individuals based upon availability and accessibility (Hartras, 2010). It is very common in action research to use the latter form of sampling, specifically convenience or purposive sampling, as we are typically drawing our participants from our classroom or from within the context that we teach.

This preceding list of considerations transitions us nicely to the final term: *research methods*. **Research methods** are those specific techniques and procedures that are used to complete the research study. In essence, it is how the approaches to research, whether qualitative, quantitative, or mixed methods, are translated into practice. When you see reference to *qualitative methods*, the writer is referring to the broad array of techniques for data collection or analysis that match this approach. For example, qualitative data collection methods include activities like observations or interviews, while qualitative data analysis methods might involve a constant comparative approach or content analysis. *Quantitative data collection methods* include rating scales, surveys, or tests that are scored numerically. Computations of descriptive and inferential statistics are the most common quantitative data analysis methods. Our point in mentioning this is to have you note that much of what you read will simply refer to the data collection and analysis processes as qualitative methods or quantitative methods, which is where some of the confusion we mentioned earlier arises.

The specific research methods you will use within the completion of your study will be influenced by your research question. For example, if you plan to conduct ethnographic research focused on a question about students' attitudes, perceptions, and beliefs about writing, there is some flexibility in the qualitative methods you can choose. You may conduct observations of students' writing processes in the classroom, but you could also conduct interviews with students, both of which are associated with qualitative methods. Each will be explained in greater detail in Chapter 5. The subsequent analysis might involve examining the observation and interview notes to look for trends or patterns, which are qualitative methods of analysis. In essence, when researchers refer to *quantitative* or *qualitative methods*, you can make certain assumptions about the set of techniques that could be used based on the descriptor.

As you begin to consider the steps necessary for your research, begin to think about these key areas. While we will introduce and briefly describe the various collection methods in this chapter, Chapter 5 will include a more in-depth explanation of the various methods that can be used within action research. Data analysis is the focus of Chapter 6, and it is in that chapter that you will finalize your research plan.

"NOTE"-ABLE THOUGHTS

Now that you've been introduced to the concept of research design, reflect on the action research study that you'd like to complete. Would you classify it as experimental, quasi-experimental, or nonexperimental? Why? How will you select the participants?

RESEARCH METHODS

We've clarified some of the differences among the terminology associated with research, and thus we'll begin to elaborate on the specifics associated with the various approaches for conducting research and introduce data collection strategies. As you read each, continue to reflect upon your research question and the types of methods and strategies that will allow you to most effectively answer this question. Keep in mind that there might be several different strategies that could work, thus potentially leading toward a mixed methods approach that combines both qualitative and quantitative sources.

Qualitative methods. Qualitative approaches and the subsequent methods used to gather and analyze data are characterized by attempts to answer *why* questions through exploration, description, and interpretation (Flick, 2009). These investigations are often completed under natural conditions, and there is a focus on collecting in-depth information relative to the topic under investigation. This information is analyzed using interpretative and inductive approaches with the researcher engaging with data multiple times, seeking to develop themes that address the research question (Flick, 2009; Grady, 1998).

One noteworthy characteristic of qualitative methods of data analysis is that researchers bring their own perspective to the examinations of qualitative data, influencing the theories and explanations for the outcomes. Subsequently, findings are non-static and change as multiple researchers engage in analysis. In fact, given the overall variance that is possible as qualitative data analysis evolves, two researchers may arrive at different conclusions from the same data, although the conclusions are likely to be related.

An inherent benefit of qualitative methods is the incorporation of multiple factors to explain the data. In comparison to quantitative methods, researchers have greater flexibility in both the implementation and analysis of qualitative data. For example, using a semi-structured interview means that a researcher can adapt some questions during the interview and can probe for additional information by asking clarifying questions as necessary. Other qualitative data collection strategies that can often be completed in schools include observations, anecdotal notes, and student artifacts (e.g., student journal). Each will be explained in greater detail in Chapter 5.

Grady (1998) proposed that the qualitative methods may be better suited for school contexts, as it is challenging to conduct investigations where the conditions are tightly controlled in a school or classroom. As you well know, for example, a teacher cannot predetermine if a student will be absent the day a test is given. Instead, the researcher can adapt as conditions dictate. This includes changing schedules to conduct interviews with students about a new math program, making observations of children using reading strategies when they are present in the classroom, or collecting and analyzing journal entries over a period of time to note consistencies and inconsistencies within descriptions of problem-solving techniques for mathematical word problems. This also means that the researcher may have more insight into the day-to-day realities and changes that occur within the classroom than if quantitative measures are used at predetermined time intervals (Grady, 1998). Finally, qualitative methods are best suited for smaller sample sizes due to the necessity of examining a significant amount of textual data, which can involve extensive coding and development of relevant thematic trends.

Quantitative methods. Quantitative approaches rely on numerical data to examine units that are measureable. The focus is on reaching conclusions using deductive reasoning, as researchers examine the relationships between defined variables in specific settings (Szafran, 2012). According to Grady (1998), when using quantitative methods, researchers focus on control and replicability. In other words, the intent is to use specific, precise procedures that can be enacted by other researchers to verify the conclusions. Given the potential for objectivity associated with numeric data, quantitative methods produce findings that are not influenced by the inherent subjectivity of qualitative methods. Descriptive research, correlational studies, and quasi-experimental designs have been the most common forms of quantitative methodologies used among the teachers we have guided in the action research process.

In their broadest senses, quantitative approaches involve implementation of an intervention, which is referred to as the independent variable, and measure the relationship with or impact of the intervention on a specific outcome, deemed the dependent variable. In layman's terms, the independent variable is the one providing the influence, and the dependent variable is the one being influenced. The benefit of being a teacher is that we have access to many forms of quantitative data that is already being collected in the classroom, from grades on homework or quizzes to scores on standardized tests. Within an action research study that uses quantitative methods, you will need to determine what you are changing or doing in your classroom, the independent variable, and the sought-after impact of the change or implementation, which would represent a potential dependent variable. For example, does the amount of in-class review for a spelling test (independent variable) have an effect on the grade (dependent variable) on the spelling test? We can also think about the relationship between two variables, which is referred to as correlational research (Salkind, 2008). Returning to our previous example, a question that might be suited to examine a correlation is: What is the relationship between the amount of time studying and scores on spelling tests?

Quantitative methods can utilize a variety of data collection measures and are not confined to simply collecting scores on tests or quizzes. There are a number of surveys that utilize responses that can be converted to interval values by computing the total scores, allowing their use for comparison purposes. There are often options available with regard to the tools we can choose, and this leads to several inherent advantages to the use of quantitative methods. Among them are the potential for consistency of measurement (e.g., the use of the same test or survey instrument), the capacity to collect and analyze large amounts of quickly and efficiently, and the variety of ways numerical data can be analyzed (Grady, 1998). Finally, there is the inherent opportunity to display results graphically in tables and charts.

One thing that we have found out over the years, which we feel needs to be mentioned, is that when quantitative methods are referenced teachers often interpret this to mean they will need to utilize some form of statistical procedure to complete their study. This has led to some anxiety, as the vast majority of those we have worked with have not felt completely comfortable with statistical analysis. While certainly statistics can be used with numerical data, it's important to note that statistical analysis is not a requirement. There are times when descriptive research will yield conclusions that are significant for practice, yet don't achieve "statistical significance," a term you may have encountered as you engaged with literature to develop your background knowledge about your chosen topic. The term simply indicates that it is highly unlikely the results associated with the comparison or correlation occurred by chance. The goal of action research is to create conclusions that are useful to a teacher researcher within the context of practice, and thus practical significance might be viewed as more important than achieving statistical significance. See Figure 4.2 for a summary of the characteristics of qualitative and quantitative approaches to research.

Mixed methods research. We briefly introduced mixed methods (or multiple methods) research earlier in the chapter, and now it is time to provide additional information about this approach. **Mixed methods research** has been characterized as having the potential to address research questions with greater precision through the combination of qualitative and quantitative methods (Creswell & Plano Clark, 2011; Teddlie & Tashakkori, 2009). Notably, it allows the researcher to use all the strategies and procedures associated with each approach to comprehensively examine a situation and arrive at conclusions that may demonstrate greater reliability and validity, which will be discussed in Chapter 5. Ivankova (2015) noted, "Researchers can gain a more thorough understanding of the research problem under investigation and get more complete answers . . . [as] qualitative and quantitative research approaches are complementary in nature" (p. 4).

Mixed methods research has been proposed to be an effective approach for action research studies due to its applicability with the multiple forms of data that are available in the classroom. James, Milenkiewicz, and Bucknam (2008) noted that researchers can "make use of all available data (both qualitative and quantitative) in order to build a rigorous, cohesive set of conclusions" (p. 81). Given the increasing focus on the use of regular quantitative assessment to demonstrate growth, Creswell (2014) described the potential uses of mixed methods, including classroom observations and narrative descriptions, to supplement findings and verify academic achievement.

	Quantitative Research	Qualitative Research
Process	**Deductive**	**Inductive**
Purpose	To explain or predict through formulation of a hypothesis that is tested within the research process; generalize results to population	To gain in-depth understanding through examination or observation; involves a search for patterns to generate a theory; does not seek to generalize to population
Design	Structured; specified in advance; seeks representative sample of participants; potential for larger numbers of participants	Flexible and evolving; involves a small number of participants specifically selected for the research
Role of researcher	"Distant"—remains separate from subjects; objective	Immersed; participant (direct or indirect); subjective
Data	Numeric	Textual
Data sources/ collection strategies	Tests, surveys, questionnaires (closed response), measureable quantities (e.g., scores)	Interviews, observations, focus groups, surveys (open-response), journal, documents, artifacts
Analysis	Examination of results to confirm or disprove the hypothesis; often involves statistics at the end of the study	Coding to determine patterns or themes; ongoing
Time requirement	Dependent on purposes of research	Often requires extended time; may proceed in successive phases
Setting	Controlled; can be natural or can be conducted in laboratory	Natural

Researchers highlight that when using mixed methods research, the research question should include both qualitative and quantitative design elements to ensure a cohesive process is utilized within the study (Creswell & Plano Clark, 2011; Yin, 2006). For example: What is the impact of a reading incentive program on students' motivation as measured by the Motivation to Read Profile instrument and described through individual interviews? Procedurally, the data collection and analysis processes used within mixed methods research do not differ from those that would be employed when using specific quantitative or qualitative methods, respectively. Yet, according to Wisniewska (2011), there are various ways for qualitative and quantitative results to be combined to produce the conclusions for the research. Of the various forms of mixed methods approaches proposed, which includes parallel, sequential, and multilevel (Teddlie & Tashakkori, 2009), we feel that the parallel is most applicable within action research, as it is most closely aligned with what a teacher would do in a classroom. Notably, parallel mixed methods research involves the simultaneous examination of data from both qualitative and quantitative sources. Sequential and multilevel approaches, on the other hand, entail analyzing one form of data before the other, with the latter involving examinations of data at various levels (e.g., student and teacher) within the process. Using the parallel form within our example research question, the teacher would intentionally examine both the survey results and the interviews together to determine the impact on motivation.

Teddlie and Tashakkori (2009) note an inherent strength of mixed methods is the opportunity to utilize both inductive and deductive reasoning simultaneously. As the results of the quantitative and qualitative data are merged, there is a greater potential for **triangulation**, which is described as using multiple sources of data to verify findings that are emerging from the various sources (Merriam, 1998). Accordingly, the procedure can help teachers develop "a new appreciation for a data-driven decision-making process" (Lyons & DeFranco, 2010, p. 149). We acknowledge that the opportunity to collect various forms of data is both helpful and challenging. It is helpful in that there is increased efficiency because the various forms of data can be collected simultaneously (Creswell & Plano Clark, 2011). Yet, this is also challenging if the teacher is attempting to individually collect all data while maintaining attention to planning and instruction. In addition, this approach can cause difficulties for the interpretation of results if the results are not complementary, which also diminishes or eliminates the potential for triangulation.

"NOTE"-ABLE THOUGHTS

In the preceding chapters, you have developed a question to guide your research and conducted a review of the related literature. Using your question, the information you found, and the preceding information, which method is most applicable for your research: qualitative, quantitative, or mixed? Why do you think this is the case?

DATA SOURCES AND COLLECTION METHODS

Now that you have identified the method that you feel is most applicable to your action research, it is time to begin to focus on the various sources of data and collection processes that are appropriate for the chosen method. Our goal in this chapter is not to describe each source of data or method of collection in detail, but to help you generate a list of potential options that will be gradually refined as you engage with the information in Chapter 5 (data collection) and Chapter 6 (data analysis). We emphasize that you should initially consider multiple sources of data as well as several data collection strategies, as this maximizes the number of opportunities to answer the question you have posed.

We've mentioned previously that teachers have access to a variety of sources of data within their everyday practices. Sometimes, however, we need to be reminded of all the sources that may help us within the research process to determine how to leverage them and to understand the scope of how they can be used to inform research in the classroom or school. Figure 4.3 lists various sources of data that may be found in a classroom. Some of the data sources occur naturally within typical school and teaching practices, while others are less likely to be used on a regular basis and some planning might be required prior to their use as a data source. The key is to consider primary sources of data that can be collected efficiently and effectively to ensure you can reliably engage in the processes as you conduct your research.

As you consider your data sources, we recommend that you concurrently consider your question as well as reflect on your current classroom practices as they relate to the

FIGURE 4.3   Classroom-Based Sources of Data

Readily Available Sources	Less Probable
Portfolios	Interviews
Journals/diaries	Questionnaires
School records—standardized test scores, report cards, attendance	Surveys
	Audio recordings
Samples of student work	Photos
Anecdotal records	Logs of meetings
Projects	Video recordings
Performances	Attitude or rating scales
Self-assessments	
Checklists	

sources in Figure 4.3. The design, which is aligned with your question, will influence the need to consider whether your data source can be used to facilitate comparisons among groups (experimental or quasi-experimental) or whether there is no group assignment present (nonexperimental). In the case of the former designs, you will need to consider data sources that offer a defined set of criteria upon which the comparisons can be based. For example, if classroom observations were utilized to examine differences in the level of student engagement within two different classes during instruction, comparisons could be more effectively accomplished using a defined observation protocol to collect data on specific student actions (criteria) as opposed to unstructured, free-flowing thoughts that vary from observation to observation. If you were focused on quantitative methods, you would administer the same instrument or test to different classes (or comparison groups) and compare the scores. Similarly, a research question framed by a quantitative method would require data that can be expressed numerically or through defined, measureable units. Anecdotal notes that describe random interactions between groups of students in the lunchroom would not likely meet these criteria. However, if the goal was to document specific categories of interaction (e.g., hostile, friendly), the researcher could employ a checklist to note how often each type of interaction occurred.

■ ■ ■ VOICES FROM THE FIELD

Sejal Pringh, 11th-Grade Teacher

I have learned through experience that when the researcher does not create specific questions or have a way of measuring the data, it is very hard to come up with a solution for the problem.

As teachers and researchers, we need to create a plan that allows us to collect useful data, not just any data. We need to be very specific first in what we want to improve, and then be very detailed in how we will collect and what we will collect if we want the process to be meaningful. In the past when I have tried to collect data to problem solve, I was not consistent in the process of how I was going to collect the data. As a result, when I went to analyze the information and develop a plan or solution, I was unable to narrow in on what was even causing the problem. I now understand the importance of taking time to reflect on the issue and then spending sufficient time identifying the problem/topic before gathering data that correlates to the problem.

Reflection on your classroom practices is also important, as we feel that the likelihood of consistent and successful data collection is enhanced when you think about what sources of information you already have and how data collection techniques can be seamlessly integrated into your regular practices (or at least with as little disruption as possible). The ultimate goal of action research is to make you a better teacher, so you may have to consider how you can effectively conduct conferences while documenting data pertinent to your study in sufficient detail in a manner that works for you individually. We sound this note of caution given the novice researchers with whom we've worked who have focused specifically on qualitative techniques and often underestimated the time necessary to use these techniques and quickly became overwhelmed trying to collect too much data. Being aware of your situation, context, and the various characteristics of the sources will help you develop an effective data collection plan.

"NOTE"-ABLE THOUGHTS

Look at the sources of data listed in Figure 4.3. Are there other sources that might be available that are not in the list? Can you think of additional forms of data that might assist you within your research? Make a list of them for future consideration.

ETHICAL CONSIDERATIONS IN ACTION RESEARCH

Researchers who conduct investigations in various contexts are held to ethical standards of research, yet these same ethical principles are especially important in the design and implementation of a study that will be completed within your own classroom (Hesse-Biber & Leavy, 2011). As a teacher and action researcher, there is the necessity of playing two roles in the classroom. On one hand, you are responsible for the instruction and well-being of the children in your classroom. On the other, you are a researcher who is trying to systematically collect data to measure the impact of an intervention on some specific outcome. Given these potentially confounding roles, the teacher could intentionally or unintentionally interfere with participation as well as the results (Nolen & Vander Putten, 2007). The National Institute of Health (NIH) (Emanuel, Abdoler, & Stunkel, n.d.) compiled a set of general principles for conducting ethical research and for the protection of participants that must be adhered to within the research process. In sum the research should have

- social value—provide benefits to health and well-being,

- scientific validity—produce results that are beneficial and increase knowledge,

- fair subject selection—utilize procedures that ensure equal opportunities for individuals to be selected for participation (assuming they match the criteria or characteristics sought),

- favorable risk–benefit ratio—benefits of research outweigh the risks,

- independent review—individuals not connected to the research have an opportunity to review it,

- respect for enrolled subject—includes continued monitoring of well-being and active communication with them, and

- informed consent—agreement to participate.

We believe most of the categories are generally self-explanatory when coupled with our explanation, but informed consent may be a new concept that includes some specific parameters, and we will discuss it in greater detail.

Informed consent. An important part of the research process is **informed consent**, which is designed to prevent (or limit) situations where the subject feels compelled to participate as opposed to doing so out of free will. To reinforce the necessity of this within your classroom, you must consider the relationship you have with your students. Ultimately in any teacher/student relationship, the teacher holds the power. The question comes to bear if a student or several students refuse to participate in your study. Certainly, the more participants, the greater the potential for substantive conclusions, and thus you are likely to be motivated to recruit as many students as possible. However, given your position, students may elect to participate out of fear of negative repercussions. Collecting informed consent is a method to limit this possibility by expressly addressing the details necessary to increase the likelihood of voluntary participation.

Informed consent contains specific information that allows the participants to assess the research study and subsequently participate of their free will as a result of their understanding of the study. There are certain elements inherent in an informed consent document: competence, disclosure, understanding, and voluntariness (Emanuel et al., n.d.). *Competence* refers to a participant's capacity to understand the study, including its requirements, and to make a decision regarding whether to participate. Disclosure involves sharing all information about the study, including goals, benefits, and risks, with the student. The subject must also be informed exactly what participation in the study involves. This contributes to understanding, which must be confirmed and acknowledged within the informed consent process. Finally, it must be clear on the informed consent form that participation is voluntary and that the option to opt out of participation is always present. In regard to the latter, the process for doing so should be expressly described. An example of a letter of consent is provided in Figure 4.4 to allow you to see how each of these elements appears in context.

TECH CONNECTIONS

How many times have you received notification from one of your devices indicating that an update is available or required? Before the actual installation of the update can take place, we're presented with the opportunity to "agree" to Terms and Conditions outlined in the document that most of us probably never read. This represents a perfect example of giving our consent, although we don't always think it could be completely characterized as "informed" because we don't actually take the time to read what is written. The idea behind informed consent in research is essentially to ensure that this doesn't happen, or at least to diminish the likelihood of it. We want participants in our research to know exactly what they will be doing and what will be required of them if they choose to join our study. There shouldn't be any fine print that would surprise or otherwise jeopardize participation. This carries over to administering surveys electronically, which is also becoming more commonplace. If you submit a proposal to an institutional review board, you'll still be required to provide evidence of informed consent, with all the related details. This "new" process simply means the participant can elect to toggle a button or click "Agree" as opposed to the traditional paper copy form. We hope, but can't guarantee, that potential participants will still read the details and objectives of your study and not treat it like another software update!

Informed consent is typically obtained after subjects have the study explained to them and agree to participate by signing a consent form. However, by law, informed consent cannot be given by children under the age of 18, which likely has ramifications for your study. In these instances, a competent adult guardian or parent must provide informed consent. The child can then provide *assent*, which means that he or she agrees to participate in your research (and that the parent has provided permission through informed consent). In your study, you may be asked to obtain informed consent from parents as well as assent from the student participants.

Action research represents a somewhat tricky situation when it comes to informed consent or assent. While teacher/researchers are technically required to obtain informed consent due to the pitfalls mentioned previously, there are some instances where the teacher may be granted an exemption. Primarily this occurs when research activities are deemed to be a component of regular professional practice or when there is a "legitimate educational interest" by school personnel (Stringer, 2014). For example, if your source of data was an assessment measure (e.g., Reading 3D or Northwest Evaluation Association's Measure of Academic Progress test, which was regularly administered as a standard form of data collection), consent may not be needed. In these instances, parental permission may suffice as long as it is communicated what data will be used, the purposes for its use, and who will use it.

A challenge surrounding consent and exemption lies with protecting the anonymity of participants. When action research is conducted in the classroom, there are a limited number of subjects and, oftentimes, there are discernible characteristics of individual students that facilitate recognition by the researcher. It is for this reason that you should be familiar with two very important terms in action research: *anonymity*

FIGURE 4.4 Letter of Consent

Dear Parent/Guardian and Student:

I am a teacher at Sunrise Elementary. I am interested in collecting information about students' attitudes toward and strategies for reading on the Internet, as they have important roles in shaping how students use the Internet and potentially impact student achievement due to the different skills used in comparison to traditional reading activities.

Study Title

Exploring Fifth- and Sixth-Grade Students' Skills, Attitudes, and Dispositions Toward Online Reading

Study Purpose and Rationale

Many of today's K–12 students naturally integrate the Internet into their everyday activities. Reports indicate that as many as 93% of children and teens use the Internet, with many regarding it as a primary tool for gathering information. Yet little is known about to how measure differences in attitude and skill toward reading online. My goal is to produce an instrument that will measure these skills and attitudes in addition to the behaviors necessary for proficient reading online. Through this research, I hope to statistically determine if the instrument I have developed is accurately measuring the above traits. If I am successful, the instrument will enable educators to more effectively assess differences in attitudes and skills and use this information to implement instructional practices that prepare students to successfully read on the Internet and participate in an age of global information sharing.

Participation Procedures and Duration

For this project, students will be asked to provide information on their general technology experiences and knowledge (i.e., the use of specific Internet tools, such as blogs, wikis, and e-mail). In addition, students will complete a 52-question survey that requires them to respond to statements about their

- personal beliefs regarding technology and reading online (e.g., I feel confident that I can easily understand information I research on the Internet);
- motivation for reading online (e.g., I enjoy the challenge of trying to find something using the Internet);
- anxiety (e.g., I cannot relax when I am reading/researching on the Internet); and
- strategies for reading online (e.g., Before I begin to research on the Internet, I think about what I am supposed to be looking for).

The survey will be taken at school, in either the regular classroom or computer lab, and is designed to take approximately 30 minutes. Students who choose not participate will remain in the classroom or computer lab and will be provided with an alternate activity during the survey completion time. Survey responses will remain anonymous; no information will be collected linking responses to students' identities. All data will be deleted at the completion of the data analysis, which is anticipated to last one year after completion of the survey.

Risks or Discomforts

There are no foreseeable risks or ill effects from participating in this study. As the respondents' identities will be anonymous, choosing not to participate will not incur any negative consequences.

Voluntary Participation

Participation in this study is completely voluntary, and you are free to withdraw at any time for any reason without penalty or prejudice from the investigator. Please feel free to ask any questions of the investigator (see contact information below) or encourage your student to do so before completing the survey or at any time during the completion of the survey. To indicate consent, please complete the information below and return this form to school with your student.

****

Consent

I have read the description of this research project, titled "Exploring Fifth- and Sixth-Grade Students' Skills, Attitudes, and Dispositions Toward Online Reading." All of my questions have been answered to my satisfaction, and I give my permission for my child to participate. I give permission to the investigator to examine my child's survey responses. I understand that upon request I will receive a copy of this informed consent form to keep for future reference.

_____   _____

Parent's Signature   Date

I have had this research explained to me and have been given the chance to ask questions. I understand what I am being asked to do. I agree to participate.

_____   _____

Child's Signature   Date

Researcher Contact Information

Principal Investigator:

John Doe

Fifth-Grade Teacher

Sunrise Elementary

Sunrise, CA 55306

Telephone: (555) 336-8547

E-mail: johndoe@sunrise.edu

---

and *confidentiality*. **Anonymity** refers to the situation when the researcher does not know or have access to the identity of the participant. **Confidentiality** relates to situations where the researcher may have access to personally identifiable information, but does not release or share the information. When data includes information that can potentially identify individual students, it is likely best to obtain parental permission. When identities can remain anonymous, permission is not likely needed. However, in any instance where there are questions, we recommend erring on the side of caution and that you work closely with a local administrator, as that individual will be most familiar with the expectations of the school or district.

INSTITUTIONAL REVIEW BOARD

Per guidelines established by the U.S. federal government, research that is conducted with direct or indirect funding from the government requires a review of proposed research by an **institutional review board** (IRB). This may include the context where your research will be conducted. The primary purpose for the institutional review board is to ensure protection of the human subjects that may participate in the research. Boards can conduct several forms of review, including a full committee or expedited, or, when certain conditions are met, there may be an exemption from review granted. Generally, the level of review required is based upon the amount of risk to participants associated with the research. Luckily for teachers, the exemption from review is the one that is most likely to apply for your situation. Research is exempt from review when the following applies:

1. Research conducted in established or commonly accepted educational settings, involving normal educational practices, such as (i) research on regular and special education instructional strategies, or (ii) research on the effectiveness of or the comparison among instructional techniques, curricula, or classroom management methods

2. Research involving the use of educational tests (cognitive, diagnostic, aptitude, achievement), survey procedures, interview procedures, or observation of public behavior (Department of Health and Human Services, 2009, p. 3)

However, these provisions change with respect to the second qualifier if the subjects can be identified, and thus it is critical that you reflect on the methods that will be used if your institution requires IRB approval.

If your district or local education agency requires IRB approval, after reading Chapters 4 and 5 you should have most of the information necessary for the application. A sample (see Figure 4.5) has been included that may demonstrate the related requirements of completing an IRB protocol. In essence, IRB requires a summary of the proposed research, the methodology to be used, including the sampling procedures and information about the proposed participants, and the proposed timeline for the research. Our example also requests information about obtaining informed consent. In some cases, you may be required to include the consent and assent forms, copies of data collection instruments, and a letter of approval from an administrator or school official.

FIGURE 4.5 Sample IRB Form

SECTION A: APPLICANT INFORMATION

Researcher's Full Name(s):	Title/Position:
Institution/Organization:	
Mailing Address:	
E-mail Address:	Daytime Phone:

SECTION B: STUDY INFORMATION

Project Title:	
Projected Start Date: _____ Projected Completion Date: _____	
Purpose(s) of Study:	
Rationale for Study:	

SECTION C: PARTICIPANT INFORMATION

Participants:	Check all that apply.
Students	□ Yes □ No
Teachers	□ Yes □ No
School administrators	□ Yes □ No
Parents	□ Yes □ No
Other (please specify):	□ Yes □ No

Participant Information	
Number of student participants	
Number of teacher participants	
Number of school administrator participants	
Number of parent participants	
Number of other participants	

Describe the subject population.
Describe the participant selection criteria.
Describe subject recruitment.

SECTION D: RESEARCH METHODOLOGY

Describe the methods and procedures to be used within the study.
Describe how data will be collected and stored (include research instruments where applicable).
Describe how data will be analyzed.
Provide a timeline for the research.

SECTION E: INFORMED CONSENT

Describe the process that will be used to obtain informed consent from the participants (include the letter of consent when applicable).

Taking Action: Developing a Preliminary Research Plan

Without a plan in place, the possibility of the success of your action research is significantly diminished. Central to the research plan is the actual design and methods to be used in the study, which is the focus of this section. To get started on your research, let's begin by considering your question. Are there elements within your question that will specifically guide the processes that will be used or the form of the data you will collect? Begin by jotting down your response to these considerations. When designing a research study, Hubbard and Power (2003) recommend an examination of the setting as part of the process of development of the research design, and thus, the next things you should think about include the following:

- What are the places where you might collect data?

- What happens in these settings? What events are common?

- What people are involved? What interactions? (Hubbard & Power, 2003, p. 17)

Active reflection on these questions can help determine the specific variables you will examine and will also narrow the focus of your study. Given the tendency of the teachers that we have worked with to choose topics that are too broad early in the development process, this is an important process. We've found that forethought on the questions we've presented limits the potential to try to plan a study that is too large in its size and scope to be effectively carried out within the parameters of everyday teaching practices. Furthermore, the questions will help you ultimately design a study that contains the right balance between structure and flexibility to maximize the likelihood of addressing the research question(s) under examination.

So far, we've covered multiple topics pertinent to the development of your overall research plan, and it is time to put this information to use as you begin to refine your thoughts regarding the specifics of your plan. Before finalizing your research plan, which will be initiated as part of the next section and completed in Chapters 5 and 6, it's important to complete a few additional organizational steps that will ultimately make the development of the plan easier.

We've included an example (see Figure 4.6) of a chart that we ask those who we guide through the process to complete to help frame their thinking. You'll note that we begin the table with a re-articulation of the problem statement, goals for the research, and research question. This is to emphasize the fact that these must be at the forefront of the development of the research plan, as the lack of alignment with the procedures will prohibit you from attaining the intended goals of your research.

The first consideration involves specifically identifying the context for your study as well as the characteristics of the participants. You've likely considered the latter a great deal as you developed your question, but you may not have articulated (or considered) all the relevant information that may impact your study. Thinking about the context will allow you to consider whether the resources are present for the research. For example, if the school is located in a rural area with limited Internet access, it may be difficult to conduct a study that requires students to complete online activities outside of school. On the other hand, if the school serves a significant number of students who are English-language learners, it may not be feasible to conduct a study that requires students to

FIGURE 4.6 Example of a Research Plan Organizer

Problem statement	
Goals for research	
Research question	
Context	
Participants	
Data to be collected	
Frequency/duration of data collection	
Location of data collection	
Who will collect data	
Data analysis procedure	
Display of data/findings	

solve complex word problems (in English) as homework. Of course, this is dependent upon the actual participants and the intervention that occurs, but given the influence of the greater context, it's still an important consideration.

Focusing on the actual participants in the study, typically a teacher conducts the study with the students in the classroom and therefore has in-depth knowledge about the sample. Completing the chart is an opportunity to think specifically about your participants. For example, will you use your whole class or a subset of students who struggle with a particular skill? Regardless of the number of participants, you'll need to consider the characteristics of the participants, as evidenced by the preceding example. Furthermore, in some cases there are control groups that must be included among the participants, and you'll need to reference information about the participants who compose this group to demonstrate their similarity to the students exposed to the intervention.

This brings us to the portion of the research plan that involves the articulation of the various facets of data collection. We've only introduced you to some basic information about the various forms of data that are associated with the research methods, but we feel that you can begin to think about what is applicable for your study. Additional information presented in Chapter 5 will help you refine your ideas and provide specific rationales for your methods, and thus right now you are primarily brainstorming potential methods of collection. We require our students to develop and submit drafts of their research plan (see Figure 4.7 in our Case in Point for an example), as it forces them to think comprehensively about the time necessary for each step as they are further introduced to the multiple considerations within data collection and analysis that must be considered within the research.

DEVELOPING A PLAN OR A PRODUCT: INITIATING THE RESEARCH PLAN PROPOSAL FORM

Using our example, it's now time for you to synthesize the information we've provided and to produce the artifacts associated with this phase of the action research process.

In this case, you will use our template to produce a first draft of your research plan. As previously mentioned, the next two chapters are focused on data collection and analysis, respectively, and we feel it is important that you consider pertinent information about each before finalizing and implementing your action research plan.

To create the first draft of your research plan, you must first revisit the research statement and goals for your action research study. List those in the blanks provided along with your primary research question(s). Next, think about the context for your study and the participants. It may be necessary to gather additional information about the school or district where the action research will take place. This can often be located on a website for the respective education department for your state or municipality. While you will know the primary information about the students who will be the participants in your study, there may be characteristics that are relevant that may come from school records. As a note of caution, you should inform an administrator that you are searching for information that may not be specific to their educational performance per se. For your research question, consider the data collection strategies that could *potentially* help you answer it, taking the time to reflect upon your design, method, and those sources of data available as part of your classroom practice. Your final research plan does not have to incorporate all the strategies you list, but you still need to consider alternate approaches for future projects and/or continued action research. Choose one or two of these strategies and list them in the "Data to Be Collected" box. Think about and write examples of the specific kinds of information you plan to obtain (e.g., I will collect surveys administered at reading conferences). Given this is an action research study, you will likely be the individual to collect the data and the location will be your classroom. However, this is dependent on the overall research design, as you may, for example, have a colleague who is helping to perform the observations or you may have a control classroom that is not your own.

As a final step in this portion of the planning process, take the time to clarify whether you will need to complete an institutional board review application and, relatedly, to develop an informed consent document. To assist in this process, we recommend using the example of the consent letter provided in the Figure 4.4, changing the pertinent information to be specific to your study. Once you have completed the review of your data collection and analysis procedures at the end of Chapter 6, you should have all the information necessary to fully complete the IRB application should it prove necessary.

Evaluating Against the Standards: Are You Ready to Move On?

CHECKLIST: PRELIMINARY RESEARCH PLAN

Have you:

_____ 1. Determined the appropriate research method for your action research study?

_____ 2. Reviewed the research question to ensure it can be answered using the proposed methods?

_____ 3. Determined the potential sources of data that will be collected?

_____4. Listed the specific locations that will be used for data collection?

_____5. Inquired with an administrator or the district office to determine if a proposal must be submitted to the institutional review board?

_____6. Developed an informed consent letter or permission form (if necessary)?

As we've described in previous chapters, it's important to examine and reflect upon your responses to the questions contained as part of the checklist. If you have not considered or addressed several elements, we would caution against proceeding to the next steps in the process. This is especially relevant to those questions that address permission and informed consent. If your responses are positive, it's time to begin to focus more on the data sources and collection associated with your chosen research methods. Chapter 5 will present various methods to collect data within qualitative, quantitative, and mixed methods research.

Summary

In this chapter, we provided information that must be considered when planning the specific facets of an action research study. We introduced various terminology, including _methodology_, _research methods_, and _research design_, to help you consider what type of study should be conducted to help you answer your research question. Qualitative methods are those that use an inductive approach to develop codes and themes that describe the data, while quantitative methods are those that are more numerically oriented. Mixed methods research combines both qualitative and quantitative methods and utilizes data collection strategies associated with each. This method was noted to be well suited for action research studies, as it allows the researcher to develop conclusions that have depth as well as breadth because of the two forms of data. We mentioned various methods of data collection, including observations, interviews, student records, and surveys and questionnaires, that may be directly applicable to your classroom and may be considered as you develop your research plan. Finally, we discussed the ethical requirements of a researcher while planning and engaging in action research. We explained the difference between consent and assent and outlined the requirements associated with completing an application for an institutional review board. The chapter culminated with the completion of a first draft of your research plan.

Key Terms

Anonymity, p. 87
Assent, p. 85
Confidentiality, p. 87
Experimental design, p. 75
Informed consent, p. 84
Institutional review board, p. 87

Mixed methods research, p. 79
Nonexperimental design, p. 75
Quasi-experimental design, p. 75
Research design, p. 74

Research methodology, p. 74
Research methods, p. 76
Sampling, p. 76
Triangulation, p. 81

Case in Point: Research Plan (Pre-implementation)

One Elementary Teacher's Journey: Research Log Entry

I've thought a great deal about the various forms of data that I can collect to help me answer my research question. Looking back at the question and reflecting on what I should do, I really think a mixed methods approach might be the best way to capture the data I need. I was thinking I would like to conduct student interviews as well as collect students' oral reading fluency scores. The interviews would help me see evidence of students' thinking and determine the processes they are using while reading, and the scores would allow for the possibility of a quick comparison to see whether growth occurred. The challenge is that I am not sure I have the time to interview each child independently on several occasions, so I am somewhat hesitant to commit to this data source right now. To examine students' fluency, DIBELS is the logical choice. I already collect this data, so it will be very manageable.

In looking at the data for my class, it's clear that I have a variety of reading levels present. However, I want to really focus on the eight students who seem to be struggling the most to determine the impact of the study. When I implement the Readers' Theater, though, I will attempt to intermix the groups with different reading levels to allow the students to help each other and to interact socially. As my research progresses, I'll look and see how this is working and modify the groups somewhat, depending on the results I am seeing. I am still thinking about using stories that highlight information from various content areas as I want to spread the excitement I think will be generated by this throughout the students' day. I think this will also activate different interests. Given this is my first attempt at using the intervention, though, it may be easier to start simple and focus on our regular reading time. Typically, I meet with individual students during the time I will devote the Readers' Theater, but I think I can make the necessary adaptations to the schedule (see Figure 4.7).

FIGURE 4.7   One Elementary Teacher's Initial Research Plan

Problem statement	Several second-grade students in my class struggle with fluency (rate and accuracy) and are below grade level standards as assessed three times a year using DIBELS. I want to see these struggling students reading on grade level, according to DIBELS, by the end of the year.
Goals for research	The goals I am considering for my action research study are focused on helping my students who are currently reading below grade level to become more fluent readers so that they can read words accurately, at an appropriate rate, and with expression.
Research question	What is the effect of Readers' Theater on second-grade students' reading fluency?
Context	The context for this research is a school located in a suburban area within the city limits of a large metropolitan city. The overall socioeconomic status of the school is rated as low to middle class, with 58% of the enrolled students receiving free or reduced-price lunch. The school is primarily African American (59%), Hispanic American (20%), Caucasian (12%), Multiracial (5%), Asian American (3%), and American Indian (1%). Both genders (male, 51%; female, 49%) are fairly equal in representation of students.
Participants	Twenty-four second-grade students; 12 participants are African American, eight are Hispanic American, three are Caucasian, and one participant is multiracial; 14 boys and 10 girls; five demonstrate oral reading fluency scores below grade level.
Data to be collected	Oral reading fluency scores, student interviews
Frequency/duration of data collection	Three times over the length of the study (ORF scores), possibly weekly (interviews)

Location of data collection	My classroom
Who will collect data	Teacher
Data analysis procedure	
Display of data/ findings	

One Secondary Teacher's Journey: Research Log Entry

In order to answer my research question, I will need to determine the effect of the open investigation instructional approach on student learning and their academic achievement. To accomplish this, I would give weekly tests to assess their mastery of the science content taught each week. During the direct instruction segment, students will be given a 10-question multiple-choice test each week for eight weeks. I will use this as baseline data and then develop weekly tests using the exact same format for the next eight weeks during the intervention. I am also thinking of designing a Likert-scale questionnaire that will assess student attitude toward the class and the instructional approach. I think I may add some open-ended questions to allow students to share freely about their experiences and express additional strengths or weaknesses that I do not address with the items on the questionnaire. I think this would give me rich data and a better chance of capturing what students are thinking and feeling about the structure of our class. I would give the questionnaire in the last week of the unit that I am currently teaching using direct instruction and then again at the end of the unit that I will be teaching using the open investigation approach. I want to be able to

have data to compare student attitudes with both approaches.

By collecting these two data sources I can implement a pre-test and post-test, using the same group research design. I think the pre-test and post-test data gathered within my one class will show the effect of the open investigation approach as it compares with the direct instruction approach on student learning. I would also have pre- and post-test data from the questionnaire to examine the attitudes and perceptions of the students on the instructional approaches. I might consider looking at different readiness levels within my class and examine how the intervention affected different groups of students, but I am not sure yet how I might do this. I am also wondering if I should keep a journal to record field notes during the intervention to capture my observations and thoughts. My only concern with this is that I would need to do this consistently throughout the study, and I did not do it during the direct instruction. So, I am not sure that it would be a good source of data to use if it was only randomly collected or if only done during the intervention phase. I plan on talking these ideas through with my colleagues and professor as I continue to develop my research plan (see Figure 4.8).

FIGURE 4.8 One Secondary Teacher's Initial Research Plan

Problem statement	In a lower-level ability section of ninth-grade science, students struggle with science content and a motivation to learn. I want to see how an open investigation workshop approach impacts these students' learning and engagement during the second quarter of instruction.
Goals for research	My goal for this action research study is to implement the open investigation approach with my science class of below-level readers/writers to improve their academic achievement and motivation for learning.

(Continued)

FIGURE 4.8 (Continued)

Research question	What is the effect of an open investigation workshop approach on a ninth-grade science class with students who are lower-level readers/writers?
Context	The context of this study is a secondary school located in a suburban area near a large metropolitan city. The student body consists of 908 students. The school is classified as medium socioeconomic status, with 48% of students being eligible for free or reduced-price lunch. While the school is not Title I, it does qualify to receive state funds proportionate to the free and reduced-price lunch percentage. The student population consists mainly of Caucasian (79%), African American (17%), Asian American (2%), American Indian/Pacific Islander (1%), and other (1%).
Participants	This study utilizes one of three sections of science classes that I teach. As a result of ability grouping based on language arts skill levels, this particular group of students struggle to read and are classified as below grade level readers. The class consists of 28 students: eight have 504 plans, two have IEPs, 16 are male, and 12 are female. The majority of the class is Caucasian (20), with African American (5), Hispanic (2), and Asian American (1) students included. The majority of the students (19) have low informational text reading scores, while the remaining nine have scores in the low-medium range.
Data to be collected	Multiple-choice test, questionnaire, observations
Frequency/duration of data collection	Test—each Friday; questionnaire—baseline and end of unit; observations—ongoing
Location of data collection	My classroom
Who will collect data	Teacher
Data analysis procedure	
Display of data/findings	

Activities and Additional Resources

1. A colleague comes to you with the following research question: How does the use of manipulatives impact the math performance of fifth-grade students? What research design and research methods would be appropriate for this investigation? Make a recommendation to your colleague, providing a rationale using information discussed in the chapter.

2. Record a classroom episode or lesson using audio or audio/visual. Listen to/watch the episode and take notes about a specific facet, for example, teacher–student interactions or student engagement. Ask a colleague to do the same. Compare your notes. What was similar? What was different? What does this tell you about the need to think about how consistency (reliability) can be built into qualitative data collection?

3. Using the example in Appendix A and the information in the chapter, develop your own informed consent document that could be used within a research study.

Print Resources

Creswell, J. W. (2014). *Research design: Qualitative, quantitative, and mixed methods approaches* (4th ed.). Thousand Oaks, CA: Sage.

Davies, J. (2010). Preparation and process of qualitative interviews and focus groups. In L. Dahlberg

& C. McCaig (Eds.), *Practical research and evaluation: A start-to-finish guide for practitioners* (pp. 126–144). Thousand Oaks, CA: Sage.

Student Study Site

edge.sagepub.com/putman

- Take the practice quiz.
- Review key terms with eFlashcards.
- Explore topics with video and multimedia.

References

Creswell, J. W. (2014). *Research design: Qualitative, quantitative, and mixed methods approaches* (4th ed.). Thousand Oaks, CA: Sage.

Creswell, J. W., & Plano Clark, V. L. (2011). *Designing and conducting mixed methods research* (2nd ed.). Thousand Oaks, CA: Sage.

Department of Health and Human Services. (2009). *Code of federal regulations: Part 46, protection of human subjects*. Retrieved from http://www.hhs.gov/ohrp/policy/ohrpregulations.pdf

Emanuel, E., Abdoler, E., & Stunkel, L. (n.d.). *Research ethics: How to treat people who participate in research*. Bethesda, MD: National Institute of Health. Retrieved from http://www.bioethics.nih.gov/education/pdf/FNIH_BioethicsBrochure_WEB.PDF

Flick, U. (2009). *An introduction to qualitative research* (4th ed.). Thousand Oaks, CA: Sage.

Grady, M. P. (1998). *Qualitative and action research: A practitioner handbook*. Bloomington, IN: Phi Delta Kappa International.

Hartras, D. (2010). Qualitative research as a method of inquiry in education. In D. Hartras (Ed.), *Educational research and inquiry: Qualitative and quantitative approaches* (pp. 65–84). London, UK: Continuum International Publishing Group.

Hesse-Biber, S. N., & Leavy, P. (2011). *The practice of qualitative research* (2nd ed.). Thousand Oaks, CA: Sage.

Hubbard, R. S., & Power, B. M. (2003). *The art of classroom inquiry: A handbook for teacher-researchers* (rev. ed.). Portsmouth, NH: Heinemann.

Ivankova, N. V. (2015). *Mixed methods applications in action research: From methods to community action*. Thousand Oaks, CA: Sage.

Flick, U. (2014). *An introduction to qualitative research* (5th ed.). Thousand Oaks, CA: Sage.

James, E. A., Milenkiewicz, M. T., & Bucknam, A. (2008). *Participatory action research for educational leadership: Using data-driven decision making to improve schools*. Thousand Oaks, CA: Sage.

Kothari, C. R. (2004). *Research methodology: Methods and techniques* (2nd ed.). New Delhi, India: New Age International.

Lyons, A., & DeFranco, J. (2010). A mixed-methods model for educational evaluation. *The Humanistic Psychologist, 38*, 146–158.

McNiff, J., & Whitehead, J. (2002). *Action research: Principles and practice* (2nd ed.). London: Routledge.

Merriam, S. B. (1998). *Qualitative research and case study applications in education*. San Francisco, CA: Jossey-Bass.

Nolen, A. L., & Vander Putten, J. (2007). Action research in education: Addressing gaps in ethical principles and practices. *Educational Researcher, 36*, 401–407.

Salkind, N. J. (2008). *Exploring research* (7th ed.). Upper Saddle River, NJ: Prentice Hall.

Stringer, E. T. (2014). *Action research* (4th ed.). Thousand Oaks, CA: Sage.

Szafran, R. (2012). *Answering questions with statistics*. Thousand Oaks, CA: Sage.

Teddlie, C., & Tashakkori, A. (2009). *Foundations of mixed methods research: Integrating quantitative and qualitative approaches in the social and behavioral sciences*. Thousand Oaks, CA: Sage.

Wisniewska, D. (2011). Mixed methods and action research: Similar or different? *Glottodidactica, 37*, 59–72.

Yin, R. K. (2006). Mixed methods research: Are the methods genuinely integrated or merely parallel? *Research in the Schools, 13*, 41–47.

CHAPTER 5

Methods of Data Collection

GUIDING QUESTIONS

After reading this chapter, you should be able to answer the following questions:

- What are the differences between validity and reliability? How can data be collected to ensure reliability and validity?

- How are data collection methods categorized?

- What forms of qualitative data collection methods can be used within action research? What are the characteristics and considerations for using these methods?

- What forms of quantitative data collection methods can be used within action research? What are the characteristics and considerations for using these methods?

CHAPTER AIMS AND GOALS

This chapter is focused on extending the information introduced in Chapter 4 through a more detailed description of the forms of data collection that could be used within your action research investigation. The chapter begins with a brief review of the various different approaches for conducting research. Following this introduction, we present various forms of data collection categorized within each of the respective approaches. Using your research question as a guide will be important as you develop an understanding of what each form of data collection can offer. The chapter also specifically addresses validity and reliability as it relates to data collection. At the end of the chapter, you will have gathered the necessary information to develop a plan to guide your data collection throughout the action research process.

SETTING THE CONTEXT: CHOOSING DATA COLLECTION METHODS

In Chapter 4, we introduced you to information necessary to help you begin to draft a plan to guide your research, including sources of qualitative and quantitative data (see Table 5.1). As part of the process, we asked you to consider the question: What forms of data can I collect to answer my research question? Thinking about that question and your tentative plan, let's briefly review the characteristics associated with the research methods you may be considering for your action research investigation before describing the various forms of data collection in greater depth.

Recall that qualitative approaches are focused on exploring, describing, or interpreting information relative to a particular area under study (Flick, 2009). Through these processes, qualitative research seeks to answer *how*, *why*, and *what* questions. Data sources often (though not always) consist of some form of textual data, obtained either directly from a source (e.g., written reflections or field notes) or through transcription of verbal interactions (e.g., interviews or focus groups). Data is collected under natural conditions (e.g., in the classroom), and conclusions are formed through repeated examinations of the data to help the researcher develop interpretations and themes related to the research question (Flick, 2009; Grady, 1998). Among the advantages of qualitative approaches are the opportunities to view or interact with participants in a natural setting, the depth of information that can be obtained through the accompanying data collection strategies, and the inherent flexibility within the ability to adjust the research to the specific setting. On the other hand, challenges associated with qualitative studies include the amount of time necessary to collect and analyze data, the lack of generalizability to other contexts, and the potential subjectivity associated with the researcher's conclusions.

Quantitative approaches, on the other hand, focus on the collection of data that is in measureable units using a specific, replicable process. Researchers employing quantitative methods use descriptive or inferential techniques to examine the relationships between defined variables in specific settings (Szafran, 2012). The intent is to find evidence or support for a hypothesized outcome. Quantitative data can be collected in a variety of ways, including scores on assessment measures (e.g., tests and quizzes), through the administration of questionnaires or surveys that feature scaled or interval responses, or using defined protocols that yield data that can be expressed in numerical form. When encountering quantitative approaches, you'll likely see references to interventions, and independent and dependent variables. The advantages of quantitative research include the ability to collect and analyze large amounts of data quickly and efficiently, objectivity in the conclusions, ease of replication, and the potential to share results graphically. Potential disadvantages, on the other hand, include the lack of depth in the results (e.g., potential inability to answer *why* questions) and dependence on the instrument used to provide valid and reliable results.

Finally, mixed methods approaches utilize a combination of the qualitative and quantitative methods (Creswell & Plano Clark, 2011; Teddlie & Tashakkori, 2009). Mixed methods offer researchers the opportunity to combine the strengths of each of the aforementioned approaches by incorporating the multiple forms of data that may be present within a research context, which is especially relevant when we consider the multiple sources of data that are often present in a classroom. For example, instead of relying solely on grades, a teacher may conduct interviews or observations, or collect surveys to gain a greater understanding of *how* and *why* questions. Mixed methods approaches increase opportunities to triangulate data—that is, to use information from multiple sources to develop a more refined, detailed set of conclusions. Using concurrent procedures, data can be collected from qualitative and quantitative sources at the same time, increasing efficiency. However, there is an increase in the amount of data that must be analyzed to arrive at conclusions, and the researcher must be adept at synthesizing information from the two sources to develop accurate conclusions.

VALIDITY AND RELIABILITY

As we further refine your ideas for data collection, it's important to introduce two key terms you are likely to encounter that are important within the process. These are *validity* and *reliability*. When a something has **validity**, it is deemed to measure what it is intended to. For example, if you were examining students' knowledge of the state capitals, a blank map of the United States might be a valid way to measure this knowledge. However, the same map would not be a valid way to measure students' ability to convert improper fractions. **Reliability**, on the other hand, has been referred to as "consistency of measurement" (Szafran, 2012, p. 18). In other words, you are likely to get the same or similar scores across multiple instances of measurement of some variable. Going back to our previous example, the blank map assessment would be deemed reliable if students with similar levels of knowledge consistently demonstrated the same or similar scores on the assessment. When an instrument does not demonstrate reliability, it means the scores fluctuate across students or administrations of the test.

Reliability and validity are inextricably mixed within the research process, as you don't want one without the other. If I develop a reliable measure, it should produce consistent results, but if it is not valid, it is not measuring what it is supposed to. On the other hand, I can have an instrument that measures what it is supposed to (valid), but if participants' scores vary widely from administration to administration, it may not be reliable. As a teacher, it's important that the assessments you develop and use effectively capture the true capabilities of your students. The same holds true as you engage in the action research process. Teddlie and Tashakkori (2009) recommend considering two questions for reflection when considering reliability and validity:

- Am I truly measuring what I intend to measure?

- Is my measurement consistent and accurate?

Capturing whether the processes used for an action research study produce reliable and valid results is different based on the methodology used for the research, and thus we'll further describe each construct relative to qualitative and quantitative approaches before commencing our discussion of data collection strategies.

"NOTE"-ABLE THOUGHTS

Reflect upon the strategies that you have proposed for your data collection in the initial plan you created in Chapter 4. Do you think they are reliable and valid? How do you know? If you are not sure, how do you think you will be able to determine this?

Reliability. When using qualitative methods for your research, the form of reliability referenced most often is inter-rater reliability. **Inter-rater reliability** describes the situation where the observations produce the same or similar codes and themes within the analysis of qualitative sources of data. If we considered establishing inter-rater reliability as part of an action research study that involved collecting data through observations, two (or more) observers would independently observe the same activity using the same protocol, or observation procedure, producing qualitative (likely textual) data that described the episode. The observers would then consult with each other afterwards and examine their percentage of agreement on the coded behaviors to determine an estimate of inter-rater reliability. Inter-rater reliability is expressed as a decimal that conveys the percentage of agreement. Inter-rater reliability estimates with values between .75 and 1.00 are noted to be excellent, while those between .60 and .74 are considered to be acceptable (Cicchetti, 1994). Of note, some researchers (see Cohen, 1960) have dismissed this method of quantifying inter-rater reliability as being an inadequate measure. However, given that it continues to be utilized in research studies and is a relatively effective way to capture the agreement between the observers, we feel it is acceptable for use within most action research studies.

Within quantitative analysis, *reliability* has been referred to as "the degree to which a test consistently measures whatever it is measuring" (Gay, Mills, & Airasian, 2006, p. 139). Unlike qualitative research where reliability generally involves the researcher in some capacity, quantitative research assesses the reliability of the instrument being used to collect the quantitative (numerical) data. There are multiple forms of reliability associated with instruments used for the collection of quantitative data, including the following:

- **Stability reliability** represents similar performance when data collection using the instrument occurs on different occasions (separated by an adequate amount of time).

- **Equivalent (or alternative) forms reliability** involves using forms of the test that contain different versions of the same items with the results on the two forms consistent over time.

- **Test–retest reliability** represents consistency in scores when respondents complete the test on multiple occasions over a period of time (Popham, 2009).

As with inter-rater reliability, reliability associated with quantitative measures is expressed as a decimal, which is referred to as a **reliability coefficient**. This value, which is expressed on a scale of 0 to 1, represents the consistency of results across repeated administrations. While it's important to note that no test or instrument is perfectly reliable, meaning it has a reliability coefficient of 1.00, "coefficients at or above 0.80 are often considered sufficiently reliable to make decisions about individuals based on their observed scores" (Webb, Shavelson, & Haertal, 2007, p. 81).

Threats to reliability are those factors that could cause errors in your research. While you are likely to encounter some challenges as part of the research process, we present the following list to help you minimize it. Our list is not exhaustive, but it contains those threats that we feel you are most likely to encounter with action research:

- Subject reliability: factors related to the subjects (i.e., students) in your classroom, including fatigue or mood during the data collection period

- Situational reliability: conditions within the context where the data collection occurs (e.g., an announcement or classroom interruption during administration of an instrument or technology problems during an electronic administration)

- Instrument reliability: questions are poorly worded or incomprehensible to students

- Data processing reliability: misinterpretations during collection or miscoding during analysis

The primary goal within your research is to minimize the likelihood that you will encounter the threats. Being in a school environment, there are many factors that are out of your control, but being aware of these four threats can help you proactively adapt your research.

Validity. As mentioned previously, validity is the degree to which an instrument or collection strategy measures what it is supposed to (Gay et al., 2006). As with reliability, however, validity is multifaceted, and there are various forms to consider. **Construct validity** is present when an instrument measures an intended concept or construct. Within **content validity**, the instrument measures the intended subject matter of the content and takes into account all aspects of a situation. Lastly, **criterion validity** is the degree that scores on an instrument correlate with scores on a similar instrument measuring the same or similar construct (Thorndike & Thorndike-Christ, 2011). These are general forms of validity; however, there are also differences in how validity is characterized and measured within each of the respective research methods.

Given the potential for subjectivity within qualitative methods, there has been a long-standing debate regarding establishing validity using these methods. As opposed to strictly describing validity as a construct, qualitative methodologists, including Lincoln and Guba (1985) and Maxwell (1992), began to use *trustworthiness* to describe what essentially amounted to validity. Lincoln and Guba went on to further establish validity criteria that included credibility (extent findings are believable), transferability (applicability of results to other contexts or to other people), dependability (extent findings are stable and replicable), and confirmability (findings are objective and not a result of researcher bias or perspective).

Validity within a study that utilizes quantitative methods is primarily related to the instruments being used to measure the construct. If you are using an instrument that has been commercially produced or has been vetted through the research process, there will (or should) be information about its validity within a publication or administration manual/directions. Validity should receive extensive consideration when you create your own instruments and use them to generate data for analysis. There are multiple forms of validity, but we'll focus on those that are most applicable in the teaching context. **Face validity** involves the examination of an instrument to determine if it measures what it says it is supposed to. For example, a test on the Civil War contains questions that only address the Civil War and not the Revolutionary War. Face validity can be established by giving the instrument to a trusted colleague or expert for a visual examination. For this reason, face validity is probably the easiest to establish. Similarly, content validity involves examinations of the items on the instrument, but this time the examination is focused on whether the items encompass the range of questions necessary to adequately measure the construct or knowledge. Using the previous example, content validity would not be established if a test was supposed to demonstrate knowledge of the Civil War, yet only included questions about John Wilkes Booth. Less likely in a classroom setting is the establishment of convergent validity. **Convergent validity** is focused upon using statistical measures (correlation) to show that your instrument is well aligned with another instrument that has already proven reliable. It might mean taking a test developed by a publisher and adapting or revising it to form your own version, then having the students take both and comparing the results. Correlation is a statistical measure that will be explained in Chapter 6, and thus you'll obtain additional information about how to ensure your newly created instrument achieves the range (.5–.7) necessary to demonstrate high correlation with the original.

■ ■ ■ VOICES FROM THE FIELD

Mark Barnes, Ninth-Grade Teacher

I like to design and write my own tests. I think I am best suited to know what my students have learned over the course of a unit as I planned most of the curriculum as well as the instructional activities. I try and change these each year based on what I teach as I adapt them to the students in my room for that particular year. Recently I had a long conversation about the validity and reliability of my tests with another teacher in my building who is enrolled in the same graduate program that I am. In our conversation, she told me that my tests are valid, but that I could not prove that they were necessarily reliable. While normally this wouldn't be a big deal to me, I admit I got a little mad at first. What did she mean telling me that my tests weren't reliable? Of course they are! My strong performers who seem to grasp the concepts

the best almost always score better than those who sometimes struggle. I thought that is what reliability meant—that I could depend on the test to show me who knew the content. However, I realized that my idea of reliability may have been a little off and that changing my tests each time they were administered limited my ability to refer to them as reliable. I really had no way to compare them from year to year or administration to administration. I was relying on my gut to confirm what I thought was already true. After I thought about this more, I knew that if I wanted to use my tests in my action research study, I needed to really think about making sure they were valid and reliable. I will need to figure out a way to give the same test a few times or possibly create a couple of versions that have slightly different editions of my questions.

As with reliability, there are various threats to validity. For example, if your sample is too small, as it might be within an action research study, the study results may be different when additional studies are conducted with larger samples. Similarly, although less applicable within action research, sampling procedures (see Chapter 4 for a review of sampling) are a threat to validity. If the action research study is employing a control group, care should be given to finding participants who are closely matched with those receiving the intervention. Failure to obtain matched (or similar) samples means that results may be skewed toward one group or another based on the characteristics of the members. Finally, nonrepresentative data and the lack of a methodologically sound study, including data analysis techniques, can invalidate study results.

"NOTE"-ABLE THOUGHTS

What threats to validity and reliability are present within your research? Discuss your study with a colleague to determine if there are hidden threats that could disrupt the data collection process or create the potential for noncredible findings.

SOURCES OF DATA

We've discussed the categories of research that you will be conducting and given some basic information about the potential sources of data for each. However, to ensure you can definitively choose the source of data and have enough information about the data collection process associated with the source, we'll now provide additional information about more commonly used sources for qualitative and quantitative research. We will direct most of your attention toward the data sources that we believe have the greatest applicability within the action research process, but we will also mention some less common ones. Prior to these descriptions, however, we feel it is important to remind you that research should never come at the expense of teaching, and thus you should thoughtfully reflect upon how your data collection techniques can be seamlessly integrated into your regular practices, or at least with as little disruption as possible. We've divided the discussion of the various forms of data collection into qualitative and quantitative data sources (see Table 5.1).

QUALITATIVE DATA SOURCES

Observations and anecdotal notes. While observations and anecdotal records are not the same form of data collection, per se, they both involve watching and recording

TABLE 5.1 Sources of Qualitative and Quantitative Data

Qualitative	Quantitative
Interviews	Surveys/questionnaires
Surveys/questionnaires	Tests
Observations	Quizzes
Anecdotal notes	School records—standardized tests, report cards, attendance
Meeting logs	
Journals	Classroom assessment scores
Artifacts/documents/projects	Artifacts
Checklists	Rating scales
Video/audio recordings	
Photographs	

information that relates to a given period of time in a specific context. Observations are the more formal of the two, as we will describe, while **anecdotal notes** (see Figure 5.1) result from observations but are usually shorter episodes where the teacher quickly jots a few notes about a student or situation.

Grady (1998) described **observations** as "looking with a purpose" (p. 22). The goal of an observation is to record exactly what is happening in a specific context within a specified timeframe. This allows the researcher to use observations in a range of situations to examine a variety of behaviors and note

- performance of a specific skill,

- preferred learning styles,

- on-task/off-task behavior,

- interaction patterns,

- problem-solving/higher-level thinking abilities, and

- level of involvement in discussions/attentiveness (Costa & Garmston, 2002; Henning, Stone, & Kelly, 2009).

Furthermore, depending on the situation, the observer can examine multiple class configurations (e.g., whole class, small group, or an individual).

FIGURE 5.1   Examples of Anecdotal Notes (using sticky notes in a folder)

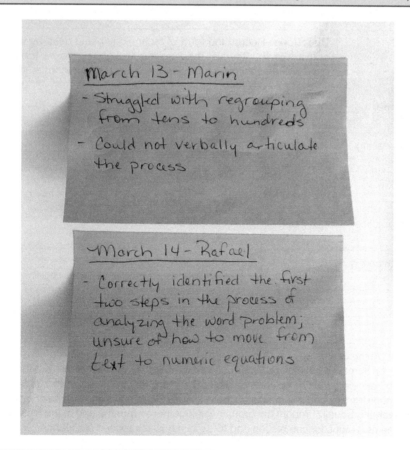

Observations can vary in format on a continuum from unstructured to structured. The level of explicitness in the observation process is generally used to categorize the location on the continuum. Structured observations are those that explicitly state when and how the observations will occur as well as precisely what behaviors are being examined (Ivankova, 2015). They may use interval techniques, which address how often the observer will record the behaviors under study (e.g., every five minutes or every minute). A common form of structured observation is the checklist, where behaviors are simply checked off if they are observed within the structure of the protocol being used. The advantage of the use of the checklist is that the researcher can simply focus on the specific behaviors that represent the focus of the data collection. See Figure 5.2 for an example of a completed structured observation protocol. Unstructured observations, on the other hand, allow the researcher to simply record what is seen without focus on predetermined events, behaviors, intervals, or people. This format offers great flexibility, but also can be challenging given the possibility of missing important aspects of the situation that may provide valuable data. Grady (1998) noted the structured observation as being more effective for the novice researcher, while experienced observers may be better prepared to use an unstructured protocol. Structured observation protocols would be considered the most trustworthy (objective) and reliable due to the level of detail and explicitness used to guide the observation. In essence, different observers would look for the same behaviors at the same intervals and focus on the identified participants.

FIGURE 5.2 Completed Observation Form

Students are using:	**Directions:** Record the form of technology being used by the students at five-minute intervals, marking the appropriate boxes for each being used at the specified interval. Use the last row to record any comments.				
	Interval				
	1	2	3	4	5
Word processing software	✓	✓	✓	✓	
Presentation software					
Skill and practice software					
Social networking tools			✓	✓	
Internet	✓	✓	✓	✓	
None					✓

Comments: At the beginning of the observation, the students were in various stages of finalizing their projects. Some were typing the information into a Word document before entering it into the wiki, and others were looking up the final facts that were required to fill in the gaps. Gradually, several groups transitioned to focusing on the wiki about 15 minutes into the observation (Interval 3). The teacher gradually brought the group back together toward the end of the lesson to review some of the next steps for completion and to explain how to proceed after lunch.

Depending upon the format and goals of the observation, suggestions about what to record vary. Henning et al. (2009) recommend that you establish goals and consider *who*, *when*, *where*, and *how* questions prior to commencement of the actual observations. They also recommend considering the form the notes may take. For example, the focus may lie on writing short bits of information, similar to what might be recorded as part of the anecdotal record. On the other hand, the goal might be to record observations with such a level of detail that the notes can be analyzed with minimal revision. These may be akin to the notes that many teachers use when conducting reading or writing conferences that allow the teacher to track progress over a defined period of time. Hubbard and Power (2003) recommend writing down as much information as possible without directing attention toward conventions. This will allow the researcher to gain as much information as possible. However, much more time is necessary for the collection process as notes become more detailed. The teacher observer must determine what works best within the context of the classroom to facilitate the collection of the data necessary without preventing the observer from carrying out the necessary teaching responsibilities. We've found notebooks, clipboards with paper, and sticky notes in folders provide effective ways to record information on a moment's notice and easily serve the task of recording necessary information.

As a final bit of advice, it is important to remain objective when recording observations within the action research process. This is sometimes challenging because we tend to want to look for confirmation of our expectations or want to judge during the observation. Refraining from engaging in either of these behaviors, however, allows us to remain objective and, in turn, helps the findings to demonstrate greater credibility.

When considering whether to conduct observations as part of your research, it's important to note the advantages and disadvantages. Observations can be very effective for capturing the many nuances of the classroom, including nonverbal signals and cues, and have the potential to provide a more comprehensive picture of the classroom context. They can easily be used in conjunction with other forms of data, and many teachers are already familiar with the various uses and formats. Disadvantages of observations include the potential time necessary to collect and document behaviors or actions pertinent to what is being studied, the potential to miss events or other elements of the classroom due to the focus necessary to document evidence, and the potential to observe with predetermined perceptions or biases, which could influence the results.

Interviews. Interviews represent an opportunity to speak with participants directly. Interviews can be conducted with individuals or with groups (e.g., a focus group about a specific topic), dependent upon the primary goal associated with the activity. There are several types of interviews that can be conducted, with differentiation between the types primarily related to the configuration of the questions. In a formal, or structured, interview, the interviewer has a list of questions that are used to guide the interview (Flick, 2009). These questions are asked in the same order, and, in general, there are no follow-up or probing questions asked within the interview. One would consider these to lead to the most reliable data and to facilitate the most efficient comparisons among subjects. Semi-structured (or semi-standardized) interviews can use a previously established set of questions. However, there is less adherence to the predetermined structure for the questions, and the interviewer may revise both the questions and the order as well as ask follow-up questions as necessary (Flick, 2009). This form of interview is most often used with action research, as it is very similar to conferences that some teachers conduct with students on a regular basis. Finally, the unstructured or informal interview utilizes an open-ended format where questions are generally not written down, although they may be an outline to ensure topics of interest and those under investigation are accessed (Teddlie & Tashakkori, 2009). In an unstructured interview, the interview proceeds in a natural fashion akin to a conversation as the researcher asks open-ended questions and uses the responses to generate follow-up queries.

To conduct effective interviews, there are a number of behaviors and considerations researchers must keep in mind (Hubbard & Power, 2003). First, the interviewer should begin with simple or less-threatening questions to establish rapport with the participant. This builds comfort and can be the mechanism that activates interest in the topic/conversation. When interviewing students, the interviewer should be flexible and adapt as necessary to ensure the sought-after information can be obtained. To this end, it is a recommended practice to record the interviews to listen to at a later time. When attempting to take notes on the participant's responses, it is easy to miss key information, and the recording can assist the researcher in identifying key statements. Finally, the interviewer must be adept at listening to what is said as well as the manner in which it is said. Sometimes verbal inflections or nonverbal cues can convey key states of mind or attitudes that require follow-up questions.

■ ■ ■ VOICES FROM THE FIELD

Amber Smith, Second-Grade Teacher

As a researcher and a teacher, I need to be very specific first in what I want to improve, and then be very detailed about how and what I collect to ensure the data collection process is meaningful. In the past when I have tried to collect data to problem solve, I was not consistent in the process of how I was going to collect the data, and when I went to analyze the information and develop a plan or solution, I was unable to narrow in on what was even causing the problem. I learned that when the researcher does not create specific questions or have a way of measuring the data,

it is very hard to come up with a solution for the problem. As teachers and researchers, we need to create a plan that allows us to collect useful data, not just any data. I now understand the importance of taking time to reflect on the issue and then spend sufficient time identifying the problem/topic before gathering data that correlates to the problem. I have decided that when I conduct the interviews for my action research study, I will create either a checklist or scale to allow me to zoom in on the issue and learn why the issue is happening.

While individual interviews are an effective way to collect data, group interviews can facilitate more in-depth data, as they allow individuals to speak directly to each other, potentially leading to deeper insights through interactions among participants. It is this direct communication among the participants or between the interviewer and participant that sets the stage for effective interaction, and thus one of the most important considerations within the interview process is how to build rapport with (or among) the participant(s). Without rapport, the participant may not develop the comfort level necessary to share information. We advocate formatting the group interview more as a conversation than as a formalized interview to keep all participants at ease and to heighten the potential for interaction.

Personal contact and the ability to attend to conversational nuances and ask follow-up questions are key advantages of interviews as a data collection method. Other advantages that occur within the context of two-way communication include modification of the interview protocol as it proceeds to seek clarity within responses or to expand upon responses that do not contain adequate information (Henning et al., 2009). This leads to greater utility than surveys. However, interviews do have some inherent disadvantages. They are time consuming and mean that the researcher can only access a limited number of participants. Given this situation, great care must be directed towards ensuring those chosen can provide the relevant data necessary to provide insights pertinent to the research question. Finally, effective interviewing is a skill that must be developed through experience as the researcher learns to interpret responses and adapt questions as necessary to control both the flow of the interview and the topics under discussion.

Journals and reflective logs. Journals and reflective logs are written records that convey data relative to specific attributes within a particular setting context. For example, journals and logs allow the researcher to obtain descriptions of the context, including the participant's thought processes, potentially helping the researcher "uncover meaning, develop understanding, and discover insights relevant to the research problem" (Merriam, 1988, p. 118). These methods of data collection can also be used to capture information on daily activities (especially those that may not be noticed if not documented) in combination with self-reflection. Additional unique attributes of journals and logs include the potential to convey data on the context where participants are operating (e.g., provide first-person accounts or document background knowledge); to lead to additional questions to be asked in both research and as follow-up in interviews or things to look for within observations; and to trace change and development over time (e.g., examine drafts to note changes as progress is made or examine reflections to see how thinking has changed, because they can be placed side by side for analysis). Journals and logs are especially useful as a form of supplementary research data, especially when used in conjunction with other sources like interviews or observations, as participants may be more willing to express information in writing than within a face-to-face interaction.

The overall process for analysis of journals and logs is iterative, as it is with most qualitative sources. The key in this process is to examine enough documents to form interpretations of what is revealed and, subsequently, to ensure understanding is produced. The researcher must engage in a systematic examination of the text to find information that is pertinent to the topic/question and separate it from extraneous information (Corbin & Strauss, 2008). Analysis can occur at the line, phrase, sentence, or paragraph levels to develop themes and codes by asking "how is _____ similar to _____" or "how is _____ different from _____" as part of the analysis. As with most thematic analysis, the multiple examinations of the data result in the formation of codes and categories that encompass the data. When used in conjunction with other types of data collection, these codes and themes can be used across sources to add to their potential relevance and meaning for answering the research question. This process may also lead to additional questions that could be highlighted if used in conjunction with other collection methods such as interviews.

One unique advantage to using journals and reflective logs is their overall efficiency. For example, they are less time-consuming than interviews and observations, and the researcher does not have to be physically present to administer the prompt. There is also greater potential for trustworthiness due to the lack of social interactions. Finally, journals and logs offer opportunities to capture information over an extended time period and for repeated views of the same information over time. One inherent disadvantage of journals and logs, especially in early grades, is the reliance on writing. Students who lack the proficiency or will to write in detail may not include sufficient information, resulting in imprecise or incomplete records.

Less common qualitative sources. There are additional qualitative data sources that you can consider using within your action research, but these are not used as frequently as those we have previous described. These include video and audio recordings, photographs, and focus groups. Video and audio recordings can be used to supplement several qualitative sources, including interviews and observations, but they can also function as data collection techniques on their own. Either source allows the researcher to engage with the collected data on multiple occasions, providing the opportunity to record notes and revise them, as the source is reexamined. Challenges sometimes arise within video recordings, however, as participants may not act naturally under the recognition that they are on camera or they may avoid being on camera altogether. Photographs are useful when it is necessary to collect observable information about participants, such as dress or appearance, or about objects of significance within the research. They allow the researcher to capture a single moment for analysis but do not allow the researcher to construct relative conclusions about anything more than the observable information in the photo. Finally, focus groups are analogous to group interviews with data sources representing the researcher's notes or transcription of all dialogue. Focus groups are an economical, fast, and efficient method for obtaining data from multiple participants (Krueger, 2000). They also offer an opportunity to triangulate with other data sources. They are best used when the research has limited time or resources to conduct individual interviews and when discussions between participants can be utilized to help the researcher obtain data that will lead toward an understanding of the situation being examined. Groups, which should range from 6–12 participants (Krueger, 2000), can be created by the researcher or previously existing. A key consideration with the focus groups is that participants have something in common that is aligned to the research being conducted. Focus groups are slightly more challenging to conduct than interviews, as, in addition to having effective listening skills, the researcher must be able to moderate and facilitate the ongoing group interactions. On the other hand, groups can be nonmoderated, which means they proceed without direct participation by the researcher. This allows the researcher to collect data from conversations that unfold naturally.

QUANTITATIVE DATA SOURCES

Surveys and questionnaires. Surveys and questionnaires represent tools for systematic data collection that do not provide any face-to-face contact with the participants. While they do not allow for direct interaction, Henning et al. (2009) note that one distinct advantage of using surveys and questionnaires is the larger sample size that can potentially be engaged in the data collection process. Depending on your action research project, this may or may not be relevant. If you seek to get information only from and about your class, access to a larger sample has limited value. However, if you want to compare your class to all other fourth grades in the district, then surveys and questionnaires represent an efficient mechanism to do so.

The type of survey or questionnaire you administer depends on the data that you wish to collect. Some instruments include open-response questions, where the respondent answers specific questions about the topic at hand, with written comments that could range from a single word to several paragraphs (See Figure 5.3.) These types of surveys or questionnaires would be more aligned with a qualitative methodology. On the other hand, scaled or forced-response questions could request that the respondent pick a specific response from among a previously generated list. Generally (but not always), when this format is used, the researcher is interested in analyzing the data using a quantitative technique.

There are many surveys and questionnaires that have been developed to access information about a variety of topics, including attitudes and beliefs that are relevant for the teacher and researcher. Often during the literature review, you will come across instruments that have been used in past investigations to access information about the topic under study. When this is not the case, it may be necessary for you to develop your own. To engage in this process, you must consider the information being sought, the type of question (open, forced response, or combination) that will provide access to the information as well as its alignment with your research question, and who the instrument will be administered to. The latter will be especially impactful, as you will have to consider the respondents' ability to read and respond to the questions. Once developed, it is suggested that you conduct a pilot administration to ensure the instrument meets the expectations for data collection (e.g., directions and questions are clear, anticipated completion time is accurate). Using this information, revisions can be made as necessary. It is also important to consider reliability and validity, which were introduced earlier in this chapter.

Henning et al. (2009) note that surveys and questionnaires can be powerful data collection tools, especially in combination with other measures, such as an observation or

---

FIGURE 5.3   Examples of Open-Response Survey Questions

Answer each of the following questions to the best of your ability.

1. How comfortable do you feel solving chemical equations?
2. How frequently are you required to solve chemical equations in your chemistry class?
3. What strategies have you found most helpful for solving chemical equations?
4. How do you check your equation to ensure it is balanced?
5. When you are at home, how often do you study chemistry?
6. What resources do you use to study chemistry and, specifically, to study solving chemical equations?
7. What do you see as the most important skill or strategy that students should be taught to help them solve chemical equations?
8. Have you heard of Dalton's law of definite proportions? If so, what is the primary idea behind the law?

work sample. Used as the sole data collection instrument, however, they may not provide enough depth within the information obtained due to a lack of ability to ask for additional information. Items that are written with the open-response format may address some of this, but respondents may be more concise because of the necessity of writing instead of speaking answers. Additionally, some of the efficiency in scoring is lost, as the researcher must code and interpret responses. Forced-response items, on the other hand, can certainly be scored quickly and efficiently, yet the predetermined responses may not accommodate for all potential answers, and, given the lack of depth, conclusions may be limited.

Records and artifacts. Rather than discuss all of the potential school- and teacher-specific forms of data collection that may be possible, we've decided to address multiple forms of data that can originate with the teacher and school simultaneously. We view records and **artifacts** as including school records, assessment data (standardized and teacher-created), and classroom artifacts. Acknowledging these come in a variety of formats and can be used in multiple ways, we felt that what is collected and how it is examined within the confines of the research question is very specific to the context of the teacher or school. As a result, we'll present general information for you to consider as you determine whether to use these within your action research study.

School records are tools that can be accessed by teachers for a variety of purposes, but, in relation to action research, we believe that their primary use is in establishing the context or historical perspective relative to a participant. For example, one could examine the frequency of student absences, report card grades for prior years, or scores on standardized achievement measures. Notably, this information could be combined with other data sources to contribute to the "bigger picture" or to provide additional insights into previous performance. As a single data source, school records would likely provide less than adequate information about an intervention specific to your classroom.

Assessments, which include standardized or teacher-made tests, may provide a more comprehensive picture of student performance when administered within the timeframe for the implementation of the action research intervention. This is especially relevant when these assessments have been used to establish baseline information or within a pre- or post-test format, but this is less likely if one relies on the standardized measures that occur once per year as part of a broader assessment plan. Given the data-driven focus of schools, there is a greater likelihood that your school may administer standardized tests, such as the Measures of Academic Progress or DIBELS, at defined intervals during the school year, which may ultimately help you within your study. If your intervention aligns with these testing periods, you have a built-in data collection mechanism. The challenge, however, is that it may be hard to develop conclusions specific to the teaching practices that led to changes, as these assessments are not designed to measure the curriculum or teaching strategies used within a particular school context. In this way, materials created or adapted by the individual teacher are likely to provide more accurate information relative to the day-to-day environment. Not only can the teacher use materials that are specific to the intervention and research question, but there is also the potential alignment of the data collection tool with individualized learning goals, potentially leading to more in-depth conclusions relative to how the intervention specifically contributed to the results.

Shae Little, Third-Grade Teacher

My action research study was focused on examining the effect of a weekly stem question on reading comprehension in a third-grade classroom. While planning the study, my goal was to incorporate as many forms of data as I could that were already being collected in the classroom. Given that my school asks that teachers to review each student's growth using our progress monitoring assessment, this became a starting point for me. I also wanted to use written comprehension questions that feature the common stems that are designed to help students begin to learn to construct responses to open-ended, comprehension questions. For those students who demonstrate a lack of willingness or capacity to write answers, I still have the opportunity to collect the information by verbally asking the same questions to determine whether or not they are capable of orally answering the question. What I haven't quite decided is whether I want to treat the questions as a qualitative source or quantitative source. I thought about analyzing the responses for themes to determine if students were able to construct a response using the stems. I am not sure that will give me enough information overall, though, so I am also considering developing a rubric that I can use to rate student answers. My thinking is that I would give 0 points for an answer that fails to address the question; 1 point for an answer that partially addresses the question but does not have any textual support for the answer; 2 points for an answer that partially answers the question and attempts to support the answer with textual information; and 3 points for an answer that effectively addresses the question and supports the answer with information from the text. I could use this to numerically show growth over time using a graph. Given these are already in place, it simply becomes a matter of how to best leverage my needs with our common practices. Knowing that more data means better information, but also more analysis, I am still working through balancing these competing interests.

Many of the benefits associated with teacher-created assessments, notably tests, carry over to the use of documents and artifacts produced by the students within the data collection process. Given the wealth of materials at your disposal, including student projects, journals, drawings, and homework, there are certainly many possibilities within the data collection process. Taking into account the specific intervention, you have the opportunity to shape the artifact(s) to meet the need for effective measurement of the outcome. The advantages of access and alignment are offset with several potential challenges. The first, subjectivity, could be present as you examine more items (e.g., journals, written artifacts) that require analysis techniques that are largely qualitative. As we've mentioned, as the teacher and researcher, you may "read" the data in such a way as to confirm what you expect to see as opposed to what is verifiably present. Furthermore, there is the potential that you would have to examine a variety of information that is unnecessary or irrelevant to your research question. This increases the amount of time necessary to winnow out what is specific to your research.

Attitude and rating scales. Conceptually similar to surveys and questionnaires, **attitude scales** offer the researcher the opportunity to collect information on participants' feelings, attitudes, or evaluations in a measurable unit (see Figure 5.4). There are a variety of scales available to researchers, each with its own properties and with the capacity to both measure associations between variables as well as potentially demonstrate cause and effect relationships, although this is more challenging and less likely. When using scales, there are four levels of data that can be collected: nominal, ordinal, interval, and ratio. **Nominal data** is information that can be classified into categories and that allows the researcher to provide frequency counts of the number of cases that fit into a particular category. In an educational context, a question associated with a scale collecting nominal data might be something like, "What is your favorite subject in school?" This would be followed by specific options for the participant to choose from. Scales designed to collect **ordinal data** involve measurement on a continuum, whereby a rank (order) is indicated. For example, participants might be asked to rank their favorite subjects in school. Ordinal data does not provide information on the intervals between the ranks. In other words, you don't know if something that is ranked first is only slightly "better" in the views of the participant or significantly better. Scales written to collect ordinal data allow the researcher to examine statistics such as the mean and mode or to determine rank order correlations (relationships). Scales that collect **interval data** improve upon the ranks provided by ordinal scales, as within interval data we have the ability to "see" differences, as there are equal units of measure between data points. A response difference between 2 and 3 represents the same distance as one between 6 and 7. This is an important distinction because it allows the researcher to compute the mean and the standard deviation. Doing so opens up a number of possibilities for statistical analysis, including measurement of correlations, and completion of t-tests and analyses of variance, which will be discussed in Chapter 6. Again using the example of subjects in school, we may administer a questionnaire about attitudes toward mathematics that involves the computation of the sum of the responses. In looking at the responses, we

---

FIGURE 5.4   Example of an Attitude/Rating Scale Using Likert-Scale Questions

Motivation to Conduct Research Using the Internet

Indicate a response to each of the statements below that best matches your reaction to the statement.

1. I enjoy the challenge of trying to find something using the Internet.
   Strongly Agree   Agree   Undecided   Disagree   Strongly Disagree

2. I like it when I am completing research using the Internet and it makes me think.
   Strongly Agree   Agree   Undecided   Disagree   Strongly Disagree

3. I am more thorough in my research using the Internet when I know that I am going to be graded.
   Strongly Agree   Agree   Undecided   Disagree   Strongly Disagree

4. When my research using the Internet gets challenging, I will continue to try so that I can learn the information.
   Strongly Agree   Agree   Undecided   Disagree   Strongly Disagree

5. I will continue my research using the Internet, even when I have trouble, because I know I will find the information eventually.
   Strongly Agree   Agree   Undecided   Disagree   Strongly Disagree

6. I don't complete very much research using the Internet because I get distracted.
   Strongly Agree   Agree   Undecided   Disagree   Strongly Disagree

could interpret differences among the sums to be approximate differences. Finally, scales that collect **ratio data** represent the most effective measurement, as this form of data has the properties of interval but also includes a point of origin (or zero score). This means that the research can compare the relative distance between responses as well as the magnitude of the response. In other words, going back to the previous example of measuring the attitudes toward mathematics, a response score of 10 is twice the magnitude of one that is 5.

As with the quantitative data collection techniques we have addressed so far in the chapter, collecting data through attitude or **rating scales** is advantageous due to the efficiency and ease of collection. The researcher can capture a great deal of information through the administration of these measures in a relatively short amount of time. The challenge comes in choosing the correct scale for your data collection. Depending upon your question, you may need to collect a specific form of data to facilitate comparisons among respondents that will allow you to develop conclusions relative to your chosen intervention. There are many freely available scales that have been published in various outlets, and we would recommend beginning your search in the available literature to determine if you can locate one that would suit your needs. If the scale is published, it is more likely to have information about its reliability and validity. On the other hand, you may consider creating your own scale. While in some cases this may be advisable, especially if your primary data will be nominal or ordinal, creating interval and ratio scales is a more challenging endeavor and one that may require some advanced knowledge of statistics to truly create something that captures the information you need.

Observations. While observations are typically associated with qualitative techniques, quantitative observations can be utilized when the research wishes to capture information about "how much," "how many," or "how often" something happens within a particular setting. Often, this form of observation uses a checklist or follows a specific protocol, especially when comparisons are sought as part of the research. For example, when considering the former, a researcher could utilize a checklist to record each time a student calls out answers without indicating a wish to speak to track how many times this happens in one instructional period. Alternatively, an observation protocol checklist can be used to track whether a lesson was presented in a specific sequence of steps or to track how often a teacher asks a question that represents a check for understanding. In each case, there is a specific focus on documenting a unit that can be measured numerically, whereas a qualitative observation entails recording multiple details about various aspects of the context being examined within the research.

There are certainly a variety of means for data collection as part of an action research study. We have elected not to address all possible sources or methods of collection, so there may be other sources that are applicable to your processes that are described in the additional resources we've provided. Our advice would be to consider using several sources, at least initially, to ensure you can measure the impact of your intervention and answer your research question. If the data collection is not sustainable, it may be necessary to refine the collection process as necessary as opposed to reaching the conclusion of the data collection period and realizing that what you collected is insufficient for answering the research questions.

Suppose you were attempting to answer the following research question: How does the use of cooperative learning groups impact fifth-grade students' understanding of the water cycle? What forms of data could be collected to answer this question? Provide a rationale for each of your selections.

TAKING ACTION: SELECTING DATA COLLECTION METHODS

In Chapter 4, you were able to develop a preliminary version of your research plan, albeit without specific information about your methods of data collection. After reading this chapter, you should have a greater understanding of the various methods of data collection at your disposal. Now it is time to put this information to use and to begin to refine your thoughts regarding the specifics of your plan. We feel that before moving forward with your research plan, it's important to complete a few additional organizational steps that will ultimately make the development of the plan easier. It is very likely that you have been asked to write some form of story or piece of writing in the past that has required you to consider the five *W* (who, what, when, where, why) and one *H* (how) questions. We've found that these same questions can be used to provide you the opportunity to think about a research plan, notably the data collection. We've included Figure 5.5 as a form of organizer to help you think critically about the data you will need to collect as part of your study. This format was chosen because we feel it clearly allows the researcher to examine each of the specific components separately, while the narrative format used in a "typical" action research report or paper necessitates a search for the specific details. We've also found that answering these questions as part of the action research process has helped our teachers/researchers identify potential pitfalls and make adaptations to their proposed process prior to starting it, limiting the changes that were needed during the process.

We've included the example of the research chart (see Figure 5.6) that we began in Chapter 4 with some of the missing details about the data collection process completed. We've also incorporated an additional example (see Figure 5.7) to help you gain some perspective about what this would look like in a project being conducted in a different subject area. Now that you have had an opportunity to reflect on the various questions that must be considered as part of the data collection process (see Figure 5.5), we'll focus on five of the questions (what, how, when, where, who) within the research plan template.

Once you have established the specifics around the data collection process within your study, it becomes important to begin to consider a timeline for implementation, with direct consideration for the amount of time necessary to reasonably accomplish the steps included in the research plan for the data collection. This is more challenging than it appears. We've seen many novice researchers propose research plans that addressed all of the necessary considerations, yet their proposed timeline did not allow enough time for the full scope of the data collection or too little time for analysis. The latter was more likely when qualitative or mixed methods were used, as the teacher/researcher was not fully aware of the amount of time required to engage in the multiple examinations of the data necessary to develop the themes and codes associated with this type of research. We

FIGURE 5.5   Organizer for Data Collection

WHAT data are you collecting?

- What different sources of data are best aligned with your research question?
- How much data do you need to answer this question?
- Is there previously existing data that can be used, or does all data need to be collected from participants as part of the study?

WHY did you choose to collect this data?

- What do you hope to learn?
- Does what you hope to learn match what is described in your question?
- What methods of analysis are aligned with this data?

WHO is going to collect the data?

- Will you be responsible for collecting all sources of data?
- How will you engage in data collection and maintain effective teaching practices?
- Is there a colleague or trusted peer who can assist with data collection?

HOW will the data be collected?

- How will you collect the data?
- How structured and systematic will the collection be?
- What unforeseen circumstances could prevent the data from being collected?

WHERE is the data going to be collected?

- Will any organizational structures need to be put in place to ensure it is possible to collect the data in this location?
- Does the location for data collection need to be the same each time?
- How can you build data collection into the normal activities of the classroom?

WHEN is the data going to be collected?

- How often will data collection need to occur?
- Is the duration of the collection procedures (daily and long term) sufficient for the data collection?
- Is the time allocated for collection sufficient to gather and record the necessary data using the strategies selected?

require our students to develop and submit their research timeline (see Figure 5.8 for an example), as it forces them to think comprehensively about the time necessary for each step. It also provides a visual representation that allows them to "see" where potential shortcomings may lie. Finally, the timeline facilitates examination of whether the resources necessary for completion of the project will be available.

DEVELOPING A PLAN OR A PRODUCT: REVISING THE RESEARCH PLAN PROPOSAL FORM AND CREATING A TIMELINE

Before completing the information on data collection and developing your first timeline, take another look at your question and reflect upon whether the methods of data collection represent the best place to continue in your quest to develop the plan that will guide your action research. Ultimately, your question will specifically lead you to determine the type of data that must be collected, as different sources and processes will

Problem statement	Several second-grade students in my class struggle with fluency (rate and accuracy) and are below grade-level standards as assessed three times a year using DIBELS. I want to see these struggling students reading on grade level, according to DIBELS, by the end of the year.
Goals for research	The goals I am considering for my action research study are focused on helping my students who are currently reading below grade level to become more fluent readers so that they can read words accurately, at an appropriate rate, and with expression.
Research question	What is the effect of Readers' Theater on second-grade students' reading fluency?
Context	The context for this research is a school located in a suburban area within the city limits of a large metropolitan city. The overall socioeconomic status of the school is rated as low to middle class, with 58% of the enrolled students receiving free or reduced-price lunch. The school is primarily African American (59%), Hispanic American (20%), Caucasian (12%), Multiracial (5%), Asian American (3%), and American Indian (1%). Both genders (male, 51%; female, 49%) are fairly equal in representation of students.
Participants	Twenty-four second-grade students; 12 participants are African American, eight are Hispanic American, three are Caucasian, and one participant is multiracial; 14 boys and 10 girls; five demonstrate oral reading fluency scores below grade level.
Data to be collected	Dynamic Indicators of Basic Early Literacy Skills (DIBELS) Score (Oral Reading Fluency)—easy and effective method to collect the score using a numerical indicator; already collected within classroom, so teacher and students are familiar with administration and completion.
Frequency/duration of data collection	DIBELS: pre-test, midpoint assessment (week 3), post-test (week 5)
Location of data collection	My classroom
Who will collect data?	Teacher
Data analysis procedure	
Display of data/ findings	

FIGURE 5.7   Example of a Research Plan Organizer

Problem statement	Students can compute correct answers in math, but cannot explain how they arrived at that particular conclusion.
Goals for research	To develop students' capacity to successfully express their thought processes, their understanding, and their logic behind mathematical principles. To incorporate writing across the curriculum through the use of math journals.
Research question	How can using writing journals in the mathematics classroom improve students' ability to understand and express mathematical concepts and problem solve?

Context	The context for this research is an elementary school in a low-income suburb in a large southeastern city. The neighborhood and school population is predominantly Hispanic and African American. Approximately 90% of the students in the school are eligible for free or reduced-priced lunch. A significant percentage of the students receive ESL services and accommodations.
Participants	Twenty-two fourth-grade students will participate in the research. Nine are African American, eight are Hispanic, and five are Caucasian. The participants include 12 boys and 10 girls. Sixteen students speak English as their first language.
Data to be collected	Illinois Board of Education, Mathematics Classroom Assessments Journal entries Observations
Frequency/duration of data collection	Illinois Board of Education, Mathematics Classroom Assessments (pre- and post-test) Journal entries (weekly; eight weeks) Observations (ongoing; each student once per week for eight weeks)
Location of data collection	Classroom
Who will collect data	Teacher
Data analysis procedure	
Display of data/findings	

FIGURE 5.8 One Elementary Teacher's Journey: Action Research Timeline and Activities

Informed Consent

Two weeks prior to pre-test	Develop research plan/informed consent
One week prior to pre-test	Informed consent letter sent home and returned

Data Collection

Day 1	Complete DIBELS oral reading fluency assessment for eight students (pre-test)
Week 1	Implement Readers' Theater (week 1)
Week 2	Implement Readers' Theater (week 2)
Week 3, Day 1	Complete DIBELS oral reading fluency assessment for eight students (midway)
Week 3	Implement Readers' Theater (week 3)
Week 4	Implement Readers' Theater (week 4)
Week 5	Complete DIBELS oral reading fluency assessment for eight students (post-test)

facilitate different types of conclusions relative to the action research study (Henning et al., 2009). Concurrently, however, you must consider several additional questions:

- How long will the research last?

- What resources are needed to answer the question?

- What resources and support are available?

- What obstacles could prevent completion of the study?

It's important to consider these early in the process, as failure to do so may create the necessity of significant modifications to the plan later, potentially limiting the quality and relevance of the findings.

RESEARCH PLAN

To continue creating your research plan, we recommend that you review what you have already completed before progressing to outlining the specifics for your data collection and developing the timeline. Once you are satisfied that you have addressed each area with sufficient detail, focus on the data collection strategies that will be used within your action research to answer your question. There may be some consideration of alternate approaches that remain, but this version of the research plan should be more refined and focused in terms of the overall data collection methods to be used. List your strategies in the "Data to be collected" box. For this draft, we recommend that you go a step further than the last one, where you listed specific kinds of information, to actually describe the rationale for use of each strategy. Be specific: Describe how the strategy will help you answer the question(s). Include information that addresses how often the data collection will occur and the total duration of the data collection activities within the research process. If you have reflected upon the techniques you will use for your data analysis, you can incorporate them now. However, Chapter 6 is focused upon analysis, and thus you may decide to wait until you decide precisely how the analysis will be conducted.

TIMELINE

Now that you've articulated the majority of the elements contained in the action research process, it is time to develop a timeline that depicts this process. As previously mentioned, the greater the level of detail that can be included in this timeline, the more likely you are to be successful in accurately defining the most appropriate periods necessary for the various activities for your research. For the timeline, include a detailed plan for the development and collection of an informed consent document, for implementation of your data collection strategies, listing the collection procedures for all sources. Sometimes it is easier to look at when you plan to conduct the collection of baseline data and when the data collection activities will conclude, and insert formative activities within the intervening timeframe. At other times, your ongoing data activities are already prescribed because they occur naturally within the context of your classroom, so there is little to no choice in how this is completed. The intention behind the timeline is simply to help you determine whether you have a sufficient amount of time to complete the activities necessary to effectively address your research question and develop the relevant conclusions. Of note, in Chapter 6, you will add the proposed time period necessary for analyzing the data, so it is not necessary to add this information now. Finally, we suggest outlining the daily or weekly procedures that will be used within the implementation of the plan; however, these may evolve as you continue to refine your research plan as part of the activities within Chapter 6.

EVALUATING AGAINST THE STANDARDS: ARE YOU READY TO MOVE ON?

CHECKLIST: RESEARCH PLAN (REVISED) AND TIMELINE

Continuing from the research plan you started in Chapter 4, have you:

_____ 1. Determined the appropriate research method for your action research study?

_____ 2. Reviewed the research question to ensure it can be answered using the proposed methods?

_____ 3. Determined the research design that will be used?

_____ 4. Listed the specific locations that will be used for data collection?

_____ 5. Detailed the specific procedures that will be used for data collection?

_____ 6. Developed a plan to organize the data as it is collected?

_____ 7. Considered how you might examine/analyze the data once it is collected?

_____ 8. Reviewed your proposed timeline to ensure the activities can be completed within the proposed timeframe?

_____ 9. Inquired with an administrator or the district office to determine if a proposal must be submitted to the institutional review board?

_____10. Developed an informed consent letter or permission form?

As we've described in previous chapters, it's important to examine and reflect upon your responses to the questions contained as part of the checklist. If you have not considered or addressed several elements, we would caution proceeding with the implementation of your plan. This is especially relevant to those questions that address permission and informed consent. If your responses are positive, it's time to begin to focus more on the data analysis associated with your chosen research methods. Chapter 6 will present various methods to analyze qualitative, quantitative, and mixed methods research.

SUMMARY

In this chapter, you were introduced to two terms, *reliability* and *validity*, which are important to consider as part of the data collection process (as well as later in your analysis). In layman's terms, *validity* refers to whether the construct represents or measures what it is supposed to, while *reliability* denotes consistency of measurement.

We briefly reviewed the classifications of research: qualitative, quantitative, and mixed methods. You were then introduced to various methods of data collection associated with each type. Qualitative data collection methods include observations, anecdotal notes, interviews, journals, and focus groups, among others, while quantitative researchers may use methods like surveys, questionnaires, school artifacts (e.g., tests, records), and attitude and rating scales. Mixed methods research utilizes data collection strategies associated with each. The various forms of data collection should be thoughtfully considered in terms of the scope, time, and context of your action research study. We included the template in Figure 4.6 as a means to help you organize and think critically about the various facets that will be necessary to complete your action research.

Key Terms

Anecdotal notes, p. 105

Artifacts, p. 112

Attitude scales, p. 113

Construct validity, p. 102

Content validity, p. 102

Convergent validity, p. 103

Criterion validity, p. 102

Equivalent forms reliability, p. 101

Face validity, p. 102

Inter-rater reliability, p. 101

Interval data, p. 114

Interviews, p. 107

Journal, p. 109

Nominal data, p. 114

Observation, p. 105

Ordinal data, p. 114

Rating scales, p. 115

Ratio data, p. 115

Reliability, p. 100

Reliability coefficient, p. 101

Stability reliability, p. 101

Survey, p. 110

Test–retest reliability, p. 101

Validity, p. 100

Case in Point: Revising the Research Plan and Timeline

One Elementary Teacher's Journey: Research Log Entry #2

In my last entry, I wrote that I was thinking about using a mixed methods approach incorporating interviews and oral reading scores (from DIBELS). Now that I have had a chance to look over the data collection process and reflected about my classroom, I am not sure I can still conduct interviews. I only have a certain amount of time each day, and I'm afraid I would be trying to rush the students through their responses instead of letting them really describe their thinking and the processes they were using while reading. In an effort to overcome this potential problem, I began to think about having the students keep daily reading journals. They could write in them while I was

finishing up with small groups and there would be a lot more time for them to add the details I am looking for. I could collect them periodically, probably once per week, and take them home to read them. The more I thought about it though, I began to realize it might be too much to have the students practice the Readers' Theater and write in their journals. Plus, I am not sure I have the time to read and respond to each of their entries, so I decided that I would focus on what I thought would be the best measure of their improvements in fluency— DIBELS. As I wrote last time, this makes the most sense because I already collect this assessment at regular intervals, so this will not only be manageable, but using the oral reading fluency portion will help me note improvements over the duration of the study.

As far as a timeline, after administering DIBELS as the baseline (pre-test) measure, students will engage in the activities associated with Readers' Theater for four weeks. Since this is my first action research study, I decided to start simple and focus on our regular reading time. Typically, I meet with individual students during the time I will devote the Readers' Theater. However, I will modify my plan and try to meet with various students and groups three or four times a week (Monday–Thursday) and work with students individually, in partners, or in small groups, as necessary, to increase their fluency for the passages. During this specific time, we will tackle any difficulties by scaffolding with reading strategies such as sounding out, context clues, word segmentation, and so on.

I am going to intermix the groups with different reading levels to allow the students to help each other, but these will be flexible groups. Progress monitoring (DIBELS) will take place before we began Readers' Theater, midway through our time together, and at the end of the four-week period. The midpoint data will play an important role in determining how the process proceeds. I have adjusted my research plan (see Figure 5.6) to reflect all of these changes; now I just have to think about the specific ways that I am going to analyze my data.

My initial timeline for the project is that the data collection will be conducted over four weeks (see Figure 5.8). Beginning with week 1, Readers' Theater will be implemented daily during our readers' workshop. On Mondays (45 minutes), we will be selecting our reading material, becoming familiar with the passage, and discussing the storyline. On Tuesdays (45 minutes), we will be reading all roles with partners and independently, and choosing roles. On Wednesdays (45 minutes), we will be coaching each other, getting into character, and practicing our lines. Thursdays will be our main day to rehearse together and add our own dramatic touches and interpretations to our roles. Fridays will be performance day, where the students perform in front of parents, staff, and peers.

One Secondary Teacher's Journey: Research Log Entry #2

In my previous entry, I was considering using a pre-test, post-test one group research design to examine the effect of the open investigation instructional approach on my students who are lower-level readers. As I continue to reflect on my classroom and the data collection procedures, I am convinced that the collection of the weekly test scores and the attitude questionnaire will give me the data I need to answer my research question. I think my data collection methods are manageable and will not require too much additional time outside of what I normally do to cause difficulty with implementation. I usually give a weekly test to assess student learning, so this will fit our schedule and allow me to compare data to previous learning outcomes. After sharing my initial plans with peers and my professor, I have decided that I will include approximately two open-ended questions on the questionnaire. It was agreed that this would give me qualitative data that could explain why students were ranking items on the questionnaire as they did. This would be simple to add and wouldn't require too much extra time to gather or analyze. Plus, it might add some very valuable insights. My idea for keeping field notes during the intervention phase was also thought to be valuable and would add another source of data to either support, explain, or refute what the quantitative measures were communicating. During the intervention phase, I will take time each day/week to write down some of my impressions, observations, and notes about the class sessions and how they are progressing. This data will be useful as formative data that will inform instructional decisions and changes to the process as the intervention is implemented. It also may prove to be extremely valuable as I am interpreting my results and considering implications for future practice. My research plan and timeline for the project are starting to take shape (see Figures 5.9 and 5.10).

FIGURE 5.9   One Secondary Teacher's Action Research Plan

Problem statement	In a lower-level ability section of ninth-grade science, students struggle with science content and a motivation to learn. I want to see how an open investigation workshop approach impacts these students' learning and engagement during the second quarter of instruction.
Goals for research	My goal for this action research study is to implement the open investigation approach with my science class of below-level readers/writers to improve their academic achievement and motivation for learning.
Research question	What is the effect of an open investigation workshop approach on a ninth-grade science class with students who are lower-level readers/writers?
Context	The context of this study is a secondary school located in a suburban area near a large metropolitan city. The student body consists of 908 students. The school is classified as medium socioeconomic status, with 48% of students being eligible for free or reduced-price lunch. While the school is not Title I, it does qualify to receive state funds proportionate to the free and reduced-price lunch percentage. The student population consists mainly of Caucasian (79%), African American (17%), Asian American (2%), American Indian/Pacific Islander (1%), and other (1%).
Participants	This study utilizes one of three sections of science classes that I teach. As a result of ability grouping based on language arts skill levels, this particular group of students struggles to read and are classified as below grade-level readers. The class consists of 28 students: eight have 504 plans, two have IEPs, 16 are male, and 12 are female. The majority of the class is Caucasian (20), with African American (5), Hispanic (2), and Asian American (1) students included. The majority of the students (19) have low informational text reading scores, while the remaining nine have scores in the low-medium range.
Data to be collected	Multiple-choice test—quantitative measure, easy to administer and collect, minimal data storage necessary
	Questionnaire—Likert-scale with two additional open-ended questions to assess student attitude toward the class
	Observation notes—qualitative source, may provide additional information to reinforce trends identified in other sources
Frequency/ duration of data collection	Multiple choice test (weekly; eight weeks)
	Questionnaire (week 1, week 8)
	Observation notes (ongoing)
Location of data collection	My classroom
Who will collect data	Teacher
Data analysis procedure	
Display of data/ findings	

FIGURE 5.10   One Secondary Teacher's Action Research Timeline and Activities

Informed Consent

Two weeks prior to intervention	Develop research plan/informed consent
One week prior to intervention	Informed consent letter sent home and returned

Data Collection

Final week of direct instruction approach learning unit	Compile weekly tests over the eight-week period; distribute and collect student attitude questionnaire
Week 1	Implement open investigation approach—week 1 test collection
Week 2	Implement open investigation approach—week 2 test collection and researcher field notes written and compiled
Week 3	Implement open investigation approach—week 3 test collection and researcher field notes written and compiled
Week 4	Implement open investigation approach—week 4 test collection and researcher field notes written and compiled
Week 5	Implement open investigation approach—week 5 test collection and researcher field notes written and compiled
Week 6	Implement open investigation approach—week 6 test collection and researcher field notes written and compiled
Week 7	Implement open investigation approach—week 7 test collection and researcher field notes written and compiled
Week 8	Implement open investigation approach—week 8 test collection, researcher field notes written and compiled, and collect student attitude questionnaire

Activities and Additional Resources

1. You have decided that you would like to create your own assessment to measure students' knowledge of scientific elements. Describe what you will need to consider as you construct the instrument to make sure it is valid and reliable.

2. Consider the following situation: A teacher administers the same U.S. History test to three classes. The average grades for the three classes are as follows: 82.8, 97.3, and 67.9. Using this information, the teacher concludes the test is not a reliable measure. Is the teacher making a correct assumption? Why or why not?

3. Two teachers are collaborating on an action research project. One suggests that an observation checklist will provide the greatest information about a student's off-task behavior because it will reveal how many times the off-task behavior happened over a specific interval. The other teacher advocates for a more open-ended, holistic observation tool because she feels the observer needs to collect information about the context to accurately determine the causes for the behavior. Which teacher do you support and why? If possible, suggest an alternate form of data collection to help them collect the information about the student's off-task behavior.

4. While planning your action research study, you decide that you need to be able to compute the mean to effectively compare measures. What forms of data measurement (nominal, ordinal, interval, or ratio) would be necessary within your variables to ensure this was possible? Which levels would not allow you to compute the mean? Be sure to explain your reasoning.

Print Resources

Creswell, J. W. (2014). *Research design: Qualitative, quantitative, and mixed methods approaches* (4th ed.). Thousand Oaks, CA: Sage.

Davies, J. (2010). Preparation and process of qualitative interviews and focus groups. In L. Dahlberg & C. McCaig (Eds.), *Practical research and evaluation: A start-to-finish guide for practitioners* (pp. 126–144). Thousand Oaks, CA: Sage.

Flick, U. (2014). *An introduction to qualitative research* (5th ed.). Thousand Oaks, CA: Sage.

Ivankova, N. V. (2015). *Mixed methods applications in action research: From methods to community action.* Thousand Oaks, CA: Sage.

Web Resources

Madison Metropolitan School District, Classroom Action Research: http://oldweb.madison.k12.wi.us/sod/car/carhomepage.html

Student Study Site

edge.sagepub.com/putman

- Take the practice quiz.
- Review key terms with eFlashcards.
- Explore topics with video and multimedia.

References

Cicchetti, D. V. (1994). Guidelines, criteria, and rules of thumb for evaluating normed and standardized assessment instruments in psychology. *Psychological Assessment, 6,* 284–290.

Cohen, J. (1960). A coefficient of agreement for nominal scales. *Educational and Psychological Measurement, 20,* 37–46.

Corbin, J., & Strauss, A. (2008). *Basics of qualitative research: Techniques and procedures for developing grounded theory* (3rd ed.). Thousand Oaks, CA: Sage.

Costa, A. L., & Garmston, R. J. (2002). *Cognitive coaching.* Norwood, MA: Christopher Gordon Publishers.

Creswell, J. W., & Plano Clark, V. L. (2011). *Designing and conducting mixed methods research* (2nd ed.). Thousand Oaks, CA: Sage.

Flick, U. (2009). *An introduction to qualitative research* (4th ed.). Thousand Oaks, CA: Sage.

Gay, L. R., Mills, G. E., & Airasian, P. (2006). *Educational research: Competencies for analysis and applications* (8th ed.). Upper Saddle River, NJ: Merrill Prentice Hall.

Grady, M. P. (1998). *Qualitative and action research: A practitioner handbook.* Bloomington, IN: Phi Delta Kappa International.

Henning, J. E., Stone, J. M., & Kelly, J. L. (2009). Using action research to improve instruction: An interactive guide for teachers. New York, NY: Routledge.

Hubbard, R. S., & Power, B. M. (2003). *The art of classroom inquiry: A handbook for teacher-researchers* (rev. ed.). Portsmouth, NH: Heinemann.

Ivankova, N. V. (2015). *Mixed methods applications in action research: From methods to community action.* Thousand Oaks, CA: Sage.

Krueger, R. A. (2000). *Focus groups: A practical guide for applied researcher* (3rd ed.). Thousand Oaks, CA: Sage.

Lincoln, S. Y., & Guba, E. G. (1985). *Naturalistic inquiry.* Thousand Oaks, CA: Sage.

Maxwell, J. A. (1992). Understanding and validity in qualitative research. *Harvard Educational Review, 62,* 279–300.

Merriam, S. B. (1988). *Case study research in education: A qualitative approach.* San Francisco, CA: Jossey-Bass.

Popham, W. J. (2009). Unraveling reliability. *Educational Leadership, 66,* 77–78.

Szafran, R. (2012). *Answering questions with statistics.* Thousand Oaks, CA: Sage.

Teddlie, C., & Tashakkori, A. (2009). *Foundations of mixed methods research: Integrating quantitative and qualitative approaches in the social and behavioral sciences.* Thousand Oaks, CA: Sage.

Thorndike, R. M., & Thorndike-Christ, T. M. (2011). *Measurement and evaluation in psychology and education* (8th ed.). Upper Saddle River, NJ: Pearson.

Webb, N. M., Shavelson, R. J., & Haertal, E. H. (2007). Reliability coefficients and generalizability theory. In C. R. Rao & S. Sinharay (Eds.), *Handbook of statistics, Vol. 26* (pp. 81–124). Amsterdam, The Netherlands: Elsevier.

PHASE III

Enacting

CHAPTER 6

Analyzing the Data

GUIDING QUESTIONS

After reading this chapter, you should be able to answer the following questions:

- What is generalizability?
- How does a researcher determine the appropriate techniques for data analysis within an action research project?
- What is the best way to organize data for analysis?
- How is qualitative data reduced, analyzed, and interpreted?
- What are descriptive statistics? When are they appropriate measurements?
- What are inferential statistics? What statistical tests can be used to measure inferential statistics?
- What is triangulation, and how can it be used to strengthen the conclusions associated with an action research study?

CHAPTER AIMS AND GOALS

Chapter 6 is designed to extend information presented in Chapters 4 and 5, and to help you finalize your research plan through describing the methods that can be used to analyze your data. After a brief review of reliability and validity, we will introduce generalizability and its applicability to action research, then progress to outlining qualitative and quantitative techniques for data analysis, describing the processes for analysis and interpretation within each methodology. We will also explain mixed methods approaches that utilize both qualitative and quantitative methodologies to triangulate the analysis. The chapter will culminate with the completion of your research plan.

Setting the Context: Analyzing Your Data

Working with teachers over the years, we've come to realize that when the words *data analysis* are uttered or seen, their first inclination is to immediately think about statistics. Data analysis, however, encompasses a variety of techniques, many involving interpretations of themes or trends that do not involve a single calculation. For some, this knowledge may be a relief, yet the numbers-oriented people among us will continue to seek out methods to calculate relationships or the impact of an intervention through some form of mathematical analysis. When conducting action research, it is important to remember that the function of data analysis is to help us determine whether our intervention is successful. We can collect copious amounts of data, but if we fail to take the time to critically examine it in some organized format (or at all), it is essentially meaningless and does not lead us toward new insights in relation to the question that we are attempting to address. Given that teachers and school personnel are increasingly being asked to collect data and use it for decision-making purposes, it's important to become well versed in the methods for the related analyses.

In Chapter 5 we introduced you to reliability and validity in our descriptions of data collection procedures. However, these constructs are influential within your data analysis, as failure to pay attention to them impacts the conclusions formed as part of the analysis. For example, if you have selected an instrument that is not a valid measure of a particular topic, regardless of the appropriateness of your selected method of data analysis, it is unlikely that you will reach conclusions that deliver an answer to your selected question. If we consider qualitative research, if two researchers are conducting observations and have not directed attention toward establishing inter-rater reliability prior to their analysis, they may code certain behaviors differently, limiting their capacity to discover trends and themes within the data.

Remember, reliability represents the degree a measurement tool generates consistent and steady results. In other words, if you administer a test to a group of students on several occasions, those with similar levels of knowledge will score similarly on each administration. We summarized the various forms of reliability in the previous chapter (e.g., inter-rater, test–retest, and equivalent forms), and would recommend referring back to Chapter 5 for a refresher if necessary. Reliability is a prerequisite for validity. In other words, for an instrument to effectively measure what it is supposed to, the instrument should consistently demonstrate similar or the same results. *Validity*, as you'll recall, describes whether an instrument or procedure measures what it is proposed to. Content validity, construct validity, and criterion validity are some of the more common forms. One form of validity that we have not mentioned previously that is applicable to your analysis is theoretical validity (Maxwell, 1992). This form of validity is focused on the accuracy of the explanation for the conclusions. It is especially relevant when using qualitative methods for action research, as it is easy to fall prey to wanting to see positive results from our teaching practices or intervention. As a result, we may seek to explain behaviors or results in such a way that we extend beyond what our data analysis actually reveals. We discourage this practice and urge you to report only what you discovered directly in the data. Otherwise, the results and conclusions you report won't have the validity necessary to be meaningful.

GENERALIZABILITY

Generalizability extends from research that is both reliable and valid. **Generalizability** represents the process of explaining the behavior of a larger sample (or population) as a result of conducting a study with a smaller set that appears to exemplify the characteristics associated with the population. Generalizability can apply to the particular setting where the research was conducted, referred to as internal generalizability, or in a new setting, representing external generalizability. Acknowledging that generalizability is an important consideration within traditional research studies and that you should be familiar with it, it is generally not the focus of action research studies. The inherent goal of your study is to develop a greater understanding of your personal teaching context, identified as your classroom or school, and to help your students make academic (or social) gains as a result of a direct intervention. While you may gain some insights that apply outside of your specific context, you will likely need to conduct additional research to generate findings that are truly generalizable.

PREPARING FOR DATA ANALYSIS

After our review of the terminology that is important within the research process, it is time to begin to address various aspects associated with data analysis. You developed your preliminary research plan as part of Chapters 4 and 5. One central consideration that is not articulated in the research plan is how you will manage the data you collect. This is an important consideration within the overall process, and thus it warrants a brief discussion. Arguably, if you are administering a pre- and post-assessment that coincides with data collected as part of your regular teaching activities, this is a relatively simple process. It is very likely that you have an electronic gradebook or spreadsheet that you already use. However, where the situation becomes challenging is when you are collecting observations or another form of qualitative data that requires you to hold on to large amounts of textual data over an extended period of time. When this is the case, you will need to determine another mechanism to organize your data. To some degree this is a personal preference based on your own organizational tendencies. We've seen qualitative data from observations entered into spreadsheets that are color-coded by date, student, and subject to ease sorting and to add visual cues. We've also observed anecdotal records kept on sticky notes inside folders for each individual student. In the latter case, analysis was actually conducted by placing the notes on the wall and manipulating them under theme headings as they evolved. One teacher we worked with kept all her data in a word processing document and used Wordle (www.wordle.net) to generate a "word cloud" of the most common terms. She subsequently used this information as she developed themes within her analysis. As your research proceeds, there is an element of trial and error as you determine the most effective methods to keep and organize data—there is no one-size-fits-all method and no single piece of advice that works for everyone. Essentially, you have to use what works best for you. Our recommendation is simply to think proactively about this process, before collecting the first piece of data, to ensure you don't become overwhelmed trying to do so after the research has commenced. See the Tech Connections box for additional suggestions on useful tools for use with your data storage and analysis.

TECH CONNECTIONS

Few people would argue that our ability to store data and conduct data analysis has certainly been enhanced by the various technological tools that are now available to us. No longer do we have to store data in paper and print form, but we can enter it into various programs, which will not only store it but can also help us organize it in a variety of ways. Similarly, the need to calculate descriptive or inferential statistics by hand is eliminated through some of the tools listed below. A more recent addition to our capabilities includes several programs that will aid us in identifying themes in qualitative data, although we still feel the researcher should engage in some level of analysis to ensure additional themes or codes pertinent to the research question are not missed.

Electronic Data Storage and/or Analysis Tools:

Quantitative Analysis

Excel—Spreadsheet program that is produced and distributed by Microsoft as part of the Office software bundle.

Google Sheets—Cloud-based spreadsheet that provides accessibility anywhere an Internet connection is available. Free with a Google account.

Zoho Sheet—Cloud-based spreadsheet that allows users to access and use local files on their computer as well as Google Sheets files. Free with sign-up for Zoho account.

IBM SPSS Statistics—Computer software designed specifically for quantitative analysis. Available for purchase only.

Qualitative Analysis

NVivo—Computer software that is available for purchase that is specifically designed for qualitative data analysis.

Dedoose (www.dedoose.com)—Dedoose is a web-based tool that can be used for analyzing data, including text, audio, and videos, from qualitative and mixed methods research. Requires user to purchase an account.

Wordle (www.wordle.net)—Wordle is a web-based word cloud generator that is useful for examining preliminary patterns in qualitative data that may guide future analysis.

"NOTE"-ABLE THOUGHTS

Take a few moments and write down the method(s) that you are considering to organize and store your data. As you read the descriptions of the data analysis processes, continue to reflect on whether your selected methods will be feasible within the greater research plan.

QUALITATIVE ANALYSIS

When primarily text-based data is collected through observations, interviews, or examination of artifacts and documents, we learned in Chapter 4 that we would characterize the method used for analysis as being qualitative (see Table 6.1 for a review of quantitative and qualitative methods). Choosing to collect these forms of data is a commitment to a concurrent process of data collection and analysis as opposed to two activities that are completely separate. Boeije (2009) reinforces this, noting:

Qualitative analysis is the segmenting of data into relevant categories and the naming of these categories with codes while simultaneously generating the categories from data ... to generate theoretical understanding of the social phenomenon under study in terms of research questions. (p. 76)

In other words, you will engage in simultaneous collection and analysis through ongoing assessment and examination as your study proceeds (Creswell, 2012). This constant cycle of collection and analysis represents opportunities for researchers to gain preliminary insights and adapt the research to address a deficiency in data collection or trend that is noted within the initial analysis (Herr & Anderson, 2005).

Various methods of qualitative analysis exist (e.g., grounded theory and constant comparative methods), but they share the general characteristics associated with processes that involve **inductive analysis**. This form of analysis represents the systematic development of categories and themes that originate from the interpretation of data (Creswell, 2014; Mertler, 2012). Within the interpretive process, the researcher must examine the data set as a whole, often several times. As these examinations occur, there is a deliberate effort to sort and categorize as consistencies between individual pieces of data are noted. As a very simple example, suppose your students were required to keep science journals while participating in a unit about the scientific method. Reading through the journal entries, you noted that students consistently defined the problem, but many entries lacked predictions prior to beginning experimentation. In this scenario, each journal entry might be considered an individual piece of data and perhaps you use "lack of prediction" as a category for statements that originated within the data.

Once categories are developed, the researcher continues to examine them for the presence of a broader theme that demonstrates ways the data is interconnected. Continuing the previous example, as you continue to read the entries, you note that the students who were not making predictions were those who received their

TABLE 6.1   Review of Differences Between Research Methods

Qualitative Methods	Quantitative Methods
Observations, interviews, artifacts/documents	Survey, questionnaire, scores (e.g., tests)
Inductive (exploratory, theory formulation)	Deductive (hypothesis testing)
Text-based	Numerical
Fewer participants	Larger potential number of participants
Greater depth of analysis	Greater breadth within analysis
Greater time expenditure necessary for collection and analysis	Diminished time (in comparison to qualitative) necessary for collection and analysis
Coding, development of themes	Statistical tests/analysis

instruction from a substitute when you were at a district-level meeting and others who are pulled from the classroom each day during science instruction. In recognizing this, you've noted how the data is interconnected and potentially created an explanation for the conclusions. Again, this is a very simplistic example that does not fully address all of the nuances of qualitative analysis, but it provides some background for new researchers. It is important to note that seldom does qualitative analysis represent a stress-free process for the novice researcher, as it is easy to become overwhelmed by the amount of text to examine, especially when working with large samples. That's why action research represents a good way to dive into this form of analysis!

We have found Creswell's (2012) approach for analyzing qualitative data to be especially helpful for providing guidance within the qualitative analysis process for the teachers we have worked with. Within this approach, data collected from the qualitative sources (e.g., interviews, observations, or artifacts) is first gathered into a clear, readable form. For many researchers, this means the process must begin by transcribing the information to effectively prepare it for analysis. Creswell recommends the use of a codebook to facilitate the organizational process, but the data can be held in various forms, including those that we mentioned previously (e.g., spreadsheet, sticky note). Once the data is transcribed, it is organized according to the research questions. Some researchers further subdivide the data based on the collection method. For example, for each research question they make note of the source of the data, for example, data from surveys, data from observations, or data from interviews.

Following the organizational activities, **coding** begins as the researcher engages with the raw text data accumulated through the qualitative data sources and seeks to generate categories and themes that will continue to guide analysis. Please note that when we mention coding, we are referring to the process for "identifying a meaningful segment of text . . . for some minimal representation of meaning" (Guest, MacQueen, & Namey, 2012, p. 52). In other words, coding data involves finding bits of information that are seemingly aligned and combining them to form groups or categories. According to Craig (2009), it is this process "that truly creates the picture of events" (p. 189). The goal of coding is to take the potentially large amounts of textual data and refine it so that it is represented by a significantly smaller number of categories (Strauss & Corbin, 1998). When coding, it is important to use clear labels for the categories, as you will need to continually examine them within the process. Explicit labels that convey meaning of information ensure this process can proceed most effectively and efficiently. Using an iterative process where the data, codes, and themes are revisited and compared multiple times with previously collected and new data, the researcher attempts to make refinements to the codes and themes used for categorization. There are also direct attempts to interpret and generate meaning from what is revealed, and the researcher engages in reflection regarding the alignment with the original research questions. Once no new codes or themes appear as additional data is collected and examined, which is referred to as saturation, the researcher tests the categories against the data and determines the most effective way to convey the findings.

Carlos Rivera, 11th-Grade Teacher

My action research study was focused on examining peer feedback on student writing using online discussion boards. Given that the posts made to the discussion board provided a substantial amount of textual (qualitative) data, I knew that I had to code the responses in such a way that would make it digestible in order to analyze it efficiently. I spent some time thinking about the basic categories that I would need that would confirm similarities and differences. Once I identified the categories to use for coding, I combed through the data and used tally marks to record the frequency of responses that matched the categories. I focused on the specific comments that mentioned elements of revisions that we discussed in class as one of the main categories. Along with that I tagged some sub-themes to ensure I was able to code the feedback accurately. Many of the suggestions for revisions fell within the editing category (e.g., missing punctuation or misspelling), but there were also a number that addressed specific suggestions for and corrections to the content. Lastly, I spent some time combing through the list of adjectives and descriptors that were used to illustrate various points about the writing and concluded the majority of them were positively oriented, but had limited relationship to the "must have" traits of good writing. Through this experience, I found that once I created the categories for coding it provided me an easy way to record the frequency using tally marks and I was also able to view the data in an organized manner.

While the process we have described generates the codes and themes from what is revealed in the data (inductively), qualitative data analysis can occur using predetermined codes developed after a review of the literature or based on specific categories (Creswell, 2014). For example, if we were examining student discussions about controversial historical events, we could specifically look for utterances that demonstrate content knowledge or specific levels of Bloom's Revised Taxonomy. You could also look at students' response patterns to determine if participation is equally distributed or whether patterns were observed based on student characteristics or group qualities, for example, on-task versus off-task (Henning, Stone, & Kelly, 2009).

In summary, qualitative data analysis involves examinations of data that is primarily textual in nature, as it is collected through observations, interviews, or open-ended surveys. Through an iterative process of collection and analysis, the researcher seeks to interpret the data and develop a theory or framework to explain the question under study. This is contrasted with quantitative analysis, which involves numerical data and is concerned with hypothesis testing. This form of analysis will be explained in the following section.

QUANTITATIVE ANALYSIS

Quantitative analysis has been identified as a primary method used to analyze data produced through action research studies (Tomal, 2010). This form of analysis, which includes the use of numeric strategies (i.e., statistics) to arrive at conclusions, would be categorized as having a greater degree of objectivity than qualitative analysis. It represents a method to take large amounts of numeric data and effectively examine it for trends, patterns, and potential relationships. As we describe the processes that can be used within quantitative analyses, we will focus on the two broad categories of statistics most often in action research studies: descriptive and inferential. Subsequently, we'll describe various types of strategies and analyses within each category that can be used to help you arrive at conclusions.

Descriptive statistics. Descriptive statistics are the metrics that many of us have some familiarity with (e.g., mean, median, range) as well as others that we may have heard of but cannot always define, like variance and standard deviation. The benefit of analyses that incorporate descriptive statistics is that a researcher can take a large amount of data and quickly gain a sense of how spread out the data is or what the mean value is, that is, what the average result is. In short, descriptive statistics represent an effective and efficient method to gain information about numeric data sets.

We referred to the *mean* in the previous paragraph, but it's important to recognize that in statistics, many of the terms we are familiar with (like *mean*) actually fall into a broader classification. For example, mean, median, and mode are classified as **measures of central tendency**. While we are more concerned that you retain your familiarity with the primary terms, it is important to know that measures of central tendency yield general trends in data and are presented as a numeric value that establishes what is standard about the data under study (Creswell, 2012). Ideally we'd like to use *average* in our description, but we hesitate to do so because most of us associate *average* with the *mean,* and while measures of central tendency include the mean, they also encompass median and mode (Mills, 2011; Tomal, 2010). As a refresher on these three terms, **mean** is the average of all the numbers in a data set. It is the most commonly computed measure of central tendency (Tanner, 2012). The **mode** represents the value that occurs most frequently in a group of data (Tanner, 2012). Finally, when all numbers are placed in order, the **median** is the "point below which half the scores in the group occur" (Tanner, 2012, p. 22).

Many researchers focus on the mean when they report the results of their studies, and we expect that this is something you are likely considering. However, it's important to note that when using measures of central tendency, you need to be aware of outliers, or values that are very high or very low in comparison to the rest of the data set. For example, if you have the following six scores on a test, 89, 88, 90, 89, 91, and 51, the last score (51) would be considered the outlier. Outliers can have a significant impact on the mean of the set, more so than the median or mode, and this may lead to conclusions that don't truly reflect the data. Generally, the presence of an outlier can be confirmed through visual analysis of the data set. Should you suspect the potential inclusion of an outlier in your data set through this visual analysis, we suggest calculating all three measures of central tendency. If the mean is significantly different than the median or mode, you've likely confirmed an outlier (or an error in calculation). Referring back to the data set above, the median and mode are both 89, while the mean is 83. When outliers are present in a data set, you can (a) choose to statistically adjust for it, which we don't necessarily recommend, as it generally involves complicated statistical measures; (b) remove the outlier, which is also not recommended as it may impact your findings; or (c) acknowledge our recommendation and include all three measures in your reporting to provide the most accurate picture of the data.

Measures of variability, on the other hand, may not be as familiar or readily recalled as measures of central tendency. Measures of variability provide information about how individual scores differ from each other within a set of scores (Creswell, 2012; Mertler, 2012). In essence, measures of variability provide information about how well the mean represents the data. There are several measures that can be calculated to provide this information. **Range** represents the difference between the highest and lowest value within the data set. While it provides a quick method to examine the spread of the data, it is strongly influenced by outliers, or numbers far from the mean. Thus, other methods are more descriptive. **Variance** is the sum of the squared distance of each score from the mean divided by the total number of scores. The variance is large if the scores within a data set are spread out and smaller if the scores are more concentrated around the mean. As with range, variance is influenced strongly by outliers or scores that deviate significantly from the mean, but the differences are not as sizable. Finally, **standard deviation** refers to the average distance of scores away from the mean (Creswell, 2012). This measure is not as influenced by outliers as the others and provides us information that can help us determine how close scores are to the mean. Standard deviation is important to keep in mind when using inferential statistics, as many tests require normally distributed data. Visualizing the bell or normal curve (see Figure 6.1), 68% of scores should fall within one standard deviation above and below the mean within data that meets this requirement (Creswell, 2012; Tomal, 2010).

Given the various measures at your disposal, choosing which ones to report is something that you must consider as part of your overall data analysis. For measures of central tendency, the form of the data is an important deciding factor. Recall from Chapter 5, there are four forms of data that can be collected: nominal, ordinal, interval, and ratio. Nominal data is best reported using the mode, while ordinal data can be described using the median and range (or minimum and maximum values). Mean and standard deviation are typically used to represent interval and ratio variables, but researchers can also calculate mode, median, and range with these forms of data.

FIGURE 6.1 Normal Distribution

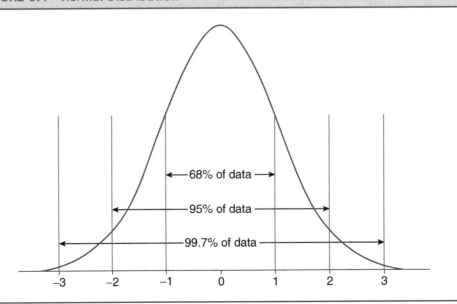

One inherent advantage in the use of descriptive statistics is the capability to depict various facets of the data, such as frequencies or sample characteristics, using graphs, charts, or tables. For example, if I am a teacher and want to show the performance of my class on identifying the number of states over the course of the school year, I can create a line graph that depicts the mean number of states correctly labeled on a map each month. Using this graph, I can quickly visualize how the class improved as the year progressed as well as note how much progress occurred by comparing the mean at the beginning of the year to the mean at the end of the year. Considering the type of data that you will collect can influence the chart or graph that can be used to graphically represent your data, but you should also think about the most effective method to convey the data. Pie graphs can be used to depict all four types of data. However, given each element is shown as a slice of the pie, too many elements result in a visual where differences are not as readily discernible. Bar graphs are primarily used to report nominal and ordinal data, with relative frequencies within the attributes being measured depicted by the height of the bar. A third type of graphic representation that may not be as familiar to you is the histogram. We've found that histograms are often mistaken for bar graphs, but there are some fundamental differences between the two. First, a bar graph (see Figure 6.2) has space between each bar because the data is not continuous, while the histogram (see Figure 6.3) does not show spaces between the bars, which are also referred to as bins (Szafran, 2012). This is because the histogram is used for interval and ratio (continuous) variables and the horizontal axis is a number line as opposed to a discrete data category. As a result, histograms reveal the relative frequency among data as well as the distribution of the data as one scans the breadth of data along the horizontal axis.

Inferential statistics. In our experiences, inferential statistics are those that most teachers readily associate with research. However, as we have established, research can include

---

FIGURE 6.2 Bar Graph of Participant Responses

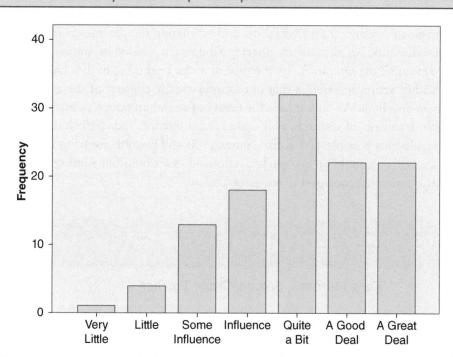

FIGURE 6.3 Histogram of Participant Responses (Interval Data)

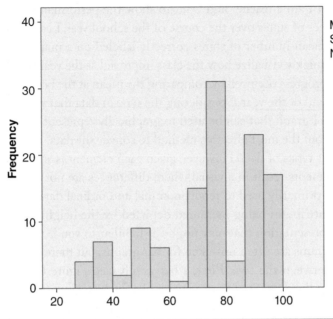

Mean = 72.96
Std. Dev. = 22.655
N = 124

many types of data and many forms of analysis. Contrary to qualitative analysis, which involves inductive reasoning, **inferential statistics** involve **deductive analysis**, which is focused on testing hypotheses about differences or observed relationships. The intent of inferential statistics is to extend the findings associated with a particular sample, or subset of a group, to the population from which it was drawn or to make generalizations from specific conditions to more general ones. In other words, the sample is used to represent a larger population, and properties of the sample are inferred to embody the population. In educational research, this might mean measuring kindergarten readiness of a sample of students from all 50 states and estimating the parameters (e.g., mean and standard deviation) of all students entering kindergarten based on statistical techniques used to examine the sample. As we mentioned at the beginning of the chapter, the challenge within action research is that our sample usually consists of the students in our classroom or school. We do not have the luxury of a random sample, which is considered the "gold standard" of research, as it makes the inferences (generalizations) associated with populations possible. Given this context, it is still possible for us to use inferential statistics, but we should be extremely cautious in describing our findings, focusing on the participants that took part in our research.

■ ■ ■ VOICES FROM THE FIELD

Kara Manwell, Second-Grade Teacher

In determining the methods I would use to analyze the data I had gathered, I referred back to my original question, "What effect does repeated reading have on students' oral reading fluency and reading progress?" Because my study would entail numerical data only, I knew my data analysis technique would be quantitative. When I first began collecting the data, I placed students' baseline and weekly oral reading fluency scores on a large sticky note for each student. Likewise, I listed students' initial and post-strategy scores on the running records on each student's sticky note. This method was fine for collecting and organizing my data initially, but it did not take me long to realize that I would need a better process to analyze the collected data. In thinking about what I had access to and what I felt I had the most knowledge of, I decided to utilize a spreadsheet to simplify, summarize, and organize the results of students' assessments. After entering each student's scores on each measure, I used the formulas to find the mean of the students' scores. This helped me to find the central tendency and actual value of these students' scores. Since I did not have any extreme or outlier scores to skew the data, the mean seemed like a simple and understandable way to reduce the data. I found the mean score for each student's growth after four weeks of implementing the repeated readings. I also found the mean score for all of the students combined for the baseline oral reading fluency and each of the four weeks of progress monitoring while the intervention was conducted. For the students' pre- and post-reading level comparison, I created a bar graph to show the compared reading levels of students before and after the implementation of the repeated readings. Each technique I chose not only fit well with the data, but was a measure that provided me the insights I needed to judge the success of the intervention.

While not required within all action research studies, investigations that will incorporate the use of inferential statistics can include a hypothesis, which represents a prediction about the effects of an intervention on a specific variable within a sample. The intent is to determine whether there is sufficient evidence from the sample to extrapolate findings to a defined population. Given our research is primarily focused on our own classrooms, this doesn't necessarily apply in action research; however, it's important to be familiar with the terminology in case you encounter it within the research articles you are examining as part of your review of literature. As we mentioned, the hypothesis is a prediction, and there are two types present within a hypothesis test: the null hypothesis and the alternative hypothesis. The former is the one that is tested as you implement your procedures, and it is written from the perspective that there are no differences between the variables being tested. For example, if you were comparing the test scores of one class that received an intervention with scores from another that did not, the null hypothesis would be written to reflect that there was no difference in the mean scores of the two groups. The alternative hypothesis, on the other hand, is what most researchers hope to be true—that the scores are actually different. The statistical test used within the research determines whether the null hypothesis is rejected, indicating the differences between the means of the two groups is unlikely to be the result of chance, or whether we fail to reject the null hypothesis, which means the two groups are statistically similar. See Figure 6.4 for how the two hypotheses are depicted using the Greek letters common within statistical notations. For an action research study, the substantive hypothesis (Kerlinger & Lee, 2000), which makes predictions about specific variables, should be sufficient for most purposes. Rather than Greek notation (see Figure 6.4), the substantive hypothesis flows directly from the rational or research purpose. For example, within our previous example, we know one class is receiving the intervention and the other is not, and thus the substantive hypothesis would be written to reflect the predicted outcome, for example, "Participation in the intervention will affect students' test scores."

FIGURE 6.4 Common Greek Notations Used Within Statistical Analyses

It's All Greek to Me

Eventually during your journey as a researcher, you're going to encounter the variety of symbols associated with statistics. This extends from the hypothesis through the results. While we don't expect you to be experts after reading this text, we felt it would be helpful to show you a few of the more common symbols that you may encounter as you read various literature and research and inform you what each is associated with.

Hypothesis

We mentioned the development and use of a hypothesis within our description of inferential statistics. While this seems simple enough, some literature, especially dissertations, incorporates the Greek letters typically associated with statistics. When this is the case, a hypothesis might look something like: $H_0: \mu_1 = \mu_2$, with H representing the hypothesis and μ symbolizing the population mean. This is the null hypothesis. Essentially, this demonstrates that the two means are hypothesized to be equal. The alternative hypothesis, on the other hand, where the scores are actually different, looks like this: $H_1: \mu_1 \neq \mu_2$. Generally speaking, researchers are hoping to prove that the null hypothesis is not true, as equal means would indicate that an intervention was not successful.

Sample versus Population

You'll note below that the symbols are differentiated by whether they represent the sample or population. The population represents all individuals of the demographic group the study is targeting, while the sample is a subset intended to represent the population and includes the participants of the study. The goal of various quantitative methodologies is to examine the sample and generalize to the population.

Symbol	Represents
n	Sample
Y	Variable
$\bar{Y}$	Sample mean
s	Sample standard deviation
μ	Population mean
σ	Population standard deviation
α	Significance level

While noting that action research is often exploratory as opposed to judging whether a difference arose from chance, teachers should still be familiar with inferential statistics to ensure they can accurately examine and interpret information from published studies that might be encountered while reviewing literature (Tomal, 2010). Inferential statistics can be useful within action research when the teacher seeks to compare students' scores on an instrument or assessment or to establish some type of relationship between variables. Common inferential statistics include the t-test, analysis of variance, correlation, and chi-square test. It is important to note that these three forms of analysis can only occur when the variables being investigated are continuous, or can be measured along a number line or interval. What follows is a very basic description of the previously mentioned tests that can be performed in a study that seeks to integrate inferential statistics. There are a number of resources or statistics texts available should you choose to use a different approach or encounter a statistical procedure that you are unfamiliar with. We recommend Creswell (2012) or Szafran (2012) as sources for your examination.

The most frequently applied form of inferential statistics of the teachers we have worked with has been the **t-test**, which compares the means of two groups or scores. There are actually several forms of t-test that are applicable for action research. One, an independent measures t-test, compares the means of two groups using a common measure. It would be most applicable in a situation similar to our previous example where one class was receiving an intervention while another class was not and, using scores from the same instrument, the means of the two groups were compared after the intervention to see if there was a difference. The paired t-test, on the other hand, is most often used to compare the same group under different conditions (e.g., pre-intervention and post-intervention) (Tomal, 2010). This comparison would be most relevant if you wanted to administer a pre-test to a group of students, implement some instructional intervention, then conduct a post-test assessment. The substantive hypothesis for a study using this form of analysis might be: differentiated instruction will affect students' knowledge of Greek roots in vocabulary words. The t-test would enable you to determine if there was a statistically significant growth (improvement) when the means of the pre- and post-assessments were compared.

An **analysis of variance** (ANOVA) is similar to the t-test; however, the difference is that the comparison is run on the means of three or more groups (Mertler, 2012; Mills, 2011). Comparisons can be conducted between groups to note whether differences are present, which is referred to as a one-way ANOVA. A repeated measures ANOVA, on the other hand, compares the scores/performance of a single group at several points in time to determine whether statistically significant changes have occurred. In each case, the ANOVA does not indicate where the difference lies; additional tests must be performed to determine this information. These tests, referred to as post-hoc analyses (meaning they were conducted after the ANOVA) are simply t-tests comparing differences between each group or administration. When using most programs for statistical analysis, you can set up the ANOVA in such a way to ensure the post-hoc tests are run automatically, helping you identify where the specific differences occurred.

The final analysis that we will discuss determines the relationship between two variables. Referred to as **measures of association**, examining the relationship between variables provides information regarding how variables are linked (Szafran, 2012). For example, we might want to examine if the amount of studying per night and grade point average are connected. Perhaps our hypothesis is that when students increase the amount of studying each night, their grade point average increases. I think most of us would answer affirmatively, but it's important to note that when using measures of association, we can't say that the increase in studying caused the increase in the grade point average. We can only say that there is a relationship—when the number of minutes per night devoted to studying increased, so did the grade point average. Without additional tests that control for various factors, we can only describe the relationship that exists. This is referred to as a correlation, which is the most commonly used statistical analysis to document this relationship. The correlation coefficient, which results from the afore-mentioned test, shows the strength of the relationship through a value between -1.0 and 1.0. The closer to either extreme, the greater the correlation, while a correlation coefficient close to zero means there is little or no relationship. In the case of our previous example, if both figures increased, the value would be positive. On the other hand, if the value of one variable increased while the other decreased, the correlation coefficient would be a negative number, which indicates an inverse relationship. There are additional measures that can be computed to demonstrate relationships between variables, but our experiences have shown that computation of a correlation coefficient, also referred to as the Pearson product-moment correlation coefficient, is the most effective and easiest to use. The inherent advantage within the use of inferential statistics is the ability to analyze the data quickly and efficiently using statistical procedures. These procedures do not require advanced statistical software, and, in most cases, researchers can use Microsoft's Excel or similar software to complete the various statistical tests. On the other hand, a disadvantage of using statistics in action research is the specialized knowledge that is sometimes required to both plan for and conduct the comparisons necessary to demonstrate the impact of the intervention. Furthermore, inferential statistics are particularly sensitive to small sample sizes, which could be the case in many action research studies, as it becomes more difficult to obtain statistical significance. That written, we always encourage our students to step out of their comfort zone if inferential statistics are applicable in helping them answer their question and if the various requirements of the proposed statistical test are met. Don't shy away from statistics—take advantage of them to help you make informed, data-based decisions that could be used to help you and others improve student achievement.

MIXED METHODS APPROACHES TO DATA ANALYSIS

As mentioned in Chapters 4 and 5, mixed methods approaches allow researchers to integrate quantitative and qualitative data analysis strategies to generate conclusions (Creswell & Plano Clark, 2011; Teddlie & Tashakkori, 2009). Descriptions of the approaches utilize words like *merging* and *connecting* to describe the related analyses (Creswell & Plano Clark, 2011). Through the combination of techniques, the result is often more stable conclusions, as there is the capacity to develop depth as well as breadth through analysis.

Teddlie and Tashakkori (2009) note one advantage of mixed methods is the opportunity to utilize both inductive and deductive reasoning simultaneously. There is a greater potential for triangulation (confirmation) from the various sources, as mixed methods approaches allow crosschecking and verification of data to confirm or support findings. Hinchey (2008) reinforces this point in stating, **triangulation** "is simply a sophisticated way of naming the commonsense principle that the more evidence there is to support a finding, the more credible the finding" (p. 96). Accordingly, the procedure can help teachers develop a new appreciation for using data within their decision-making processes.

The actual procedure used to analyze the data may differ. For example, it may be necessary to perform separate analysis based on the method, and then attempt to combine the findings based on the comparison of what each yielded individually. Ivankova (2015) described first conducting the quantitative analysis, then using results from this initial analysis to set direction for qualitative analysis as an effective way to conduct the mixed methods analysis. In this way, the qualitative results can expand upon or explain the findings associated with the quantitative analysis. Regardless of the order of analysis, however, the opportunity to collect and analyze various forms of data is both helpful and challenging. It is helpful in that there is increased efficiency because the various forms of data can be collected simultaneously (Creswell & Plano Clark, 2011). Yet, this is also challenging if the researcher is attempting to individually collect all data while maintaining attention to planning and instruction. In addition, this methodological approach can cause difficulties for the interpretation of results if the results are not complementary, which also diminishes or eliminates the potential for triangulation.

We close this section on the various forms of data analysis that can be used within action research studies with attention toward the identification of criteria that you will use to judge the success of your action research. We feel it's important to note that *success* is a relative term. While the only data to support the following statement is our own experiences, these experiences have shown us that teachers are often focused on external metrics, like having the "right" answer or conducting a study where the change is clearly significant and impactful. However, within action research, sometimes change occurs incrementally, and we advocate that teachers reflect on the practical significance (as opposed to statistical significance if quantitative methods are being used). In that regard, you are the sole determinant of whether you were successful. I (Mike) conducted a study that resulted in the students answering, on average, two more questions correctly on an exam after the intervention. The result was not statistically significant, but improvement was demonstrated, and I cannot ascertain how that improvement might have grown over the course of a year if the students continued to use the strategies they were taught correctly. We recommend stepping back for a moment and reflecting on what the analysis reveals. There is certainly growth as a teacher in doing so. If the results were not what were anticipated, that is okay. In later chapters we'll discuss how to develop an action plan to help you think about future action research studies and how you can maximize the knowledge gained through each iteration of the action research cycle.

TAKING ACTION: SELECTING THE METHOD OF DATA ANALYSIS

Hopefully you have now begun to reflect upon the data analysis procedures that have been outlined within the chapter. As part of your ongoing construction of your research plan, it will be necessary to finalize the collection methods and identify the relevant forms of analysis associated with the data you are collecting. We've provided information on some of the more common techniques and noted references that can be examined should you require additional resources for more in-depth analysis. Hubbard and Miller (2003) propose that statements detailing the processes to be used for the data analysis should begin with "I will" statements. For example,

- I will analyze my teaching notes to identify significant patterns or events that may indicate the influence of social interactions on overall growth.

- I will analyze the writing in the students' math journals for patterns among the techniques or problem-solving approaches used to solve conceptually similar problems.

- I will use a paired samples t-test to determine if there was significant growth from pre-test and post-test scores.

We are not as concerned with the format for the statement, but we believe that it is helpful to articulate all facets of the analysis process to ensure you can complete the relevant activities within the proposed timeline for your research. Our final consideration within the application of the analysis is the methods that will be used to convey the findings of your research. Dependent upon your selected method, potential sources include matrices, charts, graphs, figures, and presentation software (e.g., PowerPoint slides). The format is generally dictated by the source. For example, you are less likely to display qualitative data as a graph, but this is not out of the realm of possibility, as you could show the number of instances of critical thinking that occurred, as measured through observation, as the study progressed. As with organization, presentation of the results of the analysis is based upon your preferences and overall knowledge of the various tools and methods at your disposal.

USING FORMATIVE DATA

One thing that we ask the teachers we work with to do is keep a journal or log as they engage in the action research process. In the journal, we ask them to record their progress and note significant events that occur during implementation of the action research plan. This record of progress identifies the strategies and solutions that were implemented and documents the progress over time. Some of the teachers use the journal to compile a file that includes the actual materials used with students during the implementation stage. We feel the journal keeps them focused on examining progress throughout the study as opposed to simply thinking about the data prior to implementation and then again at completion. Just like we view formative data as an important component within the learning process, we feel that our own reflections represent a form of formative data that can inform minor changes to the processes used within the action research. For example, suppose you log your thoughts and record the amount of time you are engaging in observations during the school day. Looking at the journal, you determine that you are spending too much time in this process, causing your teaching to suffer. As a result, you may need to consider how to modify this process to ensure you have the ongoing data necessary to help you make adaptations as well as engage in the summative analysis that concludes one cycle of the action research loop and begins the consideration of the next.

DEVELOPING A PLAN OR A PRODUCT: COMPLETING THE RESEARCH PLAN PROPOSAL FORM AND TIMELINE

Over the past three chapters, we have described various pieces of information pertinent to data collection and analysis. In Chapter 4 you constructed a preliminary research plan, and in Chapter 5 the details that described the specific plan for data collection were added. However, to date, the research plan has not addressed the method of data analysis that will be used within your research. While acknowledging that collection and analysis are inherently linked, we felt it was better to introduce them separately to allow you to think carefully about the overall process for your study. As a result, we recommend that you take a moment to revisit the plan and reflect upon whether the proposed collection methods remain applicable for your study. Will the methods encompass the data necessary to reach a conclusion relative to your question?

If you answered affirmatively, it's time to finalize your data analysis and enter it into the research plan. Think about the data you plan to collect—is it quantitative, qualitative, or both? If it is quantitative, you will need to consider whether the data is nominal, ordinal, ratio, or interval, and determine the most applicable statistics or statistical procedure to conduct. Additionally, think about the graphic displays that could be used to help you form conclusions and show information necessary to answer your research question. What additional resources might be necessary (see Tech Connections) to conduct the analysis? If you are collecting both qualitative and quantitative data, you will need to focus on how you will combine the analysis of the two forms of data to develop your results.

Once you have finalized your method of analysis, revisit the research plan and record this information. In addition, describe how you will display the data and findings from your analysis. For example, you may use a histogram to depict students' scores from the test that was administered within your study, or you may use a pie chart to represent the demographics present in your classroom. In terms of the results, think about whether figures or tables are necessary to highlight various aspects of your analysis, such as might be the case if you used an analysis of variance. Next, it's time to update the timeline. As a reminder, quantitative analysis is less time-consuming than qualitative, but it is crucial that you give yourself enough time to conduct the necessary analysis to answer your question. We generally recommend allowing two to three weeks for qualitative or mixed methods analysis; however, this is dependent upon the number of participants and the amount of data that was collected. There is no simple rule of thumb, but it is better to overestimate than underestimate.

EVALUATING AGAINST THE STANDARDS: ARE YOU READY TO MOVE ON?

Note that we have repeated many of the questions that were included in Chapter 4. Again, we think it is important to revisit what you originally presented and then extend it to include the forms of data analysis that will be used in the study. Once the research plan and timeline are established, you are ready to implement your study.

CHECKLIST: RESEARCH PLAN AND TIMELINE

Have you:

_____1. Reviewed and reflected upon the research method for your action research study?

_____2. Reviewed the research question to ensure it can be answered using the proposed methodology?

_____3. Detailed the specific procedures that will be used for data collection?

_____4. Developed a plan to organize the data as it is collected?

_____5. Determined the form of analysis that will be used to analyze the data once it is collected?

_____6. Considered how you will store the data for the duration of your study?

_____7. Reviewed your timeline to ensure the activities can be completed within the proposed timeframe?

_____8. Considered how you will present the findings of the analysis at the conclusion of the study?

SUMMARY

In this chapter, you were introduced to a variety of information that will help you determine the most effective process for analyzing the data collected as part of your action research study. Remember, *validity* means an instrument or strategy measures what it is supposed to, while *reliability* indicates consistency of measurement when using the same instruments or methods in similar situations (Mertler, 2012). Both concepts are important within the research process, regardless of whether qualitative or quantitative methods are used. Generalizability, on the other hand, is the potential to extend the findings from a sample to the population. It is an inherent goal associated with inferential statistics. In qualitative data analysis, researchers engage in concurrent collection and analysis, forming interpretations and judgments as the process proceeds. This means there is some subjectivity within the analysis, and the researcher must be cognizant of staying neutral during the analysis to ensure the conclusions accurately reflect the data. Quantitative data analysis, on the other hand, involves using descriptive or inferential statistics to test hypotheses using primarily numerical data. Researchers associate a greater degree of objectivity with quantitative techniques. Finally, the analysis in mixed methods approaches involves a combination of the two forms. After finalizing your analysis procedures, your preparation is complete and it is time to implement your study!

Key Terms

Analysis of variance, p. 141

Coding, p. 133

Deductive analysis, p. 138

Descriptive statistics, p. 135

Generalizability, p. 130

Inductive analysis, p. 132

Inferential statistics, p. 138

Mean, p. 135

Measures of association, p. 141

Measures of central tendency, p. 135

Measures of variability, p. 136

Median, p. 135

Mode, p. 135

Range, p. 136

Standard deviation, p. 136

T-test, p. 141

Triangulation, p. 142 (see also Chapter 4)

Variance, p. 136

Case in Point:
Final Research Plan and Timeline

One Elementary Teacher's Journey: Research Log Entry #3

I've thought more about the process I want to use to answer my research question. As I wrote in my last entry, I really wanted to collect student journals, but I didn't think that I would have the time to really read and respond to the journal entries. I decided that I would focus on collecting data using the oral reading fluency portion of DIBELS since we already use it the school. The more I thought about this, the more I had this feeling that I wouldn't really have all the information I wanted to really determine if the intervention was a success. As I looked back across the ways I could collect data, I was struck by the fact that I already conference with my students weekly as part of our balanced literacy block and it really wouldn't be a stretch to make notes in the conferences as I was watching the groups practice for the performances each Friday. As a result, I decided that I would incorporate these notes into my analysis to see if they would help me get a better sense of how the students were responding to using Readers' Theater over the course of four weeks. This means that I will have more data to look over (using just the analysis of variance would have been really easy!), but in the end, I think it will help me figure out if I am going to continue to use this method.

In terms of my analysis, after reviewing the statistics text my professor gave me, I have decided that I will use a repeated measures analysis of variance since there will be three data points to compare. Luckily, I have a great professor who is also willing to help me analyze the results if there are differences to see where they might come from. For my qualitative analysis (see Figure 6.5), since I am going to use sticky notes to collect my records, I will first organize them by student and read through all the notes to determine if there is any pattern that stands out regarding both positives and challenges with respect to fluency (but I'll also probably look to see if anything stands out about the children's ability to work with each other). After I have done this once or twice, I'll start to really look for any patterns that emerge across students from the notes and move the notes accordingly to start to develop my themes. I am estimating that if I work on this pretty steadily, I can have it done within two weeks (see Figure 6.6), but I have given myself a little extra time in case things get busy at school. Once I figure out if there are qualitative themes, I'll go back to the results of the ANOVA and combine all of the data.

FIGURE 6.5   One Elementary Teacher's Final Research Plan

Problem statement	Several second-grade students in my class struggle with fluency (rate and accuracy) and are below grade-level standards as assessed three times a year using DIBELS. I want to see these struggling students reading on grade level, according to DIBELS, by the end of the year.
Goals for research	The goals I am considering for my action research study are focused on helping my students who are currently reading below grade level to become more fluent readers so that they can read words accurately, at an appropriate rate, and with expression.
Research question	What is the effect of Readers' Theater on second-grade students' reading fluency?
Context	The context for this research is a school located in a suburban area within the city limits of a large metropolitan city. The overall socioeconomic status of the school is rated as low to middle class, with 58% of the enrolled students receiving free or reduced-price lunch. The school is primarily African American (59%), Hispanic American (20%), Caucasian (12%), multiracial (5%), Asian American (3%), and American Indian (1%). Both genders (male, 51%; female, 49%) are fairly equal in representation of students.
Participants	Twenty-four second-grade students; 12 participants are African American, eight are Hispanic American, three are Caucasian, and one participant is multiracial; 14 boys and 10 girls; five demonstrate oral reading fluency scores below grade level.
Data to be collected	Dynamic Indicators of Basic Early Literacy Skills (DIBELS) Score (oral reading fluency [ORF])
Frequency/duration of data collection	DIBELS: pre-test, midpoint assessment (week 3), post-test (week 5) Anecdotal records
Location of data collection	My classroom
Who will collect data?	Teacher
Data analysis procedure	I will use a repeated measures analysis of variance to analyze the change in fluency over time. I will analyze weekly anecdotal records for each student and across students by examining the data for patterns and grouping this information together to note if trends are revealed in the data.
Display of data/ findings	Display ORF scores for each individual student using a line graph that shows pre-, midpoint, and post-test data; create a visual (PowerPoint) that depicts results of ANOVA as well as qualitative themes that emerged (with representative quotes where applicable)

FIGURE 6.6   One Elementary Teacher's Final Action Research Timeline and Activities

Informed Consent

Two weeks prior to pre-test	Develop research plan/informed consent letter
One week prior to pre-test	Informed consent letter sent home and returned

Data Collection

Day 1	Complete DIBELS oral reading fluency assessment for eight students (pre-test)
Week 1	Implement Readers' Theater—week 1; collect daily anecdotal records
Week 2	Implement Readers' Theater—week 2; collect daily anecdotal records
Week 3, Day 1	Complete DIBELS oral reading fluency assessment for eight students (midway)
Week 3	Implement Readers' Theater—week 3; collect daily anecdotal records
Week 4	Implement Readers' Theater—week 4; collect daily anecdotal records
Week 5	Complete DIBELS oral reading fluency assessment for eight students (post-test)

Data Analysis (Incorporate Anecdotal Records)

Completed one week after post-test	Organize data for analysis; conduct preliminary review of data
Completed three weeks after post-test	Develop initial categories for anecdotal records
Completed four weeks after post-test	Combine quantitative and qualitative results; finalize analysis

One Secondary Teacher's Journey: Research Log Entry #3

I am still feeling committed to my initial thinking about the research design for my action research study (see Figure 6.7). I believe the best design will be a pre-test and post-test, using the same group. There will be no control group used in this study. The raw data collection will come from two major assessment methods. The first is a weekly, multiple-choice format summative assessment consisting of 20 questions used to assess learning during the week. The multiple-choice test was given every Friday for eight consecutive weeks during the direct instruction unit and will be used to set a baseline to compare to. The second eight weeks I plan to continue to give a multiple-choice test each week to document student learning

during the intervention of using the open investigation workshop format strategies. In order to analyze this data, I will collect, compile, graph, and analyze the students' raw scores on the tests. I think I will first create a data table of average test scores each week, and then create a line graph to see the trends in the scores as a whole class across both the baseline data and the intervention data. I am now considering that I might also like to examine the trends in the scores across groups of students within the class (a low, medium, and high group based on Lexile reading level). This would provide me with the opportunity to have another level of analysis. I could calculate the average gain per reading score (low, medium, or high). This would allow me to see how the format is affecting the learning as a whole class and also individual groups of students. To do this, the pre-test and post-test gains will be charted so students with different reading scores can have overall gains compared. I am not completely sure how to analyze my observational field notes that I will collect, but I believe one way this data will be useful is that it might help me explain any unusual trends that occur in the data or pinpoint what may have been happening at any one week that might influence the test scores. Therefore, I plan to keep this data source and use it as it helps me to understand what the data is conveying.

The second major source of data I plan to use is an anonymous Likert-scale questionnaire with two additional open-ended questions to assess student attitude toward the class. I will be collecting an attitude questionnaire at the end of the direct instruction unit and at the end of the open investigation workshop instructional unit. The Likert-scale data will be averaged for each item and for an overall score. The scores across the two formats will be compared and any trends noted. The Likert-scale survey will be on a 5.0-point scale. I should be able to present whether my students' attitudes improved, stayed the same, or declined. I will then need to read through the open-ended questions for each format several times and identify themes in the responses. Once I identify themes I will go back to the raw data and record how many times those themes were expressed. I will then rank the themes by order of incidence to allow the most prominent ideas to be identified and presented. I am pretty excited about my research plan thus far, and I am looking forward to getting started on the timeline presented in Figure 6.8.

FIGURE 6.7 One Secondary Teacher's Final Research Plan

Problem statement	In a lower-level ability section of ninth-grade science, students struggle with science content and a motivation to learn. I want to see how an open investigation workshop approach impacts these students' learning and engagement during the second quarter of instruction.
Goals for research	My goal for this action research study is to implement the open investigation approach with my science class of below-level readers/writers to improve their academic achievement and motivation for learning.
Research question	What is the effect of an open investigation workshop approach on a ninth-grade science class with students who are lower-level readers/writers?
Context	The context of this study is a secondary school located in a suburban area near a large metropolitan city. The student body consists of 908 students. The school is classified as medium socioeconomic status, with 48% of students being eligible for free or reduced-price lunch. While the school is not Title I, it does qualify to receive state funds proportionate to the free and reduced-price lunch percentage. The student population consists mainly of Caucasian (79%), African American (17%), Asian American (2%), American Indian/Pacific Islander (1%), and other (1%).
Participants	This study utilizes one of three sections of science classes that I teach. As a result of ability grouping based on language arts skill levels, this particular group of students' struggles to read and are classified as below grade-level readers. The class consists of 28 students: eight have 504 plans, two have IEPs, 16 are male, and 12 are female. The majority of the class is Caucasian (20), with African American (5), and Hispanic (2). The majority of the students (19) have low informational text reading scores, while the remaining nine have scores in the low-medium range.
Data to be collected	A multiple-choice test consisting of 20 questions used to assess learning each week
	An anonymous Likert-scale attitude questionnaire with two additional open-ended questions to assess student attitude toward the class
	Observation field notes

(Continued)

FIGURE 6.7 (Continued)

Frequency/duration of data collection	The multiple-choice test will be given every Friday for eight consecutive weeks during the direct instruction unit and will be used to set a baseline of data. The second eight weeks (primary investigation) I plan to continue to give a multiple-choice test each week to document student learning during the intervention of using the open investigation workshop format strategies. The questionnaire will be collected at the end of the direct instruction unit (week 1 of study; see timeline) and at the end of the open investigation workshop instructional unit. Observation field notes—ongoing
Location of data collection	My classroom
Who will collect data	Teacher
Data analysis procedure	I will compile student raw scores and utilize descriptive statistics (mean scores) to analyze the multiple-choice tests and the attitude questionnaire. The test data will be examined for both whole group and within group varying abilities to determine difference between pre- and post-mean scores. The Likert-scale data will be averaged for each item and for an overall score. The scores across the two formats will be compared and any trends noted. I will analyze weekly researcher field notes and open-ended questions from the attitude questionnaire by examining the data for patterns and grouping this information together to note if trends are revealed in the data.
Display of data/ findings	A table of mean test scores each week, and a line graph to show the trends in the whole class/varying ability group scores across both the baseline data and the intervention data. A pre- and post-bar graph will be used to display the Likert-scale data from the attitude questionnaire. The qualitative data will be presented in a narrative format that presents the themes, and representative quotes from the raw data will provide a rich description of the themes identified.

FIGURE 6.8 One Secondary Teacher's Final Action Research Timeline and Activities

Informed Consent

Two weeks prior to intervention	Develop research plan/informed consent letter
One week prior to intervention	Informed consent letter sent home and returned

Data Collection

Final week of direct instruction approach learning unit	Compile weekly tests over the eight-week period; distribute and collect student attitude questionnaire
Week 1	Implement open investigation approach—week 1 test collection
Week 2	Implement open investigation approach—week 2 test collection and researcher field notes written and compiled
Week 3	Implement open investigation approach—week 3 test collection and researcher field notes written and compiled
Week 4	Implement open investigation approach—week 4 test collection and researcher field notes written and compiled
Week 5	Implement open investigation approach—week 5 test collection and researcher field notes written and compiled
Week 6	Implement open investigation approach—week 6 test collection and Researcher field notes written and compiled

Week 7	Implement open investigation approach—week 7 test collection and researcher field notes written and compiled
Week 8	Implement open investigation approach—week 8 test collection, researcher field notes written and compiled, and collect student attitude questionnaire

Data Analysis

Completed one week after post-test	Organize data for analysis; conduct preliminary review of data; create tables and graphs; examine observational field notes for potential explanations for trends in data
Completed two weeks after post-test	Develop initial themes for open-ended questions and rank themes in order of prominence
Completed three weeks after post-test	Combine quantitative and qualitative results; finalize analysis

Activities and Additional Resources

1. Conduct a search for a research article in your local library or online. Read the article and locate the Methodology or Procedures section. Identify whether it uses qualitative or quantitative methods, and write a short paragraph summarizing the methods and your rationale for your answer.

2. A colleague has recently concluded a series of interviews with parents to determine their perceptions about a series of computer-based activities students completed out of school. She recorded each interview, but she is not sure how to compile or analyze all the information and comes to you for advice. In your own words, describe the steps and processes necessary to complete the data analysis.

3. You are a member of a team of biology teachers at your high school. You choose to conduct an action research study that examines the impact of using a science journal on students' understanding of the relationships between the structures and functions of cells. Two classes will use the journals, and two classes will not. Which form of analysis would be best suited for examining this data? Suppose the research was modified so that approximately one-third of the students would write in the journals and participate in experiments, one-third would only write in the journals, and the remaining third of students would not write in journals or participate in experiments. Would the same form of analysis be applicable? If not, describe why this is the case and what form of analysis would now be necessary.

Print Resources

Field, A. (2013). *Discovering statistics using IBM SPSS Statistics*. Thousand Oaks, CA: Sage.

Flick, U. (2014). *An introduction to qualitative research* (5th ed.). Thousand Oaks, CA: Sage.

Gay, L. R., Mills, G. E., & Airasian, P. (2006). *Educational research: Competencies for analysis and applications* (8th ed.). Upper Saddle River, NJ: Merrill Prentice Hall.

Teddlie, C., & Tashakkori, A. (2009). *Foundations of mixed methods research: Integrating quantitative and qualitative approaches in the social and behavioral sciences*. Thousand Oaks, CA: Sage.

Student Study Site

edge.sagepub.com/putman

- Take the practice quiz.
- Review key terms with eFlashcards.
- Explore topics with video and multimedia.

References

Boeije, H. R. (2009). *Analysis in qualitative research*. Thousand Oaks, CA: Sage.

Craig, D. V. (2009). *Action research essentials*. San Francisco, CA: Jossey-Bass.

Creswell, J. W. (2012). *Educational research: Planning, conducting, and evaluating quantitative and qualitative research* (4th ed.). Upper Saddle River, NJ: Merrill Prentice Hall.

Creswell, J. W. (2014). *Research design: Qualitative, quantitative, and mixed methods approaches* (4th ed.). Thousand Oaks, CA: Sage.

Creswell, J. W., & Plano Clark, V. (2011). *Designing and conducting mixed methods research* (2nd ed.). Thousand Oaks, CA: Sage.

Guest, G., MacQueen, K. M., & Namey, E. E. (2012). *Applied thematic analysis*. Thousand Oaks, CA: Sage.

Henning, J. E., Stone, J. M., & Kelly, J. L. (2009). *Using action research to improve instruction: An interactive guide for teachers*. New York, NY: Routledge.

Herr, K., & Anderson, G. L. (2005). *The action research dissertation: A guide for students and faculty*. Thousand Oaks, CA: Sage.

Hinchey, P. H. (2008). *Action research: Primer*. New York, NY: Peter Lang.

Hubbard, R. S., & Miller, B. M. (2003). *The art of classroom inquiry: A handbook for teacher-researchers*. Portsmouth, NH: Heinemann.

Ivankova, N. V. (2015). *Mixed methods applications in action research: From methods to community action*. Thousand Oaks, CA: Sage.

Kerlinger, F. N., & Lee, H. B. (2000). *Foundations of behavioral research* (4th ed.). Fort Worth, TX: Harcourt College Publishers.

Maxwell, J. A. (1992). Understanding and validity in qualitative research. *Harvard Educational Review, 62,* 279–300.

Mertler, C. A. (2012). *Action research: Improving schools and empowering educators*. Thousand Oaks, CA: Sage.

Mills, G. E. (2011). *Action research: A guide for the teacher researcher* (4th ed.). Boston, MA: Pearson.

Strauss, A., & Corbin, J. (1998). *Basics of qualitative research: Techniques and procedures for developing grounded theory* (2nd ed.). Thousand Oaks, CA: Sage.

Szafran, R. (2012). *Answering questions with statistics*. Thousand Oaks, CA: Sage.

Tanner, D. (2012). *Using statistics to make educational decisions*. Thousand Oaks, CA: Sage.

Teddlie, C., & Tashakkori, A. (2009). *Foundations of mixed methods research: Integrating quantitative and qualitative approaches in the social and behavioral sciences*. Thousand Oaks, CA: Sage.

Tomal, D. R. (2010). *Action research for educators* (2nd ed.). Lanham, MD: Rowman & Littlefield.

PHASE IV

Adaptation

CHAPTER 7

Reflecting on Results and Planning for Action

GUIDING QUESTIONS

After reading this chapter, you should be able to answer the following questions:

- What are the five typical outcomes of action research?

- Why is reflection important within the action research plan?

- What is the function of a plan for action?

- How do I create a plan for action?

- What are potential and viable new questions to pursue in subsequent cycles of the action research?

- How do I formulate a discussion that presents my conclusions, implications for practice, and plans for action?

CHAPTER AIMS AND GOALS

At this stage of the action research process, you have put together an action research plan and implemented the plan by gathering and analyzing data, and now the question arises, "What do I do next?" The time has come for you to reflect on your results, draw conclusions and implications for practice, and finally, develop action steps based on what you have learned from your study. It is the time to put the "action" into action research. As you proceed through this chapter, you will develop an understanding of

- the five typical outcomes of action research;

- the importance of professional reflection as you seek meaning in your data;

- how to extend your data analysis by making connections to personal practice, the professional literature, and broader educational issues or priorities;

- the purpose and function of planning for action; and

- how to develop an organized and systematic plan for action.

As you develop a plan for action, you will also have the opportunity to generate new questions that have emerged from your study and target appropriate lines of inquiry for future cycles of the action research. This chapter will guide you to think deeply about what you have learned, make relevant connections to personal and broader implications for practice, determine appropriate action steps that are systematically developed, and plan for future study. This is an exciting time in the action research process because it is time when all of your planning and effort to study your practice will result in intentional and purposeful change to your practice. The goal of action research—to improve instructional practice—is achieved when you implement action steps based on new understandings and insights from your systematic study. This chapter will focus on assisting you in planning for change and improvement to your practice.

SETTING THE CONTEXT: REFLECTING ON THE RESULTS OF ACTION RESEARCH

When you began the action research process you identified a "problem of practice" that interested or challenged you in some way within your classroom, school, or educational setting. Most likely the motivation to engage in this inquiry was centered on the hope that you would resolve the "problem of practice" or at least arrive at a better understanding of the problem to allow for eventual resolution or situational improvement. As you begin to reflect on your results, it is important to consider the typical outcomes of action research conducted by teachers. In most situations, the intended outcome of engaging in action research is for the teacher to do something different in the future based on what was learned. However, there are cases where teachers may discover from their results that what is occurring is working well and there is no need for change (Johnson, 2008). Therefore, the plan for action may be to do nothing. Although this is a possibility, it is only one potential outcome. Johnson (2008) outlined the following five typical outcomes of action research studies:

1. A greater understanding of the situation or child under investigation or of students in general is developed.

2. A new problem is discovered.

3. A plan, a program, or an instructional method is found to be effective.

4. A plan, a program, or an instructional method is found to need modification.

5. A plan, a program, or an instructional method is found to be ineffective. (pp. 136–137)

"NOTE"-ABLE THOUGHTS

As you examine your data analysis, which of Johnson's (2008) typical outcomes best aligns with your results? Record in your researcher's log a statement that asserts what your results show in terms of one of the outcomes above, and provide several supportive, data-based statements to justify the asserted outcome.

IMPORTANCE OF REFLECTION

Before we go further in thinking about the results of the action research, let's discuss the reflective processes you have engaged in and will continue to develop as you move deeper into the examination of your study outcomes. A commitment to ongoing reflection throughout the action research process is necessary for practitioners who hope to achieve improvement of practice and professional growth (Sagor, 2000). The role of a reflective practitioner is one that teachers engaged in action research must value and understand. In the mid-1980s, Donald Schön clarified what is involved in reflective thinking by observing how practitioners think in action. Schön (1984) developed the terms **reflection on action** and **reflection in action** to describe two forms of reflective thinking in his "epistemology of practice" model. According to Schön, reflection in action involves the constant interaction of thinking and doing, resulting in the modification of ongoing practice in such a way that learning occurs. Much of this thinking may remain unconscious and unspoken; however, when unanticipated problem situations arise, reflection in action may be detected as the reflective practitioner engages in reframing the problem and improvising on the spot so that the experience will be perceived differently. In contrast, reflection on action is viewed as teachers' thoughtful consideration and retrospective analysis of their actions to gain understanding from experience. It is the process of deliberate and systematic thinking back over the experience once it is complete. Reflection on action is a conscious effort that often results in the practitioner being able to articulate their learning and communicate it with others (Leitch & Day, 2000). Together, reflection on action and reflection in action constitute the professional attributes of the reflective practitioner.

As you work through the various stages of the action research process, you will find that you will use both of these reflective processes, moving from one to the other. For example, as you were collecting data you were constantly evaluating whether the data you gathered would be useful, whether the data collection strategies you were using were effective, whether adjustments or clarifications were needed to instruments and protocols, and so on. This is reflection in action, and it allows for flexibility and responsiveness to changing conditions and unanticipated situations. However, as you proceed in this chapter you will be primarily engaged in reflection on action as you retrospectively consider and analyze the action research plan, the results, and your personal and professional learning in order to formulate implications for practice and future action steps. Without sufficient time and focus dedicated to both of these forms of reflection, potential professional learning from the action research is diminished.

ACTION RESEARCH

CONSTRUCTING MEANING FROM RESULTS

Let's begin utilizing the reflection on action process by considering the personal and professional learning that has occurred. The first key question to reflect on is, "What did I learn?" You will want to consider this question in depth by thinking of what you learned about (a) yourself as a teacher; (b) curriculum; (c) instruction; (d) student learning and motivation; (e) the particular method, strategy, or program being studied; and (f) any other key concepts or factors relevant to your work. As you are reflecting on your learning, you may find that it is useful to organize your thoughts around categories such as these to promote deeper exploration of your learning outcomes. As you identify what you have learned, you will also want to connect the different aspects of your learning with potential **implications for practice**. These implications, which are influenced by the meanings you construct from your data, will assist you in generating ideas about how to teach in a particular way. The statements you make about how you might change your teaching practices, in light of your results, are the implications for future teaching. It is appropriate at this time to make note of any and all implications that might be drawn and to consider a variety of alternatives or possibilities within your thinking.

Once you have generated what you have learned and potential implications for your practice, you can evaluate your ideas against your personal and professional prior experience and by soliciting feedback on your ideas from "critical" friends or collaborative colleagues engaged in the study. During your reflection, it is sometimes common to raise more questions than answers as you explore your learning. Make note of these questions and share these as well with colleagues to assist you in gathering differing perspectives and insights on your ideas and questions. It is extremely valuable at this point to seek the advice of "critical" friends after spending time in reflection on your results. If you are conducting the action research within a collaborative team, it is often helpful to have all team members engage in individual reflection on their learning and then bring the ideas and questions to a collaborative sharing and reflection session. Following the opportunity to share and discuss your learning with others, you are able to reflect on another compelling question, "What did others see that I did not or could not, and how will I use that knowledge to continue to refine and improve my teaching?"

"NOTE"-ABLE THOUGHTS

In your researcher's log, create a double-sided journal entry and record and organize your reflections on what you learned with appropriate headings on one side (e.g., Self as Teacher, Curriculum, Student Motivation). On the other side, write related implications for practice and questions that you have generated. Once this is complete, you will be ready to begin informally sharing your reflections on your learning with others. Revise or extend these initial reflections following your discussion with others.

A second key question to reflect on is, "How does what I learned from the study connect with the current literature?" As you reflect on your own learning and the insights and perspectives you gain from critical "friends" and colleagues, it is essential to go back to your review of the literature from Chapter 3 to connect what you are learning to what is already known. The idea of situating your results in the existing theory or research will deepen your reflection and is a critical element of a systematic study. For example, if you find that the initial actions you took have results that are very similar to those of other researchers, then you know there is support for your analysis and that you are most likely on the right track. It allows you to borrow from the authority of others who have also studied the topic before you to strengthen the claims that you will make for the action that you took. However, if your results contradict prior research, then you will need to develop a provocative new question about why your study yielded such different results. This situation will provide you with something interesting to talk about with colleagues and with other researchers. Either way, what you learn from your specific action research study can become part of a larger conversation among educators and researchers (Rust & Clark, n.d.). By contextualizing your results in the literature, you will be able to draw more robust interpretations that link to broader issues and provide meaning to your work.

"NOTE"-ABLE THOUGHTS

How do your results support, contradict, or extend the theory and/or research you uncovered about your topic in Chapter 3? How can you make connections to the existing knowledge about the topic that will provide meaning and substance to your ability to discuss the results of your study with others? As part of your researcher's log, identify places in your reflections that support, contradict, or extend prior research or literature, and make note of these connections.

A third key question to reflect on is, "How successful was my action research plan in accomplishing my goals and objectives and in resolving my problem statement?" As you reflect on your results, it is important to review your original problem statement as well as the implementation plan, its goals, and objectives. The final stage of reflecting on your results should include reflection on your expectations, what you did well, what you might do differently next time, and how you could improve in using the action research process. You want to analyze more completely what was successful and what was not, if and how you accomplished your goals and objectives, and if and how you resolved your problem statement. You may find you strayed from your original goals and objectives, or even away from your problem statement as stated. Often, this occurs because you found successes or challenges in unexpected ways that have taken you on a different course. Be prepared to discuss any implementation variations, because you may learn you solved a problem you did not know you had and/or achieved something that was as good as, if not better than, what you originally conceived. When you review your implementation plan, make sure to analyze and evaluate any strategies you might eliminate, revise, or replace. You will want to consider any and all changes you could have made or did make to improve your study overall.

Sarah Kennedy, Third-Grade Teacher

After closely analyzing the data and the results of my action research study, I believe that the intervention of including journal writing in my third-grade math class was a success. The results support many of the studies I reviewed and presented in my literature review (Bangert-Drowns, Hurley, & Wilkinson, 2004; Baxter, Woodward, & Olson, 2005; Kostos & Shin, 2010). I believe that the increase in test scores from the pre-test to the post-test showed enough improvement that this intervention was well worth the time and effort. I felt that the students greatly benefited from the opportunity to express themselves through writing. My ability to closely monitor the students' progress helped the individual students to direct their own learning. However, using writing in math class was difficult at times. Not only was it very time-consuming to respond to each journal entry, but it also took up valuable class time. In spite of these challenges, I believe that the positive outcomes were worth the time invested. Through keeping my personal research logs, I could see growth for my individual students and growth among my class as a whole. Through this study, the writing prompts forced the students to pause and think more deeply. For my highest-achieving students, it forced them to really analyze why their particular methods of problem solving were successful and effectively communicate their reasoning. For my average students, the journals helped them to organize their thoughts for problem solving. The explanatory prompts required them to review their own learning and evaluate how well they knew the material. These students really benefited from dissecting the different parts of the problems and creating a problem-solving strategy. For my low-achieving students, the journals forced them to identify the important parts of the problem. I encouraged these students to draw a picture of the situation if they could. This often helped them to understand the main parts of the problem. These students (along with the rest of the class) really benefited from my responses to their entries so that they could see where their process was successful and unsuccessful.

There are two main changes that I would make to this action research project if I were to conduct it again. First, I would make the intervention longer. This particular intervention is a very slow process, and sometimes it was difficult to accurately judge the growth. With only grading the journal responses once a week for five weeks, I only had brief snapshots of a very complicated process. If a student simply did not understand the prompt for the day that I graded the journals, it did not necessarily mean that they were not showing overall growth in their problem-solving skills. An increase in the amount of time for the study implementation would provide a better opportunity to document change. The other main change that I would make would be to start this journal writing process at the beginning of the year. Most elementary math curriculums spend most of the first semester basically in review of the year before. Therefore, these concepts are easier for the students to grasp. At this time, I feel that we would have more time to devote to the direct instruction of journal writing and problem-solving skills. The students struggled with the new concept of writing in the journals as well as the mathematical concepts they were learning (fractions). Therefore, I believe that the students would have performed better on the journals if they had been introduced to them at the beginning of the year when the mathematical concepts are being reviewed.

As you are reflecting on the action research plan, you will also want to identify the limitations within your study. Did you experience contextual or time limitations that interfered with the implementation of the study as you ideally conceived it? Were there elements of the study design that inhibited or prevented you from being able to fully address your statement of the problem? Were there threats to either the reliability or validity of the study that you were unable to reduce or eliminate? Do you have philosophical or personal biases that may have influenced your interpretations of the results? Qualitative researchers seldom claim that their reports are totally unbiased; instead, they put forth a concerted effort to let the reader know what their perspectives and biases are and clearly present their research methods to allow the reader to evaluate for him or herself the potential usefulness of the results (Stainback & Stainback, 1988). As you discuss your results, you will want to clearly present the limitations of the study and how you attempted to mitigate those limitations or how you plan to do so in future studies. It is also important to make sure your claims are situated in your particular context and bound to your classroom, school, or educational setting. Be careful as you present your results to others not to over generalize or use language that establishes claims beyond the scope of your study. For example, making a statement like "Readers' Theater is an effective strategy for improving reading fluency" is a claim that overgeneralizes the results of an action research study. Rather, stating, "In my second-grade classroom, Readers' Theater improved the reading fluency of six of my below grade-level students" is a more specific and justifiable claim based on a classroom action research study.

■ ■ ■ VOICES FROM THE FIELD

Jeff Myers, 10th-Grade English

In my action research study, I examined my students' perceptions of the culturally responsive curriculum materials and resources I had incorporated into a unit of study. I was very enthusiastic about the connections and thoughtful reflections my students had made with the materials and resources presented to them. I shared my written reflections in my graduate class and with great confidence proclaimed that if students' cultural backgrounds were represented in the curriculum, there is a positive effect on students' perceptions of the learning experience and their motivation to engage in classroom activities. However, my professor was quick to challenge my claim and asked if my study design could support the statement. I realized that I had overstated my results. I will need to be careful when I am speaking about my study to make sure to keep my excitement in check and be clear that my results are only reflective of the small sample of students that I collected data from in my classroom.

Overall, the intended outcome of thoughtful and engaged reflection on action should be the ability to communicate about what is of importance and value in your study. You want to find meaning in your data analysis and clearly address the "So what?" question. What do I now know or understand about the problem of study? Why is this important? How will it impact my classroom practice? How does what I have learned connect to broader educational issues or problems? What will others find interesting or compelling about my results? How can I improve my use of the action research process in the future? These questions will push you to focus on what matters, which builds personal engagement and motivation for the time and effort required by the action research process. Reflecting on your results will allow you to extend your data analysis by making connections to personal practice, the professional literature and broader educational issues or priorities, and the effectiveness of the action research plan that you implemented.

"NOTE"-ABLE THOUGHTS

Spend time reviewing your written reflections and implications for practice as you have recorded them in your researcher's log. You will want to prioritize your reflections to identify the most important and valuable insights that you have gained from the project.

These ideas will be what you will want to share as you begin to prepare a discussion of the results. You want to be able to present the ideas that make the most compelling discussion of what you have learned and how it will impact your instructional beliefs and practices.

GENERATING NEW QUESTIONS FOR FUTURE STUDY

The final component of reflection on action is to think about if and how your findings can help you develop a new set of questions that merit exploration. One amazing thing about teacher action research is that every research project seems to bring up multiple other projects that are worthy of exploration. What questions came out of your research that could be addressed in a future action research project? You may have begun to think of these questions as you collected or analyzed the data, but now is the time to think in greater depth about what remaining areas of research could help fill the gaps or extend your current research project. By outlining these questions, discussing them with "critical" friends or collaborative partners, and reflecting on their value toward ongoing improvement of practice, it will push you to continue to engage in a cycle of inquiry that is characteristic of teacher action research.

Planning for action. After a period of reflection on action (involving both individual and collaborative thought, sharing, and deliberation) of what the data analysis revealed about the identified problem of practice, you will now begin planning for action. Taking informed action, or developing a **plan for action**, is the final step in the action research process. Taking informed action steps is not an unfamiliar task for teachers or other educational professionals. When educators write lesson plans or develop academic programs, they are engaged in an action planning process. However, what makes planning for action particularly satisfying for the teacher is that with each piece of data uncovered the educator gains greater confidence in the wisdom of the action steps that are planned. Although all teaching can be classified as trial and error, action researchers find that the research process liberates them from continuously repeating their past mistakes. In addition, with each improvement of practice, action researchers gain valid and reliable data to justify the changes they are implementing within their classrooms or educational settings (Sagor, 2000).

In order to create appropriate action steps, you will need to examine your results, the reflections you recorded on what was learned, and the implications you identified for your practice. As you consider what you now know or understand, you can begin generating potential action steps you wish to take as a result of your learning. As you identify potential action steps, you should evaluate the ideas based on your ability to present a rationale for the action based on evidence and data. You will also want to carefully consider any limitations, drawbacks, or unintended consequences that may result from implementing the potential action in your practice (Sagor, 2000). Again, it is important to share your ideas with "critical" friends or collaborative partners involved with the action research. Their perspectives and insights are often invaluable in developing thoughtful and appropriate action steps.

TECH CONNECTIONS

Throughout the previous sections, we have continually encouraged you to discuss, share, and engage in reflective dialogue with "critical" friends or collaborative action research partners to promote deeper reflection and thinking about your results and plans for action. We believe this promotes stronger and more thoughtful outcomes for your study. However, within the realities of professional duties and daily schedules, finding time to connect in person with peers to engage in face-to-face dialogue is often a challenge. To support ongoing opportunities for feedback and critical inquiry, you may want to consider establishing online collaborative forums. These types of forums allow document storage and collaborative editing and comments. We regularly use Google Docs to upload and share documents with those we wish to collaborate with and invite them to provide insights, feedback, and critical questions on the documents in the form of tracked changes or comments. All participants have access to the document and to the ideas, questions, and feedback of the other participants in the forum. Technology tools, like Google Docs, allow participants to contribute and engage in reflective dialogue when it is not possible to meet, or they can function as a means to extend the thinking and discussion beyond the time limits of face-to-face meetings.

As you engage in planning for action, it is essential that you remain systematic and organized in your thinking. This is what separates what teachers do while engaged in action research from what practitioners do on a day-to-day basis as they make decisions about students, curriculum, and instruction in their classrooms. You will first want to make sure that the action steps you generate align with the original research questions that were developed or with new research questions that emerged during the reflection on action process. You should plan how the action steps will be carried out and who will be responsible for implementing them. You will need to consider if there is anyone who needs to be consulted or informed about the actions you are planning. It is important at this time to determine what data will be collected to allow you to evaluate the effects of the actions as well as who will collect the data. It would be valuable to establish a timeline for the implementation of the potential action steps and determine any resources that will be needed. Planning for action requires not only that action steps are created but also that a plan is in place for implementing and evaluating these actions. In the Taking Action section that follows, you will be involved in applying these planning for action ideas to your action research project work.

"NOTE"-ABLE THOUGHTS

It is important to think through potential action steps before moving forward with creating an implementation plan for them. In your researcher log, list any potential action steps you are considering and jot down ideas that present a rationale for the actions and any potential limitations, drawbacks, or unintended consequences of each of the actions. Now, you are ready to identify the action steps that have strong potential for bringing positive improvement to your practice.

■ ■ ■ VOICES FROM THE FIELD

Sarah Kennedy, Third-Grade Teacher

After developing and implementing my action research plan on my own, I began discussing my findings with my colleagues during team planning meetings. The other teachers helped me to analyze my findings and develop the next plan of action. My work was now becoming shared work as other teachers wanted to engage in extending the action research project across the grade level. It was decided that our research question would be the same, "How can writing journals improve students' ability to understand and express mathematical concepts and problem solve?" We decided to begin the next phase of the research at the beginning of the next school year. The participants would now come from all of the third-grade classrooms. This will bring the total number of participants to 64 students. This should give us much more reliable data than just my class of 18 students. We decided to continue to use a pre-test and a post-test. The pre-test would be administered the first week of school. The pre-test question for each grade will be chosen by the teachers, and must be approved by all the teachers in the team. This will help to make sure that it is a reliable measure. As a team, we have decided to use the same rubric from the Illinois Board of Education to grade the pre-test, post-test, and any graded journal entries. We have also decided to stay with the star motivation method that I used in my initial study and to grade the students' entries once a week. Each teacher also believed it was a good idea to continue to respond to all the journals.

To address the time constraints and limitations of the original study, we will initiate the study at the beginning of the year and spend the first four weeks of school giving the students direct instruction on journal writing in math and specific problem-solving strategies. This was not possible in my original study and was determined to be a hindrance to the effectiveness of the intervention. We will then continue the study for approximately 12 weeks, until the end of the first semester. This will give us a lot more data that will result in more reliable statistics. This will also give the students much more time for growth.

This new action research plan, as an extension of the original research, will hopefully address most of the issues faced in the original research. As we, now as a team of teachers, are conducting this research, I confidently expect our students to continue to grow in their knowledge and understanding of mathematics and their ability to express their ideas and problem-solving strategies through writing.

TAKING ACTION: CREATING A PLAN OF ACTION

It is essential to be organized in your thinking during the planning for action phase. To assist with this, you may want to consider developing a Steps to Action chart (Mills, 2011). This chart will align your selected action steps to your research questions with attention to who will carry out the action, who will need to be consulted, what data will be collected, the timeline for implementing the actions, and any resources that are needed. An example of a Steps to Action chart (which has been adapted from Mills, 2011) is shown in Figure 7.1.

FIGURE 7.1   Steps to Action Chart Example

Research Questions With Summary of Findings	Actions to Be Taken	Who Is Responsible for Implementing Actions?	Who Needs to Be Consulted?	What Data Will Be Collected?	Timeline	Resources Necessary

---

DEVELOPING A PLAN OR A PRODUCT: COMPLETING A PLAN OF ACTION

This chapter has guided you through the process of reflecting on your results and planning for action as key components of teacher action research. You have generated conclusions and implications for practice, and organized your thinking to create a strategic plan for action. As you consider all that you have learned by engaging in action research, you will want to communicate with others, either formally or informally, the outcomes of your study (Creswell, 2005). To do so, teachers may develop their new insights into a written discussion of the results of their project. If the nature of your work only requires informal communications with colleagues or interested others, then you may find that outlining your conclusions and implications for practice and preparing a Steps to Action chart will suffice to guide your informal sharing and to prepare you for the next stage of the action research process. However, if you plan to share your results more formally with colleagues, administrators, course instructors, and/or the broader educational community, you will need to prepare a written discussion of your results. To formulate a clearly written discussion, you will have to select what is most important and meaningful from your reflections, provide evidence to support your claims, connect to implications for personal practice as well as broader educational issues and related literature, and present your ideas for how to improve and extend your study in the future. To assist you in developing a written Discussion of Results, the Case in Point: Reflecting on Results section of this chapter provides two examples from both an elementary and secondary action research study that you have been following throughout the text. After examining the examples provided, you should now develop a written discussion that communicates the outcomes of your study. When complete, the written discussion should address

- how this process impacted your personal practices and future instruction,

- a discussion of the results in light of what the literature review revealed and future potential investigations,

- what changes you could have made to improve your study overall, and

- how you will move forward with a plan of action based on your current findings.

EVALUATING AGAINST THE STANDARDS: ARE YOU READY TO MOVE ON?

To evaluate your work thus far, you may use the checklists in this section to carefully review the narrative discussion section you have created to present your conclusions, implications for practice, and the plan for action before formally sharing it with others or moving forward to the next chapter.

CHECKLIST: SELF-REFLECTION

Consider the following questions to help you determine relevant conclusions and implications for practice:

_____ 1. Is the outcome of my study presented as it relates to my goals, objectives, and my statement of the problem?

_____ 2. Do I provide evidence to support my claims?

_____ 3. Do my colleagues find my claims credible?

_____ 4. Do I discuss my claims as they relate to the research and educational literature I uncovered during Chapter 3?

_____ 5. Will others find my claims or assertions useful?

_____ 6. Are the key concepts I learned presented?

_____ 7. Do I present what I learned about my own teaching?

_____ 8. Do I present my "aha!" moments and/or successes?

_____ 9. Is there discussion of what did not go well and/or was not as successful as I had hoped?

_____10. Do I discuss what needs improvement or what I would do differently next time?

_____11. Are there clear and explicit implications presented that demonstrate how what I have learned will affect my future practices?

_____12. Do I take the opportunity to share new questions that emerged from the study that I would like to pursue in future action research studies?

CHECKLIST: ACTION PLAN

Consider the following questions as you develop your action plan:

_____ 1. Did I generate appropriate action steps that align with my research questions and the learning outcomes from my study?

_____ 2. Is there a plan for what data will be collected to evaluate the actions taken?

_____ 3. Is there a plan for who needs to be consulted about the action steps planned?

_____ 4. Is there a plan for who will collect the data?

_____ 5. Is there a plan for when the data will be collected?

_____ 6. Have the necessary resources to carry out the action steps been identified?

SUMMARY

This chapter has focused on how to (a) reflect on your results, (b) draw conclusions and implications for practice, and (c) develop action steps based on what you have learned from your study. Reflecting on results requires reflection on action as you look back on what you have learned from implementing the action research plan. Reflection on action is important to find meaning in your data by making connections to personal practice, the professional literature, and to broader educational issues or priorities. Taking informed action, or "planning for action," is the final step in the action research process and is designed to bring improvement to practice. As you engage in planning for action, it is essential that you remain systematic and organized in your thinking. The chapter concludes by preparing you to write a narrative discussion that presents your conclusions, implications for practice, and plans for action in order to effectively communicate with others about what is of importance and value in your study.

Key Terms

Implications for practice, p. 157

Plan for action, p. 161
Reflection in action, p. 156

Reflection on action, p. 156

Case in Point: Reflecting on Results

In Chapter 5, you were able to see the complete research plans created by Margaret Curtis to study the effect of using Readers' Theater on the reading fluency of her second-grade students and by Matt Wells to study the effect of an investigative approach to the teaching and learning of science on his ninth-grade students. Their analysis of the data collected and presentation of the results is included in the full report found in Appendix A. Here, you will be given the opportunity to examine how they reflected on their results and crafted a narrative discussion of their conclusions, implications for practice, and plan for action (see Figures 7.2 and 7.3).

One Elementary Teacher's Journey: Research Log Entry #4

FIGURE 7.2 An Elementary Teacher's Reflection on Results Log

Reflecting on Results:

The original question I was seeking an answer to was: "What is the effect of Readers' Theater on second-grade students' reading fluency?" The data from the three administrations of DIBELS showed that the students did grow overall as fluent readers. Most students' oral reading fluency and reading rate increased, and they maintained or increased in prosody (some students more than others). No student misread more than eight words on the post-test, which was a slight decrease from the midpoint administration, but after reflecting on their reading, the students were able to identify the words they missed. As a teacher, this served as more practical information than the total number of errors (which most likely were not corrected at the time because the students were racing the clock). Though the post-test results were not as significant as I had hoped, there was an increase in their overall reading fluency and I was pleased to see the students grow as readers in the sense that they became more self-aware when reading and could explain what "fluent reading" looked like and sounded like.

I was able to find multiple other positive effects of using this strategy as an intervention. The students' level of interest and motivation to read increased, and they were able to work cooperatively with others to improve their fluency. Students expressed their excitement to be a part of Readers' Theater, and sought out opportunities outside of our regular reading time to practice reading their lines. The students felt a sense of accomplishment when reading fluently during the weekly performances for the class. The audience members were very attentive as the readers read at a good pace and with expression.

A research question that developed as a result of this action research was, "What is the correlation between fluency and comprehension of text read by struggling readers?" The students in my class who struggle with reading fluently also struggle in the realm of comprehending text. I wish I had investigated the link between the two in this study, but I think this gives me additional motivation to keep the intervention going. Moving forward, I think this is going to be the specific area I examine first as part of my action plan. As part of this, and given the amount of time spent implementing the intervention was shorter compared to other studies mentioned in my review of literature, I would like to see Readers' Theater used consistently quarterly or maybe even throughout the year to see if the results would be more significant than what I saw over the five weeks. This is something that can not only be done in my classroom, but in other second-grade classrooms as well. Scripts could be reused and revised over time to meet the needs of the specific children in the classroom. Students could create their own scripts to demonstrate their learning of various texts and concepts, and this would likely be an additional tool to motivate students in the classroom.

In the future, I also would like to try using Readers' Theater as a tool to integrate reading with other content areas, such as science. This method of repeated reading and reflection would most likely increase the students' awareness and understanding of vocabulary words, and could be a strategy used to introduce a unit, while giving struggling readers extra exposure to certain concepts and words. To make the action research more cohesive, a pre-test could be given containing unit vocabulary words, Readers' Theater scripts containing these words and concepts could be used throughout the intervention, and the same pre-test could be administered as a post-test at the end of the study to get an even better idea of whether the intervention was successful.

Readers' Theater proved to be a motivating way to get this group of second-grade students interested in reading. Each student showed more interest in reading the text within the scripts than with other timed reading activities done previously in the year. The peer coaching that took place throughout the week was also helpful for the students who normally found distractions when reading alone. I will continue to use Readers' Theater in the classroom as it proved to be an engaging and effective strategy that will help prepare my students for future grade levels where the focus is on reading to learn.

One Secondary Teacher's Journey: Research Log Entry #4

FIGURE 7.3 A Secondary Teacher's Reflection on Results Log

Reflecting on Results:

After compiling and analyzing the data I collected, I am able to report both positive and unanticipated negative results. Overall, the data show that the students did over time increase their learning of the content through the open investigation workshops. However, I was also interested to see if there were any differences in effects among the varying levels of learners in my class. As I predicted, the low-reading students did show an increase in their scores, but not as high as I hoped. My observational field notes reveal challenges these students experienced during the intervention and may help explain these results, such as their difficulty adapting to a new learning format, attention span problems due to new-found freedom, and social anxiety from speaking and learning from peers. The low-medium reading level student scores remained about the same during the first weeks of workshop. This group formed a majority of students who were fascinated with workshop freedoms and were excited and motivated by the new method, but failed to concentrate on the actual policies and procedures until well into week 2. Their scores started coming up the following week and continued to improve. The few high-reading students in the class actually showed a decrease in scores. This was counterintuitive to what I expected, but the root of the problem exposed itself early. These students used to work well ahead of the other students, but due to the peer interaction in the workshops they focused mainly on only the current activities and did not get into the extension activities. They also seemed to be enamored with the new format and spent quite a bit of time initially working through the social dynamics and issues involved in working in a team format. Overall, the three different averages and the class average stabilized and began to climb in weeks 15 and 16. Moving the whole class to this format was difficult, and there were times that I wanted to throw in the towel and give up on the intervention but the results of the class average graph are very encouraging.

The results of the pre-/post-attitude questionnaire demonstrated an increase from a 2.0 following the direct instruction to a 4.2 following the open investigation workshop as an overall class average. This large overall increase in student attitude toward the class is the most significant finding of the study. My observational notes are evidence of the sheer enjoyment of the class for both the students and the researcher. The class, which seemed so difficult to teach and manage, transformed into a class that was easy to teach and easy to manage and had happy students. The entire atmosphere of the class changed. Students who were just trying to get through the day now showed up to class excited and with the correct classroom supplies. Some students even began the written work in the morning before school voluntarily instead of walking the halls socializing. I don't know of any higher evidence than that of a student being engaged in the class. Something that I am very passionate about also began to change in the room in the last four weeks: my high-, medium-, and low-performing students all began working as teams. I had students hanging around after class wanting to continue to engage in discussion and class work on many occasions. I recorded that students would say things like "I actually think I like science now" and "This class is so much more fun than any of our other classes." On the open-ended questionnaire, the majority of the students expressed that they hoped the workshop format would continue because they liked it better and they enjoyed learning the content by working as a team. This alone is worth the change, and if the scores continue to climb as these students get acclimated to their new learning environment then it seems to be the way I should teach science to all my students in the future.

My results are supported and can be better understood by the literature on the topic. Lee et al. (2010) and Fogelman, McNeill, and Krajcik (2010) both express the positive impact of inquiry and technology incorporation to a positive learning environment. The students in this research showed gains other than those that were specified by the research question. For example, my field notes reveal that they began to work with the technology in the centers and collaborated on projects, which are both 21st-century learning skills. In addition, O'Neill's (2010) views were confirmed when students who took ownership of their education had a more positive view of their science class experiences. When examining the results as compared to the Marx study, one has to consider the longitudinal nature of the Marx et al. (2004) study. My research project had an eight-week modification, while the Marx study analyzed data at the end of the first through third years. The students in my study were static for the first two weeks of the intervention, but they began to show improvement for the last several weeks. I believe they were on a positive trajectory that would continue if implemented over a longer period of time. Fogelman et al. (2010) stated that the instructor's experience also

ACTION RESEARCH

may contribute to the success of open inquiry and that an inexperienced inquiry instructor would see smaller gains than an experienced direct instruction teacher. This may also explain the limited academic gains in this study. While I have taught the other two sections with open investigation, they behaved very differently than this section. As I spend more time with these students who are lower-level readers, I anticipate that I will get better at providing appropriate scaffolding to support their reading/writing and better manage their engagement in the workshop format. The findings of the multiple researchers listed were consistent with this study. Student learning, attitude, collaboration, pride, and technology use all improved during the study. The major concern in my results was the lower scores in the high-reading range students, which I believe may improve with adjustments I can make with further study. I think my study extends the current research literature because I was able to look at the effects of the approach on different levels of learners. This understanding is needed in the literature, and there is limited research on this aspect of the topic.

Though the research project progressed without any major derailments, it did have some hurdles to overcome and bumps along the way. There are some things I wish I could have anticipated ahead of time. The first was switching the class over to a full workshop too quickly. As you can read in my field notes, students had some serious management issues until they learned the routine. This took about two weeks, with only a few relapses along the way. In the future I believe that a day-to-day gradual release during the period would shorten this window to about one week. I believe this would produce higher test results sooner. Another concern is a student with an IEP who I created plans to work with, but due to management issues I really didn't have the opportunity to devote as much time to her as I would have liked. In the future a more developed plan and maybe even another instructor might help. The final change is related to the length of the lab day during the week. The students struggled with 90-minute lab procedures once a week, and I had to modify it soon into the research project. I removed the full-day lab and replaced it with mini labs, across three days per week. I think if this had been arranged from the beginning it would have helped in the transition.

Future research I would like to conduct relevant to the current study would be to study how the higher-level students are impacted by working with the lower-level students in the workshop approach. I am teaching a section of primarily high-level readers and a section with primarily lower-level readers with only a few higher-level readers and would like to set up a new study and compare the data. I would set up an identical unit with identical assessments and test both sections. If the high-level readers in the low-reader grouping have lower scores than the high-level readers in the high-level group then the cause of this should be examined. I would set up the research design, would collect data, and would have to consult my principal as well as the students' parents who are participating. Once data is gathered, it can be charted and analyzed. The timeline would be a full unit, which would take approximately six to eight weeks.

As I reflect on the results of my action research project, I feel an overwhelming sense of satisfaction with the project and the results of it. The students are thrilled to come to class every day, and I love teaching it. I spend extra hours in the classroom and really enjoy preparing the learning experiences for the workshop approach. I have a renewed sense of teaching, and I am happy that I am beginning to figure out how to make this work with all my students. Seeing this group of students, who are so used to struggling, devour a lesson with intrinsic motivation makes the time invested so worthwhile.

Activities and Additional Resources

1. Go to www.teachersnetwork.org/tnli/research and examine other examples of teachers' written discussions of their results. Use the checklists provided in the Evaluate Against the Standards section of the chapter to evaluate examples from your field and/or level of instruction.

2. As you discuss your results with "critical" friends and colleagues, determine additional audiences for sharing your project. Who might also benefit from understanding the results of your study? Where would be appropriate opportunities to disseminate your work? Identify where and with

whom you will share the results of your action research study.

3. Reflection in action and reflection on action were two types of reflective thinking discussed as important to the action research process. The following quote was presented in this chapter: "These two processes together, in Schön's terms, form the core professional artistry of the reflective practitioner" (Leitch & Day, 2000, p. 180). Do you agree with this quote? Explain.

Print Resources

Brookfield, S. D. (1995). *Becoming a critically reflective teacher.* San Francisco, CA: Jossey-Bass.

Moon, J. A. (1999). *Reflection in learning & professional development: Theory & practice.* New York, NY: Routledge-Falmer.

Schön, D. A. (1987). *Educating the reflective practitioner: Toward a new design for teaching and learning in the professions.* San Francisco, CA: Jossey-Bass.

Student Study Site

edge.sagepub.com/putman

- Take the practice quiz.
- Review key terms with eFlashcards.
- Explore topics with video and multimedia.

References

Bangert-Drowns, R. L., Hurley, M. M., & Wilkinson, B. (2004). The effects of school-based writing-to-learn interventions on academic achievement: A meta-analysis. *Review of Educational Research, 74,* 29–58.

Baxter, J. A., Woodward, J., & Olson, D. (2005). Writing in mathematics: An alternative form of communication for academically low-achieving students. *Learning Disabilities: Research & Practice, 20,* 119–135.

Creswell, J. W. (2005). *Educational research: Planning, conducting, and evaluating quantitative and qualitative research* (2nd ed.). Upper Saddle River, NJ: Pearson Education.

Fogelman, J., McNeill, K. L., & Krajcik, J. (2010). Examining the effect of teachers' adaptations of a middle school science inquiry-oriented curriculum unit on student learning. *Journal of Research in Science Teaching, 48*(2), 149–169.

Johnson, A. P. (2008). *A short guide to action research* (3rd ed.). Boston, MA: Allyn & Bacon.

Kostos, K., & Shin, E. (2010). Using math journals to enhance second graders' communication of mathematical thinking. *Early Childhood Education Journal, 38,* 223–231.

Lee, H., Linn, M. C., Varma, K., & Liu, O. (2010). How do technology-enhanced inquiry science units impact classroom learning? *Journal of Research in Science Teaching, 47,* 71–90.

Leitch, R., & Day, C. (2000). Action research and reflective practice: Towards a holistic view. *Educational Action Research, 8,* 179–193.

Marx, R. W., Blumenfeld, P. C., Krajcik, J. S., Fishman, B., Soloway, E., Geier, R., & Tal, R. T. (2004). Inquiry based science in the middle grades: Assessment of learning in urban systematic reform. *Journal of Research in Science Teaching, 41,* 1063–1080.

Mills, G. E. (2011). *Action research: A guide for the teacher researcher* (4th ed.). Boston, MA: Pearson.

O'Neill, T. B. (2010). Fostering spaces of student ownership in middle school science. *Equity and Excellence in Education, 43,* 6–20.

Rust, F., & Clark, C. (n.d.). *How to do action research in your classroom: Lessons from the Teachers Network Leadership Institute.* Retrieved August 1, 2015, from https://www.naeyc.org/files/naeyc/Action_Research_Booklet.pdf

Sagor, R. (2000). *Guiding school improvement with action research.* Alexandria, VA: Association for Supervision and Curriculum Development.

Schön, D. (1984). *The reflective practitioner: How professionals think in action.* New York, NY: Basic Books.

Stainback, S., & Stainback, W. (1988). *Understanding & conducting qualitative research.* Dubuque, IA: Kendall Hunt.

CHAPTER 8

The Action Research Report: Sharing Results

GUIDING QUESTIONS

After reading this chapter, you should be able to answer the following questions:

- Who is the audience of my action research report?

- What is the most appropriate format for my action research report?

- How do I organize and write the action research report?

- How do I disseminate my action research report?

- What are the potential challenges I may face when moving forward with the action research process?

CHAPTER AIMS AND GOALS

You have put a tremendous amount of time, energy, and thoughtful reflection into improving an aspect of your professional practice through engaging in the action research process. In Chapters 2 and 3, you began with an area of focus, developed a statement of the problem and research question(s) to guide your inquiry, and then engaged in a systematic review of related literature to help you refine and frame your inquiry within a broader understanding of the professional literature. In Chapters 4, 5, and 6 you created a plan of action, implemented the plan, and collected, organized, and analyzed your data. In Chapter 7, you reflected on your results and wrote a discussion narrative to capture how you interpreted the results/findings, in light of both your personal understandings and connections with the professional literature. This allowed you to establish implications for your current practice, while also developing a plan of action steps to guide your future inquiry. Hopefully, the time and energy devoted to this pursuit of a deeper understanding of the teaching and learning process has yielded powerful new insights and inspired and renewed your commitment to systematically studying and reflecting on your professional practice.

It is now time to pull all of these pieces together to create an organized report of your action research to allow you to share the outcomes of your investigation with others. At the closing of the last chapter, you were asked to begin initiating discussions about your results with "critical" friends and colleagues to determine additional audiences for sharing your project and appropriate opportunities to disseminate your work. In this chapter, we will explore these ideas more deeply to identify where and with whom you will share the results of your action research study. The chapter will provide a variety of formats for organizing and sharing your work to allow you to select the one most suited for your goals and audience. The formats discussed can be used individually to meet immediate and local needs or can be developed in steps to build toward a more developed and formal report that could be "publishable" to allow your work to be shared more widely. You will be provided with resources and tips to help you identify appropriate professional journals that may be a good fit for publishing your work.

Sharing your results is the final step in the first phase of the action research process. There is great value in finalizing your thinking and preparing to share your work with others. The process of writing and communicating about your study promotes deep engagement with the topic and allows for additional critique and problem solving with others in a professional community of learners, which we will discuss in Chapter 9. Although additional commitment and time is required to accomplish this final step, we believe that it is necessary before moving forward with the challenges that arise with implementing future action steps and additional lines of inquiry as you continue in the action research process. So, get ready to make important decisions regarding your work, such as who you will share it with, what you will want to share, and how you would like to share it. By sharing the outcomes of your action research study, the time, energy, and commitment you invested in the project will culminate with a sense of satisfaction, accomplishment, and a renewed professional curiosity.

SETTING THE CONTEXT: DETERMINING THE AUDIENCE, FORMAT, AND OUTLET

The purpose of sharing your work is so that others can learn from it and adopt or modify your ideas to their own situations, in terms of both the content as well as the inquiry processes utilized. The first question you must answer is: Who will be the audience of my action research report? This is not always a simple question to answer because often there are multiple audiences that you may find yourself writing for. Zuber-Skerritt (1996) suggests that the issue of the audience of action research reports is problematic because there are likely three audiences—each of equal importance. One audience is the colleagues with whom you may have collaborated in carrying out the research reported. Another audience is interested colleagues or administrators in other institutions, or in other areas of the same institution, for whom the problem of practice presented may address a common or similar situation or topic of concern in their area of work. "But the third, and perhaps most important audience, is ourselves. The process of writing involves clarifying and exploring ideas and interpretations" (Zuber-Skerritt,1996, p. 26). As McNiff (1990) articulately expresses

> In writing I tap my tacit knowledge. I externalize [sic] my thoughts-at-competence through my action-at-performance. My writing becomes both symbolic expression of thought (this is what I mean) and the critical reflection on that thought (do I really mean this?). My writing is both reflection on action (what I have written) and reflection in action (what I am writing). The very act of making external, through the process of writing, what is internal, in the process of thinking, allows me to formulate explicit theories about the practices I engage in intuitively. (p. 56)

It is important to recognize the value of the writing of your **action research report** to extend and develop your thinking about your work. It has the power to enhance and refine your personal theorizing about teaching and learning and therefore impact your **praxis**, or the practice that is formed at the intersection of reflection and action. However, when writing the report keep in mind that you are writing for others to understand the nature and the value of the work you engaged in. Therefore, it is important that your writing is clear, concise, and well organized. In addition, you need to make sure you address the "So what?" question for the audience you are writing for. What is important about these results? Why is this work valuable to the reader of the report? Are there practical implications, policy implications, or both? These questions may shape the audience that you target for the research report, or you may modify or tweak the implications and conclusions sections of the report for different audiences that you share it with. Ultimately, the action research process should enrich, empower, and improve your own professional practice, but when you take the responsibility to share what you have learned with others, you have the opportunity to make a broader professional impact (see Figure 8.1). Think carefully about where your work can have the greatest impact.

The most obvious people to share your research with are the colleagues in your school or course. They already know that you are doing research, and you have kept them informed because either you wanted to work collaboratively or you needed additional perspectives or "critical" friends to challenge or question your emerging ideas. Some people may already perceive the value of what you are doing and want to learn from it themselves, and may even wish to begin their own action research. You could make your final report available in digital or print copy, or ask for time to present at a faculty meeting, or circulate a two-page summary (see Case in Point: Action Research Summary). Perhaps ask your administration to announce publicly that your work is available, so that action research as a form of professional learning is seen as normal practice in your school. With the current emphasis on collaborative, inquiry-based professional development, you could find yourself in a position of academic leadership (McNiff & Whitehead, 2009). Action researchers have the potential to set a precedent for collaborative learning in their schools, especially if their research is relevant to improving the quality of teaching and student learning.

Of course, if you are completing this action research study as part of a program of study for initial or advanced degree programs, you will need to share and present your

FIGURE 8.1 Audiences for Action Research

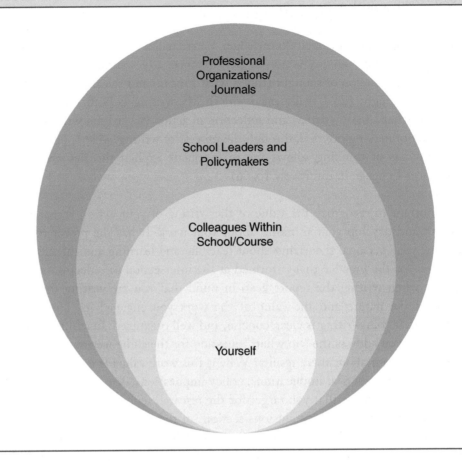

Professional Organizations/ Journals

School Leaders and Policymakers

Colleagues Within School/Course

Yourself

report to classmates and faculty. You may even have the opportunity to engage in academic symposiums or online webinars in your academic environment to present to broader audiences.

Aim to let other people outside your immediate network know about your research. For example, perhaps district-level school administrators, professional development leaders or organizers in your school system, local or state school boards, or members of legislature may be interested. Send them a copy of your report, and say you would be happy to talk with them about your work (McNiff & Whitehead, 2009). Policy implications of your research may be of critical interest for these particular types of audiences, and you will want to make sure these aspects of your results are clearly presented in the report you share. The Taking Action section of this chapter will assist you in creating procedural or policy recommendation statements.

Another audience for consideration should be members of professional organizations that have specific interests in your topic or in teacher action research (e.g., National Council for the Social Studies, International Literacy Association, National Council for Teachers of Mathematics, National Science Foundation). You may also want to look for state- or local-level professional organizations that exist in your area of interest. Most professional organizations have many different ways to disseminate information to their members. For example, you could write a proposal to present your report at the organization's annual meeting/conference. If you would like to focus on a smaller audience within the professional organization, most often have special interest groups that coordinate roundtables or poster sessions at their conference where you might consider presenting. In addition, they have established ways to communicate outside of their annual conference, such as newsletters, websites, and/or blogs, which connect and inform these network communities about current research. You can search the websites of the professional organizations that may have interest in your work to locate contact information for related special interest groups and to find guidelines for submitting proposals for conference presentations.

Finally, you will want to consider publication opportunities as a way to reach additional audiences who may have interest in your work. Educational journals, book chapters, or conference proceedings are potential publication outlets. Getting your action research report published will require persistence and determination on your part as well as important understandings related to academic and journal writing. To support you in this endeavor, there are suggestions and tips for getting published presented later in the chapter.

"NOTE"-ABLE THOUGHTS

As you consider your action research project, decide who you would like to share your results with. Make a list of potential audiences within and outside your school community that you think would find your work interesting. Don't limit yourself to only sharing your work with those in your immediate environments. With some extra effort, you can prepare your report in a way to allow it to reach wider audiences and have potentially greater impact. Believe in your work and dream big!

ACTION RESEARCH REPORT FORMAT

After identifying potential audiences for your action research, the second question you must consider is: What is the most appropriate format for my action report? Henning, Stone, and Kelly (2009) note, "There is no uniform or standard format for action research reports. For some action research projects, a more informal presentation, such as a narrative summary, a PowerPoint presentation, or an artistic display may best serve the purposes of the researchers and the study" (p. 150). In the sections that follow, we offer guidance and tips to create an action research summary and PowerPoint presentation. However, we also offer guidance on preparing a more developed and formal version of an action research report that is structured similarly to reports of educational research articles. We believe a more developed and structured approach to action research best reinforces your learning of the analytical thinking processes associated with action research (Henning et al., 2009). In addition, the action research report format is best suited for advanced degree projects and is most easily adjusted for a variety of publication outlets.

Sarah Kennedy, Third-Grade Teacher

After completing my action research project, I began to share the results with my colleagues. First, I presented the research to my peers in my graduate-level action research class at Southeastern State University. My work was well received by my peers and my professor. After the presentation, my professor encouraged me to consider submitting a proposal to present my research at the 2016 Annual NCARE (North Carolina Association for Research in Education) conference that would be held on our campus in February. This made me nervous because I have never presented at a research conference, but I am excited that she found my work compelling and recommended this opportunity to me. I looked into the process for submitting a proposal on the NCARE website and found that I had all the necessary information already in my report. I have decided to give it a try and submit a proposal. I also presented my research to the other teachers at my school during a staff meeting. The other teachers at my school were very interested in my study and asked really good questions. As a result, there are teachers in several grade levels interested in implementing my intervention and we plan to examine the results across several grade levels next fall. It is amazing how this project is continuing to grow as I share it with others!

Before we discuss the various formats you may use to share the results of your action research, let's examine how a traditional educational research report would compare to an action research report (see Table 8.1). This examination will allow you to see how a formal action research report differs in its organization and intent from a more traditional educational research report. If you refer back to Chapter 1, comparisons for traditional educational research and action research were made. At this point, it may be helpful to examine how a research report for traditional research would be structured as compared to action research to build your understanding of how action research is similar and different from traditional educational research in its purpose, audience, and approach. These insights will also help you determine similarities and differences in how the reports are organized and written. In a traditional educational research report, it would be common to have sections titled: Introduction, Review of Theoretical Framework/Literature Review, Methodology, Results, and Conclusions and Recommendations. However, the names and total number of sections often vary according to the type of research. In the action research report format that we present, we have organized the headings to reflect the steps and sections presented throughout this text to allow you to pull all of your work up to this point together to form the action research report.

"NOTE"-ABLE THOUGHTS

What are the similarities between a traditional educational research report and an action research report? How are they different? Look back to the researcher's log that you have kept throughout the process; which sections of the action research report do you have mostly complete? Which ones do you still need to develop? Hopefully, you will recognize that to complete the report it is now a matter of pulling all of your work together in an organized fashion and finalizing your thoughts for others to read and understand what you have learned through your investigation.

TABLE 8.1 Comparison of Traditional Educational Research Report and Teacher Action Research Report

Traditional Educational Research Report	Action Research Report
Introduction • Statement of the Problem • Purpose of the Study • Research Questions or Hypotheses • Limitations and Delimitations	Introduction • Area of Focus • Statement of the Problem • Description of the Research Context • Research Questions
Review of Theoretical Framework and Related Literature	Background for the Study/Review of Related Literature
Methodology • Participants • Data Collection • Data Analysis Procedures	Research Plan • Description of the Intervention or Innovation • Data Collection and Considerations (informed consent)
Results	Data Analysis and Reflection (Interpretations and Implications of Results/Findings)
Conclusions and Recommendations	Action Plan and Policy Recommendations (if appropriate)
References	References
Appendices	Appendices

ACTION RESEARCH SUMMARY FORMAT

It is often desirable to prepare a two-page summary of your action research study to share with some audiences. These summaries often have similar headings to a more formal action research report, but they would only include the main ideas and would be written in a concise manner. The purpose of these summaries is to give the audience the gist of your study along with the major findings, implications for practice, and action steps. The **action research summary** is conducive to sharing print copies across an audience or in tighter space restrictions like newsletters, web pages, or e-mail communications. This format is also an appropriate way to introduce certain audiences to your work and then allow them the opportunity to request the full action research report, if they desire. Preparing a summary of your action research study will also allow easy transfer into a conference or grant funding proposal. Finally, if given the opportunity to present your study to an audience, the two-page summary is an effective handout to provide. We've presented two examples of what this two-page summary could look like in our Case in Point: Action Research Summary section for the chapter.

ACTION RESEARCH PRESENTATION FORMAT

You may have the opportunity to verbally present your work to an audience either inside or outside your school context. Developing a structured dialogue about your work requires you to engage in making sense of your findings and brings coherence to your study. Presenting your work requires you to organize your materials for others. In addition, responding to questions from the audience forces you to address issues you may not have thought about, and helps you to see the value of your work for other people

(Henning et al., 2009). We recommend Activity 2 in the Activities and Additional Resources section and that you attend professional conferences and watch good presenters to see how they relate to an audience, respond to questions, use technology, and generally conduct themselves.

When presenting your study, a PowerPoint, Prezi, or other type of presentation software can be useful to guide and support the verbal presentation. The presentation software will allow you to summarize the key points and provide visual supports like charts or graphs to display data and findings. The visual supports and display of the data assist in keeping the audience engaged in the presentation and often stimulates questions and comments from the audience. It also helps you stay focused and on track while providing a plan for adhering to any time limitations you may have been given for the presentation. You may also want to experiment with constructing webpages using free sites such as Weebly or Wix. These user-friendly website design tools help you to organize and present information in a digital format for sharing with others. Other digital tools like VoiceThread or LiveBinder provide additional ways to organize the information from your study and optimize the visual and sensory effects that digital media has to offer. You can explore all of these options as potential ways to organize and present your work using the links provided in the Tech Connections box below.

When it comes time to present your study, you will want to do so with care and rehearse beforehand. Never read the report to an audience; this can be boring and agonizing for them. Stay relaxed and confident. Your audience is knowledgeable, so no need to talk down or up to them. The audience is generally interested in what you have to say; otherwise, they would not have made the effort to come to your presentation. Be honest and engaging without being overly dramatic or making generalizations that can't be supported by your research design. Make sure you are prepared to use the technology you have selected, and make sure it works. Set up well in advance and avoid fumbling with your computer while talking through your ideas. If the technology fails, stay positive and focused (Henning et al., 2009). If you should encounter other technical difficulties, having the two-page summary handout will be particularly useful to guide your talking points and allow you to seamlessly carry on with the presentation.

TECH CONNECTIONS

Below are multiple resources that can be used to present your work to various audiences.

- LiveBinder: http://www.livebinders.com—online information organization system

- MS Office PowerPoint: https://products.office.com/en-us/powerpoint—slide presentation software

- Prezi: www.prezi.com—presentation software that uses motion, zoom, and spatial relationships

- VoiceThread: https://voicethread.com—presentation website that creates collaborative spaces with video, voice, and text commenting

- Weebly: www.weebly.com—free online website building tool

- Wix: www.wix.com—free online website building tool

WRITING THE ACTION RESEARCH REPORT

As stated earlier in the chapter, we believe the writing process involved in compiling a full action research report stimulates and reinforces your learning of the analytical thinking processes associated with action research. It requires deep processing of your ideas and understandings to best organize and communicate the significance of the results and translate the implications for practice for you personally as well as for others collectively. In the Developing a Product section of the chapter, you will be presented with an outline for how to produce a full action research report. As you begin organizing and writing your action research report, it is important to observe certain conventions and keep some general principles in mind.

Before you actually begin to write, you should recognize that all research reports constitute an elaborate answer to four basic questions:

1. What was the purpose of the study?

2. How was the data collected and analyzed?

3. What did the researchers find when they collected the data?

4. What do the findings mean?

Therefore, as you write you want to make sure that you provide the answers to these basic questions. Doing so enables the essence of the study to be conveyed to the reader much more succinctly and effectively (Henning et al., 2009).

Action research reports, unlike many "academic" papers, are typically written in the first person as a result of several factors: the significance of the participation of the teacher as well as the personal nature, reflexivity, and individuality of the work (Somekh, 1995). However, it is important that within this voice you maintain a focus on writing for a reader, not for yourself. This suggestion is critical but often overlooked in report writing. It is your responsibility, as the author, to ensure that your reader can read your text with ease. Too many writers assume that their reader will automatically understand what they are writing about, which is not often the case. The only thing your readers know about your work is what they see on the page. Make sure that you guide them through your text so they know what you mean to say and what they are supposed to understand. For this reason, write in a clear and concise way. Produce a text that is attractive and fluent, which speaks with authority, but without grandiose language. The action research report should be written in the everyday, commonsense language of the participants. Finally, make sure that the content and approach are appropriate for an action research report. The content deals with how you were trying to improve your learning in order to improve your practice. You should take an autobiographical approach to the report through which you offer an account for what you are doing and why you are doing it. In the end, you should produce an explanatory text, not only a descriptive text. This means that the entire text will stand as an explanation for what you are doing and why you are doing it (McNiff & Whitehead, 2009).

Sherri Mayfield, Sixth-Grade Teacher

I found the most difficult aspect of writing the final report was determining what was really important to say because I had so many thoughts and ideas that I generated throughout my study. I think it can be easy to get lost in all of the data and in your reflective thinking. I kept asking myself what is really meaningful here or what would others most benefit from understanding about my work. The feedback I received from my professor that was most useful was to make sure that my research report was clearly aligned across the report from my presentation of my research questions, to the data collection strategies, to the findings. I really found it helpful to make sure that I was tying everything back to my research questions. This helped keep me focused. I also asked the "So what?" question over and over in my mind to help me determine what I wanted to emphasize in my writing. Although it was time-consuming to write the final report, I did find it valuable in helping me to clarify my thinking and come to a deeper understanding of why my work was valuable.

PUBLISHING YOUR WORK

After writing and presenting the action research report to others, you may decide to share your work more broadly and publish your results with an educational journal. This is an exciting prospect, but one that requires a significant level of commitment to achieve success. Keep in mind the research is complete and you have the report written; it is now just understanding how to prepare the manuscript for publication and taking the time to do so.

McNiff and Whitehead (2009) offer valuable insights to getting articles published. The first rule of getting published is to know what you want to say, why you want to say it, and to whom you want to say it. The key to success is knowing who you are writing for and then writing for them. You may have heard the concept of "writing for a market." This means getting to know your readers and what they like reading. To accomplish this, you need to make yourself familiar with what other people are writing for them. This involves doing your homework prior to submitting your article. The homework would involve reading previous volumes of the journal to get a feel for the style of a particular journal. Then write your article in a way that is appropriate and in alignment with the publication. You will want to read the "Notes to Contributors" or locate the "Submission Guidelines" provided by the journal to support you in writing in an appropriate style and format for the journal. Also submit your material in exactly the way that editors request; failure to do so may mean your material is rejected immediately.

Rejection, however, is not always as final as it seems. Sometimes it is a normal part of the publication process, and you should be prepared to edit your work. For example, if you have submitted your manuscript to a peer-reviewed journal, it will be sent out to reviewers. Reviewers' ratings and comments are often returned to authors, and you should pay close attention to the feedback you receive. This feedback can provide important suggestions for you to improve your work. Even if you don't elect to rework the paper entirely in light of the comments, you may need to consider modifying portions of it. If required to revise and resubmit the work to the editor, you will want to make note of all the changes that you made to the manuscript as they relate to the reviewers' feedback. Also be prepared to shorten the paper. This can be painful, but it is a common request, and you have to be prepared to meet the print limitations of the journal. Anything you must cut at this stage can be used in another article, so effort and important insights can still be shared. If the article is rejected by the journal, read the feedback carefully and submit a revised manuscript to another journal that may be a better fit for your work (McNiff & Whitehead, 2009).

Getting published is not always easy, but it can be done. It is like any new adventure: there is a learning curve that must be overcome and a need for practice and improvement based on feedback. McNiff and Whitehead (2009) wrote, "The key to publishing is a small amount of talent and a lot of hard work. The talent comes naturally. The work comes from the belief that you have something worth saying, and the determination and tenacity to say it" (p. 178).

"NOTE"-ABLE THOUGHTS

What are potential publication outlets for your study? Examine the chart of action research journals and content area journals provided in Appendix B. Identify at least three possible outlets. Visit the website links provided and determine if there are any viable options. Rank order the possible outlets, and make a plan for publication submission.

TAKING ACTION: CRAFTING THE ABSTRACT AND POLICY IMPLICATION STATEMENTS

In several spots in this chapter, we've asked you to think back on the previous actions and activities that you've engaged in during the process of this research. Before developing the products that we've previously described, we're going to ask you to look back at your researcher's log one more time to see all of the steps you have engaged in to this point and think about how they align with the various forms of dissemination that were included in our list of possibilities. In doing so, you should recognize that you've generally completed work on multiple sections, including the Introduction (area of focus, statement of the problem, description of the research context, and research questions), the Synthesis of Literature, the Research Plan (participants, description of the intervention or innovation, data collection), Data Analysis and Reflection (interpretations and implications of results/findings), and the Action Plan (specific plan of action steps). However, you still need to

- write an abstract,

- update the research plan to indicate activities in the past tense,

- elaborate on the implications (including a discussion of changes to the study),

- write a conclusion, and

- compile a complete reference list and check it against APA guidelines for formatting.

While this to-do list includes a few more steps that will require attention to some specific details, you've now done the bulk of what is needed to share your work with others. We'll specifically discuss writing the abstract and elaborating on implications shortly to help you continue to diminish the work that remains.

WRITING AN ABSTRACT

As a first step in this process, we are going to focus on writing an **abstract**, which is a required component of the majority of publication outlets you will encounter. While we know your focus may not be on publication, we've found this exercise to be beneficial for the teachers we have worked with, as it helps them concentrate on the "big ideas" from their study, and share them in a concise, concentrated format. The abstract is important, as it is the first piece of information the audience will encounter about your study. In essence, it gives the reader a first impression of the study, letting readers decide whether to continue reading and showing them what to look for if they do. In the case of a summary or presentation, the abstract could be shown prior to the Introduction or as the first slide of the presentation. The following are some general guidelines you should refer to when creating an abstract:

- It should be concise (200 words or less).

- It should accurately report the information from your study.

- It expresses the purpose/problem under study, the methodology, two or three major findings, and the implications.

As a general rule of thumb, each of the respective items shared in the final bullet point should be expressed in one or two sentences. The abstract should not include extensive citations, information not addressed with your study or its description, or definitions or detailed descriptions of terminology.

We recommend beginning your construction of the abstract by identifying key terms and important phrases or sentences in what you have written to date. This will inevitably result in too much information, but that is okay at first. The key becomes further examining the information you've gathered to determine what is most important to share and set the first impression. Consider questions like "What does the reader absolutely have to know?" or "What can I share within the primary narrative or text?" Be prepared to engage in this process several times, continually editing and refining until you can convey the information in such a way as to achieve the 200 words or less standard (or whatever the criterion is for the journal or presentation outlet that you are writing for). Be advised, we've written for various outlets that require abstracts to be as few as 100 words or less. It's challenging when composing for that particular length, but with careful consideration and a little "word smithing," it is achievable.

ELABORATING ON IMPLICATIONS

In Chapter 7, you reflected on your results and created an action plan. Taking action based on your results is a fundamental aspect of action research. You determined actions you will take within your practice to improve teaching and learning based on what you learned from your study. It is possible that, in addition to implications for your practice, there are also potential **policy implications**, which are action statements developed to inform policy, that resulted from the study. If so, as you share your results, you will want to be able to clearly present and articulate these implications to those who have decision-making power and can utilize your results to inform policy or consider procedural changes. When writing your recommendations, it is even more imperative to be clear, concise, and specific, as these are actions you hope others will take to more broadly address the problem or issue you studied. Use the following tips and examples (Short, 2004) found in Figure 8.2 to assist you in crafting effective policy recommendation statements:

- Present concrete action statements.

- State specifically who can undertake such actions, and explain how the action will solve the problem or issue you identified.

- Recommendations you suggest should follow directly from your research data, reflections, and conclusions.

Once written, be sure to reread your results as well as the recommendation statements to ensure they are aligned and that your recommendations don't extend beyond information that can be associated directly with the results. We recommend policy or procedural statements be presented in the Implications section of the action research report, summary, and presentation you create; however, we have also seen these recommendations within the Action Plan section. The choice is often dependent on whether you are primarily making suggestions (Implications) or whether you will actual implement and examine approaches associated with them (Action Plan).

FIGURE 8.2 Procedural or Policy Recommendation Statement Examples

1. **Provide time for collaboration.** Teachers need time to work with others to examine program effectiveness, discuss student needs, and plan instructional strategies. At the administrative and district level, teachers should be given the opportunity to have collaborative planning time during the school day *or* they should have contracts that provide the teacher the option to work an extended day with added time for this collaborative planning.

2. **Involve teachers in the process of selecting curricular programs.** One program or set of materials does not fit all children. The district and school administration should ask teachers what kids need and involve them in the curriculum decision-making process.

3. **Provide specific goals and standards expectations.** However, allow teachers to modify and adjust programs and materials to match the needs of their particular student population. If the district and local administration effectively communicate this policy with teachers, then there will be a stronger commitment from teachers and better learning outcomes for all students.

4. **Provide teacher training on the effective integration of music in the curriculum.** Utilizing music effectively can increase student retention of information and is aligned with current brain research on cognition. Therefore, professional development coordinators should offer opportunities for teachers to learn effective techniques for incorporating music into the learning process.

Developing a Product: Creating the Action Research Report Outline, Presentation, and Summary

We've written this chapter to be outcomes oriented. That is, our focus has been directed toward helping you consider the various ways that you could share your work with others. The emphasis now shifts to creating the products that you will use to do so as we help you develop an action research report outline, a summary, and a presentation.

ACTION RESEARCH REPORT OUTLINE

Rather than composing the full action research report as part of the chapter, we'll refer you to Appendix A, where you can find two examples of action research reports in their entirety. Instead, we'll help you construct a general outline that will assist you in the organization of your report as well as in developing the summary and presentation.

The outline in Figure 8.3 should be used in the creation of the final action research report. We've included various considerations within each section that reinforce what

---

FIGURE 8.3   Research Report Outline Considerations

Action Research Report Outline

1. Abstract
2. Introduction
   a. Statement of the Problem
   b. Research Questions
3. Synthesis of Literature
   a. Educational/Personal Significance and Question Integration—This should describe the personal and professional reasons for conducting the research, including an explicit connection to contextual factors in the school/learning environment (i.e., multiple intelligences, cultures) that contribute to the necessity of the research. Essentially, it should establish the purposes. This should set the stage for everything that follows, as you want each portion of the synthesis to relate back to the research question(s).
   b. Discussion of Research and Research Analysis—For this section, you summarize the pertinent information on the topic and past research that has been conducted. The discussion of research should describe the topic in-depth, including methods/strategies where applicable, and the results of other investigations. You should describe and analyze literature that both supports and contradicts your chosen intervention. If there isn't any literature that reflects the latter, explicitly state that research has not shown evidence to the contrary. However, analysis should be clear as to why there is a lack of contrary evidence.
   c. Reflection on Literature—You've established the rationale for your study and described previous research; now write about your experiences in light of what the research revealed.
   d. Conclusion and Synthesis—This is essentially a paragraph to summarize all that you have written about in the previous sections.
4. Research Plan
   a. Context for Research—This describes the participants and context for the research.
   b. Data Collection Strategies and Rationales—This describes what data you collected, how you collected it, and why you selected this collection strategy and form of data.

---

c. Activities/Procedure—This describes in detail when and how the activities for the research were conducted. This should include informed consent and specific points of data collection (pre-assessment, formative assessment, and summative assessment).

d. Process of Data Collection—You should include the exact processes you enacted to collect data as well as the information that was collected.

e. Informed Consent—Information in this portion of the assignment should describe how you collected the informed consent from participants (if necessary).

5. Data Analysis

a. Data Analysis—Describe how the data was analyzed, specifically addressing the results of any quantitative tests that you administered. All graphs, charts, and so on that you used to make sense of the data should be included. If you focused on qualitative data, describe how you developed your generalizations and theories.

b. Formative and Summative Assessment Data Information must clearly describe how formative data was used within the process of your action research project. This can easily incorporate or encompass your reflective logs, as anecdotal evidence can be used to note progress.

6. Reflections and Implications—This should encompass a description of how what you found within the action research project compared with findings that were reviewed in your search for relevant literature. Were your findings consistent with prior research? How might this inform what research you may consider in the future? This section should lay the foundation for the action plan.

a. Self-reflection—This should be a synthesis of the reflective logs as well as your initial thoughts about your action research project after completion.

b. Implications for Personal Practice—Describe how the results of your action research impacted your practices relative to the area you chose to investigate. This should extend what was begun as part of the Data Analysis and Reflection and provide your final thoughts regarding your future instruction and research.

c. Implications for P–12 Learning—You should attempt to answer, "How will the results of your action research study impact P–12 learning?" This should link instruction and learning based upon the formative and summative data that was collected. Specific recommendations should be made for various populations of students (linked to the information on contextual elements described in the Significance portion of the synthesis of literature).

d. Implications and Recommendations—Are there policy or procedural implications for school-wide, district-wide, and/or state-wide policies? The implications should be discussed, and concrete actions should be presented as policy recommendations. It should be clear who should undertake the actions, and an explanation for how these policy changes would solve the problem you identified should be articulated. Make sure there is a clear linkage between your research conclusions and the recommendations you present. Incorporate what was developed in the Taking Action: Applying Theory to Practice section above.

7. Action Plan and Policy Recommendations

a. Discussion of Changes—What would you change about the research you conducted? How could the investigation have been improved?

b. Plan of Action—Describe how you will enter the next phase of action research. What research will you conduct moving forward based on the results of what you found within this action research project?

8. Conclusions

a. Summary of study and concluding remarks that highlight thoughts you want to leave the reader with—the major insights or wonderings you are taking from the study.

9. Reference List

10. Appendices

a. Copies of research permission forms, written surveys, interview questions, and so on (forms used in the research or as part of the curricular engagement).

was presented in the various chapters in the book to help you determine whether the information you include fits within the relevant area and whether the details you have elected to include address the primary considerations pertinent to the section.

ACTION RESEARCH PRESENTATION

Note for each element of the presentation addressed below in Figure 8.4, we have indicated the chapter of the relevant source of information that can be used in the preparation of the slide. In general, the information involves a synthesis of information that may encompass multiple pages in the previous format. If you have multiple graphs/tables/figures, you can include more slides than what is included in the total below. The purpose of the presentation is to support the sharing of your action research and to provide others with information about your results.

FIGURE 8.4   Elements of the Presentation

1. Abstract (1 slide; Chapter 8)

2. Research Question(s) (1 slide; Chapter 2)

3. Rationale (1or 2 slides; Chapters 2 and 3)

4. Synthesis of Literature (3–5 slides; Chapter 3)

5. Research Plan (2–4 slides; Chapters 4 and 5)

    a. Description of participants

    b. Description of intervention or innovation

    c. Data collection

6. Data Analysis and Results (2–6 slides; Chapter 6)

7. Reflections and Implications (2–5 slides; Chapter 7)

8. Action Plan (1 or 2 slides; Chapter 7)

ACTION RESEARCH SUMMARY

Short (2004) recommends the following when writing an action research summary:

- Provide key points that are short and succinct. Lists and bullets often make it easier to grasp key points.

- Tables and graphs, and other graphic organizers, add visual interest and allow you to concisely present significant data from the study.

- Do not overload the pages—put spaces between sections, use at least 12-point font, and have at least one-inch margins.

The major headings of the summary report can be the same as the headings used in the outline of the formal action research report presented earlier. The example action research summary reports presented in the Case in Point: Action Research Summary section later in the chapter can be a useful guide to presenting your work in this summary format.

You may also want to engage in Activity 2 in the Additional Resources and Optional Activities section of the chapter to examine additional examples of this format.

EVALUATING AGAINST THE STANDARDS: ARE YOU READY TO MOVE ON?

CHECKLIST: ACTION RESEARCH REPORT

_____1. Is the report written in first person?

_____2. Are the area of focus, context of study, and research questions sufficiently developed and prominently presented early in the report so that the reader knows the intention of the study?

_____3. Is the report an explanatory text, not just a descriptive text? Does the entire text stand as an explanation for what you are doing and why you are doing it?

_____4. Does the review of the literature show that you are knowledgeable about the topic and that you are informed about the problem of practice that you are investigating?

_____5. Are the data collection and analysis procedures clear and succinct so that others could replicate your study?

_____6. Is the report written in a clear way for the reader to understand what the findings of the study mean? Have you effectively communicated the significance of the results? Were you able to establish connections back to the review of the literature?

_____7. Is there evidence of depth of reflection in action and reflection on action throughout the report? Do you clearly present how the findings of the study will impact your practice? If there are policy implications from your study, are those presented as recommendations that can be implemented by others?

_____8. Did you describe the next phase of your action research?

CHECKLIST: ACTION RESEARCH SUMMARY

_____1. Are key points presented in a short and succinct manner?

_____2. Are bullets and lists used appropriately?

_____3. Is the summary visually interesting, with graphs and tables to present data?

_____4. Is there plenty of white space on the page and is the text sized to be easily read?

_____5. Is the summary two pages or less?

_____6. After reading the summary, can these basic questions be answered: What was the purpose of the study? How was the data collected and analyzed? What did the researchers find when they collected the data? What do the findings mean?

Moving Forward: Potential Challenges

This marks the end of the first phase of the action research process. The next step is to enact the ideas for the research you want to conduct moving forward based on the results of this action research project. Your research may continue along the same lines of inquiry, or your reflection on your results may be taking you in a different direction. Whether staying the course or asking new questions, it is important to note that as you move forward with future phases of your action research, there are certain challenges you may face. A common dilemma as you move further into the action research process is to run into a lack of resources to continue the work. You may want to consider at this point pursuing funding to support your efforts. You have developed a project with a strong rationale, research plan, and initial outcomes and results from the first phase of the work. This can be used to develop a solid grant proposal to support the next phase of your inquiry. Many professional organizations, local agencies, civic organizations, and community foundations provide grant funding opportunities that may help you secure the resources you need to move forward. Invest the time to research and identify potential funding sources. Often, you can make only minor adjustments to your written report or summary to meet the proposal requirements for the funding request. Many funding sources are often eager for strong proposals, and securing the funding may not be as difficult as you may think.

Another typical challenge you may face is resistance to change from colleagues, administrators, or policymakers. Your work has resulted in change to your practice, and you may have even generated recommendations for broader policy changes. Your task is to share your new insights and present your recommendations as clearly and confidently as you can; however, do not be dismayed if others are not as eager for change. Change often involves risk and, if it happens, it usually takes time. A final common challenge faced by teachers is making time for ongoing action research within their practice. Time is one of our most valued commodities, and we have to make difficult decisions with this limited resource. Nevertheless, it is true that we make time for what we value. We hope that as you have experienced the value of action research during the first phase of implementation, you will continue to make time for it on an ongoing basis within your practice. Again, it is our hope that the time, energy, and commitment you invested in the action research process will culminate with a sense of satisfaction, accomplishment, and a renewed professional curiosity that will motivate and inspire you to continue your efforts as a researcher into the future.

Summary

The effort you have invested in writing up your action research study will have many benefits. It has required you to spend additional time organizing and thinking through your study to determine what is most valuable about your work and what you want to communicate with others about your learning from the process. You have gained a deeper understanding about a problem of practice, student learning, yourself as a teacher and researcher, and how to effectively communicate your ideas with others. Others within and outside your school context will benefit from learning about your work and may even be inspired to adopt/modify your insights or choose to engage with you or in their own inquiry into their practice. You are aware of the many opportunities that exist for sharing the outcomes of your work, and you have developed a plan for who you want to share your work with, what you will share, and how you will share it. It is important to remember that with the digital age, the opportunities for disseminating your ideas are bounded only by your imagination or level of energy. You need to believe that you can do it, and you will. It is our hope that this action research experience will be just the beginning of your work as a teacher who systematically examines your practices through research. By problem solving around potential challenges, the systematic process of action research can become an ongoing, natural, and integral aspect of your professional practice.

Key Terms

Abstract, p. 182

Action research report, p. 173

Action research summary, p. 177

Policy implications, p. 183

Praxis, p. 173

Case in Point: Action Research Summary

You have followed the journey of an elementary and secondary teacher engaged in the action research process throughout the text. As you work on finalizing your work to allow you to share and disseminate it with others, you have the opportunity to see the complete action research report for both the elementary and secondary teachers' projects. These complete products are found in Appendix A. In Figures 8.5 and 8.6, we provide action research summaries to support you in developing this product.

One Elementary Teacher's Journey: The Action Research Summary

FIGURE 8.5 Elementary Action Research Summary Example

Introduction

What is the effect of Readers' Theater on second-grade students' reading fluency?

Fluency is an area that has been identified as vital for development of proficiency within reading. In my class, the students demonstrated varying levels of reading fluency, and the intent of this research was to provide an intervention to boost skills in this area. Readers' Theater is a fun way to get students engaged with the text they are reading repeatedly. It also provides them with a purpose to read fluently. I had hoped that by implementing Readers' Theater on a regular basis, I would see a significant improvement in the reading rate, accuracy, and prosody of my students. The purpose of this study was to determine the effects of the Readers' Theater on 24 second-grade students.

Research Plan

The elementary school's population:

- 58% of the students categorized as economically disadvantaged
- Mixed demographics, with the following ethnicities represented: African American (59%), Hispanic (20%), Caucasian (12%), multiracial (5%), Asian (3%), and American Indian (1%)

(Continued)

FIGURE 8.5 (Continued)

Participants (24 second-grade students):

- 10 females, 14 males
- 12 African Americans, eight Hispanic Americans, three Caucasians, and one multiracial participant

Intervention:

- The students' fluency scores were assessed using DIBELS to establish baseline performance levels
- The weekly Readers' Theater intervention was put in place for five weeks. Each week followed a standard protocol as students were exposed to various scripts, were assigned parts, and then worked with the teacher and peers to rehearse their lines through repeated readings.
- Fluency was assessed after three weeks of the intervention (midpoint assessment) and after five weeks (post-test)

Data Analysis and Reflection

Data from the pre-test, midpoint assessment, and post-test administration of DIBELS progress monitoring data (oral reading fluency scores) were collected.

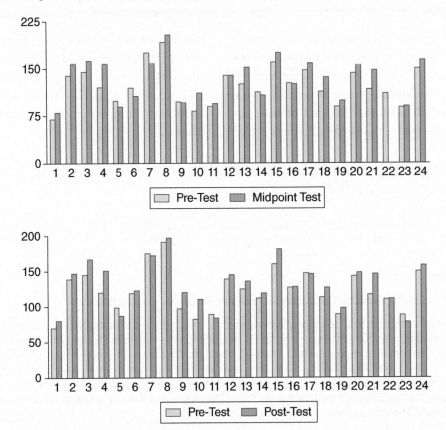

The DIBELS ORF average results showed a large increase in the groups' words read per minutes from pre-test to midpoint assessment, then a minimal increase from the midpoint assessment to the post-test. Comparing pre-test and post-test scores, students gained an average of 10.69 words per minute. On the post-test assessment, students read an average of 133.69 words per minute. The scores ranged from a low of 81 words per minute to a high of 196 words per minute. From pre-test to post-test, 19 students showed an increase in the number of words per minutes and four students demonstrated a decrease.

Conclusion

Overall, the students showed growth in the areas of reading rate and prosody. Over the course of five weeks, students became more engaged in reading, were able to master words that were unknown to them, and became more aware of not only their reading speed, but all components of fluency. With the implementation of Readers' Theater, students were able to take part in an authentic reading experience and now have a more in depth understanding of what fluent reading looks like and sounds like.

Action Plan

In the future, I plan to continue to examine the impact of Readers' Theater on students' comprehension and motivation. Furthermore, I will consider using Readers' Theater as a tool to integrate reading within other content areas, such as science. This method of repeated reading could increase the students' awareness and understanding of vocabulary words, and it could be a strategy used to introduce a unit, while giving readers extra exposure to certain concepts and vocabulary.

One Secondary Teacher's Journey:
The Action Research Summary

FIGURE 8.6   Secondary Action Research Summary Example

Introduction

What is the effect of an open investigation workshop approach on a ninth-grade science class with students who are lower-level readers/writers?

In a lower-level ability section of ninth-grade science, students struggle with science content and a motivation to learn. I want to see how an open investigation workshop approach impacts these students' learning and engagement during the second quarter of instruction. The purpose of this action research study is to implement the open investigation approach with my science class of below-level readers/writers to improve their academic achievement and motivation for learning.

Research Plan

The secondary school's population:

- Located in a suburban area near a large metropolitan city
- Classified as medium socio-economic status with 48% of the students eligible for free or reduced lunch
- Mixed demographics, with the following ethnicities represented: Caucasian (79%) African American (17%), Asian American (2%) and American Indian/Pacific Islander (1%), and other (1%)

Participants: A science class of 28 students

- eight with 504 plans, and two with IEPs
- 16 male; 12 female
- 19 have low informational text reading scores; nine have low-medium range scores

Intervention:

- The students' test scores using direct instruction were compiled over a period of eight weeks (first quarter) to have as a baseline comparison.
- Students were given the attitude questionnaire at the conclusion of the eight-week period using direct instruction to have as a baseline comparison.

(Continued)

FIGURE 8.6 (Continued)

- The open investigation workshop intervention was put in place for eight weeks during the second quarter. Each week, students completed multiple-choice tests (same format as used in the first quarter) to measure their learning of the content. I kept observational field notes during the intervention and made adjustments as needed to the structure and delivery of the open investigation workshop approach. The interventions took place during science class, five days a week, from Monday through Friday.
- At the end of the last week of implementation, the students were given the attitude questionnaire to measure their response to the intervention.

Data Analysis and Reflection

Multiple forms of data that aligned with the research question were collected and used for the analysis: qualitative field notes/research log containing observations and anecdotal notes, weekly multiple-choice test scores, data from the pre-questionnaire and post-questionnaire with both Likert-scale questions and two open-ended questions.

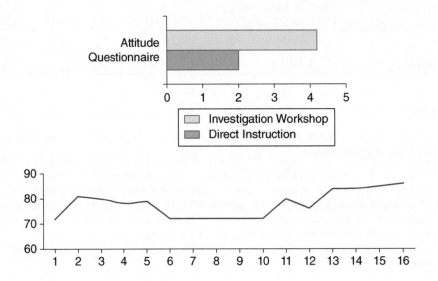

- The overall class mean score for the attitude questionnaire increased from a 2.0 with direct instruction to a 4.2 with open investigation workshop.
- The open-ended questions revealed that the students were more positive about the class experience because of the collaboration of the teams, active nature of the classes—"loved getting to *do* science and to act like scientists"—and enjoyed talking through the problem-solving possibilities.
- The trend for the weekly test scores during direct instruction (weeks 1–8) was an initial increase in scores from week 1 to weeks 2–5 and then a decline back to initial lower levels for weeks 6–8. The trend for the weekly test scores during open investigation (weeks 9–16) was a slow and level start in weeks 9 and 10 and then a (mostly) gradual increase with the highest average test scores received in weeks 15 and 16.
- Surprisingly, the higher-level students' performance was weaker initially with the open investigation method but did improve back to initial levels of achievement demonstrated with direct instruction.

Conclusion

Overall, the students showed growth in achievement and attitude with the open investigation workshop. Over the course of the eight-week intervention, students did struggle initially with the new format and were resistant to the change. I had to make many modifications to the structure of the workshop as it was implemented based on my observations and reflections during the process. There were times that I felt the workshop format was too demanding of the students and wanted to give up on it. However, as time went on and I made adjustments based on the formative data I was collecting I began to see progress in my students' ability to be actively engaged learners who took responsibility for their learning. I believe as they gained confidence and skills in what was being asked of them they began to have a more positive attitude toward their learning and this impacted their achievement in the class. The best outcome for me is that my students now love our class! I have to make them leave at the end of each class session so they will not be late for their next class! This has increased my planning but also my enjoyment of teaching this class.

Action Plan

I need to continue to make improvements to the workshop structure and function especially in regard to increasing learning outcome potential for my higher-level students in the class; however, the improvement in their overall attitudes toward learning science has convinced me to keep using this approach with this class. I also need to continue to develop scaffolding tools to support the reading and writing that is required in the ninth grade science materials for these struggling students. I believe that with appropriate and additional scaffolding I can improve all of the students' access to the material and comprehension of it. To accomplish this, I plan on sharing my study with the other ninth-grade science teachers to encourage that we use the open investigation workshop with all our students. I hope to get others interested in using this with their lower-level sections and work together to develop materials and resources to support this work with our struggling readers/writers. I think when they see (and hear from the students) how much improvement there is in student attitude toward learning science that at least two of the other teachers will want to work with me on this project. With a team approach, I believe I can sustain this method of teaching! With a few more iterations of the action research process, I may feel confident to share my work with other teachers in the district or at a professional conference.

Activities and Additional Resources

1. Go to Teachersnetwork.org and read a few more examples of action research summaries: http://www.teachersnetwork.org/tnli/research. Use the action research summary checklist in the Evaluating Against the Standards: Are You Ready to Move On? section to evaluate the summaries that you read. Use the ones that meet the evaluation criteria to guide you when writing your own action research summary.

2. Attend a local conference in your field or area of interest. Identify and attend sessions that present related work. Carefully observe the presenters, and make note of the strengths and weaknesses of the presentations. Make notes of what you will want to incorporate into your presentations and pitfalls you should try to avoid. Find roundtables and other opportunities to network with others with common interests, and find ways that they have disseminated their work. Build your confidence in attending conferences and seminars, and otherwise engaging in professional public life.

3. If you have decided to publish your work in an educational journal, you will want to seek additional resources outside the suggestions provided in this chapter to support the preparation of your manuscript. We recommend that you locate and use the following resource as you pursue the task of publishing your action research study.

Print Resources

Belcher, W. (2009). *Writing your journal article in 12 weeks: A guide to academic publishing success.* Thousand Oaks, CA: Sage.

Student Study Site

edge.sagepub.com/putman

- Take the practice quiz.
- Review key terms with eFlashcards.
- Explore topics with video and multimedia.

References

Henning, J., Stone, J., & Kelly, J. (2009). *Using action research to improve instruction: An interactive guide for teachers.* New York, NY: Routledge

McNiff, J. (1990). Writing and the creation of educational knowledge. In P. Lomax (Ed.), *Managing staff development in schools: An action research approach* (pp. 52–60). Clevedon, England: Multilingual Matters.

McNiff, J., & Whitehead, J. (2009). *Doing and writing action research.* New York, NY: Routledge.

Short, K. (2004). Writing a report of action research/teacher research. Available at https://www.coe .arizona.edu/sites/default/files/research_report_format.pdf

Somekh, B. (1995). The contribution of action research to development in social endeavours: A position paper on action research methodology. *British Educational Research Journal, 21,* 339–355.

Zuber-Skerritt, O. (1996). *New directions in action research.* London, England: Falmer Press.

CHAPTER 9

Leading a Collaborative Action Research Team

GUIDING QUESTIONS

After reading this chapter, you should be able to answer the following questions:

- What are the benefits of collaborative, school-wide action research?

- What is a community of practice?

- What is a professional learning community?

- How can technology be leveraged to develop a collaborative community?

- What are steps and considerations within the process of conducting collaborative action research?

- What role does the facilitator play within collaborative action research?

CHAPTER AIMS AND GOALS

This chapter serves to move you beyond individual action research and introduces you to considerations necessary for expanding the action research process to become a collaborative effort. Within this process, you will be introduced to communities of practice, professional learning communities, and specific structures and processes that should be considered to increase the success of the collaborative effort. We also present strategies to leverage technology within the action research process to provide flexibility and alternate means of communication. The structure of the chapter deviates slightly from the CAPES framework, as there will be no specific implementation step that you will complete after reading about the tenets of professional learning communities and school-embedded development, primarily because these processes are context specific. However, we include resources to help you determine if your current setting contains the necessary ingredients for collaborative or schoolwide action research and to help you plan what actions may be necessary to create the context for this to occur.

SETTING THE CONTEXT: ORGANIZING FOR COLLABORATIVE ACTION RESEARCH

Teaching could be characterized as a solitary practice. We go to our classrooms, shut our doors, and go about the tasks associated with helping our students learn. Within the typical teaching schedule, there are few real opportunities to engage with our peers about our teaching practices or the strategies we are using to improve our students' learning, except perhaps through a quick conversation in the hall or teachers' workroom while making copies or preparing something to be used for a lesson. To some degree, the bulk of this text is built around this paradigm as we've helped you to develop the knowledge and skills to successfully conduct your own (individual) action research. However, to have the greatest impact on student learning, teachers "cannot work and learn entirely alone or in separate training courses after school" (Hargreaves, 2003, p. 25). It is now time to begin to think about how to build upon your experiences and extend the action research process to include peers and colleagues. Revisiting several figures introduced in previous chapters, we'll help you think about how to work directly with the people in the sphere that surrounds you (see Figure 9.1) and extend the action research process to

FIGURE 9.1 Audiences for Action Research

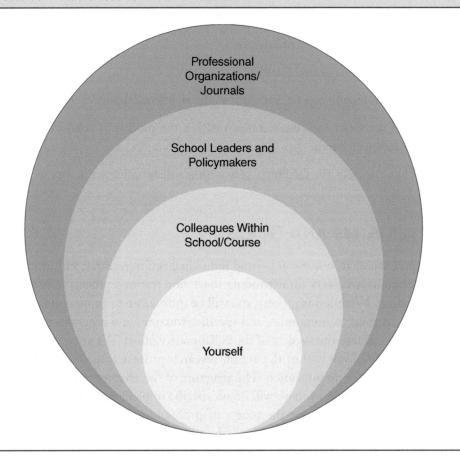

FIGURE 9.2   Collaborative Action Research Model

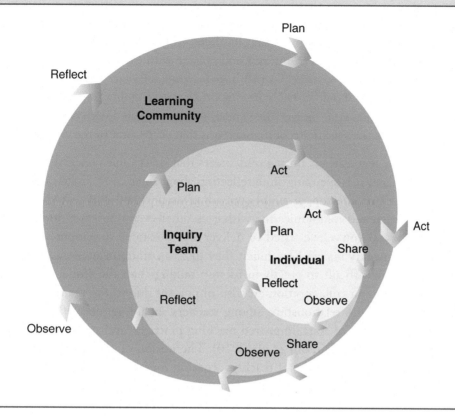

incorporate inquiry teams and learning communities (see Figure 9.2). As we move beyond individual planning for action research, we will begin to consider how teams of educational stakeholders (e.g., teachers, assistants, administrators, and counselors) can partner to engage in the iterative processes that define action research to develop curriculum or implement strategies aimed at improving student learning. Subsequently, through this collaborative activity, the number of students that can be impacted increases significantly, especially as successive iterations of the action research process are enacted.

"NOTE"-ABLE THOUGHTS

How could you connect the action research process to existing structures that support collaborative team efforts at your school?

BUILDING COMMUNITY

There is little doubt that relationships are an important factor within teaching. Our work is best accomplished when we build connections with our students, their parents, and the other adults in our building. This concept is emphasized in Westheimer's (1998) description of the characteristics of community, which encompasses "interaction and participation, interdependence, shared interests and beliefs, [and] concern for individual and minority views" (p. 12). Others (e.g., DuFour, DuFour, Eaker, & Many, 2010; Lave

& Wenger, 1998) echo this idea as they note the importance of opportunities for teachers to engage in processes that incorporate collaboration and reflection as necessary to help teachers to consider new practices. If we seek to build communities of teachers and diminish the sense of isolationism that has been so prevalent in teaching, we need to consider ways for colleagues to interact and engage with each other on a regular basis around ideas, programs, or strategies that have personal relevance to the work completed in our classroom or school. To facilitate this process, we're going to explore the broader notion of community and some of the general tenets associated with community building to help frame the specific recommendations that occur later in the chapter.

We've met very few teachers during our careers that don't value collegiality with other teachers. Whether it is spending time reflecting about their craft, discussing ways they could deliver a better lesson, or simply providing support and understanding, teachers value cooperation and communication with each other, even if it is not often present in the typical day. If you've ever tried to deliver a professional development session to teachers, you quickly realize how much they like to communicate—we've found it's sometimes more difficult to get them to stop talking than the students they teach! Communication and collaboration are also important due to the many positive outcomes associated with relationships among teachers, including more effective decision making, higher levels of trust, improved teaching practices, and sustained professional learning (Barth, 1990; DuFour et al., 2010). The notion of cooperative professional learning, which involves teams of teachers working together to enhance their professional knowledge and skills, is a natural extension of the sense of collegiality teachers value. When we are able to collaborate in work that aligns closely to our teaching, we can focus on sharing expertise and practices, and subsequently, learning from each other. Furthermore, when there is a mutual sense of support, there is an overall positive climate that permeates throughout the school, from the teachers to the students and families.

Going a little deeper, as we consider the joint discussions that can occur within a collaborative environment, we can engage in shared decision making about the skills, strategies, or curriculum that could be targeted within an action research process. This kind of collective dialogue can produce a different kind of accountability and support. Instead of externally driven consequences, we receive supportive and enabling feedback that results from shared inquiry and practices that are publicly discussed among colleagues. Hargreaves (2003) wrote, "Sharing ideas and expertise, providing moral support when dealing with new and difficult challenges, discussing complex individual cases together—this is the essence of strong collegiality and the basis of effective professional communities" (p. 109).

When we focus on co-constructing knowledge within the processes of relationship building and dialogue with our colleagues, there is an increased opportunity to support the development of a community. According to Hargreaves (2003), "It is vital that teachers engage in action, inquiry, and problem solving together in collegial teams or professional learning communities" (p. 25). Others have utilized different terms to characterize groups coming together for collaborative professional growth, including *communities of learners* (Barth, 1990), *instructional communities of practice* (Supovitz, 2002), and *communities of practice* (Lave & Wenger, 1998). Regardless of the label, participation within a teacher learning community is one of the five primary propositions of the National Board for Professional Teaching Standards (NBPTS, 2002). Activities of the community include "engaging in various forms of scholarly inquiry and artistic activity, or forming study groups for teachers" (NBPTS, 2002, p. 19). In our experiences, we have seen learning communities composed of grade-level teams, teachers of a particular content area, and even some that consist of all of the teachers at a school. For our purposes, we'll broadly define a **learning community** as a group of teachers, whether formally or informally organized, who wish to discuss and improve their practice. The teachers who are engaged in a learning community actively share information amongst the group, implement new ideas and strategies within their classroom, and then engage in conversations with other members about their experiences in an effort to share information as well as receive ongoing support.

■ ■ ■ VOICES FROM THE FIELD

Mary Olson, 12th-Grade Teacher

As a second-year teacher, I am constantly going to the other teachers on my team to ask questions about planning, the curriculum, my students, and a whole host of other things that seem to add to my daily challenges of teaching students who are already beginning to look beyond high school. I probably drive the rest of the teachers a bit crazy, but, truth be told, they always seem willing to help. Recently, I went to the lead teacher of the team to discuss what I saw as a lack of skill in reading and understanding complex text from my students. For some of my students, it's more of an unwillingness, but that is another story entirely. She mentioned that she had observed her students having similar difficulties, including limits on their ability to identify central ideas and use textual citations to support them. Given that two of the five team members were seeing similar trends, we decided to convene a team meeting to discuss the processes and strategies we were teaching students to use as they engaged with complex text.

As it turns out, four of the five us were struggling with this situation, while one teacher felt that what she had in place was working. A quick look at the data revealed that her students were doing better than the rest of ours. Rather than simply implement her strategies, though, the team lead thought it would be a good idea for each of us to observe in her classroom and then reconvene to discuss what we saw. Our plan was to use this discussion as a springboard into developing a plan that we could implement, which included not only what our instruction would look like, but what common assessments we could use to help us examine our data and how often we would examine this data. The general feeling was that a team-based approach would allow us to have additional, deliberate conversations about how we could prepare our students to be successful readers of complex text. We felt that the more we could work together, the greater the potential improvements across our students.

Given that our definition and description of *learning community* is a bit general, we've elected to briefly describe two "models" of learning communities to further help you work through the process of broadening the action research process: professional learning communities and communities of practice. We feel that various features associated with each one are very well aligned with the collaborative action research process. By describing these communities in greater detail, we think it will help build a foundation for the strategies and considerations that we share regarding the specific actions to be considered within this process as teams or communities of teachers are developed. We've included a number of resources about each that you can examine as you consider your developing knowledge about community or as you ponder suggestions we include in the chapter to guide your work.

PROFESSIONAL LEARNING COMMUNITIES

In Chapter 1, we introduced information on professional learning communities. Take a minute to see if you remember exactly what these consist of or what their purpose is. Just in case, to refresh your memory, a **professional learning community** is "a group of people sharing and critically interrogating their practice in an ongoing, reflective, collaborative, inclusive, learning-oriented, growth-promoting way" (Stoll, Bolam, McMahon, Wallace, & Thomas, 2006, p. 223). We also wrote that schools are increasingly turning to developing professional learning communities (PLCs) to create a collaborative, goal-driven atmosphere that is characterized by a focus on improved practices and increased student achievement. PLCs are aligned with the idea that learning is a social activity involving interactions among the participants within a specific setting. The latter is especially important, as multiple studies revealed that teachers seek sustained professional development focused on strategies that would be useful within their specific context of practice, for example, their classroom (Borko, 2004; Leask & Younie, 2001). Professional learning communities address these needs by bringing teachers in a school together to work collaboratively to engage in curriculum development or planning.

Within the development of a PLC, leaders and participants should maintain a focus on professional growth, cultivation of a culture of collaboration, and sustained attention directed toward results (DuFour et al., 2010). Similarly, Newmann & Associates (1996) suggested a PLC is characterized by

- development of shared values that are focused on school values and priorities;

- focus on student learning;

- ongoing reflective dialogue among teachers on curriculum, instruction, and learning;

- public sharing of teaching practices; and

- active focus on collaboration.

Combined, these traits can create a climate that leads toward the collective development of all professionals within a school. When emphasis is directed toward each of these elements within the activities associated with the PLC, the results simultaneously reflect both improvements in practice as well as demonstrated increases in student achievement.

In practice, we have seen the development of a PLC begin as an administrator, a team of teachers, or instructional specialist identified an area of challenge for students in a school. What follows is often dependent upon the individual leading the PLC as well as the context. Teachers can be asked to reflect upon their practices relative to this particular area, followed by a meeting where the staff begins a collaborative dialogue around their reflections. In this meeting, the focus can be directed toward determining new teaching methods or strategies and developing a plan to implement them to collectively address the challenge. Within the implementation process, participants engage in an ongoing discussion of the activities, including formative analysis of examples of student work to determine the effectiveness of the methods, and the teachers scaffold and support each other as necessary. Finally, as part of the overall focus on improving student achievement, the group considers the relationship between the methods and their effects relative to learning. Similar to what we've presented about the action research process, PLCs involve recursive cycles of inquiry, yet this inquiry is conducted collaboratively (DuFour et al., 2010; Stoll et al., 2006).

"NOTE"-ABLE THOUGHTS

What are some of the goals or objectives in your school's mission or school improvement plan? How could these be used to guide the action research process through the formation of a professional learning community?

COMMUNITY OF PRACTICE

Another form of community that can be used to guide teacher-driven professional development is the community of practice, or CoP (Lave & Wenger, 1991; Wenger, 1998). A **community of practice** has been shown to create the collaborative conditions necessary to focus teachers on continued self-improvement, encourage teacher interaction, and facilitate change in teachers' behaviors (Bray, 2002). Unlike PLCs, CoPs are founded within the principle that learning often occurs in informally created groups that are focused on a particular topic or issue. Within the community, there is a sense of shared purpose and "an emphasis on group learning through intentional activity, collective reflection, and participatory decision-making" (Riel & Polin, 2004, p. 16).

While not adhering to a formal structure, participants in CoPs often develop identities based upon roles they adopt in support of the goals established by the group. These identities and roles scaffold the learning of others (Jonassen, Peck, & Wilson, 1999). For example, a teacher experienced in using literature circles may mentor another teacher or small group of teachers implementing this strategy. According to Lave and Wenger (1991), "CoP requires access to a wide range of ongoing activity, old-timers, and other members of the community; and to information, resources, and opportunities for participation" (p. 101). However, it is important to point out that although there is a need for individuals to be leaders or facilitators to organize work, all members, regardless of their role, help shape the agenda. The role of the leader is facilitative, and effective leaders within a CoP provide opportunities for others to take on this role as the purposes of the CoP evolve within the practices of continuous inquiry. Given the lack of formal structure, communities of practice offer greater flexibility to engage in inquiry without adopting a particular problem-solving process or sequence of organization. A flexible structure encourages discussions about courses of action and encourages the social activities necessary for continuous inquiry. In this regard, Wenger (1998) claims, "What matters is the interaction of the planned and the emergent—that is, the ability of teaching and learning to interact so as to become structuring resources for each other" (p. 266).

The inherent goals within a CoP are that learning and the community are sustained over an extended period of time. The group's purpose evolves, and it adapts the activities conducted as the context changes. The purpose, which is generally referred to as a joint enterprise, is the tie that binds the group together, as it is shared amongst the participants. A mutual sense of purpose and a greater ownership within the context of an authentic activity legitimizes participation and therefore enhances meaningfulness (Barab & Duffy, 2000; Lave & Wenger, 1991). One challenge that we have noted in examining CoPs is maintaining a focus toward a collective goal, rather than simply individual or course-specific objectives and perspectives. It is easy to become wrapped up in your own day-to-day challenges and realities, and thus the processes and activities associated with the CoP need to be designed to encourage continual engagement, where members regularly interact about the purpose and agenda. In other words, consideration must be given toward the reasons members participate and contribute and the activities or practices that maximize membership and active participation. The capacity of the facilitator and group to respond to these fundamental questions will significantly impact the overall success of the CoP (Riel & Polin, 2004).

"NOTE"-ABLE THOUGHTS

What similarities do you notice between the professional learning communities and communities of practice? What differences?

VIRTUAL LEARNING COMMUNITIES

We've highlighted two forms of community that are prevalent in the literature on the practice (see Figure 9.3), yet given the availability of technology and the increased access to peers and resources it provides, opportunities to engage in professional learning communities have expanded. The notion of "community" is no longer confined to a single location. Schools, teachers, and facilitators can leverage technology to provide anytime, anywhere connections that stretch across a district and beyond. The emphasis is still on mutual interests and needs, yet the flexibility inherent within the use of technology-facilitated communication allows the various benefits of PLCs and CoPs to be maintained (see Ajayi, 2009; Conrad, 2005). For example, two rural schools that are otherwise geographically isolated may be able to link toward addressing a problem that may be common to them, such as students' preparation for post-secondary schooling.

Ford, Branch, and Moore (2008) referred to technology-facilitated communities as **virtual professional learning communities** (VPLCs). Various forms of technology (see Tech Connections for additional examples) can be utilized to support collaborative learning among participants. This includes learning management systems (Blackboard, Schoology) or freely available Internet sites (e.g., wikis, Nings). Interactions can be characterized by text-based collaborations (e.g., wikis, blogs) or through video-conferencing (e.g., Skype, FaceTime). Each tool allows participants to overcome geographic barriers to engage with each other, and in some cases, the technology can function as a digital repository that allows teachers to collaboratively analyze student work, noting where success has been demonstrated and where additional efforts should be addressed. Given the regular interaction among colleagues necessary within the PLCs, social networks (e.g., Facebook, Twitter) also represent an important medium. They not only provide space for communication but also broaden the potential for the discovery of new ideas through interactions with others outside the PLC.

TECH CONNECTIONS

Learning management systems: Blackboard, Moodle, Canvas, Schoology, Edmodo

Text-based collaborative tools: Wikispaces, LocalWiki, Weebly, Edublog

Social networking tools: Facebook, Twitter, Google+, Ning

Topic-specific professional social networks:

Classroom 2.0 (http://www.classroom20.com)—Technology integration

Curriki (http://www.curriki.org)—General teaching

Educators PLN (http://www.edupln.com/?xg_source=badge)—General teaching (but lots of technology)

English Companion Ning (http://englishcompanion.ning.com)—English teachers

INFOhio Learning Commons (http://learningcommons.infohio.org)—Technology

NCTE's Connected Community (http://ncte.connectedcommunity.org)—English/language arts, literacy

As you consider the use of VPLCs as an alternative to developing a site-based community, it's important to highlight one distinction between the various forms of text-based interactions. One form of interaction, referred to as synchronous, represents real-time communication, as would be the case in a face-to-face communication. For example, sending text messages might be considered a form of synchronous communication if the participants immediately type messages back and forth. The other type of communication, asynchronous, involves time delays between responses, as might be the case in e-mail. Participants in the latter are free from the time constraints of responding immediately. Each has its own benefits, yet Shotsberger (2000) notes that asynchronous communication lacks the capability to provide immediate support and may diminish the sense of community present in a group due to delays among responses. Others (see Rovai & Jordan, 2004; Zhu, 2006) would argue asynchronous interactions allow participants to access information on an ongoing basis and reflect upon it for a period of time before participation, resulting in more meaningful responses. We have used both forms of communication successfully, and, rather than belabor the arguments that accompany each, we've provided additional resources at the end of the chapter that can be used to learn more. This will allow you to form your own conclusions about which would be most effective for your purposes.

"NOTE"-ABLE THOUGHTS

Does your school utilize a learning management system? How could it be utilized to start a conversation about a particular topic with like-minded teachers in the school? Otherwise, how could a topic-specific professional social network be used to begin this conversation?

FIGURE 9.3 Characteristics of Collaborative Learning Communities

	Professional Learning Community	Community of Practice	Virtual Learning Community
Purpose	Formed to improve practices associated with a need identified by administrator, teacher, or teaching team; focus on collective inquiry or action research to impact student learning	Formed to investigate a shared interest in a particular topic or need identified by participants; focus on collaborative development for student learning	Formed to minimize time and spatial issues; focus varies by group (PLC or CoP)
Structure	More formal, goal directed, process oriented	Flexible, informal	Variable (dependent upon leader)
Leadership	Defined leader(s) or oversight	Distributed, informal	Facilitator(s)
Membership	Required; all participate in collective action and reflection within ongoing activities around particular need; roles defined by focus of inquiry	Voluntary; all participate in ongoing discussions; adopt specific roles based on area(s) of expertise within identified areas of focus	Variable; all participate in ongoing discussions and active reflection; roles vary by structure established by organizer
Communication	Face to face	Face to face	Electronic (synchronous, asynchronous)

TAKING ACTION: COLLABORATIVE ACTION RESEARCH

Considering the information presented thus far, the concepts associated with the various forms of community are consistent with Mills's (2011) expanded definition of *action research*, which encompasses "any systematic inquiry conducted by teacher researchers, principals, school counselors, or other stakeholders in the teaching/learning environment to gather information about how their particular schools operate, how they teach, and how well their students learn" (p. 5). Within **collaborative action research**, there is an expansion from the individual teacher to a focus on the practice of multiple teachers, who may represent a grade level, content area, or all the teachers at the school or district (see Figure 9.4). Kemmis and McTaggart (1992) described the process this way:

> Participatory action research establishes self-critical communities of people participating and collaborating in all phases of the research process: the planning, the action, the observation and the reflection. It aims to build communities of people committed to enlightening themselves about the relationship between circumstance, action and consequence in their own situation. (p. 35)

A variety of positive outcomes have been linked to collaborative action research, from changes in teaching practices and curriculum to renewed vigor toward the profession and related efforts (Phillips & Carr, 2006).

We elected to include the previous descriptions of professional learning communities and the community of practice, as they are well aligned with many of the principles and

FIGURE 9.4 Levels of Collaborative Action Research

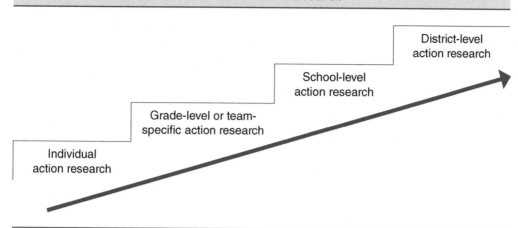

practices of collaborative action research. In each case, the process is likely to begin as a group of teachers engages in reflection and develops a set of common instructional goals to address an identified need within their practice. Our goal within this section is not necessarily to prescribe a specific process to complete collaborative research activities, as the primary steps do not change from those of individual action research. Instead, we would like to help you examine how the process of action research can be expanded to encompass additional participants, perhaps extending from the small teams to eventually include multiple schools or a district-level focus. To accomplish this, we will describe various factors you should consider as you seek to develop collaborative action research communities. Much of our discussion will focus on various facets of the process that must occur prior to starting the community; however, we will briefly describe additional aspects to think about during implementation and after completion of an iteration of the process.

BEGINNING THE CONVERSATION AND PLANNING FOR SUCCESS

Leadership. Leadership is a vital component within any schoolwide endeavor, but especially within our vision of the collaborative action research process. In providing a series of suggestions for implementation of collaborative action research, Kemmis and McTaggart (1992) note the importance of organization, including establishing who will lead the process. We concur and advocate that one of the first steps you should complete within the organizational process should be directed toward identifying who will ultimately guide the process, a position we will reference as the "facilitator" for the remainder of the chapter. Given that you have likely just completed your own action research study, we feel you definitely have the necessary knowledge of action research to fulfill this role and coordinate the planning and implementation. However, we also note that you'll need to assess your own level of comfort with regard to the overall climate of the school as well as your ability to lead prior to taking on the role.

Should you decide that you are not completely comfortable leading the effort, our recommendation is that planning and implementation should occur under the guidance of an individual, such as a building administrator or respected teacher, or a small team of individuals from within the school. Thinking about the latter, you could partner with a well-respected colleague in your school to engage in the process with you. Sometimes a lead teacher, such as a department head, is uniquely situated to fulfill these functions, as the individual is imbedded within a team and can provide encouragement within the context of practice. It is important that the individual or group of individuals ultimately selected is knowledgeable, not only about the proposed intervention and subsequent analysis but also about the school, including the climate, staff, and student population.

What makes the role of the facilitator challenging is that it is multifaceted and constantly evolving. Responsibilities will range from engaging teachers in the planning processes to providing general oversight of the activity, including maintaining the ongoing practices of reflection and modeling that are necessary as attempts are made to conduct the intervention. For this reason, the individual who is selected to serve as the facilitator must be an effective communicator who is able to consistently engage faculty in ongoing conversations about the activities or intervention. These conversations help establish what Reeves (2006) referred to as internal capacity, which is one factor necessary for successful school growth. The versatility of the facilitator is also necessitated by the fact that there is likely to be an ongoing need to adopt different roles, including coach, cheerleader, or mentor, to ensure others are taking an active role in the process. The facilitator must also possess the skills necessary to mediate attempts by teachers to try potentially new practices within the context of the activities. Finally, the facilitator should be able to communicate in a way that meets the agreed-upon norms that will be established by the group later in the process, periodically challenging members while maintaining a nonthreatening, democratic environment.

"NOTE"-ABLE THOUGHTS

Who are some of the individuals that might be best suited to act as facilitators within your school or context? Begin to create a list of these individuals and think about ways that they could be introduced to the action research process or to information about the communities we described within the chapter.

Assessing the climate and inviting critical participants. Once the group or individual that will act as facilitator is identified, the next step involves examining the overall climate for conducting the action research as well as identifying and inviting key participants. Although Lave and Wenger (1998) noted that within a community of practice the participants self-organize, the climate at your school may have a significant impact on the ability to do this. For example, if there is a professional learning community present, there is already an organizational structure in place that may enable the group to quickly progress into the planning of the work. However, when this isn't the case, the individual that is designated as the facilitator will likely have to formally or informally assess the climate in your school to determine the most effective processes for engaging teachers and proceeding with the planning stages of the action research. Ultimately, there must be a balance maintained between the needs of your school and those of the individual participants, who may come from different grade levels and subject area designations.

Starting broadly, the facilitator should consider a variety of factors that encompass the climate, including notions of power (e.g., is there distributed or shared power, or is it held by administrator/experienced staff?), perceptions, beliefs, motivation of participants, and individual personalities. Each can have a significant effect on the participation within a collaborative action research study. Acknowledging that all participants within the context should have an active, equal voice in identifying specific areas of focus, Elliott (1991) argues the emphasis should be directed toward conditions that maximize the empowerment of the group as opposed to the individual. This is not always easy. Think about the personalities in your school—is there someone who likes to take charge in conversations or has a strong personality that easily overwhelms other teachers? If so, the facilitator will need to decide upon ways to maximize the potential for

- opportunities for all participants to engage in the discussions;

- processes for distributed, democratic decision making;

- methods for the development of shared goals and responsibility for meeting the goals; and

- mutual accountability. (Morrison, 1998)

When multiple elements in the list are absent, the facilitator will need to determine necessary courses of action to address them early within the planning process. This could include conversations among participants where facilitators define norms and expectations, establish roles and responsibilities for collaborative work, model substantive communication, and provide additional resources (Ross, 2011). You may find it helpful to begin the process with small groups of collaborators, but gradually widen the community to include more and more of those involved and affected by the process. This allows the group to build momentum toward democratic outcomes, while minimizing the likelihood of the participation of strong personalities because you control membership. The key is to work to involve those most directly associated with intervention in the examination of the climate, so that they share responsibility for the whole action research process.

■ ■ ■ VOICES FROM THE FIELD

Mortimer Emerson, Seventh-Grade Teacher

I volunteered to lead my team's effort to address what was becoming a common problem among our students—talking back and being disrespectful toward teachers. At the beginning of the year, this wasn't so pervasive as I think the students were adjusting to being in junior high. However, in our weekly meetings, we've all noted that what began as a problem with a few students has magnified and now it seems most students have to get a few words in when disciplined. We've always used an agreed-upon set of consequences for the grade level, but implementation has lacked consistency. I probably tend to be stricter than Ms. McIntyre, who teaches next door. She tends to let things slide a little more than I would be comfortable with.

(Continued)

(Continued)

Recently, we held our first meeting to come up with a plan about how to address this situation. I decided to start the meeting with everyone sharing how we viewed the grade-level management plan and how we were using consequences in our classrooms. In these conversations, it became very clear that we needed to come to a better consensus about our expectations and how we reacted when students were disrespectful. Using this information, we began to look at what seemed to be working for each of us as well as what wasn't. During our discussion, Ms. Jackson, one of the more vocal members of the team, kept going back to having students compose a paragraph during recess or their free period about their action each time they talked back to one of us. Our discussion got a little tense as several members of the team (myself included) felt that this might cause the students to view writing as a punishment (most already don't like to write as it is). My focus was coming up with a plan that worked for all of us, and thus I had to keep referring back to establishing a group consensus as the lack of consistency seemed to be contributing toward the current situation. Ultimately, we developed a plan that all of us felt we could implement, including weekly meetings on Friday mornings to revisit successes and ongoing challenges. This included keeping track of the number of disrespectful comments each week. To acknowledge the solution proposed by Ms. Jackson, we agreed to develop a template that could be used to help students reflect on their actions, but that we would examine the data from our initial plan before implementing use of the template by everyone. Overall, I think everyone left our meeting ready to implement the plan as each had contributed to its development. However, I will have to make sure that I am regularly communicating with Ms. Jackson to maintain her continued buy-in given that she expressed the greatest reluctance toward the plan.

Once the climate has been examined and addressed, the facilitator begins to invite and confirm participation of key individuals. Within this prompting, the facilitator should seek to aid teachers in recognizing the importance of developing an intervention to effectively plan and implement instruction that develops students' skills and knowledge as described by curricular goals or student needs. Ownership and involvement are two important variables that influence the behaviors and attitudes of teachers, and thus providing information as to how the actions and interventions they determine to be important within the action research can benefit their students is tantamount. Failure to link teachers' perspectives or chosen activities to the intervention is likely to result in weak implementation.

On the other hand, it is critical that the facilitator realizes that teachers cannot be forced to participate. A variety of factors may influence this, including attitudes, beliefs about teaching and learning, and prior experiences. There is no set formula for obtaining participation, which is why it is beneficial for the facilitator to have established relationships with participants as well as to acknowledge the individual's position. In essence, the person selected as the facilitator must know the teachers well enough to best identify how to communicate with them in a way that will help them begin to think about the proposed action research. Our recommendations include providing relevant literature, scheduling opportunities for modeling by peers or experts, or facilitating the development of small, short-term outcomes that help the teacher(s) see progress and assess continued participation. It is also important to realize what will not be helpful in gaining support and involvement. Compliance and participation cannot be forced. Doing so will most likely cause resistance and decrease the likelihood that engagement in the process or intervention will occur. Finally, in keeping all things in perspective, we'll be frank—not all teachers need to engage in the research initially. Participation for all is an important goal to help maintain morale and to promote the effort as collaborative, but it is not necessary from the outset. As the intervention proceeds, there may be additional opportunities to engage teachers who elected not to participate, especially as the intervention demonstrates an impact.

"NOTE."-ABLE THOUGHTS

Is there anyone that comes to mind that might be reluctant to participate in this process? How could you work with them directly or through the facilitator to help them see the benefits of engaging in collaborative action research?

PLANNING COLLABORATIVE ACTION RESEARCH

Once the examination of the climate has occurred and you have gained enough participants for the action research process, it is time to begin the planning process. You are familiar with the process, as it is generally the same one used within your individual action research: an area of focus is selected, goals (or research questions) are established, and a plan is developed for implementation, including processes for data collection and analysis, and so on. Given your knowledge of the research process and the potential for you to share this knowledge with colleagues, we recommend directing your attention toward the conversations among teachers as opposed to the research plan itself. You will need a clear and explicit process for these conversations as well as established expectations for participation within the discussion, as these factors can significantly impact the steps and outcomes of the research. Expanding this to include multiple stakeholders, we recommend incorporating small and large group discussions focused upon jointly planning goals and activities as well as strategies directed toward the goals created during the process.

It has been demonstrated that teachers are not always comfortable challenging or critiquing one another due to a variety of factors, including the collegial relationships that have developed amongst them (Little, Gearhart, Curry, & Kafka, 2003). This presents a potential barrier to your discussions and a truly collaborative effort if not addressed. Thus, we advocate taking time at the beginning of the planning process to establish norms for effective group and individual conversations. These norms will guide the interaction among group members to ensure a nonthreatening atmosphere and that professional courtesy is maintained. We encourage the establishment of the norms for participation by the group as part of a larger conversation to ensure all participants have a voice. In other words, a single individual or small group should not dictate how conversations occur. We've found that generating a list of key considerations and nonnegotiable elements of communication is essential. As the elements and norms are established, the facilitator should address and model actions such as pausing (simply waiting and thinking before speaking), paraphrasing (repeating other individual's words to ensure clarity and understanding), and probing (asking questions to clarify).

Once communicative norms have been established, the group can begin to identify and plan for the primary work that will occur within the action research process. If an area for focus has not been established, initial meetings could focus on identifying a challenge, area of improvement, or potential instructional innovation relevant to "normal" teaching situations that has widespread applicability across participants. The intent is to depart from the compulsion to focus on "quick solutions and immediate results" (DuFour et al., 2010, p. 514), allowing teachers to reflect upon their daily work processes and identify steps necessary for enduring change. To maximize the potential for this to occur, it is essential to create consensus and allow the teachers to determine their professional needs or interests in relation to the school or system (Desimone, 2002). Depending upon the size of the group, the facilitator may elect to begin with large-group meetings that include breakout sessions for smaller teams. Initial tasks of the groups can focus on identifying the context for the research, the overall goals of the project, and the primary understandings to be gained. This may also include reconnaissance (e.g., a review of literature) to determine whether comparable examinations have been completed. If they have, the group's focus shifts to discovering the processes used and problems encountered. In this paradigm, teachers and school leaders, including the facilitator, can gather and discuss specific needs and concerns as well as organizational difficulties of implementation. Short- and long-term support and growth can be enhanced through these discussions, as they maximize momentum toward the creation of a community and shared vision. Collaboratively sharing their visions also ensures recognition by the participants that the entire group is responsible for ensuring success. Using the shared vision as a guide, the group can transition into developing a specific plan, which involves crafting the questions to be answered within the research process.

As with the process for individual action research, once the goals, objectives, and questions for the research are established, focus shifts to the methodology and research plan. The type of data to be collected, as you have already learned, is largely informed by the objectives; yet, it is important to consider there are potentially more data sources available, and there will certainly be significantly more data to analyze, especially if the work is conducted at the school level. It will be important not only to review the various data collection procedures that are available but also to consider the usefulness and significance of each form of data within the overall action research process and in relation to the question(s). Once the data sources are identified and methods of collection are documented, there should also be an ongoing discussion about who will monitor the data collection, how information will be transmitted to the group, including feedback about the processes, and how often the group will reconvene to discuss the data. Elliott (1991) identified the importance of the latter, as it "promotes a reflective conversation and is at the heart of any transformation of the professional culture" (p. 60). Regularly discussing data enables your group to reflect on the progress of the intervention toward the intended outcomes and provides opportunities for teachers to voice concerns or questions. As a result, small modifications can be made within the research process to address them accordingly.

The research plan is the guide for implementation of the action research. It should address each of the components identified to this point. We firmly believe that once an agreed-upon process and organization are in place, it is important to document both the process and deliverables. To enable this, we advocate that you create an action chart and/or checklist to show who has responsibility for the various facets associated with the process (see Figures 9.5 and 9.6). In Chapter 7, we referred to this as a Steps to Action chart (see p. 164), and the overall areas of focus are similar, but this is used as an organization tool for the larger process as opposed to an organizer to plan the steps encompassed within the action plan you formulated based on your results.

FIGURE 9.5 Blank Action Chart

Primary Goals	Actions to Address Goals	Individuals Responsible for Actions	Consultations or Permissions Necessary	Data to Be Collected	Timeline for Implementation	Resources Necessary for Implementation

It is very important that roles are clarified within the plan, as, whenever possible, teachers should be able to utilize their own particular strengths in the research. For example, one teacher may have skills in assessment based on work conducted as a reading specialist or another may have a particular expertise in quantitative analysis given a background in mathematics. Another teacher may have a natural ability to engage in conversations and, therefore, could be a valuable asset for interviewing. On the other hand, there may be instances where training is needed to develop skills and knowledge of individuals who are taking on new or unfamiliar tasks. We recommend that the facilitator go beyond simply "knowing" this information and actually collect data to clarify and define the various participants' skills relative to the procedures that will be carried out within the research.

The facilitator plays an active role in each of these stages, helping teachers identify and establish goals that will guide later efforts and engage them in the sought-after changes in instructional practices. Based upon the readiness for change exhibited by teachers, the facilitator may need to concurrently spark debate, challenge long-held ideals, and regularly pose questions for consideration. The facilitator's role in the process may involve working with the group to help them adjust the scope of investigation, narrowing or broadening it as dictated by the group. Our recommendation to the facilitator is that discussions or meetings should be guided by an agenda whenever possible. When there is a concrete plan of action or series of steps to be addressed within the meeting, it has the potential to increase the level of efficiency and improve results. Regular communication of the objectives and purposes of the research by the facilitator is crucial, as a lack of understanding about what is to be accomplished and how it relates to goals will contribute toward a lack of progress or advancement toward the sought-after outcomes. The facilitator should also help the group continually reflect upon whether small modifications to the objectives or questions are necessary as information is continually examined and the assumptions underlying the action research become more defined and explicit.

FIGURE 9.6 Example of an Action Chart With Preliminary Details

Primary Goals	Actions to Address Goals	Individuals Responsible for Actions	Consultations or Permissions Necessary	Data to Be Collected	Timeline for Implementation	Resources Necessary for Implementation
Students will increase achievement scores in reading and language arts by 5%	• Analyze benchmark assessment results • Identify objectives • Identify students in need of assistance • Develop strategies to improve proficiency and growth on those low objectives by providing extra help opportunities • Create pacing guides to use for all courses that are turned in at the start of the school year	• Teachers • Specialists	Principal, team leads	Benchmark assessment scores	Ongoing, biweekly meetings	• Scores • Meeting spaces • Current pacing guides

IMPLEMENTATION OF COLLABORATIVE ACTION RESEARCH

As teachers engage in deliberate attempts to implement the collaboratively established goals and plans of the intervention, the efforts should be characterized by the act–evaluate–reformulate cycle that characterizes action research (see Putman, Smith, & Cassady, 2009). As with many of the other steps completed so far, the facilitator is a vital participant in ensuring the plan is carried out effectively. The facilitator must especially demonstrate flexibility within the implementation phase, as different teachers may need varying levels of support, from simple encouragement to expert advice about the ongoing practices. The facilitator must also continually engage the teachers in ongoing dialogue within the iterations of the action research cycle. As individuals and groups come successively closer to the goal(s) identified at the outset of the process, there must be continual guidance within the process of evaluating and reformulating actions on a regular basis to help the teaching team stay on target.

"NOTE"-ABLE THOUGHTS

Which step do you see as most challenging within the act-evaluate-reformulate cycle? Why do you think this? What are some suggestions that you would make to the facilitator to address that particular challenge?

As we've mentioned previously, within the evaluation cycle examinations of data should occur within regularly scheduled meetings under the guidance of the facilitator. This ensures successful movement within the three phases. The teachers involved in the process must maintain active participation to ensure they are able to provide input on the modification of any goals, which preserves support for the process and allows examinations of whether the goals continued to be aligned with the targeted outcomes. Throughout the action research process, the group must concurrently consider teacher behaviors and student achievement, as both are relevant to continued progress toward the intended outcomes. Student data is likely to be readily accessible; however, the facilitator may need to consider informal observations amongst peers to note individual needs and progress within the process. Success should serve as a tool to create confidence in participating teachers. Furthermore, as the process continues, success could be leveraged to overcome the reluctance of those teachers who chose not to initially participate in the activities. Results may be just the prompt they need to join!

We've written about ongoing dialogue, action cycles, and observations as necessary with the collaborative action research process. However, it is also critical to note that teachers receive the opportunity to apply the proposed changes associated with the action research intervention in an environment that has very low or no anxiety associated with it. This may mean that the initial implementation cycles of the action research process are focused on small goals to enhance confidence and increase the likelihood that teachers will continue to engage in the interventions as student success is noted. These initial attempts can lead as a springboard into conversations and analyses that examine the successes and disappointments associated with the efforts. Effective leadership on the part of the facilitator can enhance the outcomes throughout the iterative processes of evaluating and reformulating goals and help the teaching team stay on target.

As mentioned previously, the facilitator may need to adopt a coaching or mentoring model to ensure consistency of implementation of the proposed intervention in individual classrooms. Within the model, the facilitator or a designee works with specific small groups over the course of time established for the intervention. Participants meet and are encouraged to share and reflect upon their practices. As relationships are established and comfort with practices increases, the facilitator can create opportunities for small-group members to begin observing each other teaching with the facilitator present. Once all team members are observed, the team reconvenes to provide feedback to each other based upon observations. Under the facilitator's guidance, the group then identifies strategies and methods for maintaining momentum toward the goals established within the research. As ongoing meetings occur, the relationships built enable conversations necessary to promote the sought-after behavioral change in teachers.

EXAMINING THE RESULTS AND PREPARING FOR THE NEXT ITERATION

Within the cycle of the action research, participants actively reflect on the results and use this reflection to plan the next iteration (Craig, 2009). While ongoing reflection helped inform practices, summative analysis can be utilized to better consider and understand the patterns and relationships that emerged within the action research. In this process, the group examines the data together and attempts to generate multiple interpretations of the results by actively generating as many different ways to connect and explain the data as possible. Looking at data from multiple angles may lead to a discovery of new information that can be used to develop new ways of responding and improving teaching practices as part of the next iteration. The facilitator can ask the group to consider questions such as the following:

- How do these patterns within the data reflect change as a result of . . .

- What might explain . . .

- What do these interactions tell you about . . .

- How does the data connect to current literature about . . .

- How does the data support implementation of . . .

- What additional data would address . . .

Generating and acknowledging multiple explanations or solutions may provide additional research possibilities for other groups of interested participants or strategies to use in various situations that occur later. As reflection provides the direction for the next action research process, it offers opportunities for more people to provide input regarding whether the individual acting in the role of a facilitator remains the same. Participants can take turns leading the efforts completed in various iterations of the action research. In fact, we encourage thinking critically about how best to develop the leadership capacity among the various participants in the research.

After discussing these various perspectives and arriving at conclusions, Stringer (2014) recommends "writing reports collaboratively" (p. 157) to ensure the multiple views can be maintained. We agree and reinforce the need to disseminate the results beyond those that participated directly in the process, especially if there are individuals who did not participate out of choice or if you plan to expand the process to additional teachers or schools. According to Hacker (2013), this dissemination may influence this participation and can stimulate implementation of the intervention into practice. Chapter 7 introduced you to various considerations within your dissemination efforts, including multiple reporting formats, and thus revisiting the chapter as a group may be necessary to create the collaborative reports.

"NOTE"-ABLE THOUGHTS

How could you connect the action research process to existing structures that support collaborative team efforts at your school?

DEVELOPING THE PRODUCT: FORMING THE COLLABORATIVE ACTION RESEARCH TEAM

You've now moved from considering action research as a process that you complete individually in your classroom to one that can involve multiple stakeholders that share similar needs or interests. Peterson (1992) wrote, "When community exists, learning is strengthened—everyone is smarter, more ambitious, and productive." Creating a collaborative action research community can enable teachers to view teaching and learning in new ways and play an instrumental role in improving student outcomes. Given that the context for collaborative action research plays a significant role in the potential for success and that we lack a prescriptive process for carrying it out (beyond the general action research formula), we've structured the "Note"-able Thoughts to help you consider some of the common situations and factors that will likely need to be addressed. With the knowledge you've gained throughout the process of reading this book, we're confident that you can play a vital role in helping to create the climate for successful collaborative action research to occur in your context of practice. Take the first steps in the process by bringing together your colleagues and having those initial conversations about how the team can work together to start investigating a topic of interest. We leave you with the strong encouragement to now go and be the change agent within your classroom or school!

SUMMARY

In this chapter, we described the importance of rethinking the solitary nature of teaching, in general, and within the action research process. You were introduced to professional learning communities and communities of practice to help you develop conclusions regarding the importance of collaboration as well as to help you begin to formulate ways to bring teachers together. The notion of community can be extended with various technological innovations that are readily available, and we provided various tools that may assist in the process. Planning collaborative research involves considering more than simply bringing people together directly or virtually, however. Teachers and instructional leaders who wish to create opportunities to work together must engage in thoughtful planning that involves many of the steps described within the individual action research process; yet, a great deal of focus must be placed on identifying a leader or group of committed individuals who will act as facilitators in the process. The facilitator plays a vital role throughout the process, from planning through reporting, considering the climate, personnel, and process for completing the action research. Engagement, involvement, and empowerment are three key pieces of the process that will be critical in achieving the ultimate goals of the action research process: improvement in practices and increased student learning.

Key Terms

Collaborative action research, p. 204

Community of practice, p. 201

Learning community, p. 199

Professional learning community, p. 200

Virtual professional learning community, p. 202

Case in Point: Developing a Collaborative Action Research Study

As we've noted multiple times in the chapter, developing a plan to conduct collaborative action research is context specific. Different teams or schools will have different needs, and thus it's difficult to establish a one-size-fits-all formula for implementation. For the Case in Point example in this chapter, we are going to deviate slightly from the elementary and secondary teacher examples that we've presented in our previous chapters. Instead, we will focus on providing a description of the preliminary considerations and steps taken in one school to engage in a collaborative action research project focused on decreasing management issues at the school. In this case, the staff, teachers, and administrators had noticed an abundance of discipline referrals at common times and in specific areas in the school (e.g., hallways during dismissal) and wanted to address the situation.

One School's Journey: Preliminary Steps in Developing the Collaborative Plan

Given the context of the management issues, the two administrators at the school, Dr. Milkens and Mr. Roos, spent several weeks gathering data from referral forms, observing, and talking to teachers and staff. What they found confirmed suspicions: common situations and locations were problematic, including arrival and dismissal times, and areas such as the hallway, the gym, and the cafeteria. An initial meeting with the staff was held by the administrators to present the gathered data. It produced a consensus that a plan needed to be developed and implemented and that data needed to be continually collected to examine the impact of the plan.

Rather than dictate specific actions, Dr. Milkens felt that the intervention plan should be developed by the teachers, as they would be the ones who would be most responsible for carrying it out. Wanting direct engagement of the staff, she deliberately selected two teachers whom she felt would be capable of leading the efforts to create and provide oversight of the eventual plan. The first teacher, Ms. Boston, had been at the school for 14 years. She was well respected by everyone in the school and was widely known for her commitment to her students. Teachers were willing to go to Ms. Boston for advice and recommendations on a variety of topics, as she would listen closely and provide honest feedback or suggestions. Her colleagues trusted her and knew that she would ultimately opt for the best course of action based on evidence, regardless of whether it was counter to what she wanted or believed. The second teacher, Mr. Tobin, was only in his third year at the school, but he had previously worked for four years in another school in the district. At his other school, Mr. Tobin had been involved in a professional learning community focused on classroom management and had been on a team that developed a school code and set of behavioral guidelines, and thus he was seen as a resident expert on management. Mr. Tobin's classes were also consistently cited as some of the best performing in the school, both academically and behaviorally, reinforcing his standing.

After an initial meeting with Dr. Milkens, Ms. Boston and Mr. Tobin decided that they were going to recommend the creation of a schoolwide management program that included specific plans and procedures for the areas in the school and times of day that appeared to be the most problematic. The goal of the plan was to diminish the number of discipline referrals during those times and in those locations. Both Ms. Boston and Mr. Tobin agreed that it would be necessary to involve their colleagues right from the beginning to create the buy-in necessary to ensure consistent implementation of the program by teachers, staff, and administrators. Given the necessity of gathering data for any intervention, the facilitators also wanted the teachers and staff to discuss various forms of data that could be collected, considering what would be meaningful to the school as well as manageable in the day-to-day activities associated with teaching.

In the first meeting with their colleagues, Ms. Boston and Mr. Tobin reviewed the data that had been gathered to re-establish the context for the necessity of the intervention that would be developed. They also presented the tentative plan of forming schoolwide procedures. In breakout groups composed of grade-level teams, the teachers were asked to discuss the data and the potential for schoolwide procedures, acknowledging

that all teachers would be asked to adhere to the plan that was developed. The facilitators then used the jigsaw approach and shifted the groups to multigrade-level teams to discuss the same topics, sharing information from the original grade-level groups. The whole group reconvened, and Ms. Boston and Mr. Tobin facilitated a conversation across the group. Within this setting, several teachers expressed concern that the schoolwide procedures would supersede what they currently had in place. While acknowledging this position, the facilitators noted that the group should look at successful practices to determine if they could be used as a potential model for procedures that would be implemented at the school level. The initial meeting ended with Ms. Boston and Mr. Tobin agreeing to examine all of the information that was compiled, and to disseminate it to the teachers and staff.

Over the course of several meetings, the facilitators helped refine and shape a vision for the schoolwide procedures, introducing literature and information gathered from other schools to provide additional foundational knowledge for the process. What began as a focus on simply creating procedures for specific areas of the school and times of day gradually shifted into a set of behavioral expectations directed toward all areas of the school that would be used throughout the day. While this didn't match the original idea of the facilitators, they were able to leverage the buy-in from the teachers to create something that was actually more encompassing than the original intent. The teachers and staff came together and developed a plan that included, among other aspects, specifically teaching expectations to their classes, weekly references to a designated expectation over the announcements with reinforcement of the expectation by teachers in their classrooms, and a system of consequences and positive reinforcement. The expectations were also to be posted throughout the school, especially in the identified areas, and in every classroom. Enforcement was distributed throughout the teachers and staff, as was the newly established focus on positive reinforcement. In the latter system, teachers and staff could give students tickets for good behavior that could be accumulated and used toward purchases from the school spirit store or entered into a weekly and monthly drawing for various items.

More challenging for the facilitators were the conversations around the data collection necessary to verify the success of the intervention. Many of the teachers felt that the number of discipline referrals and positive reinforcement tickets were all that was necessary to determine success. However, while the facilitators agreed that these were acceptable measures, Ms. Boston showed her colleagues that these were insufficient in their current form, as there was no information regarding the location where the referral or ticket were issued and, though the time of day was listed, it was often left blank. The facilitators also felt they should have some form of data from the teachers, either interview or survey data, to determine whether the teachers were teaching and reinforcing the expectations in their classrooms. They also wanted to access the

teachers' and staff members' perceptions regarding whether the intervention was successful. The position of the facilitators was supported by the administrators. This created tension, as there was some interpretation that the proposed methods would be a way to track teachers' actions. In the end, compromises were struck: the forms were revised to include location and the teachers agreed to fill in the time, and the teachers and staff agreed to complete biweekly surveys for the first eight weeks of the intervention. The plan also included the provision that at the end of the four weeks, the facilitators and teachers would discuss formative data and whether modifications needed to be made, based on the teachers' experiences and an initial analysis of the data. At the end of eight weeks, all teachers and staff would gather to examine compiled data, considering emerging patterns and what additional data might be necessary to assess the success of the intervention on changing students' behavior. With a plan in place, the staff and teachers began implementation of the intervention.

Activities and Additional Resources

1. A colleague comes to you with an idea for a collaborative, schoolwide action research study. She wants you and your colleagues to examine ways to introduce the use of science journals to improve conceptual understanding about the phases of the moon. Assess the viability of this suggestion. What information would you need to accurately assess whether the topic lends itself to collaborative action research? What are the first steps in the process of developing the group that will conduct the research?

2. Gather a group of peers and develop a list of potential topics for collaborative action research. Choose one from the list and use Figure 9.5 to develop a tentative plan of how the research to address the topic could be collaboratively conducted.

3. You've engaged a group of teachers in examining topics that may lend themselves to the collaborative action research process. However,

there is one teacher in particular who continually disagrees or challenges the rest of the group that there is a need for an emphasis on the identified areas. Discuss how you might handle this situation and what actions might be necessary to move forward within the action research process.

Professional Learning Communities and Communities of Practice

DuFour, R. (2004). What is a "professional learning community"? *Educational Leadership, 61,* 6–11.

DuFour, R., DuFour, R., Eaker, R., & Many, T. (2010). *Learning by doing: A handbook for professional learning communities at work* (2nd ed.). Bloomington, IN: Solution Tree.

Huffman, J. B., Hipp, K. A., Pankake, A. M., & Moller, G. (2001). Professional learning communities: Leadership, purposeful decision making, and job-embedded staff development. *Journal of School Leadership, 11,* 448–463.

Little, J. W. (2012). Professional community and professional development in the learning-centered school. In M. Kooy & K. van Veen (Eds.), *Teacher learning that matters: International perspectives* (pp. 22–46). New York, NY: Routledge.

Wenger, E. (2014). *Communities of practice: A brief introduction.* Available at http://wenger-trayner.com/wp-content/uploads/2013/10/06-Brief-introduction-to-communities-of-practice.pdf

Wenger, E., McDermott, R., & Snyder, W. (2002). *Cultivating communities of practice.* Boston, MA: Harvard Business School Press.

Technology-Enhanced Professional Communities

Ajayi, L. (2010). How asynchronous discussion boards mediate learning literacy methods courses to enrich alternative-licensed teachers' learning experiences. *Journal of Research on Technology in Education, 43,* 1–28.

Dede, C. (Ed.). (2006). *Online professional development for teachers: Emerging models and methods.* Cambridge, MA: Harvard Education.

Mackey, J., & Evans, T. (2011). Interconnecting networks of practice for professional learning. *International Review of Research in Open and Distance Learning, 12*(3). Retrieved from http://www.irrodl.org/index.php/irrodl/article/view/873/1682

Masters, J., De Kramer, R. M., O'Dwyer, L. M., Dash, S., & Russell, M. (2010). The effects of online professional development on fourth-grade English language arts teachers' knowledge and instructional practices. *Journal of Educational Computing Research, 43,* 355–375.

Opfer, V. D., & Pedder, D. (2011). Conceptualizing teacher professional learning. *Review of Educational Research, 81,* 376–407.

Student Study Site

edge.sagepub.com/putman

- Take the practice quiz.
- Review key terms with eFlashcards.
- Explore topics with video and multimedia.

References

Ajayi, L. (2009). An exploration of pre-service teachers' perceptions of learning to teach while using asynchronous discussion board. *Educational Technology & Society, 12,* 86–100.

Barab, S. A., & Duffy, T. M. (2000). From practice fields to communities of practice. In D. H. Jonassen & S. M. Land (Eds.), *Theoretical foundations of learning environments* (pp. 25–56). Mahwah, NJ: Lawrence Erlbaum.

Barth, R. (1990). *Improving schools from within.* San Francisco, CA: Jossey-Bass.

Borko, H. (2004). Professional development and teacher learning: Mapping the terrain. *Educational Researcher, 33,* 3–15.

Bray, J. N. (2002). Uniting teacher learning: Collaborative inquiry for professional development. *New Directions for Adult and Continuing Education, 94,* 83–91.

Conrad, D. (2005). Building and maintaining community in cohort-based online learning. *Journal of Distance Education, 20,* 1–21.

Craig, D. V. (2009). *Action research essentials.* San Francisco, CA: Jossey-Bass.

Desimone, L. M. (2002). How can comprehensive school reform models be successfully implemented? *Review of Educational Research, 72,* 433–479.

DuFour, R., DuFour, R., Eaker, R., & Many, T. (2010). *Learning by doing: A handbook for professional learning communities at work* (2nd ed.). Bloomington, IN: Solution Tree.

Elliott, J. (1991). A model of professionalism and its implications for teacher education. *British Journal of Educational Research, 17,* 309–317.

Ford, L., Branch, G., & Moore, G. (2008). Formation of a virtual professional learning community in a combined local and distance doctoral cohort. *AACE Journal, 16,* 161–185.

Hacker, K. (2013). *Community-based participatory research.* Thousand Oaks, CA: Sage.

Hargreaves, A. (2003). *Teaching in the knowledge society: Education in the age of insecurity.* New York, NY: Teachers College Press.

Jonassen, D. H., Peck, K. L., & Wilson, B. G. (1999). *Learning to solve problems with technology: A constructivist perspective* (2nd ed.). Upper Saddle River, NJ: Merrill Prentice-Hall.

Kemmis, S., & McTaggart, R. (Eds.). (1992). *The action research planner* (3rd ed.). Geelong, Australia: Deakin University Press.

Lave, J., & Wenger, E. (1991). *Situated learning: Legitimate peripheral participation.* Cambridge, UK: Cambridge University Press.

Lave, J., & Wenger, E. (1998). *Communities of practice: Learning, meaning, and identity.* Cambridge, UK: Cambridge University Press.

Leask, M., & Younie, S. (2001). Building on-line communities for teachers: Issues emerging from research. In M. Leask (Ed.), *Issues in teaching using ICT* (pp. 223–232). London, England: Routledge Falmer.

Little, J. W., Gearhart, M., Curry, M., & Kafka, J. (2003). Looking at student work for teacher learning, teacher community, and school reform. *Phi Delta Kappan, 85,* 185–192.

Mills, G. E. (2011). *Action research: A guide for the teacher researcher* (4th ed.). Boston, MA: Allyn & Bacon.

Morrison, K. (1998). *Management theories for educational change.* London, England: Paul Chapman Publishing.

National Board for Professional Teaching Standards. (2002). *What teachers should know and be able to do.* Retrieved from http://www.nbpts.org/sites/default/files/what_teachers_should_know.pdf

Newmann, F. M., & Associates. (1996). *Authentic achievement: Restructuring schools for intellectual quality.* San Francisco, CA: Jossey-Bass.

Peterson, R. (1992). *Life in a crowded place: Making a learning community.* Portsmouth, NH: Heinemann.

Phillips, D. K., & Carr, K. (2006). *Becoming a teacher through action research: Process, content, and self-study.* New York, NY: Routledge.

Putman, S. M., Smith, L. L., & Cassady, J. C. (2009). Moving beyond legislation to create and sustain intentionality in reading instruction. *The Educational Forum, 73,* 318–322.

Reeves, D. (2006). Leadership leverage. *Educational Leadership, 64,* 86–87.

Riel, M., & Polin, L. (2004). Online learning communities: Common ground and critical differences in designing technical environments. In S. A. Barab, R. Kling, & J. H. Gray (Eds.), *Designing for virtual communities in the service of learning* (pp. 16–50). Cambridge, UK: Cambridge University Press.

Ross, J. D. (2011). *Online professional development: Design, deliver, succeed!* Los Angeles, CA: Corwin.

Rovai, A. P., & Jordan, H. M. (2004). Blended learning and sense of community: A comparative analysis with traditional and fully online graduate courses. *International Review of Research in Open and Distance Learning, 5*(2). Retrieved from http://www.irrodl.org/index.php/irrodl/article/view/192/795

Shotsberger, P. G. (2000). The human touch: Synchronous communication in web-based learning. *Educational Technology, 40,* 53–56.

Stoll, L., Bolam, R., McMahon, A., Wallace, M., & Thomas, S. (2006). Professional learning communities: A review of the literature. *Journal of Educational Change, 7,* 221–258.

Stringer, E. T. (2014). *Action research* (4th ed.). Thousand Oaks, CA: Sage.

Supovitz, J. (2002). Developing communities of instructional practice. *Teachers College Record, 104,* 1591–1626.

Wenger, E. (1998). *Communities of practice: Learning, meaning, and identity.* Cambridge, UK: Cambridge University Press.

Westheimer, J. (1998). *Among school teachers: Community, autonomy, and ideology in teachers' work.* New York, NY: Teachers College Press.

Zhu, E. (2006). Interaction and cognitive engagement: An analysis of four asynchronous online discussions. *Instructional Science, 34,* 451–480.

Appendix A: Examples of Action Research Reports

Examining the Impact of Readers' Theater on Struggling Readers' Fluency Levels

INTRODUCTION

Learning to read is one of the most valuable skills students develop during their formative years in school. Research has shown students who demonstrate skill deficits in reading at the end of first grade rarely catch up to their grade-level peers (Mathes et al., 2005; National Reading Panel, 2000). According to Mathes and colleagues (2005), these students will "fall further and further behind their peers and habituate ineffective strategies for coping with reading failure" (p. 151). Given the long-term implications of reading problems and the current educational climate that is focused on yearly testing in reading, there has been an increasing awareness of the role early reading instruction plays in a child's academic success. Schools and teachers are actively focusing on methods to provide struggling students with the instruction to develop the skills necessary to read proficiently.

Fluency is an area that has been identified as vital for development of proficiency within reading. Students who become fluent readers can identify words automatically and correctly, and can focus their attention on comprehending what they read. On the other hand, the lack of fluency is often associated with reading difficulties, including comprehension (Begeny, Yeager, & Martinez, 2012; Rasinski, Blachowicz, & Lems, 2006). Osborn and Lehr (2003) stated, "Students who do not develop reading fluency, regardless of how bright they are, are likely to remain poor readers throughout their lives" (p. 2). Yet, while researchers have noted the important role of fluency and that it needs to be explicitly taught to adequately develop, it is not often incorporated into instructional programs (Kuhn & Stahl, 2003; National Reading Panel, 2000). Richards (2000) attributes this to a focus of basal readers on other areas, including word recognition, vocabulary, and comprehension. Given the compelling reasons for students to become fluent readers, it is vital that teachers recognize and determine ways that fluency can be incorporated into their instruction.

In my experiences as a second-grade teacher, I fully understand the importance of the development of reading skills as well as the role fluency plays in this process. Around third grade, students are expected to know and be able to demonstrate the fundamental skills in reading as they begin to read to learn. There is a shift from "learning to read" to "reading to learn" that is challenging for students who have not mastered some of the primary skills necessary for proficient reading. I have noticed that fluency is a common problem for many of my students who are struggling with reading. This is especially true of students who enter second grade reading below grade-level expectations. These students spend so much time focusing on each word within the text that their reading is slow and halting, and they are unable to understand or comprehend passages they are reading. As a result, I spend a significant amount of time thinking about the instructional strategies I use to help these students to read text effortlessly and accurately. This reflection has led me to explore one instructional strategy, Readers' Theater, to determine if using it in my classroom has an impact on students' fluency.

LITERATURE REVIEW

As previously described, reading fluency has a significant impact on young readers' literacy development and is a key component for becoming a successful reader. It was named as one of the five pillars of early reading education within the report issued by the National Reading Panel (NRP) in 2000. Multiple definitions of *fluency* and what constitutes fluent reading have been set forth with varying levels of specificity. For example, the NRP (2000) described a fluent reader as one who could "read text with speed, accuracy, and proper expression" (p. 3-1). Young and Rasinski (2009), on the other hand, noted fluency to be "the ability to read the words in a text with sufficient accuracy, automaticity, and prosody" (p. 4). Finally, Rasinski, Samuels, Hiebert, Petscher, and Feller (2011) defined *fluency* as "the ability to simultaneously process written texts accurately, with appropriate prosody and comprehension" (p. 75).

FLUENCY

Given there are multiple consistencies across the definitions as well as some minor variations, especially within some of the terminology, it's important to further expand on some of the traits that characterize fluent readers. One important component of fluency is automaticity. Automaticity is "the ability of proficient readers to read words in a text correctly and effortlessly" (Young & Rasinski, 2009, p. 4). The theory of automaticity notes that a reader has a limited amount of attention that they can devote to cognitive tasks, and thus while examining text, word recognition and comprehension will compete for a reader's attention (Griffith & Rasinski, 2004; Rasinski et al., 2006). Readers who are considered to demonstrate automaticity do not expend significant effort to recognize and decode words; thus they can devote attention toward constructing meaning as they read (Rasinski et al., 2006). On the other hand, students who have difficulty with decoding need to devote significant attention toward word recognition. The result is a lack of the level of automaticity necessary to be characterized as fluent (Pikulski & Chard, 2005).

Reading rate, another component of fluency, is influenced by automaticity as well as the speed a reader is able to demonstrate while progressing through text. It is often measured by the number of words read correctly in a specific time span, usually a minute, or the amount of time a reader takes to complete a passage. There are a variety of common assessments (e.g., DIBELS) that use oral reading rate as a form of curriculum-based measurement. In general, higher reading rates have been equated with more advanced skills in decoding or word recognition (Kuhn & Stahl, 2003). Students whose reading is slow and labored are likely to be judged as nonproficient, as they lack fundamental skills, including the capacity to examine sound–symbol relationships. While oral reading rarely occurs beyond the primary grades, Rasinski et al. (2011) note fluency actually affects readers throughout high school.

Prosody is the third theoretical component associated with fluency. "Text read with good prosody sounds much like daily speech, incorporating appropriate phrasing, pausing, variation in intonation patterns, rates of articulation, and pitch" (Ardoin, Morena, Binder, & Foster, 2013, p. 392). Readers who demonstrate prosody demonstrate an understanding of correct stress and intonation, along with grouping or chunking words appropriately into phrases (Tyler & Chard, 2000). As a student learns to read expressively and in a meaningful way, they are better able to construct meaning (Griffith & Rasinski, 2004). In comparison to readers who demonstrate prosodic reading, struggling readers are more likely to be characterized by reading without expression or in a monotone, lacking changes in pitch or variability of pauses between sentences (Rasinski et al., 2006).

Taken in sum, the preceding information underscores that reading fluency is an important step in the process of understanding text. Research has repeatedly shown there is a strong correlation between the construct and comprehension (Gorsuch & Taguchi, 2010; Therrien, 2004). In fact, according to Osborn and Lehr (2003), fluency serves as "a bridge between word recognition and comprehension" (p. 4). Fluent readers are not distracted by having to decode a word, so they are able to concentrate on the meaning of the text that they are reading. Thus, as students learn to read words correctly and quickly, it allows them to better comprehend what they are reading. If we understand the relationship between reading fluency and comprehension, we would expect that, as reading fluency increases, so too would reading comprehension.

It is imperative to assist students with fluency skills through intentional instruction to help them become successful readers. Fluency-based strategies have been found to enhance students' comprehension skills along with their ability to read through a passage (Begeny et al., 2012). In essence, children must be taught specific skills to become better readers. A variety of strategies can be used to develop fluency. Some of the more common ones include:

- Read-aloud—teachers read text out loud for students, modeling what proficient reading sounds like, including correct pronunciation, rate, and expression;

- Choral reading—small groups of students read a text together, with fluent readers representing a model for less fluent readers, helping the latter improve their own fluency in the process;

- Repeated reading—students reread a text or passage multiple times to assist in fluency development; and

- Guided, oral reading—a form of repeated reading that includes immediate feedback and support from the teacher.

Various research studies have proven the effectiveness of each of the strategies, but I have found that repeated readings have helped my students in our day-to-day practices as they are able to rehearse passages and correct mistakes. With this in mind, I examined additional research specific to repeated readings to gain a greater understanding of the multiple ways that it has been successfully implemented in classrooms.

REPEATED READINGS

The more we practice something, the better we become at it; hence the rationale behind repeated readings: the more students read a text, the better able they are to recognize and read the words within that text as they see them multiple times. Studies have confirmed that repeated reading increases oral reading fluency, as measured by examining the number of words read per minute (Swain, Leader-Janssen, & Conley, 2013; Yurick, Robinson, Cartledge, Lo, & Evans, 2006). Furthermore, repeated readings of text have shown improvement in increasing a student's reading accuracy along with their capacity to develop meaningful chunks of text (Tyler & Chard, 2000). This has proven true across multiple grade levels. Notably, several studies with second graders have demonstrated positive results on fluency, word recognition, and prosody (Keehn, 2003; Young & Rasinski, 2009). Osborn and Lehr (2003) proposed that while any student can benefit from specific fluency instruction, it is crucial for struggling readers. Repeated reading has also proven to be a valid strategy for use with second-language learners (Gorsuch & Taguchi, 2010) and students with disabilities (Swain et al., 2013).

The use of repeated readings in the classroom should begin with the teacher modeling a specific reading passage, discussing expression and vocabulary. Once this occurs, according to Yurick et al. (2006), as part of the repeated reading process, a fluency goal is set, and a passage of text is selected. The student reads and rereads the passage until the fluency goal is achieved. This strategy provides readers with short-term goals, such as completing the same reading faster and faster, which also may increase motivation and engagement (Cohen, 2011). While there is no single metric for the number of times the student should reread the passage, a review of research by Therrien (2004) revealed significant increases in fluency and comprehension when a passage was read at least three times. Success within the process is maximized when teachers provide explicit guidance and feedback as the student engages in practice (Ardoin et al., 2013; Kuhn & Stahl, 2003). Synthesizing many of the previously described findings, Therrien & Kubuina (2006) noted a positive impact when passages were at an instructional level where the student could achieve a goal in a reasonable amount of time, when corrective feedback in relation to word errors and reading speed needs was communicated, and when the passages were reread until a performance criterion was reached.

READERS' THEATER

There are a variety of ways that repeated readings can be implemented to help support students in their attempts to attain fluency. One instructional strategy, Readers' Theater, combines oral reading with creative performance skills. In Readers' Theater, students read directly from a script using oral expressions and gestures when presenting their lines, but without props and costumes. Casey and Chamberlain (2006) characterize Readers' Theater by noting that "students' voices are the only tool used to communicate meaning or to bring characters to life" (p. 18). Readers' Theater provides teachers with an authentic strategy to engage readers in meaningful, repeated readings that can increase reading fluency and improve text comprehension of both struggling and successful readers.

The use of Readers' Theater has been shown to have a positive impact on students' oral fluency development (Clementi, 2010; Griffith & Rasinski, 2004). Used as a short-term intervention in the primary grades, several studies revealed improvements in reading rates of more than 15 words per minute (Casey & Chamberlain, 2006; Keehn, 2003). Consistent with research on repeated readings, when implemented over a longer period, gains are even greater. For example, Griffith and Rasinski (2004) examined implementation of Readers' Theater with fourth graders for a 10-week period and found a student showed a growth of over 48 words per minute. The same student also demonstrated improvements in their silent reading comprehension. When examining the use of Readers' Theater with second-grade students, multiple studies indicated a link between using it as an instructional intervention to increase oral reading fluency and gains in overall reading achievement for second-grade students (Forsythe, 1995; Keehn, 2003; Young & Rasinski, 2009). Young and Rasinski (2009) found second-grade students' reading rates increased 65 words from fall to spring and the students gained nearly 20% in prosody, as measured by the Texas Primary Reading Inventory. Finally, Keehn (2003) examined four second-grade classrooms that implemented Readers' Theater. Two classrooms implemented Readers' Theater in conjunction with weekly mini-lessons and daily strategies to increase fluency rates, while the other two classrooms only engaged in Readers' Theater. Both groups of students showed improvement in fluency, but neither group performed significantly better than the other in regard to oral reading fluency. What is noteworthy from the results was the growth of the low-performing readers, who showed significantly greater improvements than the average and high-ability readers.

Given that the literature I have read supports repeated reading, and specifically Readers' Theater, as an effective strategy to help students increase fluency, I decided that this would be an appropriate intervention for my second graders. In addition to the benefits associated with improvement in fluency, Readers' Theater has also been shown to have an impact on motivation and engagement (Mraz et al., 2013) and I think this will be important for those students in my class who struggle with reading fluently. As soon as they start to encounter difficulties, they begin to shut down, and when that happens, my opportunities to help them become very limited or nonexistent. They also become bored very quickly when I use the same materials over the course of several days. By the third day I am usually getting eye rolls and sighs. Using Readers' Theater, I think nearly all of them will be willing to read the text several times over the weeklong period as they practice for their performance of the Readers' Theater. Given, they will also be reading in front of peers, I am hoping that this will contribute to their willingness to engage in this process. Given this context, the proposed research question guiding my work is: What is the effect of Readers' Theater on second-grade students' reading fluency?

METHODS

CONTEXT AND PARTICIPANTS

The context for this research was a school located in an urban area near a large metropolitan city. The school serves 602 students, with 58% of the students enrolled eligible for free or reduced-price lunch. The school is composed of students representing the following race/ethnicities: African American (59%), Hispanic American (20%), Caucasian (12%), multiracial (5%), Asian American (3%), and other (1%). There is fairly equal gender distribution within the school, with males representing 51% and females representing 49% of students. On recent end-of-grade tests, the school had 56% of its third- through fifth-grade students demonstrate proficiency in reading.

The classroom where this research was conducted consisted of 24 second-grade students. Ethnically and racially, the class was diverse: 12 participants were African American, eight were Hispanic American, three were Caucasian, and one participant was multiracial. The sample consisted of 14 boys and 10 girls. Six students tested below benchmark in comprehension, as reflected in progress monitoring using grade-level reading passages, while five demonstrated oral reading fluency scores below grade level.

INSTRUMENT

The Dynamic Indicators of Basic Early Literacy Skills (DIBELS; https://dibels.uoregon .edu/) is an assessment used to evaluate the development of early literacy skills for students from kindergarten to sixth grade. While DIBELS includes several components, the specific assessment used for this study was the DIBELS oral reading fluency (ORF) measure. The measure includes standardized sets of passages that have been calibrated and benchmarked at each grade level, which allows for use as a screening measure. There are also 20 alternative forms that can be used within progress monitoring at various points across the academic year. Administration involves students reading a passage aloud for one minute. At the conclusion of the minute, ORF scores are computed and indicate the number of words read correctly per minute.

PROCEDURE

Prior to implementation of the intervention, each student's oral reading fluency was assessed using a one-minute timed reading assessment. The number of words read correctly in one minute from a second-grade reading passage represented the student's pre-test fluency score. Once the pre-test assessment was completed, the Readers' Theater intervention was implemented in the classroom.

A standard format, influenced by the work of Young and Rasinski (2009), was used over the five-week intervention. The format was as follows:

- *Monday:* The students were given scripts and familiarized with them in a mini-lesson and read-aloud (this typically went along with a comprehension strategy the class was studying). After the reading, students voted for the top two roles they wanted to play.

- *Tuesday:* Individual conferences were held regarding roles and the teacher worked with the student to select and assign appropriate roles (based on reading level and interest). After being assigned a role, students would highlight their speaking parts on their script and circle any words they were unsure of. Students assigned to the same texts would read scripts round-robin style and discuss them within their group. The rest of the time was used for independent practice. Students were allowed to take the scripts home with them and practice at home if they chose.

- *Wednesday:* The teacher met with groups to review any unknown words and time was provided for additional group practices. Students engaged in peer-coaching (when possible) with a more fluent partner to rehearse their parts. The teacher also worked directly with students who appeared to be struggling (as needed).

- *Thursday:* Final rehearsal day. Students practiced with their partners and individually, then as a cohesive group as many times as needed.

- *Friday:* Students performed in front of the class while reading the lines from their scripts.

Each week, a different script was selected for the students to read based on students' interest, text difficulty or level, length of the script, and the number of parts required. The first three weeks consisted of scripts that were based on books the class had read previously, and the final two weeks included scripts from stories the students had not read prior to their assignment for the Readers' Theater performances. Flexible groups of four to seven students were used throughout the intervention, allowing for different students with multiple reading levels to be interspersed amongst the groups. Of note, during the intervention, Readers' Theater was the only change made to the students' daily curriculum.

A midpoint assessment was conducted at the end of the third week of the intervention, using one of the alternative forms of the DIBELS measures. At the conclusion of the five weeks and following the final Readers' Theater performance, a post-test was administered.

DATA ANALYSIS

Descriptive statistics were computed to help reveal trends at the class level. Graphs showing the performance of each student on pre-test, midpoint, and post-test administrations were created to allow visual examinations of changes of individual participants' ORF scores. Finally, a repeated measures analysis of variance was performed to examine whether statistically significant changes in ORF scores were present.

RESULTS

At the time of the pre-test, students were reading an average of 122.75 words per minute. The pre-test scores ranged from a low of 70 words per minute to a high of 191 words per minute. At the midpoint assessment, which was performed at the beginning of the third week of the intervention, the average words read per minute by students was 132.9. This shows an increase of an average of 10.16 words per minute over the pre-test scores. The range of scores included a low of 80 words per minute and a high of 203 words per minute.

Figure A.1 shows student performance on the pre-test and midpoint administration of the DIBELS ORF measure. Examining the data, 16 students showed positive change in words per minute read, six students demonstrated a decrease in the words read correctly per minute, and one student showed no change. Of note, one did not have a midpoint assessment score due to an absence the day of administration.

When comparing pre-test and post-test scores (see Figure A.2), students gained an average of 10.69 words per minute. On the post-test assessment, students read an average of 133.69 words per minute. The scores ranged from a low of 81 words per minute

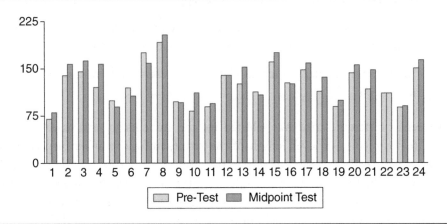

FIGURE A.1 Individual Student Change—Pre-Test to Midpoint Test

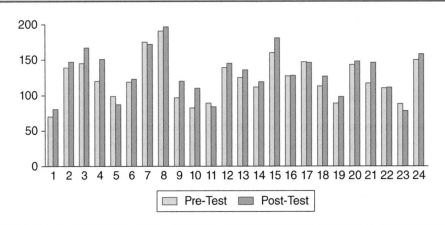

FIGURE A.2 Individual Student Change—Pre-Test to Post-Test

to a high of 196 words per minute. From pretest to posttest, 19 students showed an increase in the number of words per minutes and four students demonstrated a decrease. One student missed the post-test, and this student was removed from the final analysis.

A repeated measures analysis was used to assess changes in mean oral reading fluency scores across the action research study. The analysis revealed the presence of a significant difference, $F(2, 44) = 20.79, p < .05$, among the administrations of the DIBELS assessment (pre-test, midpoint, and post-test). Follow-up (post hoc) tests revealed significant differences between the pre-test and midpoint assessment and pre-test and post-test.

REFLECTING ON RESULTS

The original research question was: "What is the effect of Readers' Theater on second-grade students' reading fluency?" After the implementation of a Readers' Theater intervention for approximately five weeks, it can be concluded that Readers' Theater did have an impact on the fluency of students. Over the course of the study, 83% of students increased their words per minute rate. The total average words per minute gained was

10.69. With a desired increase of 37 words per minute over the course of second grade, having a 10 words per minute increase in a five-week span is significant.

The impact was differential as some students showed more growth than others. Student 10, for example, started the study reading 82 words per minute. At the end of the study, she had increased her words per minute rate by 28 words, ending the study reading 110 words per minute. Student 4, on the other hand, began the study reading 120 words per minute and increased her words per minute to 151 by the end of the intervention. On the opposite end of the scale, Student 22 read 110 words per minute at pre-test time and 111 words at the post-test, showing virtually no improvement. Of the four students who showed negative change, two had shown negative change on the midpoint assessment and two had shown positive change on the midpoint assessment.

What was noteworthy about the results was the fact that the students demonstrated their primary growth from the pre-test to the midpoint assessment and then grew very little from the midpoint assessment to the post-test. This seems to conflict with other research (Swain et al., 2013) that has shown that results generally increase more the longer the intervention is conducted. I have reflected a great deal on why this might be the case. One reason might have something to do with the texts read before and after the midpoint assessment. Prior to the assessment, students were familiar with the story and text, but afterwards, each text was new. It may be that the additional work with the script influenced the students' capacity to show growth. On the other hand, the higher gains that were seen when the strategy was first implemented may be present because it was a new practice in the classroom. Over the last two weeks, some of the novelty may have worn off, and the students may not have been reading the text as carefully or as many times as they were initially. This represents something that I will need to consider within any future studies.

Anecdotally, Readers' Theater had an effect on my students' desire to read. I noticed an increased excitement to interact with the reading each day. Students were excited every Monday to see what script they might read that week, were generally engaged in practice each day with their classmates, and came into class each day asking when we would be getting to Readers' Theater. Another noticeable benefit of the intervention was on the students' prosody. Each week, one of the first things students did with their scripts was highlight words that needed extra emphasis or expression, exclamation points and question marks, and other phrases or words that students needed to pay attention to. As the weeks progressed, there was a noticeable change to how students read their scripts. Given these prompts that the information needed to be read more closely, all of my students changed the way they looked at the script. They changed the volume and sound of their voice depending on the way the words were written. They paid attention to the details a bit more and tried to bring that out in the way they spoke. When post-test time came around, many students brought the awareness they gained for expression into reading pieces other than scripts. Post-test passages were read with more expression and prosody; however, this was not captured through my focus solely on measuring words read per minute.

PLAN OF ACTION

When thinking about my action plan and future research, I have considered both short-term and long-term plans. As an immediate focus, I would definitely like to implement the strategy for a longer amount of time to see if it resulted in greater success. As part of this process, I would like to keep track of how often each student reads the passage in school as well as determine a way to keep track of how often parts are practiced. Doing so may help me determine if there is a tipping point where reading the passages additional times may lead toward (or inhibit) increases in fluency. My intent in doing this is to help me determine a reason why my students saw gains over the first three weeks, but leveled off during the last two weeks of this action research study. I did not test the students' comprehension of the passage during the research study; I solely focused on their oral reading fluency of the passage. Through looking at the different studies others completed, repeated reading does not always improve comprehension, but it has been proven to increase students' fluency and words per minute (Young & Rasinski, 2009). Thus, as part of my short-term plan, I would like to see if Readers' Theater does help with students' comprehension as well as fluency. Questions to consider include: How much does increasing fluency affect comprehension? What other factors affect comprehension?

As I look toward action research investigations related to Readers' Theater that I would conduct in the future, I see several possibilities. Since I witnessed so many turnarounds from simply not enjoying reading to now looking forward to it, I would like to assess intrinsic motivation when Readers' Theater is used. I also focused on using fiction texts, but I think students would benefit from Readers' Theater as a tool to integrate reading within other content areas, such as science. Students could create their own scripts around the various topics, and I could use this as a tool to help increase the students' awareness and understanding of vocabulary words. Reading the scripts could give struggling readers extra exposure to certain concepts and words. Integrating Readers' Theater more solidly into the reading curriculum and other content areas could lead toward a variety of benefits that have not yet been explored.

CONCLUSION

Through this action research study, I was able to examine the impact of Readers' Theater on students' fluency and I am pleased with the results. Not only did my students demonstrate growth in their fluency, but I also saw several develop more confidence in their reading abilities. Due to these positive outcomes, I will continue this intervention with my students for the remainder of the school year. To increase the likelihood that these initial gains are sustained, I will observe, listen carefully, and analyze data to identify in which dimension of fluency students need to receive additional instructional support. I will continue to provide the necessary daily interventions and monitor progress on a regular basis to guide my instruction and adapt the scripts and processes that I am using with Readers' Theater. It is my goal that all students are reading fluently on grade level by the end of the second grade, and I am now convinced that implementation of Readers' Theater in my classroom can help me accomplish this.

References

Ardoin, S. P., Morena, L. S., Binder, K. S., & Foster, T. E. (2013). Examining the impact of feedback and repeated readings on oral reading fluency: Let's not forget prosody. *School Psychology Quarterly, 28*, 391–404. doi:10.1037/spq0000027

Begeny, J. C., Yeager, A., & Martinez, R. S. (2012). Effects of small-group and one-on-one reading fluency interventions with second grade, low-performing Spanish readers. *Journal of Behavioral Education, 21*, 58–79.

Casey, S., & Chamberlain, R. (2006). Bringing reading alive through Readers' Theater. *Illinois Reading Council Journal, 34*(4), 17–25.

Clementi, L. B. (2010). Readers Theater. *Phi Delta Kappan, 91*(5), 85–88.

Cohen, J. (2011). Building fluency through the repeated reading method. *English Teaching Forum, 49*, 20–27.

Forsythe, S. J. (1995). It worked! Readers Theatre in second grade. *The Reading Teacher, 49*, 264–265.

Gorsuch, G., & Taguchi, E. (2010). Developing reading fluency and comprehension using repeated reading: Evidence from longitudinal student reports. *Language Teaching Research, 14*, 27–59.

Griffith, L. W., & Rasinski, T. V. (2004). A focus on fluency: How one teacher incorporated fluency with her reading curriculum. *The Reading Teacher, 58*, 126–137. doi:10.1598/RT.58.2.1

Keehn, S. (2003). The effect of instruction and practice through Readers Theatre on young readers' oral reading fluency. *Reading Research and Instruction, 42*(4), 40–61.

Kuhn, M. R., & Stahl, S. A. (2003). Fluency: A review of developmental and remedial practices. *Journal of Educational Psychology, 95*, 3–21.

Mathes, P. G., Denton, C. A., Fletcher, J. M., Anthony, J. L., Francis, D. J., & Schatschneider, C. (2005). The effects of theoretically different instruction and student characteristics on the skills of struggling readers. *Reading Research Quarterly, 40*, 148–182.

Mraz, M., Nichols, W., Caldwell, S., Beisley, R., Sargent, S., & Rupley, W. (2013). Improving oral reading fluency through Readers Theatre. *Reading Horizons, 52*, 163–180.

National Reading Panel. (2000). *Teaching children to read: An evidence-based assessment of the scientific research literature on reading and its implications or reading instruction.* Washington, DC: National Institute of Child Health and Human Development.

Osborn, J., & Lehr, F. (2003). *A focus on fluency: Research-based practices in early reading series.* Honolulu, HI: Regional Educational Laboratory at Pacific Resources for Education and Learning.

Pikulski, J. J., & Chard, D. J. (2005). Fluency: Bridge between decoding and reading comprehension. *The Reading Teacher, 58*, 510–519. doi:10.1598/RT.58.6.2

Rasinski, T., Blachowicz, C., & Lems, K. (2006). *Fluency instruction.* New York, NY: Guilford.

Rasinski, T., Samuels, S., Hiebert, E., Petscher, Y., & Feller, K. (2011). The relationship between a silent reading fluency instructional protocol on students' reading comprehension and achievement in an urban school setting. *Reading Psychology, 32*, 75–97. doi:10.1080/02702710903346873

Richards, M. (2000). Be a good detective: Solve the case of oral reading fluency. *The Reading Teacher, 53*, 534–39.

Swain, K. D., Leader-Janssen, E.M., & Conley, P. (2013). Effects of repeated reading and listening passage preview on oral reading fluency. *Reading Improvement, 50*, 12–18.

Therrien, W. J. (2004). Fluency and comprehension gains as a result of repeated reading: A meta-analysis. *Remedial and Special Education, 25*, 252–261.

Therrien, W. J., & Kubuina, R. M. (2006). Developing reading fluency with repeated reading. *Intervention in School & Clinic, 41*, 156–160. doi:10.1177/10534512060410030501

Tyler, B., & Chard, D. J. (2000). Using Reader's Theatre to foster fluency in struggling readers: A twist on the repeated reading strategy. *Reading & Writing Quarterly, 16*, 163–168. doi:10.1080/105735600278015

Young, C., & Rasinski, T. (2009). Implementing Readers Theatre as an approach to classroom fluency instruction. *Reading Teacher, 63*, 4–13. doi:10.1598/RT.63.1.1

Yurick, A. L., Robinson, P. D., Cartledge, G., Lo, Y., & Evans, T. L. (2006). Using peer-mediated repeated readings as a fluency-building activity for urban learners. *Education and Treatment of Children, 29*, 469–493.

Using an Investigation Model in Ninth-Grade Science Class: Impact on Lower-Level Readers

INTRODUCTION

During professional development sessions last spring, our science team began considering moving from direct instruction to an investigation workshop approach as we were introduced to this alternative instructional model. We were presented with an investigative workshop approach as a means to assist students in acquiring deeper understandings of the content they study. In addition, it was suggested that all students enjoy and are motivated by freedom of movement throughout the room and opportunities for choice. We were intrigued by what this new instructional approach would bring to our classrooms, and our plan was to begin experimenting with the open investigation workshop approach in our science classes in the next academic year.

I teach ninth-grade physical earth science to students who are divided into three sections based on their language arts proficiencies. The rationale behind homogenous grouping based on readiness levels is that the three sections allow for differentiation during instruction on a narrower spectrum. For example, the English instructor can select a single novel to teach the whole class, versus three novels at different reading Lexile levels for each of the three core classes. As a result, I have three science sections with different reading levels. The third group, which has the lowest reading levels, struggles to grasp the ninth-grade science concepts. They also tend to be disengaged and many have a poor attitude toward learning. I have already switched the first two higher-level reading group sections to open investigative workshops with positive success during the first eight weeks of school. I am feeling more and more confident with this approach and see that it has important learning outcomes for my students. They are becoming more self-driven learners, and they seem to really enjoy being in class. They like the freedom to explore ideas, test out different hypotheses, and generate new insights within their groups. I feel that they are connecting with the concepts more than what I have experienced in the past with teaching the ninth-grade curriculum. Their test scores are good, and I hope they continue to improve as they master the skills and become more familiar with their roles and responsibilities of working in their teams. I had not yet begun to use the investigation workshop approach with my lowest reading level section of the course. I, along with my colleagues, were hesitant to introduce this new approach in our lower-level reading classes because of the behavioral problems and difficulty with attention that exists in this group of students. These students struggle with complex texts, working independently, and completing tasks. Their inability to persist with a task and work effectively with others is a challenge with an open investigation approach to teaching and learning. However, I am wondering if the direct instruction approach to teaching that is very teacher controlled is actually undermining their motivation and their sense of responsibility to their own learning.

The problem of practice that I decided to investigate within my classroom is how to effectively use the open investigation workshop approach with my students who have lower-level reading proficiency scores. I am interested in how an open investigation workshop approach impacts these students' learning and attitude toward learning during the second quarter of instruction. The research question that will guide my inquiry is: What is the effect of an open investigation workshop approach on a ninth-grade science class with students who are lower-level readers?

LITERATURE REVIEW

The National Science Education Standards call for inquiry to be the "central strategy for teaching science" (National Committee on Science Education Standards, 1996, p. 31). As a result, there has been a heavy focus on implementing more inquiry-based instruction in science classrooms. Providing teachers with professional development in the use of inquiry methods of instruction is widely advocated to promote the pedagogy in classrooms. The literature does strongly confirm that teacher beliefs, however, heavily influence the success of implementation into practice. Teacher beliefs about students, efficiency, rigor, and exam preparation can interfere with inquiry implementation (Wallace & Kang, 2004). For example, if teachers believe that some students are too immature, lazy, or unfocused to accomplish inquiry or if they believe their role is to cover the curriculum and therefore need to teach in the most efficient manner available then a transition to inquiry-based instruction will be difficult. Additional studies confirm that teacher beliefs about the nature of knowledge, teaching science, and the mandated curriculum are sometimes in conflict and can interrupt innovative practice suggested by professional development (Huberman & Middlebrooks, 2000; Munby, Cunningham, & Lock, 2000). However, recent research indicates that for those teachers who persist in promoting inquiry, either by posing interesting questions for children to answer, or by facilitating children to pose their own questions and investigations, inquiry-based learning can be a very successful practice (Wallace & Kang, 2004). One aspect of success that has been documented is that students have positive attitudes toward inquiry. Another aspect of success is that studies have shown that students engaged in inquiry-oriented instruction demonstrate academic achievement; however, there must be attention to several variables in order for inquiry-based instruction to be effective in improving student learning. These elements of success will be explored in more depth in the following sections.

STUDENT ATTITUDE AND MOTIVATION

The effect of open investigation workshop on students' attitude and motivation toward the science class is of interest in this study. A review of the literature reveals that students often express positive attitudes toward inquiry-based instruction and communicate that they like to be actively engaged in asking their own questions and investigating possible solutions to those questions (Wallace & Kang, 2004). Tuan, Chin, Tsai, and Cheng (2005) designed a study to investigate the effect of inquiry instruction on student motivation. They were particularly interested in whether there were any differences in motivational effect among students with different learning styles. Their findings indicated that after inquiry instruction students' motivation increased significantly more ($p < .001$) more than students who were taught through traditional teaching methods. They found no significant difference in motivation among the four learning styles of students after inquiry teaching. Interview data consistently showed that most students with different learning styles were willing to participate in the inquiry learning activities, but they often have different reasons for their engagement. The researchers suggest that inquiry-based science teaching can motivate students with different learning styles.

Another important focus of this action research study is to examine the effect of the open investigation workshop approach on students with lower reading proficiencies. My hope is that if their attitudes toward learning improve it may help them engage more in the class, and therefore more in the reading. Therefore, a major goal in using the inquiry-based approach with these students is to motivate them to read science material (reading online materials, instructions, etc.). A well-documented research finding is that internal motivations are positively correlated with reading achievement, and external motivations are not correlated with reading achievement (Guthrie & Coddington, 2009). In secondary school, students who read only for the reason of avoiding shame of failing or punishment show low and declining achievement (Otis, Grouzet, & Pelletier, 2005). The research shows that the reasons students choose to read are crucial. When internal motivations such as intrinsic motivation and interest prompt students' reading, students engage with the text more deeply and gain relatively high amounts of knowledge (Schiefele, 1999). However, if students' reading interests are low, their competency shows little growth and their reading quality diminishes. When reading material is made relevant for students, there is a greater chance they will become engaged and competent readers. To achieve relevance, text and activities should be connected to real-life experiences, involve hands-on activities, focus on a conceptual theme, and be culturally relevant (Vansteenkiste, Lens, & Deci, 2006).

The approach to learning that a teacher uses also impacts student motivation. A teacher who controls every aspect of instruction clearly communicates to students that their opinions and preferences aren't valued. When students are denied opportunities to make some decisions about their learning, they become a passive audience to the teacher's directives. As a result, students have no reason to read the text because they have no sense of ownership of the strategies being taught, the text used, or the knowledge presented. When it comes time to share the results of the learning experience, students feel no accountability. Often, this lack of accountability leads to failure to complete tasks and the likelihood that information is forgotten as soon as the experience is over (McRae & Guthrie, 2009).

It is also salient to consider that students are social beings that crave social interaction. They seek these interactions in all of their environments, and students may embrace collaboration with peers as a reason to read. When teachers support this need for collaboration by allowing students to share ideas and build knowledge together, a sense of classroom community is established, and existing knowledge is extended (Wentzel, 2005). Students who collaborate on a meaningful task must combine their background knowledge and skills, learn from one another, gain new perspective, and build a shared knowledge base of the material (Chinn, Anderson, & Waggoner, 2001). Grouping students of varying reading levels can also be motivating, as the struggling students gain the insight of more advanced readers, and the advanced readers develop and deepen their own understanding by explaining concepts and reading strategies to their peers (Sikorski, 2004). The more student-directed and social nature of an inquiry approach to learning establishes its potential to develop positive attitudes and motivation for science learning.

STUDENT LEARNING OUTCOMES

The effect of open investigation workshop on students' academic achievement is also a primary concern in this study. Inquiry-based instruction calls for students to build on their base of prior knowledge, create new ideas, test new theories, gather evidence, and learn from each other. There have been several studies conducted to examine the impact of inquiry-based instruction on student learning outcomes. Gormally, Brickman, Hallar, & Armstrong (2009) reported greater improvements in students' science literacy and research skills when using inquiry lab instruction. They found that students involved with inquiry gained self-confidence in scientific abilities; however, this gain was greater for students in the traditional curriculum. The researchers attributed this to the likelihood that the traditional curriculum promoted over-confidence. Interestingly, students participating in the inquiry labs valued more authentic science experiences but acknowledged that dealing with the complexity and frustrations faced by practicing scientists was challenging. The researchers suggested that this could explain why some students may resist inquiry curricula.

Marx and colleagues' (2004) study was also aimed at determining if a switch to an inquiry system would provide academic gains for students in an impoverished metropolitan school. This study switched students from conventional instruction to inquiry-based instruction, and showed large gains the first year and even larger gains the second and third years. Marx et al. (2004) went on to state that good curriculum design and collaboration with other personnel are critical to the success of the initiative. These findings were supported by another study conducted by Ojediran, Oludipe, and Ehindero (2014). These researchers investigated the impact of laboratory-based instructional intervention on the learning outcomes of low-performing senior secondary students in physics. The study adopted the pre-test and post-test control group quasi-experimental design. A total number of 194 students participated in the study. The Physics Achievement Test (PAT) was the main instrument used to collect data from students. The results of this study indicated that there was significant difference in the achievement in physics of low-performing students exposed to laboratory-based instructional intervention and those exposed to conventional teaching method. This study concluded that the use of the laboratory-based instructional intervention method of teaching should be advocated in senior secondary schools. In addition, Mooney and Laubach (2002) present large academic gains for students and improved engagement at multiple schools with an inquiry-based approach to instruction.

Additional research literature speaks positively about the gains to be made with inquiry-based learning as long as the key requirements (structure, coherent curriculum, high expectations) were met. While the Lee, Linn, Varma, and Liu (2010) study supported inquiry learning, it found that proper teacher execution and having correct materials was very important. The study showed negative gains when there were material failures or problems with teacher execution. The study concluded that well-designed inquiry units help students to understand the complex topics of science. According to Fogelman, McNeill, and Krajcik (2010), a teacher's ability to correctly deliver the curriculum was based on experience with the curriculum, and effectiveness varies widely. While switching to an inquiry-based classroom may be a necessary first step, experience with the curriculum is essential (Fogelman et al., 2010).

All of these research articles revealed some important trends. The first trend was the importance of constructing solid, coherent curriculum. Fogelman et al. (2010) stated that the instructional delivery method was not as important as the structure of the curriculum and pedagogy. A teacher who is very good at direct instruction methods will have greater gains than a teacher who is inexperienced at facilitating an inquiry workshop. The second trend in the articles was the importance of collaboration for teachers who are first starting off with inquiry-based classrooms. A third trend was the notion that inquiry-based science instruction lends itself very well to the use of technology. Research indicated that technology in the inquiry classroom had a very significant positive impact on student learning (Fogelman et al., 2010). The Waight and Abd-El Khalick (2006) study also supported use of technology in inquiry-based instruction, but noted that the complexity of some of the learning experiences often made them more difficult to conduct without a co-teacher or intervention support. Much of this literature encourages the intertwined use of technology in the inquiry-based classroom. While the technology is an important component, it is only as good as its implementation into a coherent portion of the inquiry. It should be perceived and used as a tool for learning. These studies establish that there is value in having technology in the inquiry-based classroom, but they also state that any failure in the equipment led to problems, and one article stated another potential challenge. Students working on computers can often get into individual tasks rather than working in a collaborative effort (Waight & Abd-El-Khalick, 2006). Overall, the use of inquiry-based instruction with effective integration of technology showed gains in learning outcomes, but only if the curriculum was correctly designed, delivered, and collaboratively supported.

REFLECTION ON THE LITERATURE REVIEW

Students engaged in science classes come into more difficult and deeper content as they enter secondary school. Any math or reading deficiencies quickly become apparent when reading informational text or performing math-related science research. During direct instruction students are required to read, sit, and listen for a significant amount of the period and often lose attention span part of the way through. Due to these reasons, two of my three ninth-grade science sections have been switched to open investigations. The sections are arranged primarily by their reading proficiencies, thereby grouping most students with reading difficulties into one section. The first two sections have had a relatively successful transition. Students with high reading ability are grouped primarily into one section, and they have had overwhelming success with all aspects of the class. The second section has struggled a little more with adopting self-management skills but is progressing. The third section had not been switched yet due to classroom management issues. These issues I believed may have been related to frustration with the heavy load of reading placed on them during class. I predict they will be more effectively taught using methods that include peer interaction and discussion. The addition of visualizations of complex science concepts with online technology should provide additional support to understanding the text to be read and result in improvements to students' comprehension (Lee et al., 2010). My belief is that the introduction of more workshop-oriented hands-on learning may give them another mode to learn with and in addition may stimulate more engagement, ownership, and relevance when reading is required. Part of the switch is also attempting to get these students to take more responsibility for their own learning. Student ownership should lead to a more positive view of their science class experiences, higher self-efficacy, and increased connections with science in their lives (O'Neill, 2010). With inquiry-based learning, the students have freedom within structured boundaries to choose their activities and invest themselves into the class, thereby encouraging ownership. These ideas are all supported by the literature presented in the previous sections.

O'Neill (2010) emphasized student ownership in inquiry-based learning as a rationale for more engaged learning. In the two sections I have already switched over to the open investigation workshop approach, the students have been more engaged; however, I have run into management problems when teaching inquiry lessons for the first time. Students find it easy to get disorganized when an investigation breaks down, and due to the need for the teacher to be in multiple places at once, when one problem comes up it seems that problems begin popping up all over the room. My experience verifies for me what the literature concludes, that experience and solid coherent and structured curriculum are necessary for a successful program. An instructor has to almost be able to guarantee that nothing can possibly go wrong, and that takes a great deal of preparation and experience (Lee et al., 2010). I anticipate that classroom management will be a concern in this study because this targeted group of students has difficulty with self-regulatory behaviors and persistence to task. I believe they can be successful with this approach but I know it will take diligence, persistence, and a willingness to make changes and take risks throughout the implementation.

The concerns around technology integration within the literature also make sense and encouraged me to plan carefully how I would use technology in my classroom. You simply cannot assign a student to a computer and expect something productive to come from it. A formal plan of action must be given to them if they are to utilize it effectively. Students do not have the skill set necessary to walk up to a computer and produce solid research on a topic. Computers, as with any other task, must have instructions and modeling. I cannot take for granted that most students perform most things in science for the first time.

Reflecting on my own experience as a teacher, I see lack of experience as a limiting factor going into this action research study. There are many very fluid situations where experience will let you know what to do and react faster. Although I have some experience with implementing this approach with two of my class sections, I am still new to this approach. Unfortunately, I am the only teacher who is currently taking the risk to experiment with this model of instruction with students who have the lowest reading proficiency scores. According to the literature, I will be at a disadvantage to not have a collaborative team to engage in this work with me.

Conclusion

While there are numerous articles on the benefits of inquiry-based learning in the classroom, there has been a call for additional classroom-based research that examines both cognitive and affective effects on students' learning (Wallace & Kang, 2004). In addition, research on inquiry-based instruction specifically for secondary science that focuses on students with reading difficulties was limited. This study goes further than to simply compare direct instruction to inquiry-based instruction in a ninth-grade earth science course. The results of this study will examine the effects of the open investigation workshops approach for students who have reading difficulties. This study will contribute to the existing literature base, but most importantly it will allow me to gather data to improve my abilities to meet the instructional needs of all of my students.

Methods

Context and Participants

The context of this study is a secondary school located in a suburban area near a large metropolitan city. The student body consists of 908 students. The school is classified as medium socioeconomic status, with 48% of students being eligible for free or reduced-price lunch. While the school is not Title I, it does qualify to receive state funds proportionate to the free and reduced-price lunch percentage. The student population consists mainly of Caucasian (79%), African American (17%), Asian American (2%), American Indian/Pacific Islander (1%), and other (1%).

This study utilized one of three sections of science classes that I teach. As a result of ability grouping based on language arts skill levels, this particular group of students struggles to read and are classified as below grade-level readers. The class consists of 28 students; eight have 504 plans, two have IEPs, 16 are male, and 12 are female. The majority of the class is Caucasian (20), with African American (5) and Hispanic (2). The majority of the students (19) have low informational text reading scores, while the remaining nine have scores in the low-medium range. I selected this section for the study because I was interested in understanding how the use of an open investigation approach to teaching science would impact learning outcomes for students with lower-level reading skills. The other two sections of science classes I teach, which have higher-level reading levels, already use the investigation approach. However, because of behavior management issues and resistance to independent reading and writing activities I had not implemented this model of instruction with this particular class.

Data Collection Strategies/Instrument

The research design of this action research study was a pre-test and post-test, using the same group. There was no control group. Two primary sources of data collected in this study were (a) students' reported attitude toward class and (b) actual weekly test scores. Pre-tests and post-tests were used to measure the results. The students filled out an anonymous Likert-scale questionnaire with two open-ended questions at the end of the direct instruction series, and filled out another one near the completion of the open workshop study to assess student attitude toward the class. In addition, the students were given one 20-question multiple-choice test per week for eight weeks of direct instruction. The students then switched to open investigation workshop, and the same test format was followed for the next eight weeks. The exact format of the multiple-choice tests resembled complex, critical-thinking end of grade test questions. The available answers contained more than one correct answer, and students had to choose the best answer. I also kept a researcher log during the implementation of the intervention to record field notes and observational data.

PROCEDURE

The students in this class have informational text reading deficiencies and were originally taught with direct instruction supplemented by text. The class was switched to an open investigation workshop approach to monitor the overall effect it had on the students' ability to learn the content and their attitude toward their learning experiences. The students began the academic year with a relatively rigid classroom structure using direct instruction. The 90-minute block opened up with a warm-up task (usually vocabulary words) (10 minutes), introduction of the material by the instructor (10 minutes), followed by group or round-robin reading of the chapter (30 minutes). Next, students were asked to review the end-of-chapter questions, and then the instructor chose various students to answer the questions and expand on them (30 minutes). The last 10 minutes were used for review of the objective. This direct instruction format lasted through Thursday, while Friday was reserved for testing and re-teaching. The students have experienced this type of format for years due to reading proficiency, and I wanted to study how using the investigation workshop approach would affect their learning. When switched to the workshop model, the class format changed to the following: Monday, Tuesday, and Thursday began with a lab demonstration by the instructor, which is connected to the content (10 minutes); the students were then given the learning objective for the day and the teams were assigned a station order; the students then performed their tasks in their teams at the various stations for the next 60 minutes under supervision of the instructor, followed by 15 minutes of whole group review of key ideas and information review, followed by 5 minutes of student-led discussion. The workshop stations consisted of the following: two online interactive activities, online video streaming with questionnaire/guide sheet, two hands-on stations with mini-labs, and informational text with teacher or a student with a higher reading score leading the group. While the focus of the workshop was audio, visual, and interactive modes of input, the informational text was still integrated into their learning experience. Wednesday was used for a whole group lab, which consisted of a larger teacher-guided experiment. Friday was reserved for testing and evaluation of results with the students.

DATA ANALYSIS

In order to analyze the data, I collected, compiled, and graphed the students' raw scores on the tests. I first created a data table of average test scores each week, and then created a line graph to see the trends in the scores as a whole class across both the baseline data and the intervention data. I decided to examine the trends in the scores across groups of students within the class (a low, medium, and high group based on Lexile reading level). This provided me with the opportunity to have another level of analysis. I calculated the average test score per group each week (low, medium, or high). This allowed me to see how the format is affecting the learning as a whole class and also individual groups of students. To do this, the pre-test and post-test scores were graphed to reveal trends in the data. The observational field notes data were used to help me explain any trends that occur in the data and pinpoint what may have been happening at any one week that might influence the test scores.

The Likert-scale attitude questionnaire data were averaged for each item and for an overall score. The scores across the two formats were compared and any trends noted. The Likert-scale survey was on a 5.0-point scale. I analyzed whether my students' attitudes improved, stayed the same, or declined. Then, I read through the open-ended questions for each format several times and identified themes in the responses. Once I identified themes, I went back to the raw data and recorded how many times those themes were expressed. The themes were then ranked by order of incidence to allow the most prominent ideas to be identified and presented.

RESULTS

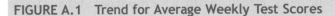

FIGURE A.1 Trend for Average Weekly Test Scores

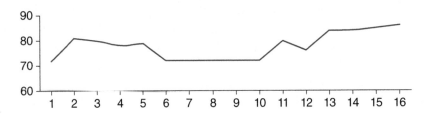

The trend for the weekly test scores (see Figure A.1) during direct instruction (weeks 1–8) was an initial increase in scores from week 1 to weeks 2–5 and then a decline back to initial lower levels for weeks 6–8. The trend for the weekly test scores during open investigation (weeks 9–16) was a slow and level start in weeks 9 and 10 and then a (mostly) gradual increase, with the highest average test scores received in weeks 15 and 16.

FIGURE A.2 Trend Scores for Lowest-Performing Readers

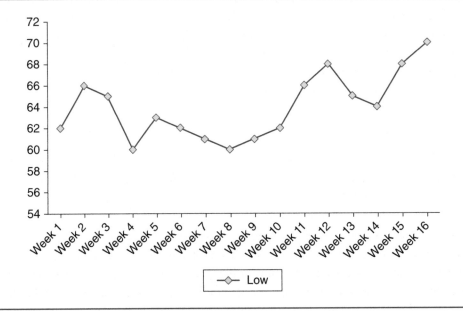

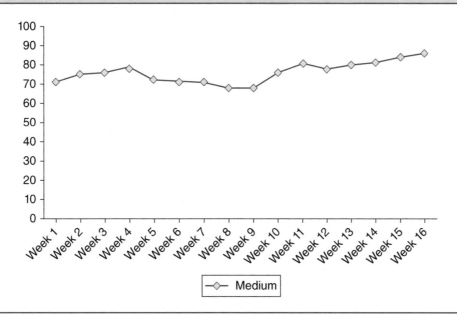

FIGURE A.3 Trend Scores of Readers With Average Proficiency

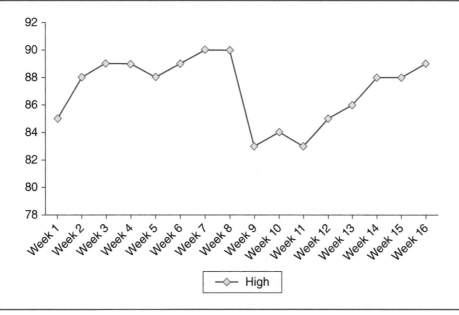

FIGURE A.4 Trend Scores for Highest-Performing Readers

The students with the lowest reading proficiencies ($n = 6$) did show an increase in scores, but inconsistently at first (Figure A.2). However, the scores were improving by the end of the intervention. The students with low-medium reading level scores ($n = 19$) dropped during the first two weeks of workshop (Figure A.3). Their scores came back up the following week and steadily improved. The few students ($n = 3$) with higher-level proficiencies (still in the low-medium range) in the class showed a decrease in scores (Figure A.4). The higher-level students' performance was weaker initially with the open investigation method but did improve back to initial levels of achievement demonstrated with direct instruction.

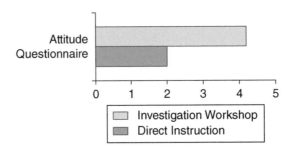

The mean class score for the attitude questionnaire increased from a 2.0 with direct instruction to a 4.2 with open investigation workshop. The open-ended questions revealed that the students were more positive about the class experience using the open investigation workshop approach. The major themes that emerged in the open-ended responses that explain their positive attitudes were (a) collaboration of the teams, (b) active nature of the classes—"loved getting to *do* science and to act like scientists"—and (c) enjoyed talking through the problem-solving possibilities. The majority of the students expressed they enjoyed the change in approach and they preferred the workshop model of instruction to the direct instruction approach to instruction. There were two students who stated that they preferred direct instruction because they liked working independently rather than in groups.

REFLECTING ON RESULTS

Overall, the data shows that the students did increase their learning of the content over time through the open investigation workshops. However, I was also interested to see if there were any differences in effects among the varying levels of learners in my class. As I predicted, the low-reading students did show an increase in their scores across the intervention, but it was inconsistent initially. My observational field notes reveal challenges these students experienced during the intervention and may help explain these results, such as their difficulty adapting to a new learning format, attention span problems due to newfound freedom, and social anxiety from speaking and learning from peers. But, I am very encouraged to see that by the end of the intervention the average scores for this group were increasing beyond what they demonstrated using the direct instruction approach. The low-medium reading level student scores also dropped during the first couple of weeks of the intervention. This group formed a majority of students who were fascinated with workshop freedoms and were excited and motivated by the new method, but failed to concentrate on the actual policies and procedures until well into week 3. Their scores started coming up the following week and continued to improve. The few high-reading students in the class actually showed a decrease in scores. Surprisingly, this was counterintuitive to what I expected but my observational notes suggested that a possible explanation for this was that these students used to work well ahead of the other students but due to the peer interaction in the workshops they focused mainly on only the current activities and did not get into the extension activities. They also seemed to be enamored with the new format and spent quite a bit of time initially working through the social dynamics and issues involved in working in a team format. Overall, the three different averages and the class average stabilized and began to climb in weeks 15 and 16. Moving the whole class to this format was difficult, and there were times that I wanted to throw in the towel and give up on the intervention but the results of the class average graph are very encouraging.

The results of the pre-/post-attitude questionnaire demonstrate an increase from a 2.0 following the direct instruction to a 4.2 following the open investigation workshop as an overall class average (Figure A.5). This large overall increase in student attitude toward the class is the most powerful finding of the study. My observational notes are evidence of the sheer enjoyment of the class for both the students and myself. The class, which seemed so difficult to teach and manage, transformed into a class that was easy to teach and easy to manage and had happy students. The entire atmosphere of the class changed. Students who were just trying to get through the day now showed up to class excited and with the correct classroom supplies. Some students even began the written work in the morning before school voluntarily instead of walking the halls socializing. I don't know of any higher evidence than that of a student being engaged in the class. Something that I am very passionate about also began to change in the room in the last four weeks: my high-, medium-, and low-performing students all began working as teams. I had students hanging around after class wanting to continue to engage in discussion and class work on many occasions. I recorded that students would say things like "I actually think I like science now" and "This class is so much more fun than any of our other classes." On the open-ended questionnaire, the majority of the students expressed that they hoped the workshop format would continue because they liked it better and they enjoyed learning the content by working as a team. This alone is worth the change, and if the scores continue to climb as these students get acclimated to their new learning environment then it seems to be the way I should teach science to all my students in the future. I did have two students who expressed they prefer the direct instruction format because they feel more successful when working independently to learn the material. They found it challenging to work together and felt they could complete the assignments with more ease and success when working alone. This didn't surprise me because I know that some students are more intrapersonal in nature and are much more comfortable and confident learning on their own. I may need to take this into consideration and provide options for some activities for students to work independently, if they desire. But, I believe that the group interaction and collaborative team approach is important for all students to experience and necessary to challenge students to grow in their interpersonal skills.

My results are supported and can be better understood by the literature on the topic. Lee et al. (2010) and Fogelman et al. (2010) both express the positive impact of inquiry and technology incorporation to a positive learning environment. The students in this research showed gains other than those that were specified by the research question. For example, my field notes reveal that they began to work with the technology in the centers and collaborated on projects, which are both 21st-century learning skills. In addition, O'Neill's (2010) views were confirmed when students who took ownership of their education had a more positive view of their science class experiences. When examining the results as compared to the Marx et al. (2004) study, one has to consider the longitudinal nature of the Marx study. My research project had an eight-week intervention, while the Marx study analyzed data at the end of the first through third years. The students' test scores in my study actually declined for the first two weeks of the intervention, but they began to show improvement for the last several weeks for all groups. I believe they were on a positive trajectory that would continue if implemented over a longer period of time.

Fogelman et al. (2010) stated that the instructor's experience also may contribute to the success of open inquiry and that an inexperienced inquiry instructor would see smaller gains than an experienced direct instruction teacher. This may also explain the limited academic gains in this study. While I have taught the other two sections with open investigation, they behaved very differently than this section. As I spend more time with these students who are lower-level readers, I anticipate that I will get better at providing appropriate scaffolding to support their reading/writing and better manage their engagement in the workshop format. The findings of Tuan et al. (2005), Fogelman (2010), Marx et al. (2004), Ojediran et al. (2014), O'Neill (2010), and Lee et al. (2010) were all consistent with this study. Student learning, attitude, collaboration, pride, and technology use all improved during the study. The major concern in my results was the lower scores in the high-reading-range students, which I believe may improve with adjustments I can make with further study. I think my study extends the current research literature because I was able to look at the effects of the approach on different levels of learners. This understanding is needed in the literature, and there is limited research on this aspect of the topic.

Though the research project progressed without any major derailments, it did have some hurdles to overcome and bumps along the way. There are some things I wish I could have anticipated ahead of time. The first was switching the class over to full workshop too quickly. As you can read in my field notes, students had some serious management issues until they learned the routine. This took about two weeks, with only a few relapses along the way. In the future, I believe that a day-to-day gradual release during the period would shorten this window to about one or two weeks. I believe this would produce higher test results sooner. Another concern is a student with an IEP who I created plans to work with, but due to management issues I really didn't have the opportunity to devote as much time to her as I would have liked. In the future, a more developed plan and maybe even another instructor might help. The final change is related to the length of the lab day during the week. The students struggled with 90-minute lab procedures on Wednesdays, and I had to modify it early into the research project. I removed the full-day lab and replaced it with mini-labs, across three days per week. I think if this had been arranged from the beginning it would have helped in the transition.

As I reflect on the results of my action research project, I feel an overwhelming sense of satisfaction with the project and the results of it. The students are thrilled to come to class every day, and I love teaching it. I spend extra hours in the classroom and really enjoy preparing the learning experiences for the workshop approach. I have a renewed sense of teaching, and I am happy that I am beginning to figure out how to make this work with all my students. Seeing this group of students, who are so used to struggling, devour a lesson with intrinsic motivation makes the time invested so worthwhile.

PLAN OF ACTION

Future research I would like to conduct relevant to the current study would be to study how the higher-level students are affected by working with the lower-level students in the workshop approach. I am teaching a section of primarily high-level readers and a section with primarily lower-level readers with only a few higher-level readers and would like to set up a new study and compare the data. I would set up an identical unit with identical assessments and test both sections. If the high-level readers in the low-reader grouping have lower scores than the high-level readers in the high-level group, then the cause of this should be examined. I would set up the research design, collect data, and would have to consult my principal as well as the parents of the students who are participating. Once data is gathered, it can be charted and analyzed. The timeline would be a full unit, which would take approximately six to eight weeks.

I also need to continue to make improvements to the workshop structure and function especially in regard to increasing learning outcome potential for my higher-level students in the class; however, the improvement in their overall attitudes toward learning science has convinced me to keep using this approach with this class. I also need to continue to develop scaffolding tools to support the reading and writing that is required in the ninth-grade science materials for these struggling students. I believe that with appropriate and additional scaffolding I can improve all of the students' access to the material and comprehension of it. To accomplish this, I plan on sharing my study with the other ninth-grade science teachers to encourage that we use the open investigation workshop with all our students. I hope to get others interested in using this with their lower-level sections and work together to develop materials and resources to support this work with our struggling readers/writers. I think when they see (and hear from the students) how much improvement there is in student attitude toward learning science that at least two of the other teachers will want to work with me on this project. With a team approach, I believe I can sustain this method of teaching! With a few more iterations of the action research process, I may feel confident to share my work with other teachers in the district or at a professional conference.

CONCLUSION

Overall, the students showed growth in achievement and attitude with the open investigation workshop. Over the course of the eight-week intervention, students did struggle initially with the new format and were resistant to the change. I had to make many modifications to the structure of the workshop as it was implemented based on my observations and reflections during the process. There were times when I felt the workshop format was too demanding of the students and wanted to give up on it. However, as time went on and I made adjustments based on the formative data I was collecting, I began to see progress in my students' ability to be actively engaged learners who took responsibility for their learning. I believe as they gained confidence and skills in what was being asked of them they began to have a more positive attitude toward their learning and this impacted their achievement in the class. The best outcome for me is that my students now love our class! I have to make them leave at the end of each class session so they will not be late for their next class! This has increased my planning but also my enjoyment of teaching this class.

References

Chinn, C. A., Anderson, R. C., & Waggoner, M. A. (2001). Patterns of discourse in two kinds of literature discussion. *Reading Research Quarterly, 36,* 378–412.

Fogelman, J., McNeill, K. L., & Krajcik, J. (2010). Examining the effect of teachers' adaptations of a middle school science inquiry-oriented curriculum unit on student learning. *Journal of Research in Science Teaching, 48*(2), 149–169.

Gormally, C., Brickman, P., Hallar, B., & Armstrong, N. (2009). Effects of inquiry-based learning on students' science literacy skills and confidence.

International Journal for the Scholarship of Teaching and Learning, 3(2). Retrieved from http://digital commons.georgiasouthern.edu/ij-sotl/vol3/iss2/16

Guthrie, J. T., & Coddington, C. S. (2009). Reading motivation. In K. Wentzel & A. Wigfield (Eds.), *Handbook of motivation at school* (pp. 503–525). New York, NY: Routledge.

Huberman, M., & Middlebrooks, S. (2000). The dilution of inquiry: A qualitative study. *Qualitative Studies in Education, 13*, 281–304.

Lee, H., Linn, M. C., Varma, K., & Liu, O. (2010). How do technology-enhanced inquiry science units impact classroom learning? *Journal of Research in Science Teaching, 47*, 71–90.

Marx, R. W., Blumenfeld, P. C., Krajcik, J. S., Fishman, B., Soloway, E., Geier, R., & Tal, R. T. (2004). Inquiry based science in the middle grades: Assessment of learning in urban systematic reform. *Journal of Research in Science Teaching, 41*, 1063–1080.

McRae, A., & Guthrie, J. T. (2009). Promoting reasons for reading: Teacher practices that impact motivation. In E. H. Hiebert (Ed.), *Reading more, reading better* (pp. 55–76). New York, NY: Guilford.

Mooney, M. A., & Laubach, T. A., (2002). Adventure engineering: A design centered, inquiry based approach to middle grade science and mathematics education. *Journal of Engineering Education, 91*, 309–318.

Munby, H., Cunningham, M., & Lock, C. (2000). School science culture: A case study of barriers to developing professional knowledge. *Science Education, 84*, 193–211.

National Committee on Science Education Standards. (1996). *National science education standards*. Washington, DC: National Academy Press.

Ojediran, I., Oludipe, D., & Ehindero, O. (2014). Impact of laboratory-based instructional intervention on the learning outcomes of low performing senior secondary students in physics.

Creative Education, 5, 197–206. doi:10.4236/ce.2014.54029

O'Neill, T. B. (2010). Fostering spaces of student ownership in middle school science. *Equity and Excellence in Education, 43*, 6–20.

Otis, N., Grouzet, F. M., & Pelletier, L. G. (2005). Latent motivational change in an academic setting: A 3-year longitudinal study. *Journal of Educational Psychology, 97*, 170–183.

Schiefele, U. (1999). Interest and learning from text. *Scientific Studies of Reading, 3*, 257–279.

Sikorski, M. P. (2004). Inside Mrs. O'Hara's classroom. In J. T. Guthrie, A. Wigfield, & K. C. Perencevich (Eds.), *Motivating reading comprehension: Concept-oriented reading instruction* (pp. 195–223). Mahwah, NJ: Erlbaum.

Tuan, H., Chin, C., Tsai, C., & Cheng, S. (2005). Investigating the effectiveness of inquiry instruction on the motivation of different learning styles students. *International Journal of Science and Mathematics Education, 3*, 541–566.

Vansteenkiste, M., Lens, W., & Deci, E. L. (2006). Intrinsic versus extrinsic goal contents in self-determination theory: Another look at the quality of academic motivation. *Educational Psychologist, 41*, 19–31.

Waight, N., & Abd-El-Khalick, F. (2006). The impact of technology on the enactment of "inquiry" in a technology enthusiast's sixth grade science classroom. *Journal of Research in Science Teaching, 44*, 154–182.

Wallace, C. S., & Kang, N. (2004). An investigation of experienced secondary science teachers' beliefs about inquiry: An examination of competing belief systems. *Journal of Research in Science Teaching, 41*, 936–960.

Wentzel, K. R. (2005). Peer relationships, motivation, and academic performance at school. In A. J. Elliot & C. S. Dweck (Eds.), *Handbook of competence and motivation* (pp. 279–296). New York, NY: Guilford.

Appendix B: Potential Publication Outlets for Action Research

GENERAL EDUCATION

Name of Publication	Journal Website/Submission Guidelines
Early Childhood Research & Practice (ECRP)	http://ecrp.uiuc.edu/authinst.html
Education Week (or Teacher Magazine)	http://www2.edweek.org/info/about/submit-commentary.html
Educational Action Research	http://www.tandfonline.com/toc/reac20/current
Educational Leadership	http://www.ascd.org/Publications/Educational-Leadership/Guidelines-for-Writers/Guidelines-for-Educational-Leadership-Writers.aspx
The Elementary School Journal	http://www.journals.uchicago.edu/journals/esj/instruct
ERIC Resources in Education	http://eric.ed.gov/submit/
Harvard Education Review	http://hepg.org/special/navigation/her-main/guidelines-for-authors
Scholastic Teacher Magazine	http://www.scholastic.com/teachermag/
Middle School Journal	http://www.amle.org/ServicesEvents/MiddleSchoolJournal/tabid/175/Default.aspx
Phi Delta Kappan Magazine	https://us.sagepub.com/en-us/nam/phi-delta-kappan/journal202327
The Urban Review	http://www.springer.com/west/home?SGWID=4-102-70-35755139-0&changeHeader=true&SHORTCUT=www.springer.com/journal/11256/submission
Young Children (NAEYC)	http://journal.naeyc.org/about/manuscripts.asp

LITERACY/READING

Name of Publication	Journal Website/Submission Guidelines
The Reading Teacher	http://onlinelibrary.wiley.com/journal/10.1002/(ISSN)1936-2714/homepage/ForAuthors.html
English Journal	http://www.ncte.org/journals/ej/write
Voices from the Middle	http://www.ncte.org/journals/vm/write

SOCIAL STUDIES EDUCATION

Name of Publication	Journal Website/Submission Guidelines
Social Studies Research and Practice	http://www.socstrpr.org
Social Education (NCSS Journal)	http://www.socialstudies.org/publications/socialeducation
Social Studies and the Young Learner (NCSS Journal)	http://www.socialstudies.org/publications/ssyl
The History Teacher	http://www.thehistoryteacher.org

SCIENCE, TECHNOLOGY, AND MATH EDUCATION

Name of Publication	Journal Website/Submission Guidelines
Teaching Children Mathematics (NCTM journal)	http://www.nctm.org/publications/write-review-referee/journals/Write-for-Teaching-Children-Mathematics/
Mathematics Teacher (NCTM journal)	http://www.nctm.org/Publications/Write,-Review,-Referee/
Mathematics Teaching in the Middle School (NCTM journal)	http://www.nctm.org/Publications/Write,-Review,-Referee/
Journal of Computers in Mathematics and Science Teaching (AACE)	http://www.aace.org/newpubs/index.cfm?fuseaction=Info.Entrance&CFID=2313913&CFTOKEN=97922705
Journal of Research in Science Teaching	http://onlinelibrary.wiley.com/journal/10.1002/%28ISSN%291098-2736/
Journal of Science Education	http://www.tandf.co.uk/journals/authors/tsedauth.asp
The Physics Teacher	http://www.aapt.org/publications/tptauthors.cfm
Science and Children (National Science Teachers Association)	http://www.nsta.org/162
Technology and Learning Magazine	http://www.techlearning.com
Information Technology in Childhood Education (AACE journal)	http://www.aace.org/newpubs/index.cfm?fuseaction=Info.Entrance&CFID=2313913&CFTOKEN=97922705

Glossary

Abstract – a paragraph, usually containing between 100 and 250 words, that provides a brief overview of the article or chapter (Chapter 3, Chapter 8)

Acting – second phase of the action research process; characterized by the implementation of the plan of action developing in the planning phase (Chapter 1)

Action research – a form of research that is based on a personally relevant topic/theme and is carried out within the context of practice to improve practices and learning. It is cyclical in nature and characterized by four primary phases: planning, acting, observing, and reflecting (Chapter 1)

Action research report – an organized report of your action research to allow the research design and outcomes of your investigation to be shared with others (Chapter 8)

Action research summary – a summary of your action research study that often has similar headings to a more formal action research report, but includes only the main ideas and is written in a concise manner (Chapter 8)

Analysis of variance – statistical test that compares the means of three or more groups or scores; often referred to as ANOVA (Chapter 6)

Anecdotal notes – informal notes that briefly describe a situation, event, or interaction; do not contain the level of detail or depth associated with formal observation protocols (Chapter 5)

Annotated bibliography – method to develop a summary/synthesis of an individual piece of literature; generally consists of three parts: citation, summary, and reflection (Chapter 3)

Anonymity – research condition where the principal investigator does not know or have access to the identity of the participant (Chapter 4)

Artifacts – any product, document, or sample that can be collected to document some specific facet of research; includes school records, assessment data (standardized and teacher created), and classroom assignments (Chapter 5)

Assent – agreement of a child who is under the age of 18 to participate in research; must be accompanied by informed consent (Chapter 4)

Attitude scales – data collection instruments designed to collect information about participants' feelings, attitudes, or evaluations in a measurable unit (Chapter 5)

Coding – process of examining textual data and finding meaningful segments of information that are seemingly aligned and combining them to form groups or categories (Chapter 6)

Collaborative action research – multiple teachers engaging together in action research who may represent a grade level, content area, or all the teachers at the school or district (Chapter 9)

Community of practice – informal group of learners focused on a specific topic or issue; focus is on interaction and shared encouragement to create individual and collective growth around the topic or issue (Chapter 9)

Confidentiality – research situation where the primary investigator may have access to personally identifiable information, but agrees not to release or share the information (Chapter 4)

Construct validity – degree to which an instrument measures an intended concept or construct (Chapter 5)

Content validity – degree to which an instrument measures the intended subject matter of the content and takes into account all aspects of a construct under examination (Chapter 5)

Convergent validity – validity established through the use of statistical procedures demonstrating alignment between instruments, at least one of which has proven reliability and validity (Chapter 5)

Criterion validity – degree scores on an instrument correlate with scores on a similar instrument measuring the same or similar construct (Chapter 5)

Deductive analysis – analysis involves testing hypotheses about differences or observed relationships with the intent of extending the findings associated with a particular sample, or subset of a group, to the population from which it was drawn or to make generalizations from specific conditions to more general ones (Chapter 6)

Descriptive statistics – numerical values that describe facets of data such as the difference between highest and lowest values or average; includes metrics such as mean, median, standard deviation, and range (Chapter 6)

Equivalent forms reliability – type of reliability present when different versions of the same items are used in multiple forms of an instrument producing similar results that are consistent over time; also referred to as alternative forms reliability (Chapter 5)

Experimental design – design that incorporates random assignment of participants to comparison groups to be used within the research (Chapter 4)

Face validity – validity present when expert review confirms an instrument measures the concepts and constructs it is intended to (Chapter 5)

Generalizability – the process of explaining the behavior of a larger sample (or population) as a result of conducting a study with a smaller set that appears to exemplify the characteristics associated with the population (Chapter 6)

Hypothesis – a proposed explanation about the possible source of the problem identified within the problem statement and the methods to resolve the situation (Chapter 2)

Implications for practice – the statements you make about how you might change your teaching practices, in light of your results (Chapter 7)

Inductive analysis – systematic development of categories and themes that originate from the interpretation of data; focused on theory generation and does not seek to generalize findings to a population (Chapter 6)

Inferential statistics – numeric values associated with specific statistical tests conducted on a particular sample, or subset of a group; attempts to make generalizations from sample to population from which it was drawn or from specific conditions to more general ones (Chapter 6)

Informed consent – the process and related document that allows the participants to assess the research study and decide whether to participate as a result of their understanding of the study (Chapter 4)

Institutional review board – group of individuals that systematically reviews research proposals using a specified set of guidelines to ensure protection of the human subjects that may participate in the research (Chapter 4)

Inter-rater reliability – the level of agreement reached between two (or more) observers when the same activity is independently analyzed using the same protocol, or observation procedure (Chapter 5)

Interval data – numeric data characterized by equal units of measure between each data point (Chapter 5)

Interviews – direct interactions between researchers and individuals or groups of participants; can be formal, semi-structured, or informal (Chapter 5)

Journal – a written record of thoughts that convey data relative the participants' thoughts, feelings, knowledge, or other attributes within a particular setting or context (Chapter 5)

Learning community – group of individuals, whether formally or informally organized, who wish to discuss and improve their practice (Chapter 9)

Mean – average of all the numbers in a data set (Chapter 6)

Measures of association – statistical test that measures the association (relationship) between variables (Chapter 6)

Measures of central tendency – numeric values that establish trends of what is standard in the data; includes measures such as mean, median, and mode (Chapter 6)

Measures of variability – numeric values that provide information about how individual scores differ from each other within a set of scores, for example, how spread out the data is from the mean (Chapter 6)

Median – value that represents the midpoint of data when it is placed in numerical order (Chapter 6)

Mixed methods research – uses a combination of quantitative and qualitative methods to address the research question; often characterized by the order of analysis (e.g., sequential or concurrent) (Chapter 4)

Mode – value that occurs most frequently in a group of data (Chapter 6)

Nominal data – data that can be classified into categories; provides frequency counts on the number of cases within a category (Chapter 5)

Nonexperimental design – design that lacks random assignment and there is no attempt to manipulate an independent variable; often associated with qualitative research (Chapter 4)

Observation – form of data collection that involves a researcher directly viewing events within a particular context within a specified timeframe; ranges from structured to unstructured (Chapter 5)

Observing – the third phase of the action research process; conducted to gather systematic and deliberate documentation of results of the acting phase of the action research process (Chapter 1)

Ordinal data – data that can be placed on a continuum characterized by rank or order (e.g., first, second) (Chapter 5)

Peer reviewed – a process that involves examination by experts in the field who note whether it meets certain levels of quality and scholarship; scholarship that has undergone peer review is typically assumed to be of higher quality (Chapter 3, Chapter 4)

Plan for Action – an organized and systematic plan that outlines action steps to be implemented based on new understandings and insights from the action research study (Chapter 7)

Planning – the first phase of the action research process where a plan of action is constructed to guide the subsequent activities of the action research investigation (Chapter 1)

Policy implications – concrete action statements developed to inform policy or suggest procedural changes to those who have decision-making power or authority (Chapter 8)

Practical significance – term used to signify that a given strategy or action that was the focus of research or an investigation has direct applicability within the context of teaching or learning (Chapter 1)

Practitioner-focused literature – publications written to provide tips and strategies that are directly applicable within a classroom or educational setting. These publications may include a theoretical basis and a synthesis of research, but are primarily written for practitioners (Chapter 3)

Praxis – the practice that is formed by a combination of critical thinking, reflection, and action (Chapter 8)

Primary source – an original document or artifact written by the individual who engaged in the processes or activities described in the document or artifact (Chapter 3)

Problem statement – a few sentences or a short paragraph that conveys information pertinent to the primary questions of who, what, and how as well as the goal of an action research investigation (Chapter 2)

Problem(s) of practice – everyday challenges that school leaders, teachers, and educators of all types face in their schools, classrooms, and educational organizations; used to identify areas of focus for action research (Chapter 2)

Professional learning community – a group of professionals (e.g., inquiry or learning teams) who gather to share and examine practices with the intent of using the collaborative atmosphere and ongoing dialogue to support ongoing growth and improvement of practice (Chapter 1, Chapter 9)

Qualitative research – approach to research that uses descriptions or illustrative data to construct an understanding of a particular situation or phenomenon; inductive reasoning is used to form conclusions as research evolves through examinations of data (Chapter 1)

Quantitative research – approach to research that utilizes numeric data to address a hypothesis about a particular phenomenon under study; involves deductive reasoning associated with theory or hypothesis testing (Chapter 1)

Quasi-experimental design – design that includes the assignment of participants to groups, but group membership is not randomly assigned (Chapter 4)

Range – difference between the highest and lowest values in a data set (Chapter 6)

Rating scale – series of questions that provide information about participants' feelings, attitudes, or evaluations in a measurable unit (Chapter 5)

Ratio data – numeric data characterized by equal units of measure between each data point with the presence of a point of origin (zero score) (Chapter 5)

Reflecting – phase of the action research process that involves examining and reflecting upon the information collected within the observing phase. Results of the phase guide the next iteration of the process (Chapter 1)

Reflection in action – reflection that occurs as you are engaged in the "action" of the action research; this thinking and doing results in changes to the ongoing practice as it is evolving (Chapter 7)

Reflection on action – reflection that occurs after you engaged in the actions of the action research; this thinking is retrospective of the action to gain a better understanding of the action research experience (Chapter 7)

Reliability – consistency of measurement (e.g., scores or answers) provided by an instrument (Chapter 5)

Reliability coefficient – numeric value that expresses the consistency of results (e.g., reliability) of an instrument (Chapter 5)

Research – systematic processes used to examine specific questions or topics with the intent of developing new knowledge or conclusions (Chapter 1)

Research-based literature – publications written to describe research or investigations into a specific topic; adheres to a general format that includes an introduction, theoretical framework and literature review, description of the methods used, results of the study, and a discussion of the results and implications (Chapter 3)

Research design – overall plan to collect the evidence necessary to reach conclusions within research (Chapter 4)

Research methodology – overarching classification of methods and design that is utilized to solve a research problem; includes underlying logic behind selection of processes (Chapter 4)

Research methods – specific techniques and procedures that are used to complete the research study (Chapter 4)

Research question – the question the researcher will attempt to answer as a result of the actions and activities conducted within the action research investigation (Chapter 2)

Sampling – the process used to select participants from among the population, or all entities that share a characteristic that is a focus of the research (Chapter 4)

Secondary source – a document or artifact that describes others' work; the authors of the secondary source did not directly participate in or observe the work described (Chapter 3)

Stability reliability – an instrument produces similar performance when data collection using the instrument occurs on different occasions (separated by an adequate amount of time) (Chapter 5)

Standard deviation – measure of variability calculated by averaging the distance of all data points from the mean (Chapter 6)

Statistical significance – associated with quantitative research methods; established numerical value that indicates it is improbable that differences or relationship between variables is due to chance (Chapter 1)

Survey – a tool used for systematic data collection that does not require face-to-face interaction; generally consists of questions/statements that candidates respond to (Chapter 5)

Synthesis of literature – culmination of all the information gathered about a particular topic; describes significance of topic and background information on the topic, including previous research where applicable (Chapter 3)

Test–retest reliability – form of reliability demonstrated when respondents complete a single version of a test or instrument on multiple occasions over a period of time with similar results (Chapter 5)

Triangulation – use of multiple pieces of data (more than two) within data analysis to validate findings; provides additional credibility to findings (Chapter 4, Chapter 6)

T-test – statistical (inferential) test that involves the comparison of the means of two groups or between two scores on the same instrument (Chapter 6)

Validity – degree to which inferences made by a researcher are supported by evidence obtained through the use of a particular instrument (Chapter 5)

Variance – measure of variability calculated by squaring the distance of each data point from the mean, calculating the sum of these squares, and dividing by the number of data points (Chapter 6)

Virtual professional learning communities – groups of individuals who utilize technology as a mechanism to support collaborative activities amongst group members; interactions can occur through audio- or video-based conferencing, text-based interactions, or a combination of the various methods (Chapter 9)

Index

Abd-El-Khalick, F., 236
Abdoler, E., 83
    see also Emanuel, E.
Abstracts, 56–57, 57 (figure), 58 (figure), 182
Academia.edu, 36, 51
Accountability, 2–3
Acting phase, 7 (figure), 8, 17, 197 (figure)
Action charts, 164, 164 (figure), 211, 211 (figure),
    212 (figure)
Action plans
    checklists, 166
    developmental steps, 164 (figure), 164–165
    professional reflection, 161–162
Action research
    audiences, 196 (figure)
    basic concepts, 5–9, 12, 74, 204
    ethical considerations, 83–85
    future projects, 161
    Hendricks's research process, 12, 13 (figure)
    individual research, 196–197, 197 (figure),
        205 (figure)
    Lewin's research cycle model, 5, 6 (figure)
    outcomes, 155, 157–158
    phases and processes, 7 (figure),
        7–8, 197 (figure)
    planning for action, 161–162
    potential challenges, 188
    professional reflection, 155–158, 160–161,
        167–169 (figure), 214
    Riel's progressive problem-solving model,
        9, 9 (figure)
    spiral model, 5, 7 (figure), 7–8
    stages, 18–19, 19 (figure)
    Stringer's action research helix, 8 (figure), 8–9
    teaching context, 11–16, 13 (figure), 14 (table)
    see also Research methods
Action research reports
    abstracts, 182
    audience, 172–173, 174 (figure)
    checklists, 187
    comparison studies, 176, 177 (table)
    dissemination, 172–175
    formats, 175–177
    importance, 173
    key elements, 47–49, 48 (figure), 49 (figure)
    outlines, 184, 184–185 (figure), 186
    policy implication statements, 182–183,
        183 (figure)
    potential challenges, 188

practical examples, 189–193 (figure)
presentation elements, 186, 186 (figure)
presentation format, 177–178
publication process and outlets, 175, 180–181
summary format, 177, 186, 189,
    189–193 (figure)
writing guidelines, 179, 181–182
    see also Investigation Model action research
        report; Readers' Theater action research
        report
Action research summary, 177, 186, 187, 189,
    189–193 (figure)
Airasian, P., 101, 151
    see also Gay, L. R.
Ajayi, L., 202
Alternative hypothesis, 139
American Psychological Association, 55
Amerine, M., 69
Analysis of variance (ANOVA), 141
Anderson, G. L., 132
Anderson, R. C., 235
Anecdotal notes, 104 (figure), 104–105,
    105 (figure)
Annotated bibliography entries, 59–60, 60 (figure),
    66, 66–68 (figure)
Anonymity, 85, 87
Anthony, J. L.
    see Mathes, P. G.
Ardoin, S. P., 223, 224
Arhar, J., 43
Armstrong, F., 23
Armstrong, N., 235
Artifacts, 104 (figure), 112–113
Assent, 85
Assessments, 112–113
Asynchronous communication, 203
Attitude scales, 104 (figure), 113–115, 114 (figure)
Audience, xiv, 172–173, 174 (figure), 196 (figure)
Audio recordings, 104 (figure), 110
Aukes, A. V., 57 (figure)
Automaticity, 222

Ball, D. L., 27
Bangert-Drowns, R. L., 159
Barab, S. A., 202
Bar graphs, 137, 137 (figure)
Barnes, Mark, 103
Barth, R., 198
Baxter, J. A., 159

Begeny, J. C., 221, 223
Beisley, R.
   see Mraz, M.
Belcher, W. L., 61, 193
Bennett, C. K., 13
Bias, 160
Bibliographies
   see Annotated bibliography entries
Binder, K. S., 223
   see also Ardoin, S. P.
Blachowicz, C., 221
   see also Rasinski, T. V.
Blackboard, 203
Blumenfeld, P. C., 68 (figure)
   see also Marx, R. W.
Boeije, H. R., 131–132
Bolam, R., 15, 200
   see also Stoll, L.
Bollen, L., 57 (figure)
Boolean operators and symbols, 52
Borg, W. R., 10, 50
Borko, H., 200
Boyd, T. A., 4
Branch, G., 202
Bray, J. N., 201
Brickman, P., 235
Brimmer, K. M., 50
Brookfield, S. D., 170
Bucknam, A., 79

Caldwell, S.
   see Mraz, M.
Canvas, 203
CAPES (context, action, product, evaluation, standards) framework, xiii, 16–19, 18 (figure), 19 (figure)
Carbonneau, K. J., 60 (figure)
Caro-Bruce, C., 12
Carr, K., 11, 204
Cartledge, G., 224
   see also Yurick, A. L.
Casas, G., 36
Case in Point examples
   action research summary, 189, 189–193 (figure)
   annotated bibliography entries, 66, 66–68 (figure)
   collaborative action research plan, 216–218
   final research plans, 146–149, 147 (figure)
   professional reflection, 167–169 (figure)
   research logs, 20–22
   research plans, 94–96 (figure), 94–95
   revised research plans, 122–123, 124 (figure)
   timelines, 124–125 (figure), 148 (figure), 150–151 (figure)
   topic development, 40–42
Casey, S., 224, 225
Cassady, J. C., 213
Chamberlain, R., 224, 225
Chard, D. J., 222, 223, 224

Checklists
   action plans, 166
   action research report, 187
   action research summary, 187
   benefits, 106
   data collection and analysis, 145
   implications for practice, 165
   preliminary research plan, 92–93
   research plan revisions, 121
   research question development, 39
   self-reflection, 165
   synthesis of literature, 65
   timelines, 121, 145
   topic development, 39
Cheng, S., 234
   see also Tuan, H.
Chin, C., 234
   see also Tuan, H.
Chinn, C. A., 235
Cicchetti, D. V., 101
Cipielewski, J. F., 50
Citation management, 59
City, E. A., 43
Clark, C., 158
Classroom 2.0, 203
Classroom environment, 29
Classroom management, 29
Clementi, L. B., 225
Coddington, C. S., 234
Coding, 133–134
Cohen, D. K., 27
Cohen, J., 101, 224
Coiro, J., 17
Collaborative action research
   act–evaluate–reformulate cycle, 213
   characteristics and functional role, 15–16, 16 (figure), 204–205
   community-building practices, 197–198
   critical participation, 206–208
   implementation guidelines, 213–214
   key elements, 205–209
   leadership and facilitation, 205–211, 213–214
   levels of research, 205 (figure)
   organizational climate, 206–208
   phases and processes, 197 (figure)
   planning guidelines, 209–211, 211 (figure), 212 (figure)
   practical examples, 216–218
   professional reflection, 214
   results dissemination, 214–215
   team-building guidelines, 215
Collaborative communities
   see Professional learning communities (PLCs)
Collins, J. S., 13
Common Core State Standards (CCSS), 3
Communication norms, 209–210
Community-building practices, 197–198
Community of practice (CoP), 200–202, 204 (figure)
Competence, 84
Conferences, 30

Confidentiality, 87
Conley, P., 224
    see also Swain, K. D.
Conrad, D., 202
Construct validity, 102
Content validity, 102–103
Convergent validity, 103
Cook, C.
    see Casas, G.
COPES (conditions, operations, product,
    evaluation, standards) model, 17, 18 (figure)
Corbin, J., 109, 133
Correlation, 141–142
Correlation coefficient, 142
Costa, A. L., 105
Council of Chief State School Officers
    (CCSSO), 3
Craig, D. V., 133, 214
Creswell, J. W., 74, 79, 80, 81, 96, 99, 125, 132,
    133, 134, 135, 136, 141, 142, 143, 164
Criterion validity, 102
Critical participants, 206–208
Cunningham, M., 233
Curriki, 203
Curry, M., 209
Curtis, Kendrick, 14

Darling-Hammond, L., 12
Dash, S., 219
Data analysis
    checklists, 145
    functional role, 129–130
    method selection and finalization, 143–145
    mixed methods, 80, 142–143
    preparation guidelines, 130–131
    qualitative methods, 77, 131–134, 132 (table)
    quantitative methods, 76, 132 (table), 134–142,
        137 (figure), 138 (figure)
    see also Investigation Model action research
        report; Readers' Theater action research
        report
Data collection
    checklists, 145
    collaborative action research plans, 210
    collection methods, 98–100
    data sources, 81–83, 82 (figure), 104 (figure),
        104–115
    mixed methods, 80, 142–143
    organizer, 117 (figure)
    preliminary planning strategies, 91–92
    quantitative methods, 76, 132 (table), 134–142,
        137 (figure), 138 (figure)
    selection methods, 116–117
    validity and reliability, 100–104, 129–130
    see also Investigation Model action research
        report
Data processing reliability, 102
Data storage, 131
Davies, J., 96, 126
Day, C., 156, 170
Deci, E. L., 234

Dede, C., 219
Dedoose, 131
Deductive analysis, 132 (table), 138
Deductive reasoning, 78, 80 (figure)
DeFranco, J., 81
De Kramer, R. M., 219
Denton, C. A.
    see Mathes, P. G.
Department of Health and Human
    Services, 88
Descriptive statistics, 135–137, 137 (figure),
    138 (figure)
Desimone, L. M., 210
Disclosure, 84
District-level action research, 205 (figure)
Duffy, T. M., 202
DuFour, Rebecca, 197, 218
    see also DuFour, Richard
DuFour, Richard, 197, 198, 200, 201, 210, 218
Duguid, P., 13
Dynamic Indicators of Basic Early Literacy Skills
    (DIBELS), 226

Eaker, R., 197, 218
    see also DuFour, Richard
Edmodo, 203
Edublog, 203
Education Resources Information Center (ERIC),
    54–55, 55 (figure)
Educators PLN, 203
Ehindero, O., 235
    see also Ojediran, I.
Electronic bibliographies, 59
Electronic resources
    see Internet resources
Elliott, J., 207, 210
Elmore, R. F., 43
Emanuel, E., 83, 84
Emerson, Mortimer, 207–208
EndNote, 59
English Companion Ning, 203
Equivalent forms reliability, 101
Ethical considerations, 83–85, 86–87 (figure)
Evaluation forms, 65
Evaluation impacts, 30
Evans, C., 4
Evans, T. L., 219, 224
    see also Yurick, A. L.
Excel, 131
Experimental design, 75

Facebook, 51, 203
Face-to-face communication, 203
Face validity, 102
Facilitation, 205–211, 213–214
Fawson, P. C., 50
Feedback, 180–181
Feller, K., 222
    see also Rasinski, T. V.
Fiarman, S. E., 43
Field, A., 151

Fishman, B., 68 (figure)
  see also Marx, R. W.
Fletcher, J. M.
  see Mathes, P. G.
Flick, U., 11, 77, 97, 99, 107, 126, 151
Fluency, 222–224
Fluent readers, 221–223
Focus groups, 110
Fogelman, J., 168, 236, 243, 244
Forced-response questions, 111–112
Ford, L., 202
Formal interviews, 107
Format, 175–177
Formative data, 144
Forsythe, S. J., 225
Foster, T. E., 223
  see also Ardoin, S. P.
Francis, D. J.
  see Mathes, P. G.
Fusarelli, B. C., 3
Fusarelli, L. D., 3

Gall, J. P., 10, 50
Gall, M. E., 10, 50
Garmston, R. J., 105
Gay, L. R., 101, 102, 151
Gearhart, M., 209
Geier, R., 68 (figure)
  see also Marx, R. W.
Generalizability, 130
Giljers, H., 57 (figure)
Google+, 203
Google Docs, 162
Google Scholar, 36, 53, 54 (figure)
Google Sheets, 131
Gormally, C., 235
Gorsuch, G., 223, 224
Grade-level action research, 205 (figure)
Grading impacts, 30
Grady, M. P., 77, 78, 79, 99, 105, 106
Graham, Brandon, 72–73
Graphic representations, 137, 137 (figure),
  138 (figure)
Greek notations, 139, 140 (figure)
Griffith, L. W., 222, 223, 225
Group interviews, 108–109
Grouzet, F. M., 234
Guba, E. G., 102
Guest, G., 133
Guthrie, J. T., 234

Hacker, K., 214
Hadwin, A. F., 17
Haertal, E. H., 101
Hallar, B., 235
Hargreaves, A., 196, 198
Hartras, D., 76
Hendricks, C., 12, 13 (figure)
Henning, J. E., 35, 105, 107, 109, 110, 111, 120,
  134, 175, 178, 179
Herr, K., 132

Hesse-Biber, S. N., 83
Hiebert, E., 222
  see also Rasinski, T. V.
Hinchey, P. H., 142
Hipp, K. A., 218
Histograms, 137, 138 (figure)
Hogan, C.
  see Casas, G.
Holly, M. L., 43
Howard, K.
  see Casas, G.
Hubbard, R. S., 90, 107, 108, 143
Huberman, M., 233
Huffman, J. B., 218
Hurley, M. M., 159
Hypothesis, 34–35, 139, 140 (figure)

IBM SPSS Statistics, 131
Implications for practice, 58 (figure), 157, 161–162
Individual action research, 196–197, 197 (figure),
  205 (figure)
Individual interviews, 107
Inductive analysis, 132, 132 (table)
Inductive reasoning, 77, 80 (figure)
Inferential statistics, 137–142
INFOhio Learning Commons, 203
Informal interviews, 108
Information sources
  annotated bibliographies, 59–60, 60 (figure)
  Internet resources, 50–53, 54 (figure),
    55 (figure)
  literature reviews, 45–50, 48 (figure), 49 (figure)
  organizer, 52 (figure)
  organizing guidelines, 58–59
  planning guidelines, 63–64
  selection guidelines, 56–57, 58 (figure)
  synthesis of literature guidelines, 60–63,
    61 (figure)
Informed consent, 84–85, 86–87 (figure)
Inquiry teams, 197 (figure)
Institute of Education Sciences, 54, 55
Institutional Review Board (IRB), 87–88,
  88–89 (figure)
Instructional materials, 29
Instructional methods, 29
Instrument reliability, 102
Internal capacity, 206
International Literacy Association, 55
Internet resources
  characteristics, 50–51
  Education Resources Information Center
    (ERIC), 54–55, 55 (figure)
  Google Scholar, 53, 54 (figure)
  keyword selection, 51–52
  online databases, 55–56
  online inquiries, 51–52
  organizer, 52 (figure)
  university libraries, 53–54
Inter-rater reliability, 101
Interval data, 114–115
Interviews, 104 (figure), 107–109

Investigation Model action research report
 action plans, 244–245
 action research summary, 191–193 (figure)
 annotated bibliography entries, 67–68 (figure)
 conclusion, 238, 245
 final research plan, 148–149, 149–150 (figure)
 initial research plan, 95, 95–96 (figure)
 introduction, 232–233
 literature review, 233–237
 professional reflection, 168–169 (figure),
  236–237, 242–244
 references, 245–246
 research logs, 22
 research methods, 238–240
 research plan revisions, 123, 124 (figure)
 research results, 240–241 (figure), 240–242,
  242 (figure)
 timelines, 124–125 (figure), 150–151 (figure)
 topic development, 42
iPads, 30
Ivankova, N. V., 79, 106, 126, 142

James, E. A., 79
Job-embedded professional learning, 15
Johnson, A. P., 155, 156
Johnson, J., 4
Johnston, S., 66 (figure)
Jonassen, D. H., 201
Jordan, H. M., 203
Jordan, Walker, 62–63
Journals, 20–22, 104 (figure), 109–110, 144

Kafka, J., 209
Kang, N., 233, 234, 238
Kasten, W., 43
Keehn, S., 69, 224, 225
Kelly, J. L., 35, 105, 134, 175
 see also Henning, J. E.
Kemmis, S., 5, 6, 6 (figure), 7, 8, 12, 13, 20,
 204, 205
Kennedy, Sarah, 159, 163, 176
Kerlinger, F. N., 139
Kettering, Charles, 4
Keyword selection, 51–52
Kostos, K., 159
Kothari, C. R., 74
Krajcik, J. S., 68 (figure), 168, 236
 see also Fogelman, J.; Marx, R. W.
Krueger, R. A., 110
Kubuina, R. M., 224
Kuhn, M. R., 221, 223, 224

Laubach, T. A., 235
Lave, J., 197, 198, 201, 202, 206
Leader-Janssen, E.M., 224
 see also Swain, K. D.
Leadership, 205–211, 213–214
Learning communities, 197 (figure), 197–203
 see also Professional learning communities
  (PLCs)
Learning management systems, 203

Learning outcomes, 157–158
Leask, M., 200
Leavy, P., 83
Lee, H., 168, 236, 237, 243, 244
Lee, H. B., 139
Lehr, F., 221, 223, 224
Leitch, R., 156, 170
Leko, C. D., 3
Lems, K., 221
 see also Rasinski, T. V.
Lens, W., 234
Levin, B. B., 12
Lewin, K., 5
Lewin's research cycle model, 5, 6 (figure)
Likert scales, 114 (figure)
Lincoln, S. Y., 102
Linn, M. C., 236
 see also Lee, H.
Literature reviews
 functional role, 45–46
 information sources, 45
 literature sources and types, 46–50, 48 (figure),
  49 (figure)
 organizer, 52 (figure)
 see also Investigation Model action research
  report; Readers' Theater action research
  report
Literature seaches, 36
Little, J. W., 209, 219
Little, Shae, 113
Liu, O., 236
 see also Lee, H.
LiveBinder, 178
LocalWiki,, 203
Lock, C., 233
Logs
 see Reflective logs; Research logs
Lo, Y., 224
 see also Yurick, A. L.
Lyons, A., 81

Machi, D., 27
Mackey, J., 219
MacQueen, K. M., 133
Madison Metropolitan School District, 42, 126
Madorey, Jeannie, 9–10
Manwell, Kara, 138–139
Many, T., 197, 218
 see also DuFour, Richard
Marion, R., 23
Marley, S. C., 60 (figure)
Martinez, R. S., 221
 see also Begeny, J. C.
Marx, R. W., 68 (figure), 168, 235, 243, 244
Masters, J., 219
Mathes, P. G., 221
Maxwell, J. A., 102, 129
Mayfield, Sherri, 180
McDermott, R., 219
McEvoy, B., 27
McKernan, J., 6, 13

McMahon, A., 15, 200
  see also Stoll, L.
McNeill, K. L., 168, 236
  see also Fogelman, J.
McNiff, J., 6, 23, 74, 173, 174, 179,
    180, 181
McRae, A., 234
McTaggart, R., 6, 7, 8, 12, 13, 20,
    204, 205
Mean, 135
Measures of association, 141–142
Measures of central tendency, 135
Measures of variability, 136
Median, 135
Mendeley, 51, 59
Merriam, S. B., 81, 109
Mertler, C. A., 7, 23, 29, 33 (figure), 132, 136,
    141, 146
Meyers, E., 23
Middlebrooks, S., 233
Milenkiewicz, M. T., 79
Miller, B. M., 143
Mills, G. E., 12, 23, 31, 101, 135, 141, 151,
    164, 204
  see also Gay, L. R.
Mixed methods analysis, 142–143
Mixed methods data sources, 99–100
Mixed methods research, 73–74, 79–81
Mode, 135
Moller, G., 218
Moodle, 203
Mooney, M. A., 235
Moon, J. A., 170
Moore, G., 202
Moore, M., 23
Moore, S. A., 50
Morena, L. S., 223
  see also Ardoin, S. P.
Morrison, K., 207
Mraz, M., 225
MS Office PowerPoint, 178
Munby, H., 233
Myers, Jeff, 160

Namey, E. E., 133
National Board for Professional Teaching
    Standards (NBPTS), 198
National Committee on Science Education
    Standards (NCSES), 233
National Council for the Social Studies
    (NCSS), 55
National Council of Teachers of English (NCTE),
    55, 203
National Council of Teachers of Mathematics
    (NCTM), 33, 55
National Education Association (NEA), 55
National Governors Association Center for Best
    Practices (NGACBP), 3
National Institute of Health (NIH), 83
National Reading Panel (NRP), 221, 222
Newmann, F. M. & Associates, 200

Nichols, W.
  see Mraz, M.
Ning, 203
Nixon, R., 7
No Child Left Behind Act (2001), 3
Nolen, A. L., 83
Nominal data, 114
Nonexperimental design, 75–76
Normal distribution, 136 (figure)
North Carolina Association for Research in
    Education (NCARE), 176
Northeast Florida Science, Technology, and
    Mathematics Center for Education, 42
"Note"-able Thoughts
  act–evaluate–reformulate cycle, 213
  action research, 7
  audience, 175
  collaborative communities, 197, 201, 215
  communities of practice, 202
  data collection, 116
  data sources, 83
  data storage and organization, 131
  facilitation, 206
  implications for practice, 157, 161
  learning management systems, 203
  literature reviews, 46, 50
  participation strategies, 209
  personal educational philosophies, 29
  planning processes, 73
  potential action steps, 163
  problems of practice, 28, 32
  professional learning communities (PLCs), 202
  publication outlets, 181
  reflective practices, 157, 158, 161
  research concepts, 3
  research design, 77
  research methods, 81
  research reports, 176
  research results, 156, 157, 161
  school system initiatives, 16
  teaching-research connection, 5, 11
  validity and reliability, 100, 104
Note-taking practices, 64
Null hypothesis, 139
NVivo, 131

Obama, Barack, 3
Observations, 104 (figure), 105–107,
    106 (figure), 115
Observing phase, 7 (figure), 8, 197 (figure)
O'Dwyer, L. M., 219
Ojediran, I., 235, 244
Olson, D., 159
Olson, Mary, 199
Oludipe, D., 235
  see also Ojediran, I.
O'Neill, T. B., 67 (figure), 168, 237, 243, 244
Online collaborative forums, 162
Online databases, 55–56
Online inquiries, 51–52
Open-response questions, 111 (figure), 111–112

Opfer, V. D., 219
Oral reading fluency (ORF), 226
Ordinal data, 114
Osborn, J., 221, 223, 224
Otis, N., 234
Outliers, 135
Outlines, 61, 63, 64, 184, 184–185 (figure), 186

Padak, G., 36
Padak, N., 36
Paired t-test, 141
Pankake, A. M., 218
Paris, A. H., 19
Paris, S. G., 19
Participatory action research
    see Collaborative action research
Pavonetti, L. M., 50
Pearson Education, Inc., 34
Pearson product-moment correlation
    coefficient, 142
Peck, K. L., 201
Pedder, D., 219
Peer-reviewed resources, 49
Pelletier, L. G., 234
Pender, L., 69
Personal educational philosophies, 28
Personal journals, 20–22
Peterson, R., 215
Petscher, Y., 222
    see also Rasinski, T. V.
Phillips, D. K., 11, 204
Photographs, 104 (figure), 110
Pie graphs, 137
Pikulski, J. J., 222
Pine, G., 36
Plan for action
    checklists, 166
    developmental steps, 164 (figure), 164–165
    professional reflection, 161–162
Planning guidelines
    action research model, 7 (figure), 7–8, 17,
        197 (figure)
    importance, 71–73
    synthesis of literature, 63–64
Plano Clark, V. L., 79, 80, 81, 99, 142, 143
Policy implications, 174, 182–183, 183 (figure)
Polin, L., 201, 202
Popham, W. J., 101
Post-hoc analyses, 141
Potential challenges, 188
Potential publication outlets, 247–248
Power, B. M., 90, 107, 108
PowerPoint, 178
Practical significance, 10
Practitioner-focused literature, 47
Praxis, 173
Presentation elements, 186, 186 (figure)
Presentation format, 177–178
Prezi, 178
Primary sources, 49–50
Pringh, Sejal, 82–83

Problems of practice, 27, 27 (figure), 155
Problem statements, 34
Professional learning communities (PLCs)
    characteristics and functional role, 15–16,
        16 (figure), 200–201, 204 (figure)
    community-building practices, 197–198
    learning outcomes, 157–158
    shared research, 172–174
Professional organizations, 55, 174–175
Professional reflection, 155–158, 160–161,
    167–169 (figure), 214
    see also Investigation Model action research
        report; Readers' Theater action research
        report
ProQuest, 56
Prosody, 223
PsycINFO, 55
Publication process and outlets, 175, 180–181,
    247–248
Purdue Online Writing Lab, 56
Putman, S. M., 17, 213

Qualitative analysis, 131–134, 132 (table)
Qualitative data sources
    anecdotal notes, 104 (figure), 104–105,
        105 (figure)
    audio recordings, 104 (figure), 110
    characteristics, 99
    focus groups, 110
    interviews, 104 (figure), 107–109
    journals, 104 (figure), 109–110
    observations, 104 (figure), 105–107,
        106 (figure)
    photographs, 104 (figure), 110
    reflective logs, 104 (figure), 109–110
    video recordings, 104 (figure), 110
Qualitative designs, 75
Qualitative methods
    basic concepts, 76–77
    characteristics, 77–78, 80 (figure), 99
Qualitative research, 11, 73
Quantitative analysis, 132 (table), 134–142,
    137 (figure), 138 (figure)
Quantitative data sources
    attitude scales, 104 (figure), 113–115,
        114 (figure)
    basic concepts, 99
    observations, 115
    rating scales, 104 (figure), 114 (figure), 115
    records and artifacts, 104 (figure), 112–113
    surveys and questionnaires, 104 (figure),
        110–112, 111 (figure)
Quantitative designs, 74–75
Quantitative methods
    basic concepts, 76–77
    characteristics, 77, 78–79, 80 (figure)
Quantitative research, 10, 73
Quasi-experimental design, 75
Questioning guidelines, 49 (figure)
Questionnaires, 104 (figure), 110–112,
    111 (figure)

Range, 136
Rasinski, T. V., 66 (figure), 67 (figure), 221, 222, 223, 224, 225, 226, 230
Rating scales, 104 (figure), 114 (figure), 115
Ratio data, 115
Readers' Theater, 224–225
Readers' Theater action research report
    action plans, 229–230
    action research summary, 189–191 (figure)
    annotated bibliography entries, 66–67 (figure)
    conclusion, 230
    data analysis, 227
    final research plan, 146–147, 147 (figure)
    initial research plan, 94, 94–95 (figure)
    introduction, 221–222
    literature review, 222–225
    professional reflection, 167 (figure), 228–229
    references, 230–231
    research logs, 21–22
    research methods, 225–227
    research plan, 118 (figure)
    research plan revisions, 122–123
    research results, 227–228, 228 (figure)
    timelines, 119 (figure), 148 (figure)
    topic development, 41–42
Reading rate, 222–223
Reading skills, 221–223
Real-time communication, 203
Records, 104 (figure), 112–113
Recursive cycle of learning behavior, 17, 18 (figure)
Reeves, D., 206
Reflecting phase, 7 (figure), 8, 17, 197 (figure)
Reflection in action, 156
Reflection on action, 156–158, 160–161, 167–168 (figure)
Reflective logs, 104 (figure), 109–110
Reflective thinking practices, 155–158, 160–161, 167–169 (figure), 214
    see also Investigation Model action research report; Readers' Theater action research report
Relationship-building practices, 197–198
Reliability, 100, 101–102, 129
Reliability coefficient, 101
Repeated readings, 224
Research
    accountability movement, 2–3
    characteristics and functional role, 3–4
    terminology, 73–77
Research-based literature, 47
Research design
    definition, 74–76
    planning stage, 90
ResearchGate, 51
Research implications, 58 (figure), 157
Research logs, 20–22
Research methodology
    classifications, 75 (figure)
    definition, 74
    guiding questions, 58 (figure)

methodological approaches, 10–11
    planning guidelines, 71–73
    see also Action research reports
Research methods
    classifications, 77–81, 80 (figure)
    data analysis, 130–143, 132 (table), 137 (figure), 138 (figure)
    data sources, 81–83, 82 (figure), 104 (figure), 104–115
    definition, 76–77
    see also Investigation Model action research report; Readers' Theater action research report
Research plans
    checklists, 121
    data analysis methods, 144–145
    data sources and collection, 81–83, 82 (figure), 91–92, 98–117, 120–122
    developmental steps, 164 (figure), 164–165
    ethical considerations, 83–85, 87
    functional role, 210–211
    institutional review board (IRB), 87–88, 88–89 (figure)
    plan organizers, 91 (figure), 118–119 (figure)
    practical examples, 94–96 (figure), 94–95, 118 (figure), 122–123, 124 (figure), 146–149, 147–151 (figure)
    preliminary planning strategies, 90–92
    professional reflection, 155–158, 160–161, 167–169 (figure)
    research methods, 72–81, 80 (figure)
    revision process, 117, 120–123, 124 (figure)
    timelines, 119 (figure), 120–121, 124–125 (figure), 145, 148 (figure), 150–151 (figure)
Research questions, 35–37, 58 (figure), 76, 90
Research reports
    see Action research reports
Research results, 58 (figure), 155–158, 164–165, 214–215
    see also Investigation Model action research report; Readers' Theater action research report
Research terminology, 73–77
Reviewer feedback, 180–181
Richards, M., 221
Riel, M., 9, 9 (figure), 201, 202
Riel's progressive problem-solving model, 9, 9 (figure)
Rikli, A., 66 (figure)
Rivera, Carlos, 134
Robinson, P. D., 224
    see also Yurick, A. L.
Rock, T. C., 12
Rogers, Bailey, 30
Ross, J. D., 207
Rovai, A. P., 203
Rupley, W.
    see Mraz, M.
Russell, M., 219
Rust, F., 23, 158

Sagor, R., 7, 12, 20, 45, 156, 161, 162
Salkind, N. J., 78
Samaras, A. P., 43
Sampling, 76
Samuels, S., 222
    see also Rasinski, T. V.
Sargent, S.
    see Mraz, M.
Scaled-response questions, 111–112
Schatschneider, C.
    see Mathes, P. G.
Schiefele, U., 234
Schön, D. A., 156, 170
School-level action research, 205 (figure)
Schoology, 203
School records, 104 (figure), 112–113
Schuler, K., 69
Secondary sources, 49–50
Self-reflection, 165
Self-regulation, 16–17
Selig, J. P., 60 (figure)
Semi-structured interviews, 107–108
Shared research, 172–174
Shared vision, 210
Shavelson, R. J., 101
Shin, E., 159
Short, K., 183
Shotsberger, P. G., 203
Sikorski, M. P., 235
Sindelar, P. T., 3
Situational reliability, 102
Smith, Amber, 108
Smith, L. L., 213
Snyder, W., 219
Social networks, 51, 203
Soloway, E., 68 (figure)
    see also Marx, R. W.
Somekh, B., 12, 179
Spiral action research model, 5, 7 (figure), 7–8
Stability reliability, 101
Stahl, S. A., 221, 223, 224
Stainback, S., 160
Stainback, W., 160
Standard deviation, 136, 136 (figure)
Standardized tests, 112
Statistical analysis, 10, 134–142, 137 (figure),
    138 (figure), 140 (figure)
Statistical significance, 10
Steps to Action charts, 164, 164 (figure),
    211, 211 (figure), 212 (figure)
Stoll, L., 15, 200, 201
Stone, J. M., 35, 105, 134, 175
    see also Henning, J. E.
Strauss, A., 109, 133
Stringer, E. T., 8, 8 (figure), 85, 214
Stringer's action research helix, 8 (figure), 8–9
Structured interviews, 107
Structured observations, 106, 106 (figure)
Student attitude and motivation, 234–235
Student learning experiences, 29–30
Student learning outcomes, 235–236

Stunkel, L., 83
    see also Emanuel, E.
Subject reliability, 102
Substantive hypothesis, 139
Summary format, 177, 186, 189, 189–193 (figure)
Supovitz, J., 198
Surveys, 104 (figure), 110–112, 111 (figure)
Swain, K. D., 224, 229
Synchronous communication, 203
Synthesis of literature
    checklist, 65
    developmental and organizational guidelines,
        60–63, 61 (figure)
    functional role, 46
    literature sources and types, 46–50, 48 (figure),
        49 (figure)
    planning guidelines, 63–64
Szafran, R., 78, 99, 100, 137, 141

Taguchi, E., 223, 224
Tal, R. T., 68 (figure)
    see also Marx, R. W.
Tanner, D., 135
Tashakkori, A., 79, 80, 81, 99, 100, 108, 142, 151
Teacher action research, 11–16, 13 (figure),
    14 (table), 16 (figure)
Teacher-made tests, 112–113
Team-specific action research, 205 (figure)
TECH Connections
    data storage and organization, 131
    functional role, 11
    informed consent, 85
    Internet resources, 51
    literature seaches, 36
    online collaborative forums, 162
    presentation format tools, 178
    virtual professional learning communities
        (VPLCs), 203
Teddlie, C., 79, 80, 81, 99, 100, 108, 142, 151
Teitel, L., 43
Test–retest reliability, 101
Text-based collaborative tools, 203
Theoretical validity, 129–130
Therrien, W. J., 223, 224
Thomas, R. A., 3
Thomas, S., 15, 200
    see also Stoll, L.
Thompson, D.
    see Casas, G.
Thorndike-Christ, T. M., 102
Thorndike, R. M., 102
Timelines, 119 (figure), 120–121,
    124–125 (figure), 145, 148 (figure),
    150–151 (figure)
Tomal, D. R., 134, 135, 136, 140
Topic Proposal Form, 37, 38 (figure)
Topic selection and development
    categories, 29–30
    checklists, 39
    focus identification, 29–32
    hypothesis formulation, 34–35

personal educational philosophies, 28
problems of practice, 27, 27 (figure)
problem statements, 34
proposal form, 37, 38 (figure)
research question format, 35–37
self-reflection, 32–33, 33 (figure), 37, 39
see also Investigation Model action research report; Readers' Theater action research report
Topic-specific professional social networks, 203
Traditional educational research, 14 (table), 176, 177 (table)
see also Action research reports
Triangulation, 81, 142
Trustworthiness, 102, 110
Tsai, C., 234
see also Tuan, H.
T-test, 141
Tuan, H., 234, 244
Twitter, 51, 203
Tyler, B., 223, 224

Understanding, 84
University libraries, 53–54
Unstructured interviews, 108
Unstructured observations, 106

Validity, 100, 102–104, 129–130
Vander Putten, J., 83
van Joolingen, W. R., 57 (figure)
Vansteenkiste, M., 234
Variance, 136
Varma, K., 236
see also Lee, H.
Video recordings, 104 (figure), 110
Virtual professional learning communities (VPLCs), 202–203, 204 (figure)
Voices From the Field
Amber Smith, 108
Bailey Rogers, 30
Brandon Graham, 72–73
Carlos Rivera, 134
Cindy Vollmer, 33–34
Gloria Waters, 46
Jeannie Madorey, 9–10
Jeff Myers, 160
Kara Manwell, 138–139
Kendrick Curtis, 14
Mark Barnes, 103
Mary Olson, 199

Mortimer Emerson, 207–208
Sarah Kennedy, 159, 163, 176
Sejal Pringh, 82–83
Shae Little, 113
Sherri Mayfield, 180
Walker Jordan, 62–63
VoiceThread, 178
Vollmer, Cindy, 33–34
Voluntariness, 84

Waggoner, M. A., 235
Waight, N., 236
Walker, T., 15
Wallace, C. S., 233, 234, 238
Wallace, M., 15, 200
see also Stoll, L.
Washburn-Moses, L., 3
Waters, Gloria, 46
Webb, N. M., 101
Weebly, 178, 203
Wenger, E., 198, 201, 202, 206, 219
Wentzel, K. R., 235
Westheimer, J., 197
What Works Clearinghouse, 55
Whitehead, J., 6, 23, 74, 173, 174, 179, 180, 181
Wikispaces, 203
Wilkinson, B., 159
Wilson, B. G., 201
Winne, P. H., 17
Wisniewska, D., 80
Wix, 178
Woodward, J., 159
Wordle, 130, 131
Writing guidelines, 179, 181–182
Writing schedules, 63, 64
Written discussions, 164–165

Yeager, A., 221
see also Begeny, J. C.
Yin, R. K., 80
Young, C., 67 (figure), 222, 224, 225, 226, 230
Younie, S., 200
Yurick, A. L., 224

Zeichner, K., 23
Zhu, E., 203
Zoho Sheet, 131
Zotero, 59
Zuber-Skerritt, O., 3, 12, 172–173